THE THEATER EXPERIENCE

NINTH EDITION

THE THEATER EXPERIENCE

Edwin Wilson

Graduate Center
The City University of New York

Boston Burr Ridge, IL   Dubuque, IA   Madison, WI   New York   San Francisco   St. Louis
Bangkok Bogotá Caracas Lisbon London Madrid
Mexico City   Milan   New Delhi   Seoul   Singapore   Sydney   Taipei   Toronto

The McGraw·Hill Companies

Mc Graw Hill

Higher Education

Front cover:

Left to right: Floyd King as Sir Amorous La Foole, Ricki Robichaux as Epicoene, and Ted van Griethuysen as Morose in The Shakespeare Theatre's production of *The Silent Woman* by Ben Jonson, directed by Michael Kahn. Photo by Richard Termine.

Back cover:

Left to right: Billy Carter as Quicksilver, Amanda Drew as Gertrude, and Michael Matus as Sir Petronel Flash in The Royal Shakespeare Company production of *Eastward Ho!* by Ben Jonson, John Marston, and George Chapman, directed by Lucy Pitman-Wallace. Photo by Donald Cooper/PhotoSTAGE.

THE THEATER EXPERIENCE

ISBN 0-07-283182-0

Publisher: *Christopher Freitag*
Developmental editor: *Caroline Ryan*
Marketing manager: *Lisa Berry*
Senior media producer: *Shannon Gattens*
Project manager: *Jean R. Starr*
Production supervisor: *Tandra Jorgensen*
Coordinator of freelance design: *Mary E. Kazak*
Lead supplement producer: *Kate Boylan*
Photo research coordinator: *Nora Agbayani*
Art editor: *Jen DeVere*
Photo researcher: *Inge King*
Art director: *Jeanne Schreiber*
Permissions: *Marty Granahan*
Cover design: *Mary Spanburg*
Typeface: 10/12 Garamond Light
Compositor: *Carlisle Communications, Ltd.*
Printer: *Van Hoffmann*

Library of Congress Cataloging-in-Publication Data

The theater experience / Edwin Wilson.—9th ed.
p. cm.
Includes bibliographical references and index
ISBN 0-07-283182-0 (pbk. : alk. paper)
1. Theater. I. Title.
PN1655.W57 2004
792–dc21   2003042089
www.mhhe.com

About the Author

Teacher, author, and critic, Edwin Wilson has worked in many aspects of theater. Educated at Vanderbilt University, the University of Edinburgh, and Yale University, he received a Master of Fine Arts degree from the Yale Drama School, as well as the first Doctor of Fine Arts degree awarded by Yale. He has taught at Yale, Hofstra, Vanderbilt, Hunter College, and the CUNY Graduate Center. At Hunter he served as chair of the Department of Theatre and Film and head of the graduate theater program. At CUNY he has been Executive Director of the Martin E. Segal Theatre Center.

Edwin Wilson was the theater critic of *The Wall Street Journal* for 22 years. In addition to *The Theater Experience,* he is coauthor with Alvin Goldfarb of *Living Theatre: A History, Theater: The Lively Art,* and the *Anthology of Living Theater,* also published by McGraw-Hill, and

he was responsible for the volume *Shaw on Shakespeare.* He was the president of the New York Drama Critics Circle and served several times on the Tony Nominating Committee and the Pulitzer Prize Drama Jury, most recently in 2003. He is on the boards of the John Golden Fund, the Susan Smith Blackburn Prize, and the Theatre Development Fund, of which he was also president.

Before turning to teaching and writing, Edwin Wilson was assistant to the producer for the film *Lord of the Flies,* directed by Peter Brook, and the Broadway play *Big Fish, Little Fish,* directed by John Gielgud. He produced several off-Broadway shows and coproduced a Broadway play directed by George Abbott. He also directed in summer and regional theater, serving one season as resident director of the Barter Theater in Virginia.

To My Wife, Catherine

Contents in Brief

Contents

PART 1   THE AUDIENCE

PART 2 THE PERFORMERS AND THE DIRECTOR

Contents

PART 4 THE PLAYWRIGHT: DRAMATIC CHARACTERS AND DRAMATIC STRUCTURE

Chapter 14 Conventions of Dramatic Structure   291

Chapter 15 Dramatic Structure: Climactic, Episodic, and Other Forms   305

PART 5   THE DESIGNERS: ENVIRONMENT, VISUAL ELEMENTS, AND SOUND

Preface

When I set out to write ***The Theater Experience,*** I realized there was a void among the introductory texts on the market. Every introductory text I had read or used approached theater from the standpoint of either the historian or the practitioner. I knew, however, that the vast majority of students studying theater for the first time would be primarily audience members. Some students might go on to major in theater, and a few might become performers, playwrights, or designers. But first and foremost, these students would most closely experience theater as part of the audience. It was with this idea in mind that I decided to orient *The Theater Experience* from the perspective of the audience. The book contains as much information about the various elements of theater as any available. It also contains an abundance of historical facts, but always these are presented in a way that can be understood and absorbed by students who, I hope, will be attending theater for the rest of their lives.

ORGANIZATION

The Theater Experience has five parts, each corresponding to an essential element of a theater event:

- The audience, which sees the event, and responds to it (Part 1)
- The performers, who bring the event alive; and the director, who guides them (Part 2)
- The type of event being performed (Part 3)
- The dramatist, who constructs the action, develops the characters, and writes the dialogue (Part 4)
- The designers, who provide the ultimate visual and audio effects of the event (Part 5).

The organization of the text has a further advantage in that it allows an instructor to arrange the parts or their chapters in any way that he or she feels comfortable.

PRODUCTION SHOTS

A hallmark of *The Theater Experience* has been its abundant production photographs, taken from professional productions in New York and many regional theaters, from colleges, and from abroad. The ninth edition incorporates over 260 color photos—the majority of which are new. These include color shots from the recent productions of *Hairspray, Topdog/ Underdog, Metamorphoses, Frankie and Johnnie in the Claire de Lune, The Producers, Harlem Song, Movin'Out,* and *La Boheme.*

BOXES

Another well-received feature of *The Theater Experience* is the sidebar, or box. Several types of boxes appear in the text. **"Getting Started in Theater"** boxes are personal statements from directors, playwrights, set designers, technicians, and others, which illustrate the diversity of talents and backgrounds of theater professionals. **"Play Synopses"** boxes are two-page spreads that provide detailed summaries of well-known plays, act by act, and are accompanied by photographs of both the playwright and the staged production. Additional boxes throughout the text present excerpts from plays, important critical quotations, warm-up exercises for actors, and much more.

APPENDIXES

Several useful appendixes are included to aid in teaching and serve as informational resources. One is a **glossary of technical terms** used in theater; a second is a lengthier description of **major theatrical forms and movements;** the third is a helpful series of **historical outlines.** The outlines, organized by nation and time period, list theatrical events on one side and developments in topics such as politics, society, and science, on the other.

NEW TO THIS EDITION
Content

Several changes and additions have been included in the ninth edition. The text has been thoroughly revised and updated, with special care to eliminate any material that is no longer pertinent while adding the most up-to-date relevant new material. These updates include not only the content in each chapter, but also careful updating of the Exploring Theater on the Web boxes that end each chapter. Specific changes to the content include:

- Three new **"Getting Started in Theater"** boxes
- Increased discussion of ceremonies, rituals, and the origins of theater
- New coverage of children's theater (Chapter 2)
- New box covering the historical status of the actor in society (Chapter 5)

- Expanded Chapter 12: "Theater of Diversity," including additional coverage of contemporary Hispanic, Feminist, Gay and Lesbian Theater and Performance Art

ORGANIZATION

The biggest change to the text's organization in the ninth edition was in keeping with the audience-centered approach of *The Theater Experience*. Coverage of "Stage Spaces" now appears in Part One: "The Audience." This change was a logical one, since one of the first things an audience member encounters is the physical space of the theater: its ambience, size and relationship to the audience. Therefore, we orient students to the physical theater along with other elements that prepare them for a theater event. (Please note: any instructor who prefers the previous order can easily delay covering Chapter 4 until the beginning of Part Five.) Another slight shift in organization is that "Dramatic Characters" has been placed before "Dramatic Structure" in Part Four. Lastly, the "Play Synopses" have been moved to the end of each Part for a more flexible format. As in previous editions of *The Theater Experience,* the organization still allows an instructor to arrange the parts and chapters in any way with which he or she feels comfortable.

CD-ROM

An exciting new element has been added to the package for the ninth edition. Now, this CD-Rom resource is included with every copy of the text purchased from McGraw Hill. The CD-ROM includes a wide variety of resources for students including

- Video clips from live theater performances. Each chapter has a video clip related to certain concepts.
- Critical thinking questions after each clip
- Multiple-Choice questions after each clip
- Nine new "Play Synopses," including *Macbeth, The Crucible,* and *Angels in America, Part One*
- *The Theatergoer's Guide*

SUPPORT FOR INSTRUCTORS

Please note: The supplements listed here and below in "Support for Students" may accompany this text. Please contact your local McGraw-Hill representatives for details concerning policies, prices, and availability, as some restrictions may apply. If you are not sure who your representative is, you can find him or her by using the rep locator at www.mhhe.com.

- Instructor's Manual: McGraw-Hill offers an Instructor's Manual to all instructors who adopt *The Theater Experience* for their courses. In addition to a full set of test questions, the IM includes a wide variety of additional resources for each chapter in the book.

- Computerized Test Bank: Test questions are available on MicroTest, a powerful but easy-to-use test-generating program. MicroTest is available for Windows and Macintosh personal computers.

Online Learning Center: *www.mhhe.com/te9*. The Online Learning Center is an Internet-based resource for students and faculty alike. Students can expand their study of theater with web links and Internet exercises for each chapter. Instructor's Resources are password-protected and offer the complete text of the Instructor's Manual, a correlation guide for *Anthology of Living Theater*, and a link to our customizable database of plays. To receive a password for the site, contact your local sales representative or E-mail us at *theater@mcgraw-hill.com*.

Additionally, the Online Learning Center offers chapter-by-chapter quizzes for testing students. These brief quizzes are separate from those offered in the Instructor's Manual; they generate instant grades; and the results can be E-mailed directly to the instructor with the click of a button. This special quizzing feature is a valuable tool for the instructor who requires a quick way to check reading comprehension and basic understanding *without using up valuable class time.*

Online Course Support: The online content of *The Theater Experience* is supported by WebCT, eCollege.com, and Blackboard. To find out more contact your local McGraw-Hill representative or visit *www.mhhe.com/solutions.*

As an adopter, you may also be eligible to use our PageOut service to get you and your course up and running online in a matter of hours-at no cost to you and without knowing HTML! To find out more contact your local McGraw-Hill representative or visit www.pageout.net.

STUDENT RESOURCES

- The McGraw-Hill *Theatergoer's Guide:* The *Theatergoer's Guide* is included on the CD-ROM with every new copy of the text. The guide is an excellent introduction to the art of attending and critiquing a play-from making theater reservations and knowing when to applaud to evaluating a performance and doing research on the Internet.
- Online Learning Center: *www.mhhe.com/te9:* McGraw-Hill offers extensive web resources for students with Internet access. Students will find the Online Learning Center of particular use with *The Theater Experience,* as for each chapter it offers glossary terms, chapter objectives, discussion questions, and on-line testing. In addition, the site hosts links to promote getting involved in theater and conducting research on the web.
- The McGraw-Hill *Guide to Electronic Research in Theater:* This brief booklet is designed to assist students in locating theater sites on the web and evaluating onsite information; it also provides guidelines for referencing on-line sources. This supplement can be packaged free with the text.

ACKNOWLEDGEMENTS

I first developed many of the ideas in this book while teaching a course in Introduction to Theater at Hunter College of the City University of New York. To my former colleagues and students at Hunter, I express my deep appreciation.

The current edition of *The Theater Experience* is the eighth edition that has featured the incomparable drawings of Al Hirschfeld as part openings. For nearly 25 years, his masterful depictions of the theater world have graced the pages of this book. Al had no peer at capturing in a few lines the motion, electricity, and elegance of live theater. Over a period that spanned seven decades he caught in an indescribable way the best in theater. Al Hirschfeld died at age 99 in the very week we were selecting the drawings that are included in this volume. I will always be grateful that Al allowed his drawings to be an important part of *The Theater Experience.*

Teachers who have used the book have contributed specific material, which I have incorporated in the text. I particularly wish to thank Susan Tenneriello, who has prepared the index for the last few editions with diligence and intelligence. I am also most grateful to Scott Walters, who prepared the Instructor's Manual; Stuart Baker, who was responsible for Appendix B and much of the material in Appendix C; Mira Felner, who not only wrote the material on women and Greek and Elizabethan theater but also made a substantial contribution to the chapters on acting; J.K. Curry, who contributed the synopsis of *Fefu and Her Friends;* Christopher Goumas, who provided invaluable assistance with the chapters on design; and Alvin Goldfarb, whose advice in many areas, especially the chapter on diversity, was, as always, enormously helpful.

McGraw-Hill and the author wish to express their thanks for the many useful comments and suggestions provided by the following reviewers:

Paul Wesley Alday, Bowling Green State University
Sidney Berger, University of Houston
Dennis C. Beck, Bradley University
Henry Bial, University of New Mexico
Claudia Billings, New Mexico State University
Sarah Blackstone, Southern Illinois University
Dan Browder, Illinois State University
Rhett Bryson, Furman University
Eric Bullis, University of Nevada, Reno
Howard Burman, California State University, Long Beach
John Callahan, Kutztown University
John Colclough, Jr., Marshall University
Armand Coutu, Okaloosa-Walton Community College
Doug Cummins, Furman University
Paul A. Daum, the University of Akron
Robert W. Dillon, Jr., Southeast Missouri State University

Armand Coutu, Okaloosa-Walton Community College
Doug Cummins, Furman University
Paul A. Daum, the University of Akron
Robert W. Dillon, Jr., Southeast Missouri State University
Ann C. Dreher, University of South Carolina
Jay Edelnant, University of Northern Iowa
Jeffrey Scott Elwell, Marshall University
Thomas H. Empey, Casper College
Gary Faircloth, East Carolina University
Pamela Fields, Scottsdale Community College
Kathleen George, University of Pittsburgh
E. Ross Genzez, Bloomsburg University
Lana Hagan, Southern Illinois University-Edwardsville
Delbert Hall, East Tennessee State University
Norman Hart, Montgomery College
Lawrence J. Hill, Western Carolina University
Elisabeth Hostetter, Stephen F. Austin State University
Jack Hrkach, Ithaca College
Joe Jeffreys, SUNY Stony Brook
Brian Jones, Indiana University of Pennsylvania
Gregory W. Justice, Virginia Polytechnic Institute
Jonathan Kalb, Hunter College
Sean R. Kelley, University of Colorado, Boulder
Janet Kenney, Morehead State University
Don LaCasse, Ball State University
David Larson, Anderson College
Robert Levy, Clarion University
Barbara Mackey, University of Toledo
Mark Mallett, Morehead State University
Dan Mangone, University of Pittsburgh
Sarah Jane Marschner, University of New Hampshire
Brenda May, Columbus State University
Margaret McCubbin, Bowling Green State University
Dale McGilliard, Middle Tennessee State University
G. David McManus, Lenoir-Rhyne College
Claudia Mohler, Appalachian State University
Michael O'Hara, Ball State University
Chris Olsen, Montgomery College
Corliss Phillabaum, University of Wisconsin-Milwaukee
Ellis M. Pryce-Jones, University of Nevada, Las Vegas
Dennis Seyer, Southeast Missouri State University
Joann Siegrist, West Virginia University
Jay Sierszyn, Waldorf College
Marvin Sims, Virginia Commonwealth University
Jim Shollenberger, University of Mississippi

Carlton Ward, Jacksonville State University
Albert F.C. Wehlburg, University of Florida
Steven L. Williams, University of Nebraska at Omaha
Bruce E. Woodruff, Baker University
Jim Wren, University of North Carolina-Greensboro

Incomparable, inimitable, irreplaceable—all apply to Inge King, who has found every photograph that has appeared in every edition of *The Theater Experience* from the beginning. She is without peer. Equally indispensable is Susan Gamer who has served as an unsurpassed copyeditor for the last seven editions in the most careful, conscientious, and committed way.

Of inestimable help at McGraw-Hill have been my two exceptional editors: Allison McNamara and Caroline Ryan. Both were helpful far beyond the call of duty, and I am deeply grateful. I am also most grateful to the publisher, Chis Freitag. In addition, I express thanks to Julie Booth who once more did a first-rate job in preparing the end-of-chapter sections on "Exploring Theater on the Web." I would like to thank Nadia Bidwell for her work on the exciting new CD-ROM that accompanies this edition. I am appreciative, as well, of the important contributions of Lisa Berry, the marketing manager, Jean Starr, the production manager, and Mary Kazak, the designer.

Introduction

Taken in its broadest sense, theater is everywhere around us. A wedding is theater; a funeral is theater. A Thanksgiving Day parade, a Mardi Gras parade, a fireworks display on the Fourth of July—all these are theater. So, too, is a presidential nominating convention, a Senate hearing, or a White House press conference. Even seemingly spontaneous, unrehearsed events, such as a high-speed automobile chase or a gunman holding hostages in a suburban home, have become a form of theater by the time they are seen on television. The person holding the television camera has framed the "shots" showing the event, and for the evening news, someone in a studio has edited the film to give it focus and make it dramatic.

More obvious forms of theater are the dramas that appear daily on television or in movies. On television, we can see a wide range of dramatic offerings. Daytime soap operas present a variety of domestic crises in family and other relationships; nighttime situation comedies depict young as well as middle-age characters in farcical and humorous encounters; hospital and police shows present the thrills and suspense of traditional melodrama.

As for movies, they provide dramatic material of many kinds: science fiction, romantic comedies, action-packed stories of intrigue, historical epics, and even film versions of such Shakespearean plays as *Hamlet, Othello,* and *Romeo and Juliet.* And then there is a combination of film and video when we watch movies at home on a DVD or VCR.

When we turn from electronic media to live performance, we see that theater has informed and influenced a popular musical form with which we are all familiar: rock and roll. Throughout its history, rock has appropriated theatrical elements. Not only do rock stars often adopt a stage persona (Britney Spears and Pink are examples), but rock concerts are highly theatrical events, using lights, sound, and properties in ways that are like multimedia stage presentations. Rock illustrates that theatrical elements have become an integral part of our popular entertainments and that we often find these elements in unexpected venues. Amusement parks like

THEATRICAL ELEMENTS: FOUND EVERYWHERE

Theater permeates many elements of the life around us. It is found in daily life, in politics, in judicial proceedings, and in all forms of entertainment. Shown here is a performance by the music group called 'NSYNC. Note the spectacular scenic and lighting effects that cover the entire stage. Included in the effects are clouds and performers suspended in the air like giant puppets. At times it is impossible to distinguish between a theater set and one devised for a rock concert or another musical presentation. (AP/Wide World Photos)

Disney World, Sea World, and Universal Studios incorporate theatrical material; most, for example, present staged productions based on films, which attract huge audiences. In cities such as Orlando, Florida, dinner theaters present entertainments incorporating Roman gladiators, medieval knights, and 1930s gangsters.

In *The Theater Experience* we will look both at the similarities and at the differences between theater on the one hand and other theatrical forms on the other. Today the vast majority of us see drama at the movies or in our homes on broadcast television or on DVD or VHS. Though these mediums are omnipresent, looked at from a broader perspective they are newcomers on the scene—movies are barely 100 years old, and television has been around for only half that time. In contrast to this, it must be remembered that we have had live theater for 2,500 years.

What's more, the drama we see on film or television owes its existence to live theater. Serious theater in any modern medium has its roots in ancient Greek theater, and there is a direct line connecting today's situation comedy on television to ancient Roman comedy. The most widely produced playwright in North America is William Shakespeare, who wrote his plays 400 years ago.

In studying live theater—its immediacy, its excitement, its various elements, its rich history—we prepare ourselves not only for a lifetime of attending theater performances but for a far better understanding of the dramas we see at a movie theater or on television. And we also see the impact that theater has had on such entertainments as theme park presentations and concerts by rock artists.

Before we plunge into the specifics of theater, however, we should take a brief look at how it relates to other art forms and to the arts in general.

THEATER: THE ART FORM

Theater is art, and as such it mirrors or reflects life. It does not try to encompass the whole of life at once; rather, it selects and focuses on a part of the total picture. As with all art, a key principle of theater is *selectivity;* through selectivity, various forms of art can achieve a clarity, an order, and a beauty rarely found in ordinary life.

The process of selection in art occurs in several ways. To begin with, any art form uses certain elements while eliminating others. For instance, music focuses on sounds produced by musical instruments and the human voice. Painting uses only visual elements: colors, shapes, and designs that can be put onto a surface, such as a canvas. Dance focuses on movements of the human body performed to the accompaniment of music. The force and effectiveness of art are due in part to its selectivity: when we look at a painting, we concentrate our full attention on the visual effect and are not distracted by other considerations.

The means by which an art form presents its material is often referred to as the *medium.* For instance, sound produced by instruments or human voices is the medium of music. In theater, the medium is the presentation of a story or another event enacted by performers: theater always involves actresses and actors on a stage playing characters. The basic encounter in theater is between the performers and the audience; but this is a special type of encounter because the performers are generally playing other people, known as *characters.* Moreover, these characters are part of a human story that has been written by a dramatist. This combination sets theater apart from other art forms.

ART IS SELECTIVE
Every art form focuses on certain elements to the exclusion of others. Painting, for example, concentrates on color, line, and design. In the performing arts, ballet focuses on movement set to music; it has no words or dialogue. An example of a ballet performance is Four Schumann Pieces *at the Royal Opera House, London.* (British Tourist Authority)

THE FOCUS OF THEATER: HUMAN BEINGS

Theater focuses on human beings, even though different plays emphasize different human concerns, from profound problems in tragedy to pure entertainment in light comedy.

Even when the performers play animals, inanimate objects, or abstract ideas, theater concentrates on human concerns. The medieval morality play *Everyman* is a good example. Although some of the roles are abstract ideas such as Fellowship, Knowledge, Good Deeds, Beauty, and Strength, the central character is Everyman, a human character if ever there was one. And the problem of the play—death coming before it is expected to come—is a universal human theme.

The human focus of theater is also illustrated in the way gods are depicted. In Greek drama, the gods sometimes appeared at the end of a play to intervene and tie up loose ends of the plot. The manner of their entrance is noteworthy: they were lowered to the playing area from the top of the

THE FOCUS OF THEATER: HUMAN CONCERNS

Painting concentrates on colors and shapes, dance on movement, music on sound; but theater focuses on encounters between human beings. Performers impersonate characters who engage in a series of personal crises and exchanges. A good example in recent years is Far Away *by playwright Caryl Churchill. The play presents an apocalyptic vision of what human beings today face in terms of deception, cruelty, and chaos. In the scene shown here, an older woman (Frances McDormand) is trying to reassure a young child (Alexa Eisenstein) that the abuses carried out by the woman's husband, which the child has witnessed, are not really what she saw, but the child knows that they are.* (© Joan Marcus)

stage house by a large lever or crane, called a *machine.* The term ***deus ex machina,*** which means literally "god from a machine," has come to stand for any device brought in arbitrarily to solve problems in a play. The gods in Greek tragedy were introduced, however, at the end, after the main characters—who were all human beings—had been through the anguish and struggle of the play.

In the modern world, human beings have lost the central place they were once believed to occupy in the universe. In the Ptolemaic view of the universe, which prevailed until the sixteenth century—when Copernicus theorized that the earth revolved around the sun—it was assumed that the earth was the center of everything. In science, we have long since given up that notion, particularly in light of recent explorations in outer space. The human being has become seemingly less and less significant, and less and less at the center of things. But not in theater. Theater is one area where the preoccupations of men and women are still the core, the center around which other elements orbit.

CEREMONIES AND RITUALS: THE IMPULSE TOWARD THEATER

Since theater is centered on human beings, it is not surprising that the impulse toward theater is universal. This has been apparent wherever human society has developed: in Europe and Asia, throughout Africa, and among Native Americans. In virtually every culture in recorded history or in anthropological studies, we find rituals, religious ceremonies, and celebrations that include elements of theater.

One aspect of theater is a presentation by *performers* in front of an *audience*—for instance, a ceremony or ritual conducted by religious leaders before members of a community.

A second aspect is *costumes,* such as those worn by priests or tribal chiefs. In some rituals or ceremonies, animals or gods are impersonated by people in costume.

Storytelling is a third aspect. In many cultures there is a strong tradition of storytellers who recite myths or legends from the past, or teach lessons by means of stories, to a group of listeners. These narrators impersonate the characters in a story; sometimes a narrator actually changes his or her voice to imitate a character.

Introduction

THE IMPULSE TOWARD THEATER IS UNIVERSAL
Throughout the world, cultures have rituals, ceremonies, and dances that include theatrical elements such as masks, costumes, and impersonations of people, animals, or spirits. Shown here is a Makishi dancer in a ceremonial dance in Zambia. Note the colorful, elaborate mask and costume. (M. and E. Bernheim/Woodfin Camp & Associates)

Ceremonies and rituals are found in every human society, and they invariably contain important theatrical elements. A ***ceremony*** is a formal religious or social occasion, usually led by a designated authority figure such as a priest or chief. Examples would include a graduation, an inauguration, or a marriage ceremony. A ***ritual*** is the acting out of an established, prescribed procedure and can range from a family event, such as an annual Thanksgiving or Christmas dinner, to the elaborate religious ceremonies of a Roman Catholic high mass or a Jewish Yom Kippur service during the High Holy Days. Because both refer to an observance that follows a prescribed course, ceremonies and rituals are closely related.

People in the west are most familiar with the kinds of ceremonies and rituals just mentioned, but important examples are found in nonwestern cultures, and these too have theatrical elements. Throughout central and western Africa, for instance, striking and imaginative costumes and masks are used in a variety of ceremonies. In a ceremony performed by the Guro tribe in the Ivory Coast, a dancer depicting an animal figure wears a large mask that combines antelope horns, an abstracted human face, and a large toothed beak. The costume consists of orange netting on the arms and bamboo reeds on the body. Other dancers wear masks and costumes appropriate to their roles.

The costumes and masks used for ceremonies in Africa are among the most beautiful found anywhere in the world, but it is not only in what people wear that we find theatrical elements; it is also in the actions of the celebrants. Frequently the participants enact a person or thing: a bird, an animal, or a spirit. In many cases the people who take part in these rituals believe that the performers are actually inhabited by the animal or spirit they portray, that they are transformed during the ceremony and become the figure they are representing. In addition, leaders and their assistants, as well as other celebrants who play key roles in a ceremony, have definite, assigned tasks and perform in a prescribed manner.

The actions of ceremonial leaders thus bear a certain similarity to those of actresses or actors in dramatic presentations, who learn specific movements and repeat dialogue from a script. Also, rituals and ceremonies generally follow a set sequence of events: the same words and actions are repeated each time, often exactly reproducing previous presentations. This sequence of events corresponds to the "script" and dramatic structure of a theatrical production. Also, the costumes and properties used in ceremonies and rituals reflect the theatrical nature of these events. Thus, some historians and anthropologists argue that theater grew out of religious rituals and ceremonies.

Exactly how and at what point rituals, ceremonies, or stories develop into the separate realm of theater is a matter of conjecture; it is enough to know that theater as a distinct art form has emerged in many different cultures going back to ancient times.

Wherever theater has become a separate art form, it has had certain essential qualities: an action or a story (the play) is presented by one group (the performers) to another group (the audience). Theater is thus an experience: a shared, indivisible event that includes both those who perform and those who observe. Like other experiences—riding a bicycle, attending a football game, falling in love—theater requires a personal presence: in this case, the presence of the audience.

THE PERMANENCE OF THE VISUAL ARTS
If they are preserved, painting and sculpture—unlike performing arts such as theater, dance, and music—are permanent and unchanging. An example is this sculpture of the Winged Victory of Samothrace *on display at the Louvre Museum in Paris, France. The torso enfolded in flowing robes and the outstretched wings appear much as they did when the sculpture was first created on the island of Samothrace in Greece around 200 B.C.E. about 2200 years ago.* (Louvre Museum/Reunion des Musées Nationaux)

THEATER AS A TRANSITORY ART

A theater performance changes from moment to moment as the audience encounters a series of shifting impressions and stimuli. It is a kaleidoscopic adventure through which the audience passes, with each instant a direct, immediate experience.

The transitory nature of theater—a quality it shares with all the performing arts—sets it apart in a significant way from literature and the visual arts. A painting, a piece of sculpture, a novel, or a book of poems is a fixed object. When it leaves the artist's hands (or, in the case of a book, when it leaves the printer's shop), it is complete. Such works exist as finished products, and their tangible, unchangeable quality is one reason we value them, in the same way that we value historic buildings or antique automobiles. In a world of change and uncertainty, they remain the same. The Winged Victory from the island of Samothrace in Greece is today almost the same majestic figure that was fashioned 2,200 years ago. When we see this statue, we are looking at a soaring figure, facing into the wind, which is essentially what the Greeks saw at the time it was created.

The essence of literature and the visual arts is to catch something at a moment in time and freeze it. With the performing arts, however, that is impossible, because the performing arts are not objects but events.

Objects—costumes, props, scenery, a script—are a part of theater, but none of these constitutes the art. Bernard Beckerman explains the difference:

> Theater is nothing if not spontaneous. It occurs. It happens. The novel can be put away, taken up, reread. Not theater. It keeps slipping between one's fingers. Stopping, it stops being theater. Its permanent features, facets of activity, such as scenery, script, stage, people, are no more theater than the two poles of a generator are electricity. Theater is what goes on between the parts.[1]

The distinction between reading a novel and attending a theatrical performance reminds us that drama is sometimes considered a branch of literature. This confusion is understandable. For one thing, plays are often printed in book form, like literature; for another, many novels and short stories contain extensive passages of dialogue that could easily be scenes in a play. But although scenes of dialogue in a novel resemble drama, and although plays appear in books, there is an important difference between the two forms. Unlike a novel, a play is written to be performed. In some respects a script is to a stage production as a musical score is to a concert, or an architectural blueprint is to a building: it is an outline for a performance.

Drama can be studied in a classroom in terms of imagery, character, and theme, just as we study a novel; but with drama, study of this sort takes place *before* or *after* the event. It is a form of preparation for or follow-up to the experience; the experience is the performance itself. Obviously, we have more opportunities to read plays in book form than to see them produced; but when we read a play, we should always attempt to visualize the other aspects of a production in our mind's eye.

One special quality of a theater performance is its immediacy. In theater, we live in what the playwright Thornton Wilder called the *perpetual present tense*. Contained in the present is the fresh remembrance of the past and the anticipation of what is to come. Robert Edmond Jones (1887–1954), an American scene designer and critic, describes it this way:

> All that has ever been is in this moment; all that will be is in this moment. Both are meeting in one living flame in this unique instant of time. This is drama; this is theater—*to be aware of the now.*[2]

As Jones suggests, the theater experience has a quality all its own; the nature of the theater experience and the elements which make up that experience will be the subject of this book.

THEATER IS ACTION
In contrast to sculpture, painting, or literature, theater is a dynamic art, changing from moment to moment as performers interact with one another. Shown here is a scene from a Royal Shakespeare Company production of Shakespeare's A Midsummer Night's Dream. *Note the physicality and movement of the performers (Nikki Aranka-Bird, Paul Chequer, Michal Colgan, and Gabrielle Jourdan, being held aloft).* (© Donald Cooper/PhotoSTAGE)

THE ELEMENTS OF THEATER

A performance results from the coming together of many elements and forces, which we will examine separately. All together, we will examine the following basic elements of theater:

1. The audience: its function, its general makeup, and the background each spectator brings to a performance.
2. The space or environment in which the theater event occurs.
3. The performances of the actors and actresses.
4. The director's supervision of the production.
5. The purpose of a theater piece and the point of view adopted by those who create it. Is the work intended as an escape from daily cares or to provoke thought? Is it serious or comic?

6. The work of the playwright in creating dramatic structure and dramatic characters.
7. The visual effects created by costumes, lighting, and scenery, along with sound.

At every point during a performance, these elements intersect; they fuse and combine to produce theater. In addition to studying the elements separately, we will look at the ways in which they join together to form the whole.

When an audience comes to see a performance, an exchange takes place between performers and spectators; the two groups engage in a form of communication or a celebration. At its best, theater affords members of the audience an opportunity to be transported outside themselves or to look deep inside themselves. In the following pages we will attempt to discover what makes this profound and magical experience possible.

SUMMARY

1. Theater is art. It reflects life, selecting and focusing on part of the total picture, and this selectivity is a key principle in theater.
2. The focus—the subject matter—of theater is always human beings.
3. The impulse toward theater is universal and has appeared wherever human society has developed. Rituals, religious ceremonies, and celebrations have certain elements of theater, including a performance in front of an audience, costumes, and storytelling.
4. Theater is a transitory art that occurs through time. A theater performance changes from moment to moment, and a theater event is created by cumulative sights, sounds, and impressions. One special quality of theater is its immediacy.
5. Basic elements of theater are the audience, the environment in which the theater event takes place, the performers, the director's supervision of performances, the purpose of a theater piece, the viewpoint of its creators, the playwright's work, and the visual and sound effects.

Part 1

The Audience

The Performer-Audience Connection

The audience forms an indispensable element in the theater equation. An important part of the audience's understanding and receptivity to a production will be the background and prior experience audience members bring to a play. ❖ August Wilson's *The Piano Lesson,* depicted here by artist Al Hirschfeld, is about an African American family in the 1930s. A brother and sister disagree sharply about whether or not to sell a piano that relates closely to the family's slave history. Any African American with a family history similar to that of the characters in the play will find an additional resonance and depth of feeling when watching a production of the play. ❖

The Audience: Its Role and Imagination

Today we are accustomed to seeing theatrical presentations in many forms: not only in live performances onstage but also on film, on television in our homes, on VCR tapes and DVD players, or on computer screens. Film, television, tapes, and computers are all products of the past 100 years, but theater existed for many centuries before that: in India, theater became well established nearly 2,000 years ago; in Greece, a fully developed theater had emerged even earlier, almost 2,500 years ago. For centuries, live theater was the only form of dramatic experience. When, around 1900, a succession of mechanical and electronic devices began to appear which could reproduce dramatic performances, many people thought theater would become obsolete.

First it was silent movies, then radio, followed by talking films, and after that television. Each of these offered theatrical presentations in a convenient form at a fraction of the cost of theater. In recent years, competition has appeared on yet another front: computers. The CD-ROM can produce scenes and sounds from plays and can even interact with the viewer.

Given the many challenges that theater has faced, its survival seems amazing. But it has survived, and in certain respects it has been greatly enriched. There has been a shift in emphasis from Broadway to off-Broadway and regional theater; in addition, multicultural theater, gender theater, and performance art have emerged as important new components of theater. Overall, theater in the United States appears surprisingly healthy. (The full range of theater in the United States will be described in detail in later chapters.)

◀ THE AUDIENCE PLAYS A KEY ROLE

Audience and performers are the two basic elements in the theater equation, and both are essential. The presence of the audience is what sets theater apart from other forms of entertainment such as film and television. Each audience is unique, especially in its reactions to what is happening on stage. This is sensed by the actresses and actors and influences their reactions. Here we see an audience attending a performance at the Globe Theatre in London. This reconstruction of the original attempts to duplicate the theater where many of Shakespeare's plays were first performed. Note the close connection between audience and the stage, making possible a true interaction between performers and audience members. (© Andrea Pistolesi/Image Bank/Getty Images)

THE RELATIONSHIP BETWEEN PERFORMER AND AUDIENCE

How has theater been able to meet so many challenges and not only survive but emerge in some ways stronger than ever? There are several answers, but perhaps the most important has to do with the "live" nature of theater. Theater is an event in which the performers are in the presence of the audience.

The Special Nature of Theater: A Contrast with Film

The special nature of theater will be more apparent if we contrast a drama seen in a theater with one shown on film or television. Both present a story told in dramatic form—an enactment of scenes by performers who speak and act as if they were the people they represent. The same actress can play Juliet in *Romeo and Juliet* by William Shakespeare (1564–1616) on both stage and screen. Not only the dramatization and the acting but also other elements, such as scenery and costumes, are often similar on stage and screen. In fact, many films and television specials have been based on stage productions: *A Chorus Line, Driving Miss Daisy, The Piano Lesson, The Heidi Chronicles, Evita, The Importance of Being Earnest*, and numerous plays by Shakespeare, including Kenneth Branagh's productions of *Much Ado About Nothing, Hamlet*, and *Henry V*, and Baz Luhrmann's *Romeo & Juliet*, and *O*, starring Julia Stiles and Josh Hartnett.

Unquestionably, one can learn a great deal about theater from watching a play on film or television. And film and television can give us many of

TELEVISION: A DIFFERENT EXPERIENCE FROM THEATER
When audiences see films or television shows, they see images—or pictures—of people on a screen rather than the people themselves. The experience, therefore, is once removed from personal contact. In this photograph, we see people watching a video presentation of Shakespeare's Henry V, *but they are looking at a screen, not the living performers, and that makes a tremendous difference in the nature of the experience.* (© Laura Dwight)

the same feelings and experiences that we have when watching a theater performance. Moreover, the accessibility of film and television means that they play a crucial role in our overall exposure to the depiction of dramatic events and dramatic characters.

Despite this, there is a fundamental difference. This does not have to do with technical matters, such as the way films can show outdoor shots taken from helicopters, cut instantaneously from one scene to another, or create the special effects of films like *Twister,* and *The Matrix,* or *Spider-Man.* The most significant difference between films and theater is the *performer-audience relationship.* The experience of being in the presence of the performer is more important to theater than anything else. With a film, we are always in the presence of an ***image,*** never a person.

The American playwright Jean-Claude van Itallie (1936–   ) has explained the importance of the actor-audience relationship in theater, and how theater differs from films and television:

> Theater is not electronic. Unlike movies and unlike television, it does require the live presence of both audience and actors in a single space. This is the theater's uniquely important advantage and function, its original religious function of bringing people together in a community ceremony where the actors are in some sense priests or celebrants, and the audience is drawn to participate with the actors in a kind of eucharist.[1]

The Chemistry of Performer-Audience Contact

Like films, television seems very close to theater; sometimes it seems even closer than film. Television programs often begin with such words as "This program comes to you live from Burbank, California." But the word *live* must be qualified. Before television, *live* in the entertainment world meant "in person": not only was the event taking place at that moment; it was taking place in the presence of the spectator. Today, although the term *live television* may still mean that an event is taking place at this moment, many so-called "live" events are actually taped and rebroadcast on one or more subsequent occasions. Also, "live" television does not take place in the *presence* of the viewer. In fact, it is generally far removed from the television audience, possibly half a world away. With television we see an image on a small tube; we are free to look or not look, or even leave the room.

The fascination of being in the presence of a person is difficult to explain but not difficult to verify. No matter how often fans have seen a favorite star in the movies or heard a rock singer on a CD or on television, they will go to any lengths to see him or her in person. Probably, at one time or another each of us has braved bad weather and shoving crowds to see celebrities at a parade, a political rally, or a concert. Even a severe rainstorm will not deter fans from seeing their favorite star at an outdoor concert. The same pull of personal contact draws us to the theater.

Audience and Performers Create Theater Together

The drama critic Walter Kerr (1913–1996) explained what it means for audience and actors to be together:

It doesn't just mean that we are in the personal presence of performers. It means that they are in *our* presence, conscious of us, speaking to us, working for and with us until a circuit that is not mechanical becomes established between us, a circuit that is fluid, unpredictable, ever-changing in its impulses, crackling, intimate. *Our* presence, the way we respond, flows back to the performer and alters what he does, to some degree and sometimes astonishingly so, every single night. We are contenders, making the play and the evening and the emotion together. We are playmates, building a structure.

This never happens at a film because the film is already built, finished, sealed, incapable of responding to us in any way. The actors can't hear us or feel our presence; nothing we do, in our liveness, counts. We could be dead and the film would purr out its appointed course, flawlessly, indifferently.

Source: Walter Kerr, "We Call It 'Live' Theater, but Is It?" *The New York Times,* January 2, 1972. Copyright 1972 by The New York Times Company. Reprinted by permission.

At the heart of the theater experience, therefore, is the performer-audience relationship: the immediate, personal exchange whose chemistry and magic give theater its special quality. During a stage performance the actresses and actors can hear laughter, can sense silence, and can feel tension in the audience. In short, the audience can affect, and in subtle ways change, the performance. At the same time, members of the audience watch the performers closely, consciously or unconsciously asking themselves questions: Are the performers convincing in their roles? Will they do something surprising? Will they make a mistake? At each moment, in every stage performance, the audience is looking for answers to questions like these.

THEATER AS A GROUP EXPERIENCE

For the audience, theater is a group experience. By contrast, certain other arts—such as painting, sculpture, and literature—provide solitary experiences. The viewer or reader contemplates the work alone, at her or his own pace. This is true even in a museum: although many people may flock to look at a single painting and are with each other, they respond as individuals, one by one. In the other performing arts, however, including theater, the group experience is indispensable. The performing arts share this trait with other communal events such as religious services, spectator sports, and celebrations. Before the event can take place, a group must assemble, at one time and in one place. When people are gathered together in this way, something mysterious happens to them. Though still individuals, with their own personalities and backgrounds, they take on other qualities as well, qualities which often overshadow their independent responses.

Psychology of Groups

Gustave Le Bon, a forerunner of social psychology and one of the first to study the phenomenon of crowds, wrote that a collection of people "presents new characteristics very different from those of the individuals composing it. The sentiments and ideas of all the persons in the gathering take one and the same direction, and their conscious personality vanishes."[2] Le Bon went on to say that the most striking peculiarity of a crowd is that although the people who compose it are different as individuals, once they have been transformed into a crowd they develop a "collective mind which makes them feel, think, and act in a manner quite different from that in which each individual of them would feel, think, and act were he in a state of isolation."[3]

Not all crowds are alike. Some are aggressive, such as an angry mob that decides to riot or a gang of young people who terrorize a neighborhood. Others are docile—passengers on an airline flight, for example. A crowd at a football game is different from a congregation at a religious observance; and a theater crowd is distinct from any of these. In spite of

THEATER IS A GROUP EXPERIENCE
In theater, the size, attitude, and makeup of the audience affect the overall experience. The theater can be large or small, indoors or outdoors, and the audience can be people of similar tastes and background or a collection of quite varied individuals. Depicted here is the audience at a performance at the Oregon Shakespeare Festival where the works of Shakespeare and his contemporaries are presented from June through September each year to a diverse audience. (© Gregory Ventana)

Chapter 1   The Audience: Its Role and Imagination   19

being different, however, the theater audience shares with all such groups the special characteristics of the collective mind.

Becoming part of a group is a crucial element of the theater experience. For a time, we share a common undertaking, focused on one activity—the performance of a play. Not only do we laugh or cry in a way we might not otherwise, we also sense an intangible communion with those around us.

When a collection of individuals respond more or less in unison to what is occurring onstage, their relationship to one another is reaffirmed. If there is a display of cruelty at which we shudder, or sorrow by which we are moved, or pomposity at which we laugh, it is reassuring to have others respond as we do. For a moment we are part of a group sharing a common experience; and our sorrow or joy, which we thought might be ours alone, is found to be part of a broad human response.

How Audience Makeup Affects the Theater Experience

Although being part of a group is an essential element of theater, groups vary, and the makeup of a group will alter a theatrical event. Some audiences are general—for instance, the thousands who attend outdoor productions such as the Shakespeare festival in Ashland, Oregon, and *Unto These Hills,* which is a play about the Cherokee Indians presented each summer on the Cherokee reservation located in western North Carolina. General audiences include people of all ages, from all parts of the country, and from all socioeconomic levels. Other audiences are more homogeneous, such as spectators at a high school play, a children's theater production, a Broadway opening night, a political play, or a performance in a prison.

Another factor affecting our experience in the theater is our relationship to the other members of the audience. If we are among friends or people of like mind, we feel comfortable and relaxed, and we readily become part of the group experience. On the other hand, if we feel alien—for example, a young person with an older group, a radical with conservatives, or a naive person with sophisticates—we will be estranged from the group as a whole. The people with whom we attend the theater—their relative homogeneity and our relation to them—strongly influence our response to the total event.

Outside events can also affect the shared experience of audience members. In the days immediately following the terrorist attack on the World Trade Center on September 11, 2001, in New York City, audiences at theatrical and other performances were aware of and sensitive to what had just occurred. Among other things, there was a loss of complacency, and a feeling of vulnerability, that had not been present before. In such an atmosphere, audiences felt a heightened sense of escape when seeing a comedy and of danger when viewing a play in which serious threats were made to characters onstage. It was an unspoken but palpable feeling shared by everyone present at many performances.

THE SEPARATE ROLES OF PERFORMERS AND SPECTATORS

In recent years numerous attempts have been made to involve members of the audience in the action of plays, with performers coming into the audience to make contact with spectators—shaking hands, touching them, arguing face to face. Spectators, too, have been encouraged to come onstage and join the action. In *Fool Moon,* which was presented on Broadway several times in the 1990s, audience members were asked to become part of the action temporarily. The performers in this production were two men from the tradition of circus clowns, Bill Irwin (1950–   ) and David Shiner (1953–), who went into the audience, engaged audience members in exchanges, and asked some of them to come onstage and take part in various segments of the performance.

How Should the Audience Be Involved?

The attempt to involve audience members directly springs from a desire to make theater more immediate and intense. In most cases, however, art requires some degree of distancing.

Imagine trying to get the full effect of a large landscape painting when standing a few inches from it: one would see only the brush strokes of a single tree or a small patch of blue sky. To perceive and appreciate a work of art, we need distance. This separation, which is called **aesthetic distance,** is as necessary in theater as in any other art.

In the same way that a viewer must stand back from a painting to get its full effect, so in the theater spectators must usually be separated from the performance in order to see and hear what is happening onstage and thus absorb the experience. If an audience member becomes involved in the proceedings or goes onstage and takes part in the action, as was the case with *Fool Moon,* he or she reverses roles and becomes a performer, not a spectator. The separation between performers and spectators remains.

There are activities applying theatrical techniques in which everyone concerned does participate; such activities point up the contrast between **observed** and **participatory** theater. In this book we are primarily concerned with observed theater; but it is helpful to be aware of participatory theater, which we will discuss in the following section.

Audience Participation through Direct Action

The issue of separation between the performer and the audience has been complicated in recent years by the rapid growth of theatrical activities in which ordinary people play roles and improvise dramatic scenes. In observed theater, the audience participates vicariously or empathically with what is happening onstage. Empathy is the experience of mentally entering into the feelings or spirit of another person—in this case, a character onstage. Sometimes an audience will not be in tune with the characters

onstage but will react violently against them. In either situation, though, members of the audience are participating empathically. They might shed tears, laugh, pass judgment, sit frozen, or literally tremble with fear. But they participate through their imaginations while separated from the action.

Theater of direct participation works differently. Those who take part are not performers in the usual sense, and there is no attempt to follow a written script. Rather, the emphasis is on education, personal development, or therapy—fields in which theater techniques have opened up new possibilities. In schools, for example, creative dramatics, theater games, and group improvisations have proved invaluable for self-discovery and the development of healthy group attitudes. By acting out hypothetical situations or giving free rein to their imagination, children can build self-confidence, discover their creative potential, and overcome their inhibitions. In some situations, creative dramatics can teach lessons which are difficult to teach by conventional means. Playwriting, too, has often proved to be an invaluable educational tool. Students who write scenes, whether autobiographical or fictional, find the experience not only fulfilling but enlightening.

In addition to creative dramatics, a wide range of other activities—*sociodrama, psychodrama,* and *drama therapy,* for example—incorporate theatrical techniques. For adults as well as children, these activities have come to the forefront as educational and therapeutic methods. In sociodrama, the members of participating groups—such as parents and children, students and teachers, or legal authorities and ordinary citizens—explore their own attitudes and prejudices. One successful approach is *role reversal*. A group of young people, for instance, may take the part of their parents while the adults assume the roles of the children; or members of a street gang will take the roles of the police, and the police will take the roles of the street gang. In such role playing, both groups become aware of deep-seated feelings and arrive at a better understanding of one another.

Psychodrama uses some of the same techniques as sociodrama, but it is more private and interpersonal; in fact, it can become so intense that it should be carried out only under the supervision of a trained therapist. In psychodrama, individual fears, anxieties, and frustrations are explored.

PARTICIPATORY THEATER: A DIFFERENT EXPERIENCE

In participatory theater, audience members, rather than simply observing, become part of the action. A good example is Euphorium, *a production that originated in London, but has played elsewhere, including the West Coast in the United States. In* Euphorium, *one person enters an environment that is like a maze attempting to simulate the experience of walking through the poet Samuel Taylor Coleridge's imagination at the moment he was dreaming up his poem "Kubla Khan." Every three minutes a spectator, equipped with a special hallucinatory helmet, enters the maze and encounters images that the poet might have imagined. The maze includes voices, music, and sound effects that are activated digitally by the presence of the spectator.* (© Antenna Theater)

A person might reenact a particularly traumatic scene from childhood, for example.

The various fields of participatory theater are fascinating, but the purpose here is to draw a distinction between participatory drama and observed drama. In participatory drama, theater is a means to another end: education, therapy, group development, or the like. Its aim is not public performance, and there is little emphasis on a carefully prepared, expertly performed presentation before an audience; in fact, just the opposite is true. In observed drama, on the other hand, the aim is an expert performance for spectators, and there must always be some separation between the performers and the audience—the "aesthetic distance" described earlier.

At times in contemporary theater, as has been noted, spectators go onstage to be part of the action, or performers come into the audience to engage in repartee with spectators. If a spectator takes part in the action, he or she has, for the moment, switched roles and become what Bernard Beckerman calls a *presenter* rather than a *presentee*.[4]

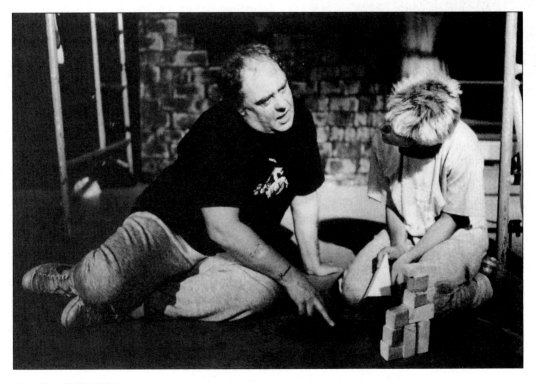

DRAMA THERAPY

Theater techniques can be used for purposes of education and therapy. A group called the Geese Company, for example, visits prisons and has convicts re-enact scenes from their own lives in an attempt to come to a better understanding of themselves. Here, the actress Pamela Daryl (right) *is listening to a prisoner unburdening painful memories of childhood in a drama therapy session* . (Steve Liss/Time Magazine/Getty Images)

THE AUDIENCE USES ITS IMAGINATION

In theater, the audience is called on to use its imagination to accept many things: ghosts, spirits, witches, imaginary objects. In playwright Tony Kushner's Angels in America, *an angel comes through the ceiling and appears to a young man with AIDS. The audience suspends disbelief in otherworldly creatures such as angels and accepts this event as part of the dramatic action. The angel here is played by Jennifer Mudge Tucker and the man by Brian McEleney.* (© T. Charles Erickson/Trinity Repertory Theatre)

THE IMAGINATION OF THE AUDIENCE

For those who create it, theater is a direct experience: an actress walks onstage and impersonates a character; a carpenter builds scenery; a scene designer paints it. For these people the experience is like cutting a finger or being held in an embrace: the pain or the warmth is felt directly and physically.

Members of a theater audience experience a different kind of pain or warmth. As spectators in a theater, we sense the presence of other audience members; we observe the movements and gestures of performers and hear the words they speak; and we see costumes, scenery, and lighting. From these we form mental images or make imaginative connections which provoke joy, laughter, anger, sorrow, or pain. All this occurs, however, without our moving from our seats.

We naturally assume that those who create theater are highly imaginative people and that their minds are full of vivid, exciting ideas which might not occur to the rest of us. If we conclude, however, that we in the audience have only a limited theatrical imagination, we do ourselves a great injustice. As we saw earlier, theater is a two-way street—an exchange between performers and audience—and this is nowhere more evident than in the creation of *illusion.* Illusion may be initiated by the creators of theater, but it is completed by the audience.

In the eerie world of William Shakespeare's *Macbeth,* when three witches appear out of the mist or when Banquo's ghost interrupts the banquet, we know it is fantasy; witches and ghosts like those in *Macbeth* do not appear in everyday life. In the theater, however, we take such fantasy at face value. In Shakespeare's own day, for instance, a convention readily accepted by audiences was that women's parts were played by boy actors. Shakespeare's heroines—Juliet, Desdemona, Lady Macbeth—were not acted by women, as they are today, but played by boys. Everyone in the audience at an Elizabethan theater knew that the boys were not actually women but accepted without question the notion that a boy actor was presenting an impression or an imitation of a woman. The film *Shakespeare in Love* afforded a fascinating glimpse of this: the actress Gwyneth Paltrow plays a young woman portraying a boy actor (in secret), while her acting partner is a young man playing a young woman portrayed by a boy (in the open).

Along with fantasy, theater audiences accept drastic shifts in time and space. Someone onstage dressed in a Revolutionary uniform says, "It is the winter of 1778, at Valley Forge," and we do not question it. What is more, we accept rapid movements back and forth in time. **Flashbacks**—abrupt movements from the present to the past and back again—are a familiar technique in films like *Citizen Kane, The Prince of Tides, A League of Their Own, Dead Man Walking,* and *Memento;* but they are also commonplace in modern drama.

A similar device often used in drama is ***anachronism.*** An anachronism involves placing some character or event outside its proper time sequence: for example, having people from the past speak and act as if they were living today. Medieval mystery and morality plays frequently contained anachronisms. The medieval play *Abraham and Isaac,* for instance, is set in the time of the Old Testament, but it makes several references to the Christian trinity—a religious concept that was not developed until centuries later. The medieval audience accepted this shift in time as a matter of course, just as we do in theater today.

In his play *Angels in America,* Tony Kushner (1958–   ) includes a number of bizarre and fantastic characters or events. For example, a character in the play called Mr. Lies is an imaginary person created in the mind of Harper, a housewife who is addicted to pills. Near the end of Part One, Mr. Lies takes Harper on a fantasy trip to the Antarctic. At the very end of Part One, an angel crashes through the ceiling and speaks to Prior, a man ill with AIDS.

In the theater, then, our imagination allows us to conceive of people and events we have never seen or experienced and to transcend our physical circumstances to the point where we forget who we are, where we are, or what time it is. How is this possible? It happens because in the theater our imagination works for us just as it does in everyday life.

Tools of the Imagination: Symbol and Metaphor

We can understand this process better if we look closely at two tools of our imagination: symbol and metaphor.

Functions of Symbols In general terms, a *symbol* is a sign, token, or emblem that signifies something else. A simple form of symbol is a sign. Some signs stand for a single, uncomplicated idea or action. In everyday life we are surrounded by them: road signs, such as an S-shaped curve; audible signals, like sirens and foghorns; and a host of mathematical and typographical symbols: $-$, $+$, \$, ¼, @ &. We sometimes forget that language itself is symbolic; the letters of the alphabet are only lines and curves on a page. Words are arrangements of letters which by common agreement represent something else. The same four letters mean different things depending on the order in which they are placed: *pear, reap, rape.* These three words set different imaginative wheels in motion and signal responses which vary greatly from word to word.

In commerce, the power of the symbol is acknowledged in the value placed on a trademark or a logo. The term *status symbol* is a frank recognition of the importance of personal possessions in conferring status on the

THE POWER OF SYMBOLS

Symbols and metaphors, though not real in a literal sense, have enormous power to influence our lives; in that respect, they become "realer than real." A forceful symbol of the gallantry, the bravery, the tragedy, and the loss of the Vietnam War is captured in the wall in Washington where the names of those who died are etched into the side of the memorial. People visiting this are put in touch with their feelings and memories because of the power of this simple but effective symbol. (© Joe Sohm/The Image Works)

owner. What cars people drive, how they dress, how they furnish their homes: these indicate what kind of people they are—at least, that is the theory.

Flags are symbols: lines, shapes, and colors which in certain combinations become immediately recognizable. At times, symbols exert incredible emotional power; a good example is a flag, embodying a nation's passions, fears, and ambitions. In the aftermath of September 11, 2001 (mentioned above), there was an outpouring of demonstrations of the American flag. Flags of all sizes appeared everywhere: on car windows, on mailboxes, and on clothes, belt buckles, and watches. Outsize flags were displayed on the facades of office buildings, on the field at sports events, and flying from helicopters above outdoor public events.

Like flags, some symbols signify ideas or emotions that are far more complex and profound than the symbol itself. The cross, for example, is a symbol of Christ and, beyond that, of Christianity as a whole. Whatever form a symbol takes—language, a flag, or a religious emblem—it can embody the total meaning of a religion, a nation, or an idea.

Functions of Metaphors A similar transformation takes place with **metaphor,** another form of imaginative substitution. With metaphor we announce that one thing *is* another, in order to describe it or point up its meaning more clearly. (In poetry, you will remember, a simile says that one thing is *like* another; metaphor simply states directly that one thing *is* another.) The Bible is filled with metaphors. The psalmist who says, "The Lord is my shepherd," or who says of God, "Thou art my rock and my fortress," is speaking metaphorically. He does not mean literally that God is a shepherd, a rock, or a fortress; he is saying that God is *like* these things.

Like symbols, metaphors are part of the fabric of life, as the following common expressions suggest:

"That's gross."

"He's off the wall."

"It's a slam dunk."

"Give me the bottom line."

"It's cool."

We are saying one thing but describing another. When someone describes a person or event as "cool," the reference is not to a low temperature but to an admirable quality. The term "slam dunk" comes from basketball, but in everyday parlance is applied to a wide range of activities that have nothing to do with sports. We can see from these examples that metaphors, like symbols, are part of daily life.

The "Reality" of the Imagination

Our use of symbol and metaphor, however, shows how large a part imagination plays in our lives. Millions of automobiles in the United States can be brought to a halt, not by a concrete wall, but by a small colored light changing from green to red. Imagine attempting to control traffic, or virtually any type of human activity, without symbols. Beyond being a matter of convenience, symbols are necessary to our survival.

The same holds true for metaphor. Frequently we find that we cannot express fear, anxiety, hope, or joy—any of the deep human feelings—in descriptive language. That is why we sometimes scream. It is also why we have poetry and use metaphors. Even scientists, the men and women we are most likely to consider realists, turn to metaphor at crucial times. They discuss the "big bang" theory of the origin of the universe and talk of "black holes" in outer space. Neither term is "scientific," but both terms communicate what scientists have in mind in a way that an equation or a more logical phrase could not.

Dreams provide another example of the power of the imagination. You dream that you are falling off a cliff; then, suddenly, you wake up and find that you are not flying through the air but lying in bed. Significantly, however, the dream of falling means more to you than the objective fact of lying in bed.

Although people have long recognized the importance of dreams in human life, in the modern period interest in dreams has been intensified as a result of the work of Sigmund Freud (1856–1939) on the subconscious. Despite variations and corrections of his theories, no one today disputes Freud's notion of the importance and "reality" of dreams, nightmares, and symbols in the human mind.

Theater functions in somewhat the same way. Though not real in a literal sense, it can be completely—even painfully—real in an emotional or intellectual sense. The critic and director Harold Clurman (1901–1980) gave one of his books on theater the title *Lies Like Truth*. Theater—like dreams or fantasies—can sometimes be more truthful about life than a mundane, objective description. This is a paradox of dreams, fantasies, and art, including theater: by probing deep into the psyche to reveal inner truths, they can be more real than outward reality.

THE IMAGINARY WORLDS OF THEATER

Realism and Nonrealism

An audience in a theater is asked to accept many kinds of imaginary worlds. One way to classify these imaginary realms is as ***realism*** and ***nonrealism.*** At the outset, it is essential to know that in theater the term *realistic* denotes a special application of what we consider "genuine" or "real." A realistic element is not necessarily more truthful than a nonrealistic element. Rather, in theater, *realistic* and *nonrealistic* denote different ways of presenting reality.

Realistic Elements of Theater   In theater, a realistic element is one that resembles *observable* reality. It is a kind of photographic truth. We apply the term *realistic* to those elements of theater that conform to our own observations of people, places, and events. Realistic theater follows the predictable logic of everyday life: the law of gravity, the time it takes a person to travel from one place to another, the way a room in a house looks, the way a person dresses. With a realistic approach, these conform to our normal expectations. In realistic theater, the act of imagination demanded of the audience is acceptance of the notion that what is seen onstage is not make-believe but real.

We are quite familiar with realism in films and television. Part of the reason is mechanical. The camera records what the lens "sees." Whether it is a bedroom in a house, a crowded city street, or the Grand Canyon, film captures the scene as the eye sees it.

Theater too has always had realistic elements. Every type of theater that is not pure fantasy has realistic aspects. For example, characters who are supposed to represent real people must be rooted in a human truth that audiences can recognize. During the latter part of the nineteenth century, in keeping with social and political changes that were occurring at the time, realistic elements became increasingly predominant. The emphasis in theater was not on fairy tales or make-believe, on kings or knights in armor in faraway places, but on what was happening to ordinary people in familiar surroundings.

Realism became the dominant form of European drama in the late nineteenth century when three playwrights—Henrik Ibsen (1828–1906) of Norway, August Strindberg (1849–1912) of Sweden, and Anton Chekhov (1860–1904) of Russia—produced a number of strongly realistic plays. To-

REALISTIC AND NONREALISTIC THEATER CONTRASTED

These scenes illustrate the difference between two approaches to the make-believe of theater. The play Frankie and Johnny in the Clair de Lune *by Terrence McNally, features a realistic apartment in which Johnny (Stanly Tucci), a middle-aged cook, has an encounter with Frankie (Edie Falco), a waitress in a diner. The set, the costumes, the dialogue all resemble those in real life. By contrast, the other photograph shows a quite unrealistic set. It was designed by the director/designer Robert Wilson for his production* The Days Before: Death, Destruction and Detroit III. *The set, the masks, all the elements make no attempt to be realistic, but, on the contrary, are completely arbitrary and imaginative.* (© Sara Krulwich/ The New York Times), (© James Hill/The New York Times)

gether they set the pattern for the next century in this type of theater. Their dramas presented characters with life histories, motives, and anxieties that audiences could immediately recognize as believable from their own experience and observation. The housewives in Ibsen's plays, the quarreling couples in Strindberg's, and the dispossessed families in Chekhov's—all were characters who spoke, dressed, and behaved as would be expected of real people.

When we are so readily able to verify what we see before us from our own experience, it is easy to identify with it and to accept its authenticity. For this reason, realistic theater has become firmly established in the past 100 years, and it seems likely to remain so.

Nonrealistic Elements of Theater   Nonrealistic elements of theater include everything that does not conform to our observations of surface reality: poetry instead of prose, ghosts rather than flesh-and-blood people, abstract forms for scenery, and so forth. Again, we find a counterpart in films and television. Movies like *ET,* the *Signs, X-Files,* and *Buffy the Vampire Slayer* use special effects to give us otherworldly creatures, rides through outer space, or encounters with prehistoric monsters. The *Star Wars* trilogy had computer-generated characters, which became famous but also created controversy over questions of ethnic identity.

In theater, the argument for nonrealism is that the surface of life—a real conversation, for instance, or a real room in a house—can never convey the whole truth, because so much of life occurs in our minds and imagination. If we are depressed and tell a friend that we feel "lousy" or "awful," we do not even begin to communicate the depth of our feelings. It is because of the inadequacy of ordinary words that people turn to poetry, and because of the inadequacy of other forms of daily communication that they turn to music, dance, art, sculpture, and the entire range of symbols and metaphors discussed earlier.

In theater, symbolic expression takes the form of nonrealistic techniques. A sense of being haunted by the past can never be portrayed in a simple description as vividly as it can be by a figure like the ghost of Hamlet's father, or Banquo's ghost appearing before Macbeth. Nonrealistic theater offers an opportunity to present these inner truths—reality that is "realer than real."

A wide range of theatrical techniques and devices fall into the category of nonrealism. One good example is the **soliloquy,** in which a solitary character speaks to the audience, expressing in words a hidden thought. In real life, we might confess some of our inner fears or hopes to a priest, a psychiatrist, or our best friend; but we do not announce such fears out loud for the world to hear as Hamlet does when he says, "To be, or not to be . . ."

Another example is **pantomime,** in which performers pretend to be using objects that are not actually present, such as drinking from a cup or opening an umbrella. Many aspects of musical comedy are nonrealistic.

Realism and Nonrealism: A Contrast

The distinction between realistic and nonrealistic techniques in theater becomes clearer when the two approaches are examined side by side. This distinction is present in all aspects of theater.

Realistic Techniques	Nonrealistic Techniques
STORY	
Events which the audience knows have happened or might happen in everyday life: Blanche DuBois in Tennessee Williams's *A Streetcar Named Desire* goes to New Orleans to visit her sister and brother-in-law.	Events which do not take place in real life but occur only in the imagination: in Kushner's *Angels America*, a character in a housewife's mind takes her on an imaginary trip to the Antarctic.
STRUCTURE	
Action is confined to real places; time passes normally as it does in everyday life: in the hospital room setting in Margaret Edson's *Wit*.	Arbitrary use of time and place: in August Strindberg's *The Dream Play*, walls dissolve and characters are transformed, as in a dream.
CHARACTERS	
Recognizable human beings, such as the family—the father and two daughters in David Auburn's *Proof*.	Unreal figures like the ghost of Hamlet's father in William Shakespeare's *Hamlet* or the three witches in *Macbeth*.
ACTING	
Performers portray people as they behave in daily life: the men on a summer holiday in the country house In Terrence McNally's *Love! Valor! Compassion!*	Performers portray animals in the musical *The Lion King*; they also engage in singing, dancing, and acrobatics in musical comedy or performance art.
LANGUAGE	
Ordinary dialogue or conversation: the two brothers trying to get ahead in Suzan Lori-Parks's *Topdog/Underdog*.	Poetry such as Romeo speaks to Juliet in Shakespeare's play; or the song "Tonight" sung to Maria in the musical *West Side Story*.
SCENERY	
Rooms of a real house, as in Wendy Wasserstein's *The Sisters Rosensweig*.	Abstract forms and shapes on a bare stage—for example for a Greek play such as Sophocles' *Electra*.
LIGHTING	
Light onstage appears to come from natural sources—a lamp in a room, or sunlight, as in Ibsen's *Ghosts*, where the sunrise comes through a window in the final scene.	Shafts of light fall at odd angles; also, colors in light are used arbitrarily. Example: a single blue spotlight on a singer in a musical comedy.
COSTUMES	
Ordinary street clothes, like those worn by the characters in August Wilson's *King Hedley II*.	The bright costumes of a chorus in a musical comedy; the strange outfit worn by Caliban, the half-man, half-beast in Shakespeare's *The Tempest*.
MAKEUP	
The natural look of characters in a domestic play such as Lorraine Hansberry's *A Raisin in the Sun*.	Masks worn by characters in a Greek tragedy or in a modern play like the musical *Beauty and the Beast*.

People in the streets or in an office building do not break into song or dance as they do in musicals like *Guys and Dolls* and *West Side Story* or begin tap-dancing as they do in *Bring in 'Da Noise, Bring in 'Da Funk*. One could say that any activity or scenic device which transcends or symbolizes reality tends to be nonrealistic.

Combining the Realistic and the Nonrealistic   In discussing realistic and non-realistic elements of theater, we must not assume that these two approaches are mutually exclusive. The terms *realistic* and *nonrealistic* are simply a convenient way of separating those parts of theater which correspond to our observations and experiences of everyday life from those which do not.

Most performances and theater events contain a mixture of realistic and nonrealistic elements. In acting, for example, a Shakespearean play calls for a number of nonrealistic qualities or techniques. At the same time, any performer playing a Shakespearean character must convince the audience that he or she represents a real human being. To take a more modern example, in *The Glass Menagerie* by Tennessee Williams (1911–1983), and in Thornton Wilder's *Our Town*, one of the performers serves as a narrator and also participates in the action. When the performer playing this part is speaking directly to the audience, his actions are nonrealistic; when he is taking part in a scene with other characters, they are realistic.

NONREALISTIC ELEMENTS
Realism has been a major approach to theater since the late nineteenth century, but for hundreds of years before that, as well as much theater since then, theater has incorporated many unrealistic elements. One example are ghosts and various otherworldly creatures in the plays of Shakespeare. Shown here in a Royal National Theatre production of Hamlet *in London is actor Simon Russell Beale (center) encountering the ghost of his dead father (Sylvester Morand). Playing his mother Gertrude, at the left, is Sara Kestelman.*

(© Donald Cooper/PhotoSTAGE)

FACT-BASED THEATER

A popular form that has emerged in the past half century is theater based on facts. This includes documentary theater taken from court trials, congressional hearings, and interviews. Shown here is a scene from The Exonerated *developed by two young actors based on interviews with six wrongfully convicted death row inmates. Elements in the documentary drama included coerced confessions, conflicting DNA evidence, and overturned convictions. Different well-known performers took turns acting in* The Exonerated. *Seen here are Jill Clayburgh and Richard Dreyfuss.* (Sara Krulwich/The New York Times)

Distinguishing Stage Reality from Fact

Whether theater is realistic or nonrealistic, it is different from the physical reality of everyday life. In recent years there have been attempts to make theater less remote from our daily lives. For example, plays have been presented which were largely transcripts of court trials or congressional hearings. This was part of a movement called **theater of fact**, which involved reenactments of material gathered from actual events. Partly as a result of this trend, theater and life have become intertwined. Television has added to this with *docudramas*, dramatizing the lives, for example, of rape victims, convicts, and ordinary people who become heroic.

This kind of interaction—and sometimes confusion—between life and art has been heightened, of course, by the emergence of television and film documentaries, which cover real events but are also edited. In addition, today we have "staged" political demonstrations and hear of "staged news." In politics staged events have become commonplace: a presidential or senatorial candidate visits a flag factory, an aircraft carrier, or an elementary school for what is called a "photo opportunity." When news becomes "staged" and theater becomes "fact," it is difficult to separate the two.

These developments point up the close relationship between theater and life; nevertheless, when we see a performance, even a re-creation of events which have actually occurred, we are always aware on some level that we are in a theater. No matter how authentic a reenactment may be, we know that it is a replay and not the original event. Most of us have seen plays with a stage setting so real we marvel at its authenticity: a kitchen, for instance, in which the appliances actually work, with running water in the faucets, ice in the refrigerator, and a stove on which an actor or actress can cook. What we stand in awe of, though, is that the room *appears* so real when we know, in truth, that it is not. We admire the fact that, not being a real kitchen, it looks as if it were.

We are abruptly reminded of the distinction between stage reality and physical reality when the two lines cross. If an actor unintentionally trips and falls onstage, we suddenly shift our attention from the character to the person playing the part. Has he hurt himself? Will he be able to continue? A similar reaction occurs when a performer forgets lines, or a sword falls accidentally during a duel, or a dancer slips during a musical number.

We remember the distinction, also, at the moment when someone else *fails* to remember it. Children frequently mistake actions onstage for the real thing, warning the heroine of the villain's plan or assuming that blows on the head of a puppet actually hurt. There is a famous story about a production of *Othello* in which a spectator ran onstage to prevent the actor playing Othello from strangling Desdemona. Another instance was a production by the Street Theater of Ossining, New York, of *Street Sounds* by the African American playwright Ed Bullins (1935–   ). The play opens with two black policemen beating a 15-year-old black youth. At one performance, a spectator ran onstage in the midst of the beating to stop the actors playing the policemen. In each of these cases, the distinction between fantasy and reality disappeared for the spectator, who mistook the imagined event for a real one.

Most people, however, are always aware of the difference; our minds manage two seemingly contradictory feats simultaneously: on the one hand, we know that an imagined event is not objectively real, but at the same time we accept it completely as fantasy. This is possible because of what the poet and critic Samuel Taylor Coleridge (1772–1834) called the "willing suspension of disbelief." Having separated the reality of art from the reality of everyday life, the mind is prepared to go along unreservedly with the reality of art.

In this chapter we have been concerned with the role the audience plays and the imagination it uses to enter into a theater event. But there are other factors surrounding our attendance at the theater that also have a bearing on how we view the experience and how well we understand it. These include the circumstances under which a play was created and the expectations we have when we attend a performance; and they are the subject to which we turn next, in Chapter 2.

SUMMARY

1. During this century, theater has been challenged by a succession of technological developments: silent movies, radio, talking movies, television, and so on. It has survived these challenges partly because of the special nature of the performer-audience relationship.

2. The relationship between performer and audience is "live": each is in the other's presence, in the same place at the same time. It is the exchange between the two which gives theater its unique quality.

3. Theater—like the other performing arts—is a group experience. The makeup of the audience has a direct bearing on the effect of the experience.

4. Participants and spectators play different roles in the theater experience; the role of spectators is to observe and respond.

5. There is a difference between participating in theater by direct action and by observation. In the former situation, nonactors take part, usually for the purpose of personal growth and self-development. In the latter, a presentation is made by one group to another, and the spectators do not participate physically in the experience.

6. For the observer, theater is an experience of the imagination and the mind. The mind seems capable of accepting almost any illusion as to what is taking place, who the characters are, and when and where the action occurs.

7. Our minds are capable of leaps of the imagination, not just in the theater but in our everyday lives, where we use symbol and metaphor to communicate with one another and to explain the world around us.

8. The world of the imagination—symbols, metaphors, dreams, fantasies, and various expressions of art—is "real," even though it is intangible and has no objective reality. Frequently it tells us more than any form of logical discourse about our true feelings.

9. Theater makes frequent use of symbols and metaphors—in writing, acting, design, etc.—and theater itself can be considered a metaphor.

10. In theater, audiences are called on to imagine two kinds of worlds: realistic and nonrealistic. Realistic theater depicts things onstage that conform to observable reality; nonrealistic theater includes the realm of dreams, fantasy, symbol, and metaphor. In theater, realism and nonrealism are frequently mixed.

11. In order to take part in theater as an observer, it is important to keep the "reality" of fantasies and dreams separate from the real world. By making this separation, we open our imagination to the full range of possibilities in the theater.

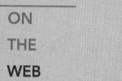

EXPLORING THEATER ON THE WEB

The Audience: Its Role and Imagination

As you examine the differences between the performer-audience relationship in film and the relationship in theater, you might find it helpful to contrast reviews of films with reviews of theater productions.

Many places on the Internet provide reviews of films. A particularly fascinating site is "Ebert & Roeper": http://tvplex.go.com/buenavista/ebertandroeper/today.html. This website posts weekly reviews and also has a search function that allows you to search by movie or person.

There are a few sites on the Internet that provide reputable reviews of theater productions. One such site is the online version of *The New York Times* (http://nytimes.com). Its theater page (http://nytimes.com/pages/arts/theater/index.html) is regularly updated with reviews of new productions.

Exercises:

1. Go to the "Ebert & Roeper" website and listen to a few reviews of films opening in your area. How are these reviews similar to theater reviews you have read? How are they different? The reviews may focus on different aspects of the film, depending on its genre. Find a review that focuses on character development. What kinds of examples do the reviewers use to comment on the acting?

2. Use the search feature on the "Ebert & Roeper" website to find a review of the film version of *Hamlet* made in 2000. You should be able to browse through several reviews of the film from various sources (e.g., the *New York Times, Los Angeles Times, Reel Views, Entertainment Weekly*). You can also access links to reviews posted by other readers. How do their perspectives on the review differ? What are some similarities? Do the reviews have any common elements? Choose three reviews and draft a chart outlining the similarities and differences among the three opinions of the same movie. What connections can be made between the expectations of the common moviegoer and those of an audience member at a theatrical event?

3. Go to the *New York Times* site and perform an advanced search in the archives for Neil Genzinger's article (August 23, 2002) reviewing the Kings County Shakespeare Company's production of *Hamlet* in Brooklyn Heights. How is the review similar to the *New York Times* film review? How is it different? How might your expectations as an audience member differ for each production?

CHAPTER TWO

Background and Expectations of the Audience

When audiences attend a theater event, they bring more than their mere presence; they bring a background of personal knowledge and a set of expectations that shape the experience. Several important factors are involved:

1. The knowledge and personal memories of individual members of the audience.
2. Their awareness of the social, political, and philosophical world in which the play was written or produced: the link between theater and society.
3. Their specific information about the play and playwright.
4. Their individual expectations concerning the event: what each person anticipates will happen at a performance. As we will see, misconceptions about what the theater experience is or should be can lead to confusion and disappointment.

◀ **RESIDENT PROFESSIONAL THEATER**

As part of the broad range of offerings for audiences, one of the most important developments of the past few decades has been the establishment of resident professional theaters in cities throughout the United States. One of the oldest regional theaters is the Guthrie Theater in Minneapolis, Minnesota. Shown here is a scene with Morena Baccarin as the Bride and Rene Millan as Leonardo from a production of Blood Wedding *by the Spanish playwright Federico García Lorca at the Guthrie.* (© Michal Daniel)

BACKGROUND OF INDIVIDUAL SPECTATORS

A background element which every member of the audience brings to a theater performance is his or her own individual memories and experiences. Each of us has a personal catalog of childhood memories, emotional scars, and private fantasies. Anything we see onstage which reminds us of this personal world will have a strong impact on us.

When we see a play that has been written in our own day, we bring with us a deep awareness of the world from which the play comes, because we come from the same world. Through the books we read, through newspapers and television, through discussions with friends, we have a background of common information and beliefs. Our shared knowledge and experience are much larger than most of us realize, and they form a crucial ingredient in our theater experience.

The play *A Raisin in the Sun* by Lorraine Hansberry (1930–1965) tells the story of a black family in Chicago in the late 1950s whose members want to improve their lives by finding better jobs and moving to a new neighborhood. But they face a number of obstacles put in their way by society. Any African American—or, for that matter, any person who belongs to a minority or to a group that has lacked opportunities—can readily identify with this situation. Such a person will know from personal experience what the characters are going through. (A synopsis of *A Raisin in The Sun* appears at

PERSONAL EXPERIENCES OF AUDIENCE MEMBERS

Audience members have individual experiences that they bring to the theater. For example, Hispanic audiences will be especially familiar with and attuned to the material in a musical revue such as 4 Guys Named Jose . . . and Una Mujer Named Maria! *The songs, the references, and the background have a special meaning and special appeal to those who know the people, customs, and history of those referred to in the music and dialog.* (© Richard Termine)

the end of Part 1.) A more recent play which evokes similar emotions is *Topdog/Underdog* (2002) by Suzan-Lori Parks (1964–   ).

We can also relate to characters and events onstage when we see plays set in other times and places. The story of Antigone, for example, was treated by Sophocles in Greece in the fifth century B.C.E. and more recently, during World War II, by the French playwright Jean Anouilh (1910–1987). A young woman, Antigone, adamantly opposes her uncle, Creon, the ruler of the state, because he is a political pragmatist who makes compromises; she is an idealist who believes in higher principles. Anyone, especially a young woman, who has ever tried to oppose corruption or complacency in an entrenched political regime will find much to recognize in Antigone. Any activity onstage that reminds us of something in our own lives will trigger deep personal responses which become part of the equation of our theater experience.

BACKGROUND OF THE PERIOD

Even when we identify closely with the characters or situation in a play, in drama from the past there is much that we cannot understand unless we are familiar with the history, culture, psychology, and philosophy of the period when it was created. This is because there is a close connection between any art form and the society in which it is produced.

BACKGROUND INFORMATION AFFECTS THE THEATER EXPERIENCE

Audience members have personal experiences that help them understand a play. For plays from other cultures, additional background information greatly enhances the experience. In fact, information can be helpful even for a play or performance from our own time and place, especially if it deals with material special to a particular group. A good example is I'm the One That I Want *written by and starring Margaret Cho. In this one-woman show, Cho, who is Korean-American, deals with problems that particularly affect gay people, as well as Asian Americans. Those who know and understand these two worlds will have a better understanding of her presentation.*
(© Carol Rosegg)

Theater and Society

Art does not occur in a vacuum. All art, including theater, is related to the society in which it is produced. Artists are sometimes charged with being "antisocial," "subversive," or "enemies of the state," and such accusations carry the strong suggestion that artists are outsiders or invaders rather than true members of a culture. To be sure, art frequently challenges society and is sometimes on the leading edge of history, appearing to forecast the future. More often than not, however, such art simply recognizes what is already present in society but has not yet surfaced. A good example is the abstract painting which developed in Europe in the early part of the twentieth century. At first it was considered a freakish aberration: an unattractive jumble of jagged lines and patches of color with no relation to nature, truth, or anything human. In time, however, abstract art came to be recognized as a genuine movement; and the disjointed and fragmentary lines of abstract art seem to reflect the quality of much of modern life.

Art grows in the soil of a specific society. With very few exceptions—and those are soon forgotten—art is a mirror of its age, revealing the prevailing attitudes, underlying assumptions, and deep-seated beliefs of a particular group of people. Art may question society's views or reaffirm them, but it cannot escape them; the two are as indissolubly linked as a person and his or her shadow. When we speak of art as "universal," we mean that the art of one age has so defined the characteristics of human beings that it can speak eloquently to another age; but we should never forget that every work of art first emerges at a given time and place and can never be adequately understood unless the conditions surrounding its birth are also understood.

Greek Theater and Culture

A study of theater in significant periods of history confirms the close link between art and society. In ancient Greece, for example, civilization reached a high point in Athens during the time of Pericles, the latter part of the fifth century B.C.E. This was the golden age of Greece—when politics, art, architecture, and theater thrived as they never had before, and rarely have since. As the Athenians of that period gained control over the world around them and took new pride in human achievements, they developed ideals of beauty, order, symmetry, and moderation which permeated their entire culture, including theater.

THEATER REFLECTS SOCIAL ISSUES
Theater reflects society. For example, gay and lesbian concerns and gender issues have become an increasingly important part of a national dialog in recent decades. The play Take Me Out *addresses these matters, along with related subjects, in a play about baseball players by dramatist Richard Greenberg. The story concerns a star athlete, an African American, who, during the course of the play reveals that he is gay. Set mostly in the baseball team's locker room, the drama deals with all the repercussions of this revelation.* (© Donald Cooper/PhotoSTAGE)

Part 1 The Audience

By the fifth century B.C.E., standard forms of drama had emerged in Greece, both for tragedies (such as *King Oedipus,* which we'll examine in Chapter 9) and for comedies. Playwrights introduced some innovations, but essentially they adhered to prescribed conventions. One of these conventions limited the number of scenes in a play: usually, there were only five scenes, interspersed with choral sections. In addition, the drama took place in one locale—often in front of a palace—and within a short span of time. Another convention reflected this society's sense of balance and order. Though bloody deeds occurred often in the myths on which most Greek plays were based, in the plays that have survived these deeds almost never took place in sight of the audience—murders, suicides, and other acts of violence usually occurred offstage. The Greek concept of moderation is reflected in still another convention of most Greek tragedies: any character in a play who acted in an excess of passion was generally punished or pursued by avenging furies. (A synopsis of *King Oedipus* can be found at the end of Part 1.)

Elizabethan Theater and Culture

Another example of the strong link between theater and society—one which stands in contrast to the classical Greek period—is the Elizabethan age in England. Named after Queen Elizabeth I, who reigned from 1558 to 1603, this period saw England become a dominant force in the world. Under Elizabeth's rule, England became a unified country; trade and commerce flourished, and with the defeat of the Spanish Armada in 1588, an age of exploration for England was under way. England was expanding confidently on all fronts, and these characteristics were reflected in the drama of the period.

THE SYMMETRY OF A GREEK TEMPLE

The formalism and sense of order of Greece in the fifth century B.C.E. are reflected in the Parthenon, on the acropolis in Athens. All art, including theater, reflects the attitudes and values of the society in which it is created.

(Greek National Tourist Office)

From medieval drama the Elizabethans had inherited stage practices that made it possible to shift rapidly in a play from place to place and from one time period to another. Using these techniques, as well as others they perfected, Shakespeare, Christopher Marlowe (1564–1593), and their contemporaries wrote plays that are quite different from the more formal drama of the Greeks. A single play might move to a number of locations and cover a period of many years. Rather than being restrictive, Elizabethan plays are expansive in terms of numbers of characters and in terms of action, and there is no hesitancy whatsoever about showing murder and bloodshed onstage. At the end of an Elizabethan play, corpses frequently cover the stage in full view of the audience. This expansiveness and this sense of adventure mirror the temper of the age in which the plays were written.

Modern Theater and Culture

Moving to the contemporary period, we find once again a tie between theater and society. Modern society, especially in the United States, is heterogeneous. We have people of many races, religions, and national backgrounds living side by side. Moreover, the twentieth century was marked by increasingly swift global communication. By means of radio, television, and computers, an event occurring in one place can be flashed instantaneously to the rest of the world. By these means, too, people are constantly made aware of cultures other than their own.

When cultures and societies are brought together, we are reminded of the many things people have in common but also of the differences among us. At the same time that we are brought together by global communications, other aspects of life have become increasingly fragmented. A number of institutions that held fairly constant through many centuries—organized religion, the family, marriage—have been seriously challenged in the century and half preceding our own day.

Discoveries by Charles Darwin (1809–1882) about evolution raised fundamental questions about views of creation held at that time: Were human beings created specially by God, or were they subject to the same process of evolution as other forms of life? People of the nineteenth century feared that if human beings had evolved, they might not occupy the unique place in the universe that had always been assumed for them. Shortly after Darwin published his findings, Karl Marx (1818–1883) put forward revolutionary ideas on economics that challenged long-held beliefs about capitalism. At the end of the nineteenth century, Sigmund Freud cast doubt on the ability of human beings to exercise total rational control over their activities. Later, Albert Einstein (1879–1955) formulated theories about relativity that questioned long-established views of the universe.

Similar changes and discoveries continued throughout the twentieth century. The cumulative effect of these discoveries was to make human beings much less certain of their place in the cosmos and their mastery of events. Today, life appears much less unified and ordered than it once seemed.

Women in Greek and Elizabethan Theaters

In considering the link between theater and society, it is worth noting that in both Greek and Elizabethan theater, although important female characters appeared in the dramas themselves, there were no female playwrights or performers. This is a result of the place women were accorded in these two cultures.

Classical Greek theater was intrinsically linked to the well-being of the state. Its themes reflected the political necessity for order and control and were intended to serve a didactic purpose, ensuring the continuation of democratic government. In Athenian society, where women were excluded from all political roles and were not even considered citizens, it followed logically that they could not participate in the creative processes of theater. In fact, we are not even certain that women were permitted to attend performances. Some classical scholars believe that women could and did attend, on the basis of contemporary accounts and some internal evidence within plays: for instance, there is an often-repeated story that some women who saw *The Oresteia* by Aeschylus (525–456 B.C.E.) had miscarriages, and a character in the comedy *The Frogs* by Aristophanes (450–388 B.C.E.) remarks satirically that all decent women committed suicide after seeing one of Euripides' plays. However, this is still a matter for debate; and it is perhaps significant that one of the more persuasive pieces of evidence for women's presence at Greek theatrical events is the fact that men were allowed to bring their male slaves: if slaves could attend, why not free women? We do know that women often acted in wandering mime troupes. These popular entertainers sang, danced, juggled, and performed acrobatics and brief comic sketches. Because of the bawdy nature of these acts, women mimes were often thought to be of low moral character. This unfortunate label was to remain with women performers for hundreds of years and is at least partly responsible for an attitude which excluded women from legitimate theater.

In Elizabethan England, despite the presence of a powerful female monarch, theater practices continued to reflect a long-standing prejudice against women. During the reign of Elizabeth, actors were raised above vagabond status, but actresses were still considered little better than prostitutes—a result of medieval and Puritan thinking. Women were thus barred from performing on the legitimate stage, and female roles (as was noted in Chapter 1) were played by boys who did much to portray feminine beauty and grace. It was not until 1660 that women were allowed to appear onstage in licensed theaters in England.

Source: Prepared by Professor Mira Felner, Hunter College, City University of New York.

These two developments—the bringing together of cultures by population shifts and communication, and the challenges to long-held beliefs—are reflected in today's theater. It is a theater of fragmentation and of **eclecticism**—the embracing of different strains. A typical theater company today performs a wide range of plays. In a single season, the same company may present a tragedy by Shakespeare, a farce by the French dramatist Molière (1622–1673), a modern drama by the Spanish writer Federico García Lorca (1898–1936), a play like *Wit* by Margaret Edson (1961–), and a new script by a young American playwright. Moreover, the dramatists of today write on many subjects and in a wide range of styles.

The three periods we have looked at—the Greek, the Elizabethan, and the Modern—are examples of the close relationship between a society and the art and theater it produces. One could find comparable links in every culture. It is important to remember, therefore, that whatever the period in which it was first produced, drama is woven into the fabric of its time.

BACKGROUND INFORMATION ON THE PLAY OR PLAYWRIGHT

Sometimes, we need additional knowledge not only about the historical period of a play but also about the play itself. For instance, a play may contain difficult passages or obscure references which it is helpful to know about before we see a performance.

As an example, we can take a segment from Shakespeare's *King Lear:* the scene in the third act when Lear appears on the heath in the midst of a terrible storm. Earlier in the play, Lear divided his kingdom between two of his daughters, Goneril and Regan, who he thought loved him but who, he discovers, have actually deceived him. Gradually, they have stripped him of everything: his possessions, his soldiers, even his dignity. Finally, they send him out from their homes to face the wind and rain in open country. As the storm begins, Lear speaks the following lines:

> Blow, winds, and crack your cheeks! Rage! Blow!
> You cataracts and hurricanoes, spout
> Till you have drenched our steeples, drowned the cocks!

In the first line, the expression "crack your cheeks" refers to pictures in the corners of old maps showing a face puffed out at the cheeks, blowing the wind.[1] Shakespeare is saying that the face of the wind should blow so hard that its cheeks will crack. In the second line, "cataracts and hurricanoes" refers to water from both the heavens and the seas. In the third line, "cocks" refers to weathercocks on the tops of steeples; Lear wants so much rain to fall that even the weathercocks on the steepletops will be submerged. If we are aware of these meanings, we can join them with the sounds of the words—and with the rage the actor expresses in his voice and gestures—to get the full impact of the scene.

In contemporary theater, playwrights frequently use special techniques which will confuse us if we do not understand them. The German playwright Bertolt Brecht (1898–1956), who lived and wrote in the United States during the 1940s, wanted to provoke his audiences into thinking about what they were seeing. To do this, he would interrupt a story with a song or a speech by a narrator. His theory was that when a story is stopped in this manner, audience members have an opportunity to consider more carefully what they are seeing and to relate the drama onstage to other aspects of life.

If one is not aware that this is Brecht's purpose in interrupting the action, one might conclude that he was simply a careless or inferior playwright. Here, as in similar cases, knowledge of the play or playwright is indispensable to a complete theater experience.

EXPECTATIONS: THE VARIETY OF EXPERIENCES IN MODERN THEATER

An expectation sometimes held by people who have not often been to the theater is that all theater experiences will be alike. In fact, audiences go to the theater for different purposes. Some spectators, like those who enjoy the escape offered by movies and television, are interested primarily in light entertainment. Audiences at dinner theaters or Broadway musicals do not want to be faced with troublesome problems or serious moral issues. They look for something which will be amusing and perhaps include music, dancing, and beautiful scenery and costumes. On the other hand, some people want to be stimulated and challenged, both intellectually and emotionally. To these audiences, a situation comedy or a light musical will seem frivolous or sentimental. It must be remembered, too, that many people like both kinds of theater. At times a person may seek light entertainment; at other times, meaningful drama.

Not only do performances vary in terms of the type of theater they offer, they also take place in a variety of settings, and this too has an effect on the nature of the experience. Fifty years ago in the United States "the theater" was synonymous with one kind of experience: Broadway. In the last several decades this has changed dramatically—further evidence of how diversity in theater reflects the overall diversity in contemporary life. To see the changes in the kinds of places theater is presented, it will be helpful to look at developments in the United States over the past half century.

Broadway and Touring Theater

Broadway is the name of the oldest professional theater in New York City: it refers specifically to plays performed in the large theaters in the district near Times Square. From 1920 until the early 1950s, most new plays written in the United States originated there, and productions in other areas were usually copies of Broadway productions. Broadway itself was confined and

BROADWAY THEATER
Productions in the major theaters in New York City—collectively known as Broadway—are usually characterized by elaborate scenic elements, first-rate acting, and scripts with wide appeal: either new works or revivals. Shown here is a scene from Thoroughly Modern Millie, *a musical set in the flapper era of the 1920s. The story concerns a young woman who comes from the Midwest to New York to make her way in the theater. The production has all the earmarks of a Broadway musical: songs and dancing, striking lighting, lavish sets and costumes.* (Sara Krulwich/The New York Times)

standardized; it consisted of an area in Manhattan roughly six blocks long and a block and a half wide. The thirty or more theaters located in these few blocks were about the same size, seating between 700 and 1,400 people, and had the same style of architecture as well as the same type of stage: a picture-frame stage (discussed in Chapter 4).

Productions sent on tour from Broadway to the rest of the country were exact replicas of the original. Scenery was duplicated down to the last detail, and New York performers often played roles they had played on Broadway. Nonprofessional theaters copied Broadway as well; acting versions of successful plays were published for colleges, schools, and community theaters, providing precise instructions for the movements of the performers and the placement of scenery onstage.

In the period after World War II, a realization grew that there were large numbers of people in the United States for whom Broadway was remote—not just geographically, but spiritually.

Because our society is diverse and complex, and because theater reflects society, it is difficult to see how any one form of theater today could speak equally to all of us. As if in response to the complexity of the modern world, in the second half of the twentieth century people began searching for new forms in theater, and for alternative locations in which to present theater.

Resident Professional Theaters

One significant development, which began in a few key cities in the 1950s and has since spread across the country, is resident professional theater, sometimes known as *regional theater.* Theater companies have been formed, and theater facilities built, for the continuing presentation of high-quality professional productions to local residents. The performers, directors, and designers are generally high-caliber artists who make theater their full-time profession.

A few of these theaters are repertory in the European tradition. In *repertory,* a theater company performs several plays on alternate nights, rather than presenting a single play night after night for the length of its run. For example, in repertory a play by Molière may appear on Monday night, a play by Beckett on Tuesday, a Shakespearean play on Wednesday, and so forth.

For reasons of economy, very few theaters in the United States find it feasible to offer true repertory. Most cities have developed theaters that present a series of plays over a given time, with each play being performed for about 4 to 12 weeks. Among the best-known of these theaters are the Arena Stage in Washington, D.C., the Long Wharf in New Haven, the American Repertory Theater in Boston, the Actor's Theater of Louisville, the Alley Theater in Houston, the Goodman Theater in Chicago, the Milwaukee Repertory Theater, the Tyrone Guthrie Theater in Minneapolis, the Seattle Repertory Theater, and the Mark Taper Forum in Los Angeles. Among African American theaters performing in repertory are the Crossroads

ALTERNATIVE THEATER: OFF-BROADWAY AND ELSEWHERE

Smaller theaters that produce experimental, avant-garde, or untested new works have developed in New York in off-Broadway and off-off-Broadway, and in similar venues across the country. Typical of the kind of theater companies that make up the alternative theater movement is Mabou Mines. Seen here is one of the founders of the company, Lee Breuer, with a puppet figure in a Mabou Mines production entitled Ecco Porco. *The play has been described as an "acid-trip collage of philosophy, mythology, corny jokes, and lyric poetry."* (Sara Krulwich/The New York Times)

Repertory Theater, the North Carolina Black Repertory, and the Saint Louis Black Repertory Company. A season of plays in these theaters will usually include both new plays and classics, and theatergoers are encouraged to buy a season subscription.

In addition to resident companies, there are now a number of permanent summer theater festivals and Shakespeare festivals throughout the United States and Canada. Among the best-known are the Shakespeare festivals at Stratford, Ontario; San Diego, California; and Ashland, Oregon.

Alternative Theaters: Off-Broadway and Elsewhere

In New York City *off-Broadway theater* began in the 1950s as an alternative to Broadway, which was becoming increasingly costly. Off-Broadway theaters were smaller than Broadway theaters—most of them had fewer than 200 seats—and were located outside the Times Square area in places like Greenwich Village. Because off-Broadway was less expensive than Broadway, it offered more opportunity for producing serious classics and experimental works.

Off-Broadway itself, however, became expensive and institutionalized in the 1960s and 1970s. Consequently, small independent groups had to develop another forum for producing plays. The result was *off-off-Broadway.* Under an arrangement with the actors' union, Actors Equity Association, professionals were allowed to perform for little or no salary for short runs in workshop productions, and for minimal salaries in longer-running productions. Off-off-Broadway shows are produced wherever inexpensive space is available—churches, lofts, warehouses, large basements—and are characterized by low-priced productions and a wide variety of offerings.

An important development in American theater is that counterparts to off-off-Broadway have been established in other major cities across the United States—Washington, Atlanta, Chicago, Minneapolis, Los Angeles, San Francisco, Seattle—where small theater groups perform as alternatives to large organizations. It is in these smaller theaters, in New York and across the country, that most experimental and new works are performed.

In addition, all across the country there are cabaret and dinner theaters in which the atmosphere of a nightclub or restaurant is combined with that of a theater; in an informal setting, guests eat and drink before watching a performance.

COLLEGE AND UNIVERSITY THEATER

A vital segment of theater in the United States is the many productions mounted by theater departments in colleges and universities. These often achieve a high degree of professionalism; they also provide excellent training for theater practitioners— and for becoming informed and appreciative theatergoers. The scene shown here is from The Rover *by seventeenth century English playwright Aphra Behn and presented at Illinois State University.* (© Peter Guither)

Children's Theater

A branch of theater that has earned an important place in the overall picture is children's theater, sometimes called *theater for youth*. Children's theater covers a wide range of activities from the most sophisticated professional organizations to semiprofessionals to improvisational groups to undertakings that are predominately amateur or educational. The aim in all cases, however, is to provide a theatrical experience for young people.

In some cases it is to offer school-age children an opportunity to see first-class productions of plays dealing with people and subjects in which they might be personally interested. In other cases, the emphasis is on dramatizing the lives of significant figures in history—Abraham Lincoln; Martin

Luther King, Jr.; Eleanor Roosevelt—or giving dramatic life to literary classics such as *Tom Sawyer* or *Huckleberry Finn*.

Other types of children's theater strive to give young people experiences in creating and presenting theater. The participants take part as actors, designers, lighting technicians, stage managers, and the like.

A number of children's theater organizations across North America have a long history and feature first-class theater spaces and production facilities. Moreover, the caliber of those responsible for their productions—performers, designers, directors, etc.—is excellent and the equal of any professional regional or not-for-profit theater. Among those in this category are the Children's Theatre Company of Minneapolis, the Children's Theatre of Charlotte, the Orange County Children's Theatre, the Nashville Children's Theatre, and Theatre Works in New York City.

College and University Theaters

In the last few decades, *college* and *university theater* departments have also become increasingly important, not only in teaching theater arts but also in presenting plays. In some localities, college productions are virtually the only form of theater offered. In other areas, they are a significant supplement to professional theater.

The theater facilities in many colleges are excellent. Most large colleges and universities have two or three theater spaces—a full-size theater, a medium-size theater, and a smaller space for experimental drama—as well as extensive scene shops, costume rooms, dressing rooms, and rehearsal halls. Productions are usually scheduled throughout the school year.

The quality and complexity of these productions vary. In some places, productions are extremely elaborate, with full-scale scenery, costumes, lighting, and sound. Colleges vary, too, in the level of professionalism in acting. Many colleges use only performers from the undergraduate theater program. If a college has a master's degree program, it will use both graduate and undergraduate performers. Colleges or universities may also bring in outside professionals to perform along with students. Most college and university theaters offer a variety of plays, including classics and experimental plays rarely done by professional theaters.

Multiethnic, Multicultural, and Gender Theaters

More and more people in the United States are becoming aware of the multiracial and multicultural aspects of our society. In the late nineteenth and early twentieth centuries, the United States was known as the "great melting pot," a term which implied that the aim of the many foreign-born people who came here was to become assimilated and integrated into the prevailing white, European culture. In the last few decades, however, many

THEATERS OF DIVERSITY: HISPANIC THEATER

Theaters of all kinds have sprung up in recent decades, representing many cultures, ethnic groups, gender orientations, and the like. Shown here is a Hispanic production by the New York–based Puerto Rican Traveling Theatre called Tiene la Muerte Atada (They've Got Death Bound Up). *It is an operatic comedy with a Uruguayan spirit that is based on a medieval folk tale. Presented outdoors in parks, it reaches an audience not usually found in more formal theaters. Note the painted faces of the performers. From left, Pietro González, Bill Blechingberg, and Ana Campos.* (© Gerry Goodstein)

people in our society have urged that, rather than embrace everyone in a common culture, we should recognize and celebrate our differences along with our shared values.

This trend toward diversity has been reflected in theater; many organizations have emerged which present theatrical productions by and for groups with a special interest. These include a number of political, ethnic, gender, and racial groups. (There is a full discussion of multicultural and gender theater in Chapter 12.)

African American Theater   One of the earliest ethnic theater movements was African American theater. It included such organizations as the Free Southern Theater, which began in New Orleans in the early 1960s; the Negro Ensemble Company, established in New York City in 1967; and the New Federal Theater, which is still active in New York. More recent groups include Jomandi Productions in Atlanta, Georgia, and the Crossroads Theater in New Brunswick, New Jersey.

GAY AND LESBIAN THEATER

Among the many kinds of alternative theater that emerged in the last part of the twentieth century were theaters centering on the gay and lesbian experience. Some groups chronicled the experience, others presented it with considerable humor, still others were more militant and political. In some cases, groups combined these approaches. An important group in the lesbian and gay theater arena was Split Britches, founded by Peggy Shaw and Lois Weaver. Seen here is Shaw in a solo performance, cross-dressing as a man, in a piece called Menopausal Gentleman. *(©Tom Brazil)*

Hispanic Theater   Theater by and for Hispanic audiences is thriving on the west coast, on the east coast, and at many points in between. One of the best-known Hispanic theaters is El Teatro Campesino in San Juan Bautista, California; in New York, three well-regarded organizations are Repertorio Español, Intar, and the Puerto Rican Traveling Theatre.

Asian American Theater   Two important Asian American theaters are the East-West Players in Los Angeles and the Pan Asian Repertory in New York.

Native American Theater   In the 1970s, Hanay Geiogamah (1945–   ) established the Native American Theatre Ensemble, which used western-type drama to express Native American values, traditions, and aesthetics.

Women's Theater and Feminist Theater   An example of a theater producing work written exclusively by women is the Women's Project, headed by Julia Miles (1930–   ). One of the early theaters that produced significant work expressing a strong feminist perspective was At the Foot of the Mountain in Minneapolis. Though that theater is no longer active, other groups are, including Split Britches in New York City.

Lesbian and Gay Theater   Organizations typical of those presenting theater by and about lesbians and gays are the Alice B. Theater in Seattle, Washington; and Theater Rhinoceros in San Francisco.

Political Theater   The theaters just mentioned frequently have a strong political component, but there are also theaters that exist specifically to espouse political causes and address political issues of many kinds. Among such groups, the San Francisco Mime Troupe has been prominent for many years.

Avant-Garde and Experimental Theater   Theater that breaks away from the mainstream tradition—*avant-garde* and experimental theater—has been a part of the theater landscape for most of this century. Movements such as expressionism, surrealism, absurdism, and theater of cruelty appeared during the first three-quarters of the century; their descendants continue into the present. Among theater movements of this kind are multimedia theater, which incorporates theater, dance, painting, and video into a single art form; and *performance art,* in which highly individual theater pieces are created by one person, or at most only a few people.

AVANT-GARDE AND EXPERIMENTAL THEATER

Aside from large professional theaters, there are many smaller theaters off-off-Broadway and in cities across the United States. Some of these are minority theaters or theaters by and for special groups: gays, lesbians, or others. Alternative theater also includes avant-garde and experimental productions. The avant-garde production shown here is Maria del Bosco, *written and directed by Richard Foreman. Foreman's work, which is highly personal and often autobiographical, features things such as imaginative costumes and sets that feature strings and lights crossing the stage as shown here.* (© Paula Court/Ontological-Hysteric Theater)

There are times when the groups described above overlap; political theater, for instance, might intersect with feminist theater. One example of the convergence of several movements is a theater piece created by the performance artist Karen Finley (1956–). In this presentation, Finley, who was nude, covered parts of her body with chocolate, which was supposed to represent human feces. The performance made a highly feminist, highly political statement. It was a protest against the treatment of women; it was a protest against traditional theater; and it was strongly political as well as theatrical.

Crossover Theater   Plays or productions from groups with a special perspective have often crossed over into a wider arena of American theater. The plays of the African American dramatist August Wilson (1945–) are regularly produced on Broadway, as was an Asian American drama, *M. Butterfly* (see Chapter 8), written by David Henry Hwang (1957–). Gay theater has been represented by such works as *Torch Song Trilogy* by Harvey Fierstein (1954–) and two musicals, *La Cage aux Folles* and *Falsettos. Angels in America,* a Broadway play by Tony Kushner (1956–) that won the Pulitzer Prize, has both political and homosexual components.

Today there is theater for almost everyone, in many kinds of places, under widely varying conditions, and for very different purposes. With theater taking so many forms, it is important in approaching the subject not to have a preconceived or rigidly fixed notion of what it is.

Chapters 1 and 2 have dealt with the part the audience plays in the theater experience. We have looked at its vital role in the performer-audience interaction, at the way it uses imagination to participate in theater, and at the background knowledge and experience that affect its experiences. In Chapter 3, we will look at the work of a specialized audience member—the critic. The critic observes a play just as ordinary spectators do but brings to his or her observations background knowledge and analytical skills which can be useful to regular audience members.

SUMMARY

1. Each individual attending a theater event brings to it a personal background of experience which becomes a vital ingredient in his or her response.

2. Theater—like other arts—is closely linked to the society in which it is produced; it mirrors and reflects the attitudes, philosophy, and basic assumptions of its time.

3. Spectators attending a play written in their own day bring to it an awareness of their society's values and beliefs, and this background information forms an important part of the overall experience.

4. A play from the past can be understood better if the spectator is aware of the culture from which it came.

5. For any play which presents difficulties in language, style, or meaning, familiarity with the work itself can add immeasurably to a spectator's understanding and appreciation of a performance.

6. With an unfamiliar work, it is also helpful to learn about the playwright and his or her approach to theater.

7. Expectations about the nature of the theater experience affect our reaction to it.

8. In the past, theater experiences were relatively uniform within any one society, but in contemporary society their time, place, content, and purpose are far more varied. Theater groups today produce works expressing the viewpoints of people of all political, ethnic, gender, and racial perspectives: African Americans, Asian Americans, Hispanics, Native Americans, feminists, gays, lesbians, and others.

EXPLORING THEATER
ON
THE
WEB

Background and Expectations of the Audience

The Internet provides a forum for opinion and information about theater productions in the U.S. and abroad. As an audience member, you can educate yourself about a production you plan to see by making use of internet resources. *Playbill Online*™ (http://www.playbill.com) hosts an online theater community that provides articles, reviews, and a live chat room for discussions about current theater happenings.

Exercises:

1. Go to "Listings" link on the *Playbill Online*™ homepage. Here you can check out what is playing on Broadway, off-Broadway, in regional theaters, on a national tour, and on the London stages, as well as what will be offered in the coming summer stock season. Search for productions opening in your area.

   If there is no regional theater close by, are there touring shows coming to your region? What are the ticket prices?

2. Return to the *Playbill Online*™ home page and click on "Theater Central" under "Links." Find a review of a performance that interests you. If you are looking for a review of a show that recently left Broadway to tour, you might check the archives of Aisle Say, (http://www.aislesay.com) or Broadway on the Net (http://www.geocities.com/Broadway/Stage/6022/) for a review of the original production.

3. Explore the web looking for sites describing some different types of theaters. Can you find a website for an off-Broadway theater (hint: start at the Off Broadway League site at http://www.offbroadway.org). An experimental theater? A community-based theater (hint: check out Cornerstone Theater in Los Angeles at http://www.cornerstonetheater.org)? How about a college or university theater? You can search for theater companies that cater to a particular audience (for example, National Theater for the Deaf [http://www.ntd.org] or Theatre Pregones [http://www.pregones.org]). Or see if you can find a theater company in another country (like Teatro La Fragua [http://www.fragua.org] in Honduras). Choose at least two sites. What are the expectations of the audience for each theater? How do these expectations differ from those in your university theater environment? Are these expectations cultural? Educational? Economic? National? Stylistic?

CHAPTER THREE

The Critic and the Audience

A *critic,* loosely defined, is someone who observes theater and then analyzes and comments on it. Ideally, the critic serves as a knowledgeable and highly sensitive audience member. Actually, most theatergoers are amateur critics. When a person says about a performance, "It started off great, but it fizzled," or "The star was terrific, just like someone in real life," or "The woman was OK, but the man overacted," he or she is making a critical judgment. The difference between a critic and an ordinary spectator is that the critic presumably is better informed about the event and has developed a set of critical standards by which to judge it.

Audiences can learn from critics not only because critics impart information and judgments but also, as suggested above, because a critic shares with an audience the point of view of the spectator. Unlike those who create theater—writers, performers, designers—critics sit out front and watch a performance just as other members of the audience do. By understanding how the critic goes about his or her task, audience members can increase their own knowledge of how theater works and make their own theater experiences more meaningful.

◀ THE CRITICS AND THE AUDIENCE

In many striking instances, audiences have made their own judgments which ran contrary to the original reception given to a production by critics. A good example is the musical Mamma Mia! *in which a story was fashioned to incorporate the songs of the singing group ABBA. Many critics felt that the end result of this hybrid musical was a bland, banal show, but audiences worldwide have flocked to* Mamma Mia!, *making it an unquestioned popular success.* (© Joan Marcus)

THEATRICAL CRITICISM

What Is Criticism?

The popular image of a theater critic is a caustic writer who makes sharp, rapier-like thrusts at performers and playwrights. Some epithets of critics have become legendary. John Mason Brown described the actress Tallulah Bankhead in a production of Shakespeare's *Antony and Cleopatra* by saying, "Tallulah Bankhead barged down the Nile last night as Cleopatra and sank." When Katharine Hepburn, who was a stage actress before she went into films, appeared in a play called *The Lake,* the critic Dorothy Parker wrote that Hepburn "runs the gamut of emotions from A to B." Before he became a playwright, George Bernard Shaw (1856–1950) was a critic, and he had harsh things to say about a number of people, including Shakespeare. Shaw wrote that Shakespeare's *Cymbeline* was "for the most part stagy trash of the lowest melodramatic order." About Shakespeare himself Shaw said: "With the single exception of Homer, there is no eminent writer, not even Sir Walter Scott, whom I can despise so entirely as I despise Shakespeare when I measure my mind against his."

The word *criticize* has at least two meanings. One is "to find fault," and that is what we see in the comments above. But *criticize* also means "to understand and appraise," and this meaning is much more important for a theater critic.

GEORGE BERNARD SHAW: CRITIC AND PLAYWRIGHT

Most people know Shaw (1856-1950) as one of the best British dramatists of the past 100 years, but he was also one of the finest critics of modern times. He reviewed the London theater for several years in the 1890s and wrote about theater for fifty years after that. Though opinionated and often caustic, Shaw had many admirable attributes as a critic. He had a wide knowledge of theater, both past and present; he understood the other arts and also political and social affairs; he had a clear set of criteria for plays and performances; and his writing style was strong, fluid, and lively.

(Culver Pictures)

Preparation for Criticism

In order to make criticism more meaningful to audiences, the critic ideally should have a thorough theater background of the kind discussed in Chapter 2. It would consist of a full knowledge of theater history, as well as other aspects of theater, such as acting, directing, and design. The critic must be familiar with plays written in various styles and modes and should know the body of work of individual writers. Also, the critic ought to be able to relate what is happening in theater to what is happening in the other arts and, beyond that, to events in society generally.

In addition, the critic should understand the production elements discussed later in this book—directing, acting, and design. The critic must know what a director does and what constitutes good and bad direction. The critic should also understand act-

"Tell me, sir, is it good or bad?"

(© The New Yorker Collection 1971 Edward Koren from Cartoonbank.com)

ing and should be able to judge whether a performer has the skills and the talent to be convincing in a role and whether the role has been interpreted appropriately. In addition, the critic should be familiar with the principles and practices of design—scenery, costume, and lighting. He or she ought to have some idea of what is called for in each area and be able to judge whether the design elements measure up in a given production.

Admittedly, this is asking a great deal of critics, and very few acquire the broad range of knowledge required; but it is an ideal to which all critics should aspire and which audiences have a right to expect of first-rate critics.

Critical Criteria

Along with a strong background, a good critic should develop criteria by which to judge a play and a production. These criteria should take the form of a set of questions to be asked each time she or he attends a performance.

 What Is Being Attempted? One of the first questions is, *What is the play, and the production, attempting to do?* This question must be raised both about the script and about the production. Regarding the script, the critic

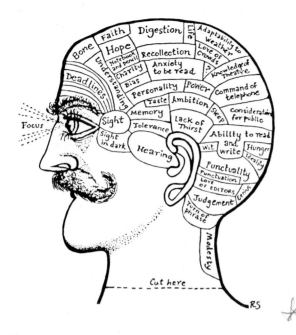

THE IDEAL CRITIC

In this drawing, the artist Ronald Searle humorously suggests the many qualities a person must have in order to be a good theater critic—everything from knowledge of the theater to adaptability to weather, from punctuality to punctuation.

(Ronald Searle, 1952)

should make clear what the playwright is trying to accomplish. Is the play a tragedy meant to raise significant questions and stir deep emotions? Is it a light comedy intended to entertain and provide escape? Is it a political drama arguing for a point of view? Good critics include in their articles background information that can be of great value to audiences.

Turning from the script to the production, the critic must ascertain what the director, the performers, and the designers are attempting to accomplish. Are they trying to carry out the playwright's intentions faithfully, or are they trying to move in another direction? For example, are they representing characters, dialogue, and situations as written, or are they altering these elements, as happens when a director wants to impose his or her own interpretation on a play?

Have the Intentions Been Achieved? A second question a critic must address is, *How well have the intentions of the playwright or the director been carried out?* A theater company may be producing an acknowledged masterpiece such as *Hamlet* or *Macbeth,* in which case the question becomes how well the play has been acted, directed, and designed. Have the performers brought Shakespeare's characters to life convincingly and excitingly? Or has the director—perhaps by striving to be too original or by updating the play and putting the characters into modern dress—distorted Shakespeare's intentions beyond recognition?

In the case of a new script, the critic must also ask how well the playwright has realized his or her own intentions. If the play is intended to probe deeper into family relationships—parents and children, or husbands and wives—how convincingly and how insightfully has the dramatist accomplished this? If the intention is to entertain, to make the audience laugh, the question must be asked: Just how funny is the play? Did it succeed in providing entertainment? Was it clever, witty, and full of amusing situations, or did it fall flat?

 Was the Attempt Worthwhile? A third question for the critic falls more into the realm of personal taste and evaluation: *Is the play or production worth doing?* Many critics think that anything which succeeds at giving pleasure and providing entertainment is as worthwhile in its own way as a more serious undertaking. Others, however, do not. In cases like this, readers must make up their own minds.

If audience members are aware of these criteria, they not only can note whether critics—in print or on television—address these questions but also can ask the questions for themselves.

Descriptive and Prescriptive Criticism

In judging a play or another theater event, critics frequently take one of two different approaches. The first approach could be called *descriptive;* that is, it attempts to describe as clearly and accurately as possible what is happening in a play or a performance. The second could be called *prescriptive,* meaning that the critic not only describes what has been done but also offers advice or comments about how it *should* be done.

These differing approaches to theater criticism were established by two theater critics in ancient times. The Greek philosopher Aristotle (384–322 B.C.E.) undertook to analyze the tragedies of playwrights like Aeschylus, Sophocles (c. 496–406 B.C.E.), and Euripides (c. 484–406 B.C.E.). Aristotle was also a scientist, and his method was chiefly to *describe* tragedy: he attempted to break it down into its component parts and to note how it worked and what effect it had on spectators.

The Roman writer Horace (65–8 B.C.E.), on the other hand, attempted not just to describe but to *prescribe* what theater should be. In other words, Horace wanted to establish rules for theater. He said, for example, that tragedy and comedy should never be mixed in the same play and that poetry should instruct as well as please the audience.

Since the time of Aristotle and Horace, critics have tended to fall into one category or the other: those who analyze and describe theater, and those who set down rules and say exactly what form plays and theater productions should follow. The second approach, it should be noted, can sometimes lead to a moralistic or overly rigid viewpoint about theater, which restricts both the creativity of theater artists and the enjoyment of audiences.

Fact and Opinion in Criticism

In reading the commentary of critics, it is important to distinguish between *fact* and *opinion.* Opinion, as suggested above, should be carefully weighed. On the other hand, facts or insights presented by a critic can be extremely helpful. Critics can often make us aware of information we might not otherwise have known—for example, by explaining a point that was confusing to the audience or noting how a particular scene in a play relates to an earlier scene. A critic might also offer background material about the playwright, the subject matter of the play, or the style of the production. Such information can broaden the audience's understanding and appreciation of theater. The more we know about what a playwright is attempting to do and why a playwright arranges scenes in a certain way, the better we will be able to judge the value of a theater event.

A good example would be an explanation by a critic of the intentions and techniques of the playwright Maria Irene Fornes (1930–) in *Fefu and*

Mel Gussow: Critic

Mel Gussow is a critic and theater writer for The New York Times *and has been a recipient of the George Jean Nathan Award in dramatic criticism.*

I have been with *The New York Times* serving as theater critic and writer about theater since 1969, but my interest in theater began when I was still in school. It came into particular focus while I was undertaking graduate studies.

While studying at Columbia University's Graduate School of Journalism, I spent my evenings in the theater. It was the 1955–1956 season, an astonishingly diverse year, with *My Fair Lady, A View from the Bridge, The Diary of Anne Frank, The Most Happy Fella*, Jason Robards in *The Iceman Cometh*,

Orson Welles in *King Lear* (he was in a wheelchair at the performance I attended), and, most important of all, the Broadway premiere of *Waiting for Godot.*

I saw everything on Broadway and many plays off-Broadway, which had become a burgeoning theatrical movement, led by the New York Shakespeare Festival, the Phoenix Theater, and David Ross's productions of Chekhov. More than anything else, that season encouraged my enthusiasm for theater— for the idea of becoming a drama critic. Earlier, at Middlebury College, I had reviewed plays for the student newspaper and had taken courses in playwriting, theater history, and Shakespeare. But that year was at the core of my theatrical education.

My professional critical life did not actually begin until the early 1960s at *Newsweek* magazine, where I wrote feature stories about the arts, movie reviews, and occasional reviews of off-Broadway shows. When T. H. Wenning, that magazine's distinguished theater critic, suddenly became ill and incapacitated soon after the Broadway opening of Edward Albee's *Who's Afraid of Virginia Woolf?* I acted as the magazine's critic. I began my regular theater reviewing at the top, with the Albee play, and then during the rest of the season covered plays and musicals across the board, from Harold Pinter one-acts to *Beyond the Fringe.* Since this was the time before bylines in news magazines, few people knew that I was a critic. But I knew I was a critic.

Her Friends. The first act of this play takes place in the living room of Fefu's New England home, which was once a farmhouse. The audience sits in one location watching the action in the living room. The second act, however, is presented differently and has an unusual structure. There are four different locations, which must be spaces in the theater other than the stage, such as backstage, offstage, in the lobby, or in a rehearsal hall. One of these locations represents a lawn outside the house, a second a bedroom, a third the study, and the fourth the kitchen. The characters in the play split up and perform separate scenes in each of the four locations. The audience is divided into four groups as well; audience members move from one location to the next until they have seen all four; the scenes in the separate locations are repeated four times so that each group of audience members can see what has happened. For the third act of the play, the audience reassembles in the main auditorium to watch a scene that takes place once again in the living room, onstage.

Among other things, Fornes uses the second act to break out of the usual theater setting. She also wants to show the fragmentation of life as well as its simultaneity. She wants the audience to get a sense of life overlapping and continuing in different places in addition to those on which we usually focus. A critic can explain Fornes's purpose and techniques so that when audience members attend a performance they will be better prepared for what they are experiencing. (A synopsis of *Fefu and Her Friends* appears at the end of Part 1.)

The Reviewer and the Critic

Another important distinction to be made with regard to theater criticism is that between *reviewers* and *critics.*

A *reviewer,* who usually works for a television station, a newspaper, or a magazine, reports on what has occurred at the theater. He or she will tell briefly what a theater event is about, explaining whether it is a musical, a comedy, or a serious play and perhaps describing its plot. The reviewer might also offer an opinion about whether or not the event is worth seeing. (Everyone has read newspaper ads with quotations from reviewers saying such things as "A play not to be missed," and "A laugh riot; the whole family will enjoy it.") The reviewer is usually restricted by time, space, or both. A television reviewer, for instance, will have only a minute or two on the air to describe a play and offer a reaction. A newspaper reviewer, similarly, is restricted by the space available in the newspaper and by the newspaper's deadline.

CRITICS PROVIDE BACKGROUND
Samuel Beckett's Texts for Nothing, *like most of his other works, proves very difficult for audiences to understand when they first encounter the piece. The play, an adaptation of a Beckett text, is set in a strange, timeless environment, typical of Beckett's dramatic universe. It is helpful to audiences if, when they go to see a production, they have background on both the playwright and the play. The actor shown here, in a production at the Classic Stage Company, is Bill Irwin.* (© Dixie Sheridan)

Reviewers are frequently limited as well in terms of experience. A television or newspaper reviewer may have a strong background in theater studies or a good deal of practical experience, but that is the exception rather than the rule. Most often, reviewers have worked at other positions at a television station or on a newspaper and have simply been shifted to this beat. In such cases their work may lack depth and may not be based on the critical criteria discussed above.

In contrast to the reviewer, the *critic* attempts to go into greater detail in describing and analyzing a theater event. Critics generally work for magazines or scholarly journals. Some critics have written entire books about playwrights, plays, and theatrical movements. A critic generally has more time to write his or her piece—perhaps several days or weeks rather than the few hours allotted to a reviewer. The critic also attempts to put the theater event into a larger context, relating the play to a category (nonrealism or realism, for instance). The critic will try to explain how the theater event fits into this framework or into the body of the playwright's work. The critic might also put the theater event into a social, political, or cultural context.

Ideally, the critic has developed a personal point of view about various aspects of theater. He or she has arrived at an idea of how plays are put together, what constitutes good acting, what is expected of a realistic play as opposed to an experimental play, and so forth.

THE AUDIENCE'S RELATIONSHIP TO CRITICISM: TWO ISSUES

As suggested earlier, when the audience combines awareness of criticism with the theater event itself, the experience can be greatly enhanced: background information and critical appraisals are added to one's own firsthand reactions. There are cautionary notes, however, of which audience members should be aware.

The Audience's Independent Judgment

Quite often critics state unequivocally that a certain play is extremely well written or badly written, beautifully performed or atrociously performed, and so on. Because critics often speak so confidently and because their opinions appear on television or in print, their words have the ring of authority. But theatergoers should not be intimidated by this. In New York City, Chicago, or Los Angeles, where a number of critics and reviewers in various media comment on each production, there is a wide range of opinion. It is not unusual for half a dozen of them to find a certain play admirable, another half-dozen to find the same play highly objectionable, and still others to find a mixture of good and bad.

What this implies is that there is no absolute authority among critics, and that audience members should make up their own minds. If a critic, for example, dislikes a certain play because he or she finds it too sentimental and you happen to like that kind of sentiment, you should not be dissuaded from your own preferences.

Analysis and Overanalysis

Another caution has to do with analysis and overanalysis. Is there a risk in a critic's being too analytical and judgmental about a theater performance? There can be, of course. Some people are so preoccupied with trying to determine what is wrong with a play or performance that they lose all sense of immediacy; the spontaneity and joy of the experience are sacrificed. Most

critics, however, find that their alertness to what is happening during a performance helps rather than hinders their emotional response to the event. After all, human beings have an enormous capacity for receiving information on several levels simultaneously. We do it all the time in our daily lives. With a little practice, the same thing can happen in theatergoing, both for audience members and for professional critics. We develop standards for theater events—a sense of what makes good theater—and we judge a performance by those standards at the same time that we lose ourselves in the overall experience.

In Chapters 1 through 3 we have examined the role of the audience and of a special audience member, the critic. Those who watch a theater performance are a necessary part of the theater equation. In Chapter 4 we turn to the space in which the audience sees a performance: The physical theater.

SUMMARY

1. Most people who attend theater events are amateur critics, making judgments and drawing conclusions about what they see.

2. The critic has several tasks: to understand exactly what is being presented, including the intentions of the playwright and the director; to analyze the play, the acting, and the direction, as well as other elements such as scenery and lighting; to evaluate the presentation—was this worth doing? does it serve a purpose? and so forth.

3. Criticism can be classified as *descriptive* and *prescriptive*. In descriptive criticism, the critic describes carefully and accurately what occurs. In prescriptive criticism, the critic undertakes to say not what does happen so much as what *should* happen in a theater production.

4. People commenting on theater can be divided into *reviewers*, who report briefly on a theater event in newspapers, magazines, or on television; and *critics*, who write longer articles analyzing in depth a performance or the work of a playwright.

5. Audience members must realize that critics, too, have their limitations and prejudices and that ultimately each individual spectator must arrive at his or her own judgment regarding a theater event.

EXPLORING THEATER ON THE WEB

The Critic and the Audience

The Internet offers many places to read reviews of current and past theatrical productions. When you are searching for play reviews by reputable theater critics, look in large-city online newspapers such as *The New York Times* (http://www.nytimes.com), the *Chicago Tribune* (http://www.chicagotribune.com), or the *Seattle Times* (http://www.seattletimes.com). *The New York Times* Arts/Living section online (http://nytimes.com/pages/arts/index.html) is a wonderful guide to New York City's arts and entertainment scene. (You will have to register to get onto this site; however, the site is free.) Clicking on the "Theater" link (left column of the page) will take you to the "On and Off Broadway" section, which provides reviews of current New York theater offerings. In addition, there is an archive of reviews by the noted critics Ben Brantley and Peter Marks (http://www.nytimes.com/library/theater). Another online newspaper with lots of theater reviews is the *Village Voice* (http://www.villagevoice.com). In the far left column, you'll find a "Theater" link, which will bring you to its current theater reviews. Use search engine at the top of the page to find archived reviews.

Exercises:

1. The *Chicago Tribune* has an online entertainment guide called Chicago Metromix (http://metromix.com). Click on the "Stage" link to find articles about the Chicago theater scene and reviews of currently running and archived productions. Use the search engine at the top of the page to find Chris Jones's review of the Steppenwolf Theatre's Art Exchange production of Ray Bradbury's *Fahrenheit 451*.

2. The *London Stage* is a newspaper established in 1880; it is one of Europe's premier theater resources. You can now access the *London Stage* online at http://www.thestage.co.uk. Go to the "reviews" link in the header, which will bring you to a page listing all current theater reviews. To the left you'll find online reviews; choose two. Do the critics address the three key criteria for criticism? Is one review more descriptive or prescriptive than the other? What conclusions can you draw from your consideration of each review? How might this affect the production?

3. Visit *American Theater* magazine's site (http://www.tcg.org/frames/am_theatre/fs_am_theatre.htm). Access the articles available online. Are they theater reviews? If yes, how do they differ from reviews you've found in newspapers? If no, what are the articles about? Are they "critical"? Explain.

CHAPTER FOUR

Stage Spaces

For those who create theater, the experience begins long before the actual event. The dramatist spends weeks, months, or perhaps years writing the play; the director and designers plan the production well ahead of time; and the actors and actresses rehearse intensively for several weeks before the first public performance.

For the spectator, too, the experience begins ahead of time. Members of the audience read or hear reports of the play; they anticipate seeing a particular actress or actor; they buy tickets and make plans with friends to attend; and before the performance, they gather outside the theater auditorium with other members of the audience.

◀ **THE ROMAN THEATER AT ASPENDOS, TURKEY**

The physical environment of a theater production is an important part of the experience. Whether the theater space is indoors or outdoors, large or small, the shape of its stage and the relationship of stage to audience will help determine the nature of the experience. Ancient Greek and Roman drama was performed in outdoor amphitheaters. Greek theaters were carved into hillsides, but Roman theaters, like the one shown here, were free standing. Note the semicircular seating area, in two sections, the semicircle at the base, which is a partial holdover of the circular orchestra of Greek theaters, and the remains of a stage façade on the left. In front of the façade, a raised stage would have run across the entire width of the space. (© Roger Wood/CORBIS)

CREATING THE ENVIRONMENT

When spectators arrive at a theater for a performance, they immediately take in the environment in which the event will occur. The atmosphere of the theater building has a great deal to do with the audience's mood in approaching a performance, not only creating expectations about the event but conditioning the experience once it gets under way.

Spectators have one feeling if they come into a formal setting, such as a picture-frame stage surrounded by carved gilt figures, with crystal chandeliers and red plush seats in the auditorium. They have quite a different feeling if they come into an old warehouse converted into a theater, with bare brick walls, and a stage in the middle of the floor surrounded by folding chairs.

For many years people took the physical arrangement of theaters for granted. This was particularly true in the period when all houses were facsimiles of the Broadway theater, with its proscenium, or picture-frame, stage. In the past half century, however, not only have people been exposed to other types of theaters, they have also become more aware of the importance of environment. Many experimental groups have deliberately made awareness of the environment a part of the experience.

An avant-garde production of Euripides' *The Bacchae,* called *Dionysus in 69,* by the Performance Group in New York, introduced the audience to the performance in a controlled manner. Spectators were not allowed into the theater when they arrived but were made to line up on the street outside. The procedure is outlined in a book describing the production.

> The audience begins to assemble at around 7:45 P.M. They line up on Wooster Street below Greenwich Village. Sometimes the line goes up the block almost to the corner of Broome. On rainy nights, or during the coldest parts of the winter, the audience waits upstairs over the theater. The theater is a large space, some 50 by 40 and 20 feet high. At 8:15 the performance begins for the audience when the stage manager, Vickie May Strang, makes the following announcement. Inside the performers begin warming up their voices and bodies at 7:45.
>
> VICKIE: Ladies and gentlemen! May I have your attention, please. We are going to start letting you in now. You will be admitted to the theater one at a time, and if you're with someone you may be split up. But you can find each other again once you're inside. Take your time to explore the environment. It's a very interesting space, and there are all different kinds of places you can sit. We recommend going up high on the towers and platforms, or down underneath them. The password is "Go high or take cover." There is no smoking inside and no cameras. Thank you.[1]

In an interview included in the book, Strang gave her own view of this procedure.

> We let the public in one at a time. People on the queue outside the theater ask me why. I explain that this is a rite of initiation, a chance for each per-

son to confront the environment alone, without comparing notes with friends. People are skeptical. Some few are angry. Many think it's a put-on. I must confess to a perverse pleasure in teasing people on a line. Many will come up and ask anxiously, "Has it already begun?" I say, "it begins before we let anybody in, but it begins when everybody is in, and really it begins when you go in." True.[2]

By having spectators enter the theater in an unconventional way, or by re-arranging the theater space itself, some contemporary groups deliberately make the audience conscious of the theater environment. But the feeling we have about the atmosphere of a theater building as we enter it has always been an important element in the experience. In the past, spectators may not have been conscious of it, but they were affected by it nevertheless. Today, with the many varieties of theater experience available to us, the first thing we should become aware of is the environment in which an event takes place. Whether it is large or small, indoors or outdoors, formal or informal, familiar or unfamiliar, it will inevitably play a part in our response to the performance.

At times scenic designers are able to alter the architecture of a theater space to create a new arrangement or configuration. If the auditorium space is too large for a specific production, balconies might be blocked off, or the rear of the orchestra might be closed in some manner. Also, the decor can be altered: bright colors, banners, and bright lighting could create a festive atmosphere in a space that is ordinarily formal and subdued.

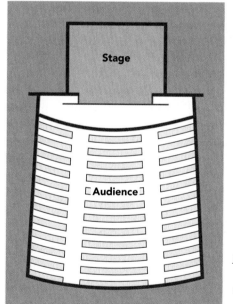

PROSCENIUM THEATER

The audience faces in one direction, toward an enclosed stage encased by a picture-frame opening. Scene changes and performers' entrances and exits are made behind the proscenium opening, out of sight of the audience.

THEATER SPACES

A consideration of environment leads directly to an examination of the various forms and styles of theater buildings, including the arrangements of audience seating. Throughout theater history, there have been four basic types of stages, each with its own advantages and disadvantages, each suited to certain types of plays and certain types of productions, and each providing the audience with a somewhat different experience. The four are (1) the **proscenium**, or **picture-frame, stage;** (2) the **arena**, or circle, stage; (3) the **thrust** stage with three-quarter seating; and (4) **created** and **found** stage spaces.[3] Today, in addition, there are all-purpose and **"black box"** theater spaces, out of which a version of any one of the other four can be created.

Proscenium Stage

Perhaps the most familiar type of stage is the proscenium, or picture-frame, stage. Broadway theaters, which for many years were models for theaters throughout the country, have proscenium stages.

The term *proscenium* comes from the *proscenium arch*, the frame which separates the stage from the auditorium and which was first introduced in Italy during the Renaissance. Although it was an arch in the past, today this frame is usually a rectangle which forms an outline for the stage itself. As the term *picture-frame stage* suggests, it resembles a large picture frame through which the audience looks at the stage. Before the 1950s there was usually a curtain just behind the proscenium opening; when the curtain rose, it revealed the picture. Another term for this type of stage is ***fourth wall***, from the idea of the proscenium opening as a transparent glass wall through which the audience looks at the other three walls of a room.

Because the action takes place largely behind the proscenium opening, or frame, the seats in the auditorium all face in the same direction, toward the stage, just as seats in a movie theater face the screen. The auditorium itself—the ***house***, or ***front of the house***, as it is called—is slanted downward from the back to the stage. (In theater usage, the slant of an auditorium or stage floor is called a ***rake***.) The stage itself is raised several feet above the auditorium floor, to aid visibility. There is usually a balcony (sometimes there are two balconies) protruding about halfway over the main floor. The main floor, incidentally, is called (in American usage) the ***orchestra***. (In ancient Greek theater, the orchestra was the circular acting area at the base of the hillside amphitheater, but in modern usage it is the

A MODERN PROSCENIUM-STAGE THEATER

In this cutaway drawing we see the audience seating at the left, all facing in the one direction, toward the stage. Behind the orchestra pit in the center is the apron on the stage; and then the proscenium frame, behind which are the flats and other scenic elements and—at the far right—a cyclorama. Overhead, scenery can be raised into the fly loft above the stage area.

main floor of the theater where the audience sits.) In certain theaters, as well as concert halls and opera houses that have the proscenium arrangement, there are horseshoe-shaped tiers or **boxes**, which ring the auditorium for several floors above the orchestra.

The popularity of the proscenium stage on Broadway and throughout the United States in the nineteenth and early twentieth centuries was partly due to its wide acceptance throughout Europe. Beginning in the late seventeenth century, the proscenium theater was adopted in every European country. Examples of eighteenth-century theaters in this style include Drury Lane and Covent Garden in London; the Royal Theater in Turin, Italy; Hôtel de Bourgogne in Paris; the Bolshoi in Saint Petersburg, Russia; and the Drottningholm near Stockholm, Sweden—a theater still preserved in its original state. Nineteenth-century proscenium theaters include the Teatro Español in Madrid; the Park Theater and Burton's Chambers Street in New York; the Burgtheater in Vienna, Austria; and the Teatro alla Scala in Milan, Italy.

A BIBIENA SET FOR A FORMAL PROSCENIUM THEATER

The standard theater throughout Europe and the United States from the eighteenth century to the early twentieth century was a formal proscenium space. The basic configuration had the audience in a downstairs orchestra, in balconies, and in side boxes facing an elaborate picture-frame stage. With this type of stage, impressive scenery and other visual effects can be created and changed behind the curtain that covers the proscenium opening. The auditorium was usually formal and ornate, with carved statues and designs, gold leaf, and red plush seats. In the eighteenth century, the Bibiena family from Italy created scene designs on a grand scale for such theaters throughout Europe. They painted backdrops with vistas which seemed to disappear into the far distance. This scene is by Giuseppe di Bibiena (1696–1757). (Victoria and Albert Museum, London)

The stage area of these theaters was usually deep, allowing for elaborate scenery, including scene shifts, with a tall *fly loft* above the stage to hold scenery. The loft had to be more than twice as high as the proscenium opening so that scenery could be concealed when it was raised, or "flown." (When pieces of scenery are raised out of sight, they are said to *fly* into the loft.) Scenery was usually hung by rope or cable on a series of parallel pipes running from side to side across the stage. Hanging the pieces straight across, one behind the other, allowed many pieces of scenery to be stored and raised and lowered as necessary.

Several mechanisms for raising and lowering scenery were developed during the period when the proscenium stage itself was being adopted. An Italian, Giacomo Torelli (1608–1678), devised a **counterweight** system in which weights hung on a series of ropes and pulleys balanced the scenery,

THE PROSCENIUM: IDEAL FOR SPECTACLE

The musical 42nd Street, *as well as numerous other large-scale musicals, is especially effective when framed by the proscenium stage opening. Both the scenery and other elements can be hidden above and around the stage, and then move into the main stage area, as if by magic. Here we see signs outlined in lights above a series of stair steps, also outlined in lights. The entire spectacle is suddenly revealed when curtains are raised and lights are turned on, making for an impressive visual display.* (© Joan Marcus)

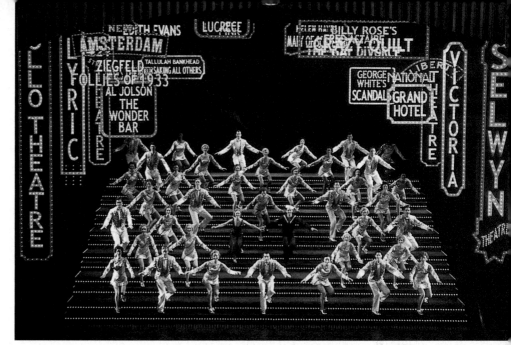

allowing heavy scenery to be moved easily by a few stagehands. Torelli's system also allowed side pieces, known as **wings**, to be moved in and out of the stage picture. By connecting both the hanging pieces and the side pieces to a central drum below the stage, Torelli made it possible for everything to move simultaneously, and in this way a complete stage set could be changed at one time.

Shortly after Torelli, a dynasty of scenic artists emerged who carried scene painting to a degree of perfection rarely equaled before or since. Their family name was Bibiena, and for over a century, beginning with Ferdinando (1657–1743) and continuing through several generations to Carlo (1728–1787), they dominated the art of scene painting. Their sets usually consisted of vast halls, palaces, or gardens. Towering columns and arches framed spacious corridors or hallways which disappeared into an endless series of vistas as far as the eye could see. Throughout this period, audiences, as well as scene designers and technicians, became so carried away with spectacle that at times the visual aspects were emphasized to the exclusion of everything else, including the script and the acting.

Although there have been many changes in theater production, and today we have a wide variety of production approaches, audiences are still attracted to ingenious displays of visual effects in proscenium theaters. This is especially true of large musicals such as *Les Misérables, The Phantom of the Opera, Aida,* and *The Lion King.* Because the machinery and the workings of scene changes can be concealed behind a proscenium opening, this type of stage offers a perfect arrangement for spectacle.

Chapter 4 Stage Spaces   75

There are other advantages to the proscenium stage. Realistic scenery—a living room, an office, a kitchen—looks good behind a proscenium frame; the scene designer can create the illusion of a genuine, complete room more easily with a proscenium stage than with any other. Also, the strong central focus provided by the frame rivets the attention of the audience. There are times, too, when members of the audience want the detachment, the distancing, which a proscenium provides.

Arena Stage

To some people, proscenium theaters, decorated in gold and red plush, look more like temples of art than theaters. These audience members prefer a more informal, intimate theater environment. A movement in this direction began in the United States just after World War II when a number of theater practitioners decided to break away from the formality which proscenium theaters tend to create. This was part of an overall desire to bring many aspects of theater closer to everyday life: acting styles, the subject matter of plays, the manner of presentation, and the shape of the theater space. One form this reaction took was the *arena stage*—a return, as we shall see, to one of the most ancient stage arrangements.

The arena stage (also called **circle theater** or **theater-in-the-round**) has a playing space in the center of a square or circle, with seats for spectators all around it. The arrangement is similar to that in sports arenas which feature boxing or basketball. The stage may be a raised area a few feet off the main floor, with seats rising from the floor level; or it may be on the floor itself, with seats raised on levels around it. When seating is close to the stage, there is usually some kind of demarcation indicating the boundaries of the playing area.

One advantage of the arena theater is that it offers more intimacy than the ordinary proscenium. With the performers in the center, even in a larger theater, the audience can be closer to them. If the same number of people attend an arena event and a proscenium event, at least half of those at the arena will be nearer the action: someone who would have been in the twelfth row in a proscenium theater will be in the sixth row in an arena theater. Besides this proximity to the stage, the arena theater has another advantage: there is no frame or barrier to separate the performers from the audience.

Beyond these considerations, in the arena arrangement there is an unconscious communion, basic to human behavior, which comes when people form a circle—from the embrace of two people to a circle for children's games, to a larger gathering where people form an enclosure around a fire or an altar. It is no coincidence that virtually all primitive forms of theater were "in the round."

A practical advantage of the arena theater is economy. All you need for this kind of theater is a large room: you designate a playing space, arrange

PLAN OF AN ARENA STAGE

The audience sits on four sides or in a circle surrounding the stage. Entrances and exits are made through the aisles or through tunnels underneath the aisles. A feeling of intimacy is achieved because the audience is close to the action and encloses it.

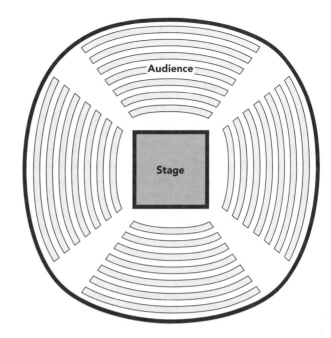

A CONTEMPORARY ARENA THEATER

The arena theater attempts to capture the intimacy and immediacy of primitive theater. It uses the barest essentials of stage scenery but the full resources of contemporary stage lighting.

rows of seats around the sides, and hang lights on pipes above, and you have a theater. Elaborate scenery is impossible because it would block the view of large parts of the audience. A few pieces of furniture, with perhaps a lamp or sign hung from the ceiling, are all you need to indicate where a scene takes place. Many low-budget groups have found that they can build a workable and even attractive theater-in-the-round when a proscenium theater would be out of the question.

These two factors—intimacy and economy—no doubt explain why arena theater is one of the oldest stage forms. From as far back as we have records, we know that tribal ceremonies and rituals, in all parts of the world, have been held in some form of circle theater. Many scholars believe that the ancient Greek theater evolved from an arena form. According to this theory, Greek tribes beat down a circle in a field of threshed grain; an altar was placed in the center, and ceremonies were performed around the altar while members of the tribe stood on the edge of the circle. This arrangement was later made more permanent, when ceremonies, festivals, and Dionysian revels—forerunners of Greek theater—were held in such spaces.

The arena form has also emerged at other times in history. Several of the medieval cycle plays were performed in the round: in Lincolnshire and Cornwall in England, and in Touraine in France, for example. In the United States in the 1940s and 1950s there was a proliferation of arena stages across the country, such as a theater started by Margo Jones in Dallas, Texas; and the Penthouse Theater at the University of Washington in Seattle.

In spite of its long history and its resurgence in recent years, the arena stage has often been eclipsed by other forms. One reason is that its design, while allowing for intimacy, also dictates a certain austerity. As I said before,

THEATER-IN-THE-ROUND: AN ARENA STAGE

One of the three major traditional stage spaces—along with the proscenium and the thrust stage—is the arena stage, or theater-in-the-round, in which the stage is at the center surrounded by audience seating on all four sides. This type of theater offers intimacy and economy, but it makes spectacular scenic effects difficult to achieve. Seen here is the Cassius Carter Theater at the Old Globe Theater complex in San Diego, California. **(Old Globe Theater)**

it is impossible to have elaborate scenery because that would block the view of many spectators. Also, the performers must make all their entrances and exits along aisles that run through the audience, and they can sometimes be seen before and after they are supposed to appear onstage. The arena's lack of adaptability in this respect may explain why some of the circle theaters which opened twenty or thirty years ago have since closed. A number survive, however, and continue to do well. One of the best known is the Arena Stage in Washington, D.C. In addition, throughout this country there are a number of *tent theaters* in arena form where musical revivals and concerts are given.

Thrust Stage

Falling between the proscenium and the arena is a third type of theater: the *thrust stage* with three-quarters seating. In one form or another, this U-shape arrangement has been the most widely used of all stage spaces. In the basic arrangement for this type of theater, the audience sits on three sides, or in a semicircle, enclosing a stage which protrudes into the center. At the back of the playing area is some form of **stage house** providing for the entrances and exits of the performers as well as for scene changes. The thrust stage combines some of the best features of the other two stage types: the sense of intimacy and the "wraparound" feeling of the arena, and the focused stage set against a single background found in the proscenium.

The thrust stage was developed by the Greeks for their tragedies and comedies. They adapted the circle used for tribal rituals and other ceremonies—this circle was called the *orchestra*—by locating it at the base of a curving hillside. The slope of the hill formed a natural amphitheater for the spectators. At the rear of the orchestra circle, opposite the hillside, they placed a stage house, or

**THRUST STAGE
WITH THREE-QUARTERS
SEATING**
The stage is surrounded on three sides by the audience. Sometimes seating is a semicircle. Entrances and exits are made from the sides and backstage. Spectators surround the action, but scene changes and other stage effects are still possible.

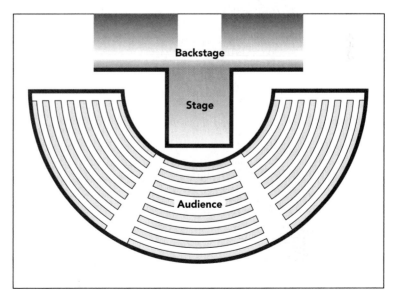

THE MODERN THRUST STAGE
PROVIDES INTIMACY

The thrust stage, with the audience on three sides, has always afforded intimacy, as well as a focal point in the stage itself. Shown here is the Festival stage at the Stratford Festival of Canada, a theater that features productions of Shakespearean plays and other classics. Note the way the seats surround the forestage on three sides, making for wrap-around closeness for the performers, but also notice the stage area at the left providing several levels of playing areas and a backdrop for the action. (Photo by Terry Manzo/Courtesy of the Stratford Festival Archives)

skene. The skene had formal doors through which characters made their entrances and exits and served as a background for the action. It also provided a place for the actors to change their costumes.

During the time of the Greek playwright Aeschylus, in the first half of the fifth century B.C.E., the skene may have been a temporary wooden structure, erected each year for the festivals. In the next two or three centuries, however, the skene became a permanent stone building, two or three stories high, with a platform stage in front. At the same time, the wooden benches on the hillsides for the spectators were replaced by stone seats.

The largest Greek theaters seated 15,000 or more spectators, and their design was duplicated all over Greece, particularly in the years following the conquests of Alexander the Great (356–323 B.C.E.) in what is known as the *Hellenistic* period. Remnants of these Hellenistic theaters remain today throughout that part of the world, in such places as Epidaurus, Priene, Ephesus, Delphi, and Corinth, to name a few.

The Romans, who took the Greek form and built it as a complete structure, had a theater that was not strictly a thrust stage but a forerunner of the proscenium. Instead of using the natural amphitheater of a hillside, they constructed a freestanding stone building, joining the stage house to the seating area and making the orchestra a semicircle. In front of the stage house, which was decorated with arches and statues, they erected a long platform stage where most of the action occurred.

Another example of the thrust stage is found in the medieval period, when short religious plays began to be presented in churches and cathedrals in England and parts of Europe. Around 1200 C.E., performances of these religious plays were moved outdoors. One popular arrangement for these outdoor performances was the **platform stage**. A simple platform was set on trestles (it was sometimes called a **trestle stage**), with a curtain at the back which the performers used for entrances and costume changes. The area underneath the stage was closed off and provided, among other things, a space from which devils and other characters could appear, sometimes in a cloud of smoke. In some places the platform was on wheels (a **wagon stage**) and was moved from place to place through a town. The audience stood on three sides of the platform, making it an improvised thrust stage. This type of stage was widely used

THE CLASSIC SPANISH STAGE

A variation on the thrust stage used in Elizabethan England is the Spanish corrales. A version of this stage, uncovered by an accident in 1953, is shown here in Almagro, Spain, where a theater festival is held each year. This is not strictly speaking a thrust stage because the audience is not surrounding the stage on the three sides of the ground floor, but it has all the other components of the Renaissance outdoor theater, with the platform stage and audience seating in boxes or balcony around three sides. (Javier Rodriguez/COVER)

from the thirteenth to the fifteenth century in England and various parts of Europe.

The next step following the wagon stage was a thrust stage which appeared in England in the sixteenth century, just before Shakespeare began writing for the theater. A platform stage would be set up at one end of the open courtyard of an inn. The inns of this period were three or four stories high, and the rooms facing the inner courtyard served as boxes from which spectators could watch the performance. On the ground level, spectators stood on three sides of the stage. The fourth side of the courtyard, behind the platform, served as the stage house.

An interesting coincidence is that an almost identical theater took shape in Spain at the same time. The inns in Spain were called **corrales**, and this name was given to the theaters which developed there. (Another coincidence is that a talented and prolific dramatist, Lope de Vega, was born within two years of Shakespeare and emerged as his Spanish counterpart.)

The formal English theaters of Shakespeare's day, such as the Globe and the Fortune, were similar to the inn theaters: the audience stood in an open area around a platform stage, and three levels of spectators sat in closed galleries at the back and sides. A roof covered part of the stage; at the back of the stage, some form of raised area served for balcony scenes (as in *Romeo and Juliet*). At the rear of the stage, also, scenes could be concealed and then "discovered." On each side at the rear was a door used for entrances and exits.

These theaters were fascinating combinations of diverse elements: they were both indoors and outdoors; some spectators stood while others sat; and the audience was composed of almost all levels of society. The physical environment must have been stimulating: performers standing at the front of the thrust stage were in the center of a hemisphere of spectators, on three sides around them as well as above and below. These theaters held 2,000 to 3,000 spectators, but no one in the audience was more than 60 feet or so from the stage, and most people were much closer. Being in the midst of so many people, enclosed on all sides but with the open sky above, must have instilled a feeling of great communion among audiences and performers. Something of the same feeling can be recaptured when one visits the recently reconstructed Globe Theatre in London.

Shortly after Shakespeare's day, in the latter part of the seventeenth century, there were two significant theatrical developments in England, in Spain, and throughout Europe:

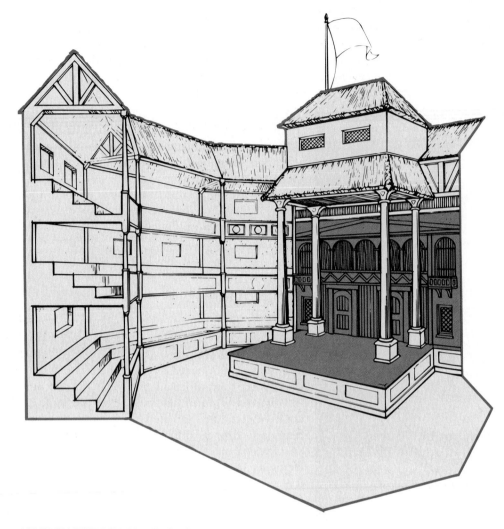

AN ELIZABETHAN PLAYHOUSE

This drawing shows the kind of stage on which the plays of Shakespeare and his contemporaries were first presented. A platform stage juts into an open courtyard, with spectators standing on three sides. Three levels of enclosed seats rise above the courtyard. There are doors at the rear of the stage for entrances and exits and an upper level for balcony scenes.

(1) the theater moved completely indoors; and (2) the stage began a slow but steady retreat behind the proscenium opening, partly because performances were indoors, but more because the style of theaters changed. For over two centuries the thrust stage was in eclipse, not to reappear until about 1900, when a few theaters in England began using a version of the thrust stage to produce Shakespeare.

The return of the thrust stage resulted from a growing realization that Elizabethan plays could be done best on a stage similar to the one for which they had been written. In the United States and Canada, though, it was not until after World War II that the thrust stage came to the fore again. Since then a number of fine theaters of this type have been built, including the Tyrone Guthrie in Minneapolis; the Shakespeare Theater in Stratford, Ontario; the Mark Taper Forum in Los Angeles; and the Long Wharf in New Haven.

The basic stage of traditional Chinese and Japanese drama (including nō theater in Japan) is a form of thrust stage: a raised, open platform stage, frequently covered by a roof, with the audience sitting on two or three sides around the platform. Entrances and exits are made from doors or ramps at the rear of the stage.

The obvious advantages of the thrust stage—the intimacy of three-quarters seating and the close audience-performer relationship, together with the fact that so many of the world's great dramatic works were written for it—give it a significant place alongside the other major forms.

Created and Found Spaces

After World War II a number of avant-garde theater artists, such as the Polish director Jerzy Grotowski, undertook to reform theater at every level. Since the various elements of theater are inextricably bound together, their search for a more basic kind of theater included a close look at the physical arrangement of the playing area and its relationship to the audience.

The Performance Group, which led spectators one at a time into the production of *Dionysus in 69* (as described earlier in this chapter), is typical in this regard. It presented its productions in a large garage converted into an open theater space. At various places in the garage, scaffolding and ledges were built for audience seating.

The Performance Group, like other modern avant-garde companies, owed a great debt to a Frenchman, Antonin Artaud (1896–1948), one of the first theater people to examine in depth the questions raised by the avant-garde. An actor and director who wrote a series of articles and essays about theater, Artaud was brilliant but inconsistent (he spent several periods of his life in mental institutions). Many of Artaud's ideas, however, were to prove prophetic: notions he put forward in the 1920s and 1930s, considered impossible or impractical at the time, have since become common practice among experimental theater groups. Among his proposals was one on the physical theater:

> We abolish the stage and auditorium and replace them by a single site, without partition or barrier of any kind, which will become the theater of the action. A direct communication will be reestablished between the spectator and the spectacle, between the actor and the spectator, from the fact that the spectator, placed in the middle of the action, is engulfed and physically affected by it. This envelopment results, in part, from the very configuration of the room itself.

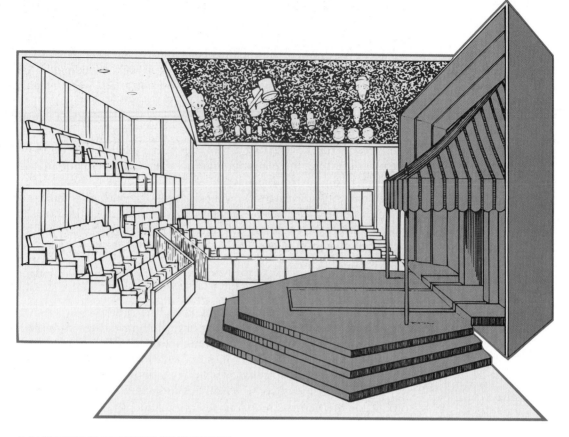

A MODERN THRUST-STAGE THEATER

This cutaway drawing of a thrust stage shows how the playing area juts into the audience, which surrounds the stage on three sides. This configuration affords intimacy, but at the back (shown here at the right) is an area that furnishes a natural backdrop for the action.

Thus, abandoning the architecture of present-day theaters, we shall take some hangar or barn which we shall have reconstructed according to processes which have culminated in the architecture of certain churches or holy places, and of certain temples in Tibet.[4]

Some of Artaud's ideas were put into practice when the movement to explore new concepts became widespread. In the generation after Artaud, Jerzy Grotowski included the physical arrangements of stage space in his experiments. Not only Grotowski but others in the avant-garde movement developed theater space in a variety of ways.

Nontheater Buildings Artaud mentioned a barn or hangar for performances. In recent years virtually every kind of structure has been used: lofts, warehouses, fire stations, basements, churches, breweries, and gymnasiums. This

practice should not be confused with the conversion of unusual spaces to full-scale theaters, which has numerous precedents in the past; historically, indoor tennis courts, palace ballrooms, and monastery dining halls have been converted into theaters. I am speaking here of using unusual structures as they are, with their original architectural elements intact, and carving out special areas for acting and viewing—as with the garage used by the Performance Group.

Adapted Spaces   One frequent practice was using a space to fit a play, rather than (as is normally the case) making the play fit the space. Grotowski, in particular, pursued the notion of finding a different, appropriate configuration for each production. In Grotowski's production of the Doctor Faustus story, for example, the theater was filled with two long tables at which spectators sat as if they were guests at a banquet hosted by Faustus. The action took place at the heads of the tables and even on the tabletops. For his production of *The Constant Prince*, a fence was built around the playing area, and the audience sat behind the fence, looking over it like spectators at a bullfight. In recent decades there have been similar attempts to deal with theater spaces in many parts of Europe and the United States.

Street Theater   One development—which was actually a return to practices in medieval Europe—is theater held outdoors in nontraditional settings. A good example is ***street theater***. Generally, street theater is of three types: (1) plays from the standard repertoire presented in the streets; (2) *neighborhood theater,* in which an original play deals with problems and aspirations of a specific

processional

ADAPTED SPACES: SITE-SPECIFIC THEATER

Another version of created or found space is the Colosseum in Rome. Built as a space for spectacles, including gladiatorial contests, it was completed in 80 C.E. and seated approximately 45,000 spectators. In recent years, parts of it have been restored, and certain enterprising theater groups have used it for dramatic presentations. Shown here is a nighttime production in 2000 by the Greek National Theater of Oedipus Rex *by Sophocles.* (**Pier Paolo Cito/AP/Wide World Photos**)

population of a city, such as Puerto Ricans, African Americans, or Italians; and (3) ***guerrilla theater***, aggressive, politically oriented theater produced by an activist group in the streets in an attempt to persuade audiences to become more politically involved. Whatever the form, the important point for our purposes is that these productions take place not in theater buildings but in places like parks, hospitals, jails, and bus stations.

In these productions, theater is brought to people who might not otherwise see it. Also, audiences in such unusual settings are challenged to rethink what theater is all about. On the other hand, there are inherent disadvantages to impromptu productions in the streets or other "found spaces": the audience must be caught on the run, and there is rarely time for more than a sketch or vignette. Nor are there facilities for presenting a fully developed work—but often that is not the purpose of these undertakings in the first place.

Multifocus Environments   An approach that sometimes accompanies these unusual arrangements is ***multifocus theater***. In simple terms, this means not only that there is more than one playing area, such as the four corners of the room (as Artaud suggested in one article), but also that something is going on in several of them simultaneously. This is somewhat like a three-ring circus, where the spectator sees an activity in each ring and must either concentrate on one or divide his or her attention among several activities.

There are several theories behind the idea of multifocus theater. One is that a multifocus event is more like everyday life; if you stand on a street corner, there is activity all around you—in the four directions of the streets, in the buildings above—not just in one spot. You select which area you will observe, or perhaps you watch several areas at one time. The argument is that in theater, you should have the same choice.

In multifocus productions no single space or activity is supposed to be more important than any other. The spectator either takes in several impressions at once and synthesizes them in his or her own mind or selects one item as most arresting and concentrates on that. There is no such thing as the "best seat in the house"; all seats are equally good, because the activity in all parts of the theater is equally important. Sometimes multifocus theater is joined with ***multimedia theater***—presentations which offer some combination of acting, films, video, dance, music, slides, and light shows.

AN ISLAND FOR SITE-SPECIFIC THEATER

In Holland, a festival, known as the Oerol Festival, has been inaugurated in which an entire island, Terschelling, for ten days in June is used by a variety of theater companies to present their pieces. Groups set up in all kinds of places on the island—taverns, barns, tents, garages, and on beaches—to offer their productions. Shown here is a production on a beach entitled Salted, *written and directed by Judith de Rijke, produced by* Tryater *of Holland, which brought together young artists from various regions to celebrate the linguistic diversity of Europe.* **(Photo courtesy of Sake Elzinga)**

All-Purpose Theater Spaces

Because of the interest in a variety of spaces in modern theater production, and the requirements of many different kinds of productions, a number of theater complexes, including many college theater departments, have built spaces which can be adapted to an almost infinite variety of configurations. Seats, lights, platforms, levels—every aspect of such a theater is flexible and movable.

In this kind of space the designers can create a proscenium, a thrust, an arena, or some combination of these. But the designers can also create corner stages, island stages, and multifocus arrangements with playing areas in several parts of the studio, sometimes referred to as a *black box* because it is often an empty rectangular space into which various audience seating and stage arrangements can be introduced.

SPECIAL REQUIREMENTS OF THEATER ENVIRONMENTS

Simply assigning a theater to a category does not adequately describe the environment; we must also take into account a number of other variables. Two theaters may be of the same type and still be quite different in size, atmosphere, and setting. The theater experience in a small off-Broadway-type thrust theater will be far different from that in a thrust theater several times larger, such as the Tyrone Guthrie in Minneapolis. Also, one theater may be indoors and another of the same type outdoors.

There are other factors that architects, producers, and designers must take into account, one of which is the human scale. No matter what the configuration, the performer is the basic scale by which everything is measured in theater. Theater architects as well as scenic and lighting designers must always keep this in mind, and audience members should be aware of it as well. When the theater environment and the stage space violate this human scale in some way, problems are created for performers and spectators.

There are also questions of appropriateness and aesthetic distance. By *appropriateness* I mean the relationship of a stage space to a play or production. *Aesthetic distance* is the principle discussed in Chapter 1 with regard to the performer-audience relationship. A large-scale musical such as *The Phantom of the Opera, The Lion King,* or *42nd Street* requires a full stage—usually a proscenium stage—and a large auditorium from which the audience can get the full effect of the spectacle. An intimate production, however, such as *Wit* by Margaret Edson, would be lost in such a large space. This play—about a female English professor dying of cancer—requires a small theater so that audience members are close enough to the action to make a connection with the characters onstage.

Rather than being limited to one type of theater building and one type of stage, theater audiences today are fortunate in having a full range of environments in which to experience theater. Taken all in all, whether single-focus or multifocus, indoors or outdoors, the recent innovations in theater milieus have added new alternatives, rich in possibilities, to the traditional settings for theatrical productions. They have also called attention to the importance of environment in the total theater experience.

In this chapter we have examined environmental factors influencing our experience at a theatrical event, including the location of the theater building, its size, its setting, its atmosphere, and its layout. In addition to a general environment in a theater building, there is a specific environment for the performer. It is to the performer—and the person who works most closely with the performer, the director—that we turn in Part 2.

SUMMARY

1. The atmosphere and environment of the theater space play a large part in setting the tone of an event.

2. Experimental theater groups in recent years have deliberately made spectators aware of the environment.

3. Throughout theater history there have been four basic stage and auditorium arrangements: proscenium, arena, thrust, and created or found space.

4. The proscenium theater features a picture-frame stage, in which the audience faces directly toward the stage and looks through the proscenium opening at the "picture." The proscenium stage aids illusion: placing a room of a house behind the proscenium, for example, allows the scene designer to create an extremely realistic set. This type of stage also allows elaborate scene shifts and visual displays because it generally has a large backstage area and a fly loft. It also creates a distancing effect, which works to the advantage of certain types of drama. At the same time, however, the proscenium frame sets up a barrier between the performers and the audience.

5. The arena or circle stage places the playing area in the center with the audience seated in a circle or square around it. This offers an economical way to produce theater and an opportunity for great intimacy between performers and spectators, but it cannot offer full visual displays in terms of scenery and scene changes.

6. The thrust stage with three-quarters seating is a platform stage with seating on three sides. Entrances and exits are made at the rear, and there is an opportunity for a certain amount of scenery. This form combines some of the scenic features of the proscenium theater with the intimacy of the arena stage.

7. Created or found space takes several forms: use of nontheater buildings, adaptation of a given space to fit individual productions, use of outdoor settings, street theater, multifocus environments, and all-purpose spaces.

8. Size and location (indoors or outdoors, etc.), along with the shape and character of a theater building, affect the environment.

EXPLORING THEATER ON THE WEB

Stage Spaces

The Internet can be used to find reproductions of different types of theater spaces (or staging practices) from specific eras, especially classical Greece and Elizabethan England. Two representative theaters of these periods are the theater at Epidaurus, which is the subject of archaeological studies as the best preserved of the classical Greek theaters; and the Globe, which has been replicated and rebuilt in England. Theater at Epidaurus (thrust stage): http://www.fhw.gr/choros/epidaurus; Globe (thrust stage): http://www.rdg.ac.uk/globe In addition, you can browse the history of the Metropolitan Opera House at http://www.metopera.org/history (can you find the drawing of the building's facade from 1883?) and read about the contemporary reconstruction of the Kreielsheimer Arena in Seattle at http://www.djc.com/special/design96/10016902.html; Metropolitan Opera House (proscenium stage): http://www.metopera.org/history/week-961021.html; Kreielsheimer Theater Seattle (arena stage): http://www.djc.com/special/design96/10016902.html

Exercises:

1. Why are certain performance spaces best suited to certain art forms? Look online for examples of performances that use different spaces: fashion shows, parades, sports events, movies, concerts, political conventions, etc. Choose at least two examples. How is each space used by performers and spectators? Why do you think each example occurs in the particular space?

2. On the basis of physical descriptions of the four basic stage arrangements noted in this chapter and the written description noted at http://www.geocities.com/ia470/primer/theatres.htm, a website for a local chapter of the International Alliance of Theatrical Stage Employees, sketch the four basic stage spaces, noting the key components that make them unique. Discuss the strengths and weaknesses regarding the use of each stage space for A Raisin in the Sun by Lorraine Hansberry. Is any one space more suited than the others to this play?

3. Look through the photo gallery for Bread and Puppet Theater at http://www.theaterofmemory.com/art/bread/photos.html (you'll have to click on NEXT to see each photo). How would you describe the performance you see in the pictures? Where does it take place? Who is performing? What kinds of costumes are used? Does the company use scenery? Is the company performing on a small scale or a large one? Why?

Play Synopsis

A RAISIN THE THE SUN (1959)

Lorraine Hansberry (1930-1965)

Chief Characters

Lena Younger, *Mama*
Walter Lee Younger, *her son*
Ruth Younger, *Walter's wife*
Travis Younger, *Ruth and Walter's son*
Beneatha Younger, *Walter's sister*
Joseph Asagai, *Beneatha's friend*
George Murchison, *Beneatha's friend*
Karl Lindner, *representative of white neighborhood*

Setting

The Youngers' apartment in a poor section of Chicago, sometime after World War II.

Background

The Youngers are a hardworking black family with dreams of improving their lives. The father worked hard all his life, but he has died, and his only legacy is a $10,000 life insurance policy which the family is about to receive. He and Mama always wanted to own a house but could never afford one.

Act I, Scene 1: It is Friday morning, and Ruth wakes the family. All of them are looking forward to the arrival of the insurance check, which promises an escape from poverty. After their son Travis goes to school, Walter tells Ruth that he has a chance to buy a liquor store with some

friends. Walter wants Ruth to persuade Mama to give him the insurance money for this new venture, but Ruth is not supportive. Walter's sister Beneatha, an aspiring doctor, enters and tells him that the insurance money is Mama's not theirs. After Walter goes to work, Mama enters. Her grandmotherly concern for Travis is a source of conflict between her and Ruth. Ruth talks to Mama about Walter's liquor store: Ruth believes that Walter needs a purpose in life, which the store could provide, but Mama, a God-fearing woman, doesn't like the idea of selling liquor. Mama wants to put some money aside for Beneatha's education and to buy a house in a nice neighborhood with the remainder of the money. Ruth suddenly becomes ill, and Mama expresses concern for her.

Scene 2: The following morning, Saturday, is cleaning day. As Mama works at home, Walter goes out to talk with his friend Willy about buying the liquor store.

Ruth comes back from the doctor very upset and tells Mama that she is pregnant. Beneatha's friend Asagai arrives with an African outfit for her to wear. Beneatha is always trying new things, like playing the guitar and pursuing her African roots. Asagai is from Africa; he is an intellectual and is attracted to Beneatha, but his attentions frighten her because she wants to find her own identity. Meanwhile, the insurance check arrives, and Mama becomes upset. It reminds her that instead of a warm, loving husband, all she now has is a piece of paper.

Marguerite Hannah (Ruth Younger), Hassan El-Amin (Walter Lee Younger) (© Richard Feldman/Huntington Theatre Company)

Walter enters excitedly talking about buying the liquor store, and Ruth storms out. Mama tries to tell Walter that she understands his frustration, but she explains to him that Ruth is pregnant and wants an abortion.

Act II, Scene 1: Later the same day. Ruth is ironing when Beneatha enters, ready for a date with George, a wealthy, successful black man. Walter is obviously jealous of George's success. Mama enters and tells everyone that she has made a down payment on a house with part of the insurance money. Ruth and Travis are happy with the news, but Walter is depressed. He believes that this is another setback to his dream of owning the liquor store. When the young people discover that the house Mama plans to buy is in an all-white section, they wonder whether they will be accepted.

Scene 2: Friday night, a few weeks later. The apartment house is strewn with packing crates in anticipation of the move to the new house. Walter has not gone to work for three days; he is spending his time in a bar. This dismays Mama, who has always worked for her children and now fears that she may be destroying her son. She therefore decides to give Walter $6,500—the remainder of the insurance money—to invest as he chooses. She tells Walter that he should act maturely and become the head of the family. He excitedly begins to talk to his son about his dreams.

Scene 3: Saturday, a week later—moving day. Ruth tells Beneatha that her relationship with Walter is better because he seems to have a new lease on life. Walter enters, followed

Hassan El-Amin (Walter Lee Younger), Esther Rolle (Lena Younger, Mama) (© Richard Feldman/ Huntington Theatre Company)

by Mr. Lindner, a middle-aged white man who has come to discourage the Youngers from moving into their new house. Walter throws him out, and when Mama comes back, they tell her about this "welcoming committee" from the new neighborhood. Mama is greatly moved when the others give her some presents for the new house. In the midst of the celebration, Walter's friend Bobo enters with bad news: Willy has run off with all their money. Walter breaks down and tells the family that he had invested the whole $6,500 with Willy. Mama is distraught, remembering all the suffering and sacrifices the family had made to pay the insurance premiums and meet other expenses.

Act III: An hour later. The mood is despairing. Beneatha fears that this is the end of all her plans. She attacks Walter bitterly, and he exits. Mama starts unpacking because now they must stay in the old house. Walter returns and tells them that he has called Lindner to make a deal. Mama

is against it: "We ain't never been that poor." Walter is about to sell out to "The Man" when his pride stops him; he tells Lindner that they have decided to move into the new house because his father earned it. The family members bustle into activity. After everyone else has left, Mama stands alone for a short while, and then exits into the future.

Discussion Questions

- *A Raisin in the Sun* was written half a century ago. How relevant, today, are the story and the struggles of the characters? How universal is the subject matter? The situation?
- Will African Americans relate more easily to *A Raisin in the Sun* than other groups? In what ways can other groups relate to it?
- Will it help to understand the play better if we know the social and political climate of the 1950s and 1960s?

Play Synopsis

FEFU AND HER FRIENDS (1977)

Maria Irene Fornes (1930—   )

(Sara Krulwich/*The New York Times*)

Characters

Fefu	Emma	Cindy
Paula	Christina	Sue
Julia	Cecilia	

Setting

A house belonging to Fefu and her husband in the New England countryside, Spring 1935.

Background

A group of women who went to college together gather at Fefu's house for a day to visit and to plan a group presentation urging educational reform. Some of the women are better acquainted than others.

Part I

The living room at midday. Fefu tells Cindy and Christina, "My husband married me to have a constant reminder of how loathsome women are." As they discuss this provocative idea, Fefu picks up a shotgun, aims out the door, and fires at her husband. Fefu explains to her shocked friends that she plays a game with her husband—she shoots blanks at him and he falls down. He has told her that he may load the gun with real bullets someday.

Julia arrives in a wheelchair, then goes off to wash up. Cindy explains to Christina the bizarre accident that led to Julia's paralysis. Julia fell down at the moment a hunter had shot and killed a deer. Julia became delirious, talking about torturers who would kill her if she did not recant. The bullet had grazed her forehead, but the doctors found no spinal cord injury that would adequately explain her inability to walk. Fefu remembers that Julia used to be afraid of nothing.

Emma arrives wearing a theatrical Turkish dress. Paula and Sue are with her. The women decide that they will eat lunch and then rehearse their presentation. Emma concentrates on the theatrical elements, suggesting which colors the other women should wear. Emma, Fefu, Paula, and Sue exit. Julia notices the gun; remarks, "She's hurting herself," apparently referring to Fefu; and has a brief seizure, blanking out for a few moments. Cecilia then arrives to complete the group.

Part II

For this section of the play, the audience is divided into four groups. Each group is taken to one of four different locations, to observe at close proximity one of four separate scenes. The events depicted in these short scenes are supposed to be occurring simultaneously in different parts of Fefu's house and on the lawn. When the four scenes are

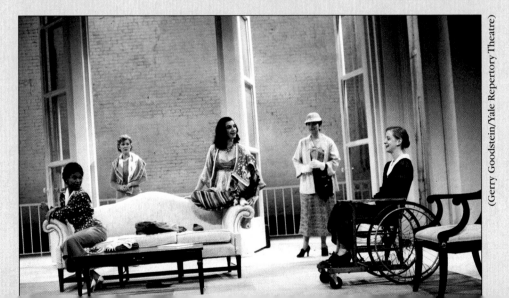

(Gerry Goodstein/Yale Repertory Theatre)

completed, each group rotates to the next location and the scenes are repeated. Each scene is played four times, so that all the audience members see every scene, but the four groups do not view these scenes in the same order.

On the Lawn: Fefu and Emma play croquet. Emma remarks that it is strange that in daily life everyone ignores the existence of genitals. Emma and Fefu agree that admission to heaven is probably determined by sexual performance on earth. Fefu reveals to Emma that she is in a state of spiritual pain. Fefu then leaves to fetch lemonade, while Emma recites a sonnet. Returning with the pitcher of lemonade, Fefu is followed by Paula and Cecilia.

In the Study: Christina and Cindy engage in idle conversation while Christina reads a French textbook and Cindy a magazine. Cindy asks Christina if she likes Fefu. Christina says she does but explains that she is frightened by Fefu's unconventional behavior. Sue comes, in, looking for Julia, and then goes off to look in the bedroom. Cindy describes a strange dream she has had in which a doctor attacks her. Fefu comes through the room and invites them to play croquet.

In the Bedroom: Wearing a white hospital gown, Julia rests on a mattress on the floor. She hallucinates. In a long monologue, she talks about her judges, who have crippled her and have the power to kill her. She says that Fefu is also in danger. Several times Julia reacts as if she has been slapped or raises her arm to ward off a blow. Her judges have taught her a prayer which states that women are evil; she is punished for not believing the prayer. Sue comes in with a bowl of soup for Julia.

In the Kitchen: Sue heats soup. Paula explains her theory of how long an affair lasts, including the time

necessary to understand what went wrong after it has ended. Sue plays with an ice cube on a stick. Then she pours a bowl of soup, puts it on a tray, and exits. Cecilia comes in and makes a cup of tea. Paula and Cecilia awkwardly discuss their past relationship. Fefu comes in for lemonade, and all three go out to play croquet.

Part III

For Part III, the entire audience reassembles and watches as a single group.

The living room in the evening. All the women are present. Cecilia discusses the need for individuals to be part of a community, but she notes that too large a community forces everyone to think at the lowest common denominator. Julia feels isolated because she hallucinates and the others do not. The women decide on the order of their presentation urging educational reform, and Emma delivers her speech on the importance of environment in education. After the program is planned, most of the women go to the kitchen to do the dishes and make coffee.

Julia and Cindy remain behind. The other women, in the midst of a water fight, run back into the living room and out again to the kitchen. A downcast Fefu is briefly alone in the

living room. Julia enters, walking, picks up the sugar bowl, and exits; then, in her wheelchair, she immediately reenters with the other women. The women reminisce about their school days. Paula, remembering her resentment at her poverty and the others' wealth, becomes upset. She leaves the room, and Cecilia goes to comfort her. After the other women go out to look at the stars, Fefu confronts Julia about having seen her walking. Julia denies walking. Julia fears that she is contagious. While Fefu repeatedly urges her to fight for her life and sanity, Julia prays that no harm will come to Fefu. Christina and Cecilia enter. Fefu gets her gun, exits, and fires the gun. Julia puts her hand to her forehead, which is bloody. Fefu reenters with a rabbit she has killed, as Julia slumps in her chair, apparently dead.

Discussion Questions

- Even with the explanations in the text and with the synopsis, can you understand what is happening in *Fefu and Her Friends?*
- What would the experience be like to be part of the audience that is split into separate groups for one section of the play?
- Is *Fefu* more meaningful to women than to men? How can men relate to the play?

Play Synopsis

(Musées Nationaux, Paris)

KING OEDIPUS (c. 430 B.C.E.)

Sophocles (c. 496–406 B.C.E.)

Chief Characters
Oedipus, *King of Thebes*
Jocasta, *wife of Oedipus*
Creon, *brother-in-law of Oedipus*
Teiresias, *a blind seer*
A shepherd, a priest, Chorus

Setting
The entire play takes place in front of the palace at Thebes in Greece.

Douglas Rain as Tiresias; Benedict Campbell as Oedipus (Cylla von Tiedemann/Stratford Festival, Ontario)

Background
When Oedipus was born, an oracle told his parents, the king and queen of Thebes, that their son would kill his father and marry his mother. Fearing this prophecy, the king and queen gave Oedipus to a shepherd to be killed. But the shepherd pitied the child and instead of killing him sent him to Corinth, where he was adopted by the king and queen. Oedipus grew up, learned of the oracle's prediction, and thinking that the king and queen of Corinth were his real parents, fled from Corinth. On the journey toward Thebes, at a place where three roads met, Oedipus argued with a man and killed him—not knowing that the man was his natural father, Laius. When Oedipus arrived in Thebes, the city was plagued by a Sphinx who killed anyone who could not answer her riddle. Oedipus answered the riddle correctly and the Sphinx died. Oedipus then became king and married Jocasta, not realizing she was his mother. Years later, the city was struck by another plague; this is the point at which the play begins.

Prologue: Oedipus enters from his palace and hears from the priest details about the plague which is devastating Thebes. The priest and the people beg Oedipus to help. Oedipus consoles them and declares that he has sent Creon to consult the oracle of Apollo at Delphi. Creon enters and reports that the oracle at Delphi has said that the plague will end when the murderer of the former king, Laius, is discovered. Oedipus is informed that there was a witness to the murder who reported that it was committed by a group of thieves. Oedipus vows to find the murderer.

Parados: The chorus prays to the gods to end the plague.

Scene 1: Oedipus swears to track down the murderer and puts a curse on him. He forbids anyone to shield or harbor him under threat of dire penalties. The blind prophet Teiresias is brought in; he knows the truth—that Oedipus has unknowingly killed his father—but does not want to tell Oedipus, who rages at him. Finally goaded to speak, Teiresias reveals the past and future of Oedipus; he says that Oedipus himself is the murderer. Oedipus, angrier than ever, cannot accept this and accuses Teiresias of plotting with Creon to gain power, but Teiresias vehemently denies this and leaves.

Ode 1: The chorus asks whom the oracle names as the murderer. It proclaims that retribution is inevitable, but it confirms its belief in Oedipus and refuses to accept the idea that he murdered Laius.

Scene 2: Creon enters to answer the charges brought against him by Oedipus. While Oedipus rages against Creon, the latter calmly urges Oedipus to be rational. Creon argues

Diane D'Aquila as Jocasta with Suppliants (Cylla von Tiedemann/Stratford Festival, Ontario)

that it is well known that he is not ambitious for power. The two men continue to argue until Jocasta enters to make peace between them. Jocasta discredits the oracle that instructs the people to find the murderer of Laius. She says that long ago the oracle was proved false because it had said that Laius would be killed by his son, but he was not—he was killed by a stranger where three roads meet. Oedipus becomes fearful that perhaps he did kill Laius after all, and he sends for the only witness to the murder.

Ode 2: The chorus says that reverence for the gods is best and speaks of the evils of pride, recklessness, and vanity. Its faith in the oracle of the gods is shaken.

Scene 3: A messenger form Corinth arrives and tells Jocasta that the king of Corinth is dead and the people there want Oedipus to be their new king. Jocasta jubilantly summons Oedipus to show him new evidence of the untrustworthiness of the oracle, which had said he would murder his father, but Oedipus

remains concerned because his "mother" still lives. The messenger tries to allay his fears by telling him that Merope, in Corinth, is not his mother—Oedipus was brought from Thebes by a shepherd when he was very young. Jocasta sees the truth and tries unsuccessfully to dissuade Oedipus from continuing his search. Seeing his determination to learn the truth, she rushes into the palace.

Ode 3: The chorus prays to the gods to help Oedipus find out about his true birth.

Scene 4: A messenger brings the old shepherd to Oedipus, who forces the hesitant man to speak. The shepherd finally admits that Jocasta told him to kill the baby because the child was destined to kill his own father but states that he pitied the child and took him far away, to Corinth; Oedipus was that boy. In despair, Oedipus rushes into the palace.

Ode 4: The chorus repeats the tale of the fall of the great man, Oedipus, and expresses its sorrow about the tragedy.

Exodos: The second messenger enters from the palace to say that the queen has killed herself. He describes how Oedipus burst into Jocasta's room, to find her hanging, dead. He pulled her down, took a brooch from her dress, and blinded himself with it. The doors to the palace open to reveal the blinded Oedipus. Oedipus blames the god Apollo for leading him to his fate. When Creon enters, Oedipus begs him to exile him, to give Jocasta a proper funeral, and to take care of his daughters, who say a last farewell to their father. The chorus warns that man should take nothing for granted, and then exits.

Discussion Questions

- From reading *King Oedipus,* what conclusions can we draw about Greek society in Athens in the fifth century B.C.E.?
- Can you find symmetry and balance in the play? In the characters? In the action? In the dramatic structure?
- Why might *King Oedipus* be called a tragedy?

Part 2

The Performers and the Director

The Actors Meet the Audience

For the audience, the most immediate contact in theater is with the actresses and actors on stage. Audiences may identify with characters, love them, or hate them, and the personal contact is with the flesh and blood performer enacting each role. ✤ This drawing by Al Hirschfeld shows a group of performers in a production of Shakespeare's *Twelfth Night* performed at the Vivian Beaumont Theater at Lincoln Center. The actors are, left to right: Paul Rudd, Philip Bosco, Max Wright, Brian Murray, Helen Hunt, and Kyra Sedgwick. ✤

CHAPTER FIVE

Acting: Offstage and in the Past

Performers, by their presence, set theater apart from films, television, and the visual arts; they serve as the direct, immediate contact which members of the audience have with theater. More than that, performers embody the heart and soul of theater. The words of a script, the characters created by a dramatist, and the scenery and costumes come to life only when an actor or actress steps onto a stage.

Frequently, acting is looked on as glamorous: successful performers are interviewed on television or written up in newspapers or magazines; books are written about them. The publicity, however, is deceptive: it disguises the fact that acting for the stage is a difficult, disciplined profession. In addition to talent and ability, it requires years of arduous training. (In Chapter 6, we will examine this training.)

Before turning to acting for the stage, however, let us look at another kind of acting: "acting" in everyday life.

◀ PLAYING A PART: IN THEATER AND IN LIFE

In life, people play many roles—as parents, teachers, students, lawyers, and so on. In theater, performers play specific roles assigned to them, and it is understood that these are not the same as a role played in real life. Nevertheless, there are similarities as well as differences that help us understand stage acting. In the picture seen here, actress Cherry Jones is quite obviously dressed for a stage role. She is wearing a Grecian-type outfit for the title role in Lysistrata *by Aristophanes at the American Repertory Theatre. The play is about a group of Grecian women who go on a sex strike with their husbands in order to force the husbands to stop fighting a war and arrive at a peace treaty with their enemies. Lysistrata leads the strike.* (© Richard Feldman/A.R.T.)

"ACTING" IN EVERYDAY LIFE

It may be surprising to realize how much "acting" is a part of our lives, beginning almost the day we are born. Two forms of acting in daily life are *imitation* and *role playing*.

Imitation

Imitation occurs when one person mimics or copies someone else's vocal patterns, gestures, facial expressions, posture, and the like.

Children are among the best imitators in the world, and we are frequently amused at a child who imitates a parent or some other grown-up: a 5-year-old girl, for instance, who puts on a long dress, makeup, and high heels. For children, imitation is more than just play-acting; it is also a way of learning—an aspect of education—and even a factor in survival. The child watches a parent open a door or walk upstairs and learns by imitation how to complete the same maneuver. Children also imitate speech patterns.

As we grow older, imitation continues to be a part of our experience: in every class in school, from elementary school through college, there is usually one person—a clever mimic—who imitates the teacher or the principal with great humor, and sometimes with cruelty. One familiar type of imitation is an attempt to copy the lifestyle of a hero—a singer, a film actor, or some other well-known personality. Examples include Elvis Presley and James Dean in the 1950s; the Beatles in the 1960s; Mick Jagger, Carly Simon,

IMITATION: A FORM OF ACTING IN EVERYDAY LIFE

Imitation and role playing are two types of acting in which everyone participates, even the very young. Shown here are two young girls imitating their elders by dressing up in hats and old-fashioned dresses while taking part in a tea party. (© Myrleen Ferguson/PhotoEdit)

Part 2 The Performers and the Director

and John Travolta in the 1970s; Michael Jackson and Cyndi Lauper in the 1980s; and Madonna, Spike Lee, and Michael Jackson in the 1990s. The imitator adopts the same wardrobe, the same stance, the same physical movements, and the same hairstyle as the hero or heroine.

Role Playing

A second type of "acting" prevalent in our daily lives is role playing. Much has been written about role playing in recent years, and a currently popular term is *role model,* referring to people whose lives, or "roles," serve as models or guides for others. Broadly speaking, roles can be classified as *social* and *personal.*

Social Roles Social roles are general roles recognized by society: father, mother, child, police officer, store clerk, teacher, student, business executive, physician, and so on. Every culture expects definite types of behavior from people who assume social roles. For many years in western culture, for example, the roles of women as secretaries or housewives were considered subordinate to the roles of men. Even when women held positions similar to those of men in business and the professions, they frequently received lower salaries for the same job. The women's movement challenged the notion of subservient roles for women. So entrenched was the idea, however, that it took an entire movement to call it into question. (One aspect of this movement was *consciousness-raising:* making people aware of social attitudes toward women.) Before changes could begin to be made in the subordinate roles women played, everyone had to understand that these *were* roles.

Role Playing Illustrated in Drama

Drama provides many illustrations of the kind of acting we do in our everyday lives. A good example is a scene from *Death of a Salesman* by Arthur Miller (1915—), in which Happy, the salesman's son, tries to be a "big shot" in a restaurant where he is about to meet his father and his brother, Biff. Happy's father has just lost his job and is on the verge of losing his sanity as well. Happy should be thinking only of his father, but he cannot resist trying to impress a woman who enters the restaurant. (Biff, Happy's brother, enters in the middle of the scene. As the scene begins, Stanley, the waiter, speaks to Happy about the woman.)

Stanley: I think that's for you, Mr. Loman.

Happy: Look at that mouth. Oh, God, and the binoculars.

Stanley: Geez, you got a life, Mr. Loman.

Happy: Wait on her.

Stanley: [Going to the Girl's table] Would you like a menu, ma'am?

Girl: I'm expecting someone, but I'd like a—

Happy: Why don't you bring her—excuse me miss, do you mind? I sell champagne, and I'd like you to try my brand. Bring her a champagne, Stanley.

Girl: That's awfully nice of you.

Happy: Don't mention it. It's all company money. [He laughs]

Girl: That's a charming product to be selling, isn't it?

Happy: Oh, gets to be like everything else, selling is selling, y'know.

Girl: I suppose.

Happy: You don't happen to sell, do you?

Girl: No, I don't sell.

Happy: Would you object to a compliment from a stranger? You ought to be on a magazine cover.

Girl: [Looking at him a little archly] I have been. [Stanley comes in with a glass of champagne]

Happy: What'd I say before, Stanley? You see? She's a cover girl.

Stanley: Oh, I could see, I could see.

Happy: [To the Girl] What magazine?

Girl: Oh, a lot of them. [She takes the drink] Thank you.

Happy: You know what they say in France, don't you? "Champagne is the drink of the complexion"—Hiya, Biff! [Biff has entered and sits with Happy]

The Goodman Theatre's Tony Award-winning production of Death of a Salesman. *Pictured are, left to right, Stephanie March as Miss Forsythe, Ted Koch as Happy Loman, and Shannon McCastland as Letta.* (© Eric Y. Exit)

Biff: Hello, kid. Sorry I'm late.

Happy: I just got here. Uh, Miss—?

Girl: Forsythe.

Happy: Miss Forsythe, this is my brother.

Biff: Is Dad here?

Happy: His name is Biff. You might've heard of him. Great football player.

Girl: Really? What team?

Happy: Are you familiar with football?

Girl: No, I'm afraid not.

Happy: Biff is quarterback with the New York Giants.

Girl: Well, that is nice, isn't it? [She drinks]

Happy: Good health.

Girl: I'm happy to meet you.

Happy: That's my name. Hap. It's really Harold but at West Point they called me Happy.

Girl: [Now really impressed] Oh, I see. How do you do? [She turns her profile]

Biff: Isn't Dad coming?

Happy: You want her?

Biff: Oh, I could never make that.

Happy: I remember the time that idea would never come into your head. Where's the old confidence, Biff?

Biff: I just saw Oliver—

Happy: Wait a minute. I've got to see that old confidence again. Do you want her? She's on call.

Biff: Oh, no. [He turns to look at the Girl]

Happy: I'm telling you. Watch this. [Turning to the Girl] Honey? [She turns to him] Are you busy?

Girl: Well, I am . . . but I could make a phone call.

Happy: Do that, will you, honey? And see if you can get a friend. We'll be here for a while. Biff is one of the greatest football players in the country.

Girl: [Standing up] Well, I'm certainly happy to meet you.

Happy: Come back soon.

Girl: I'll try.

Happy: Don't try, honey, try hard.

In this scene, Happy is pretending to be something he is not. He is "playing the role" of the successful operator—the man with numerous accomplishments and abilities, which, of course, he does not actually possess. Like imitation and similar activities, this kind of "acting" is encountered frequently in daily life. (A synopsis of *Death of a Salesman* appears at the end of Part 2.)

Personal Roles Aside from social roles, we develop personal roles with our family and friends. For example, some people become braggarts, boasting of their (sometimes imaginary) feats and accomplishments and embellishing the truth to appear more impressive than they are. Others become martyrs, constantly sacrificing for others and letting the world know about it. Still others are conspirators, people who pull their friends aside to establish an air of secrecy whenever they talk. Frequently, two people fall into complementary roles, one dominant and the other submissive, one active and the other passive.

ACTING IN LIFE VERSUS ACTING ONSTAGE

For all the similarities between acting in daily life and acting for the stage, the differences are crucial—and these differences reveal a great deal about the nature of stage acting.

Some of the differences between stage acting and acting in daily life are obvious. For one thing, actors and actresses onstage are always being observed. In real life there may be observers, but their presence is not essential to an event. Bystanders on a street corner where an accident has occurred form a kind of audience, but their presence is incidental and unrelated to the accident itself. Onstage, however, the performer is always on display and always in the spotlight.

Acting onstage, too, requires a performer to play roles he or she does not play in life. A scene between a father and his son arguing about money, or between a young husband and wife discussing whether or not to have children, is one thing when it is actually occurring in our lives, but something quite different onstage. Generally, the roles we play in life are genuine. A father who accepts his responsibilities toward his children does not just *play* a father; he *is* a father. A woman who writes for a magazine does not just *play* a magazine writer; she *is* one.

In real life, a lawyer knows the law; but onstage, an actor playing the role of a lawyer may not know the difference between jurisprudence and habeas corpus and probably has never been inside a law school. Playing widely divergent parts or parts outside their personal experience requires actors and actresses to stretch their imagination and ability. For example, a young actress at one time or another might be called on to play parts as dissimilar as the fiery, independent heroine in Sophocles' *Antigone;* the vulnerable, love-struck heroine in Shakespeare's *Romeo and Juliet;* and the neurotic, obsessed heroine in Strindberg's *Miss Julie.*

At times performers even have to *double,* that is, perform several parts in one play. In Greek theater it was customary for a play to have only three principal actors, all male; each of them had to play several parts, putting on different masks and costumes to assume the various roles. The German dramatist Bertolt Brecht wrote many plays with large casts which call for doubling. His play *The Caucasian Chalk Circle* has forty-seven speaking parts, but it can be produced with only twenty-five performers. A fascinating situation calling for doubling is written into another play by Brecht, *The Good Woman of Setzuan:* the actress playing the lead character, who becomes pregnant during the course of the play, must also play the part of her cousin—a man.

Another important distinction between acting onstage and in real life is that a theatrical performance is always *conscious.* Performers and audience are aware that the presentation has been planned ahead of time.

This underscores still another significant difference between acting for the stage and "acting" in life: that dramatic characters are not real people. Any stage character—Joan of Arc, Antigone, Oedipus, Hamlet, Willy Loman—is a symbol or an image of a person. Stage characters are fictions created by dramatists and performers to represent people. They remind us of people—in many cases they seem to *be* these people, but they are not. (We will discuss this concept in more detail in Chapter 13, on dramatic characters.)

The task of the performer in attempting to make the characters onstage *appear* to be real requires not only talent but training and discipline as well. Before we examine the training of performers in today's theater in Chapter 6, it will be helpful to look at what was required of performers in the past.

STAGE ACTING: A HISTORICAL PERSPECTIVE

Before the twentieth century, the challenges of acting were dictated by the very specific demands of the type of theater in which performers appeared.

Physical Demands of Classical Acting

Both ancient Greek theater and traditional Asian theater stressed formal movement and stylized gestures similar to classical ballet. The chorus in Greek drama sang and danced its odes, and Asian theater has always had a significant component of singing and dancing. In addition, Greek performers wore masks and Asian performers often wore richly textured makeup.

In western theater, from the Renaissance through the nineteenth century, actions onstage were not intended to replicate the movements or gestures of everyday life. For example, performers would often speak not to the character they were addressing but directly to the audience. While this approach to acting was expected and accepted as perfectly normal, it could also lead to excess and exaggeration, a tendency that more than one writer or commentator cautioned against. In Shakespeare's *Hamlet,* for instance, Hamlet's speech to the players is a good example:

(© Carol Rosegg)

(© Joan Marcus)

(© Joan Marcus)

(© Carol Rosegg)

Photo Essay

Performers Play Many Different Parts   In theater—perhaps much more than in life—performers are often called on to p
widely diverse parts. Frequently, too, actors and actresses portray people unlike themselves. The numerous roles undertaken by actress Marian Seldes are an example. Here we see her playing one of three women at three stages in one wom
life in Edward Albee's *Three Tall Women (upper left)*; a woman who with her husband deals with a fictional baby in Albe
The Play About the Baby (upper right); portraying a retired B-movie actress who embodies shabby grandeur in *Play
Yourself (lower left)* by Harry Kondoleon; and a grande dame actress in the social comedy *Dinner at Eight (lower right)*
George S. Kaufman and Edna Ferber.

Speak the speech, I pray you, as I pronounced it to you, trippingly on the tongue; but if you mouth it, as many of your players do, I had as lief the towncrier spoke my lines. Nor do not saw the air too much with your hand, thus, but use all gently; for in the very torrent, tempest, and, as I may say, the whirlwind of your passion, you must acquire and beget a temperance that may give it smoothness. Oh, it offends me to the soul to hear a robustious periwig-pated fellow tear a passion to tatters, to very rags. . . . Be not too tame neither, but let your discretion be your tutor: suit the action to the word, the word to the action; with this special observance, that you o'erstep not the modesty of nature: for anything so overdone is from the purpose of playing, whose end, both at the first and now, was and is, to hold, as't were, the mirror up to nature.

Shakespeare himself was an actor, and no doubt he had seen performers "saw the air" with their hands and "tear a passion to tatters"; here he is using the character of Hamlet to express his own desire for reasonable, convincing acting by those who performed in his plays.

In France in the seventeenth century, Molière spoke out in his short play *The Impromptu of Versailles* against excessive, absurd practices among performers. He mocked actors in a rival company who ended each phrase with a flourish in order to get applause. (The term *claptrap,* incidentally, comes from a habit of performers of that period who would punctuate a speech or an action with some final inflection or gesture to set a "clap trap"—that is, to provoke applause.) Molière criticized actresses who preserved a silly smile even in a tragic scene; he pointed out how ridiculous it was for two performers in an intimate scene (two young lovers together, for instance, or a king alone with his captain) to declaim as if they were addressing the multitudes.

In England during the eighteenth and nineteenth centuries, acting alternated between exaggerated and more natural styles. Throughout this period, every generation or so a performer would emerge who was praised for acting in a less exaggerated, more down-to-earth way. A good example is the eighteenth-century actor David Garrick (1717–1779), who was famous for his convincing style. One scholar has described the contrast between Garrick and his predecessors in playing Shakespeare's character, Richard III.

Instead of declaiming the verse in a thunderous, measured chant, this actor [Garrick] spoke it with swift and "natural" changes of tone and emphasis. Instead of patrolling the boards with solemn pomp, treading heavily from pose to traditional pose, he moved quickly and gracefully. Instead of standing on his dignity and marbling his face into a tragedian's mask, his mobile features illustrated Richard's whole range of turbulent feelings. He seemed, indeed, to identify himself with the part. It was all so real.[1]

Still, all performers before the twentieth century moved in a more formal, stylized manner than we are accustomed to onstage, in films, or on television.

.M.ʳˢ SIDDONS as LADY MACBETH.

L. Macb.—hark!—I laid their daggers ready.

ACTING IN THE PAST

Historically, acting requirements were somewhat different from those of today. Forceful, sometimes exaggerated movements and a powerful voice were two essentials for successful performers. Performers were expected to declaim their lines and strike impressive poses. Moreover, they were required to express emotions in a forceful, explicit way, often while wearing elaborate costumes. Two examples from the late eighteenth and early nineteenth centuries are shown in the pictures here. The first is an actress in the costume for a character in Athalie *by Jean Racine; the second is the famous English performer, Sarah Siddons, portraying Lady Macbeth.* (Historical Picture Archive/ CORBIS) (Private Collection/Bridgeman Art Library)

Vocal Demands of Classical Acting

Vocal requirements in the past were also different from those of modern times. The language of plays was most often poetry; and poetry—with its demanding rhythms, sustained phrases, and exacting meters—required intensive training in order for the performer to speak the lines intelligently and distinctly. There were problems of projection, too. Greek amphitheaters were marvels of acoustics, but they seated as many as 15,000 spectators in the open air, and throwing the voice to every part of these theaters was no small task.

In the Elizabethan period in England, Christopher Marlowe, a contemporary of Shakespeare's, wrote superb blank verse which made severe demands on performers' vocal abilities. An example is a speech in Marlowe's *Doctor Faustus,* addressed by Faustus to Helen of Troy, who has been called back from the dead to be with him. In the speech Faustus says to Helen:

O' thou art fairer than the evening's air
Clad in the beauty of a thousand stars;
Brighter art thou than flaming Jupiter
When he appear'd to hapless Semele;
More lovely than the monarch of the sky
In wanton Arethusa's azured arms;
And none but thou shalt be my paramour!

These seven lines of verse are a single sentence and, when spoken properly, should be delivered as one overall unit, with the meaning carried from one line to the next. How many of us could manage that? A fine classical actor can speak the entire passage at one time, giving it the necessary resonance and inflection as well. Beyond that, he can stand onstage for 2 or 3 hours delivering such lines.

The Status of the Performer: A Historical Perspective

Through the centuries there has been a wild fluctuation in the social and political position of performers. First, it must be noted that in several key periods of theater history, women were prohibited from performing at all. Two prime examples are the theater of ancient Greece—the era of the playwrights Aeschylus, Sophocles, and Euripides—and the Elizabethan age during which Shakespeare and his contemporaries wrote. In both periods women could not even appear on the stage.

The next point to be noted is that frequently in the history of acting, performers were regarded as quite low on the social scale. An early exception was the classical period in Greece. Because theater presentations were part of a religious festival, actors were treated with dignity. At the time, the most prominent figures in theater production were those who wrote the plays and those who produced them, but performers were highly respected. In the Hellenistic period, which began in 336 B.C.E., actors came even more to the forefront, so much so that by 277 B.C.E. they had established their own union, the Artists of Dionysus.

In Roman theater, women were allowed to perform, but only in a lower form of theater known as *mime*. Unlike their Greek predecessors, Roman actors, even those in more formal theater, were sometimes looked at as little better than itinerant entertainers and vagabonds. Some actors, however—such as Roscius, who performed in the first century B.C.E.—became renowned and highly regarded.

In medieval drama, especially religious drama, most performers were amateurs, drawn in many cases from craft guilds. Though most actors were men and boys, women did occasionally participate as performers. When we move to the Renaissance in Europe, acting became more professional, but the social position of actors was still problematic. Women began to appear with acting troupes in Italy and Spain; but in Spain, for instance, it was required that any actress in a company be a relative (wife, mother, sister) of one of the leaders of the troupe.

An example of the problems faced by actors in being fully accepted is the fate of the Frenchman Molière. Though he was one of the most renowned actors and playwrights of his day, France at that time had laws preventing actors from receiving a Christian burial, and thus Molière was buried secretly at night.

When women began to appear on the English stage in the Restoration period, after 1660, they were regarded by some as on a par with courtesans or prostitutes. Others, however, accepted them into high society, and one, Nell Gwynn, was a mistress of the king. During the eighteenth and nineteenth centuries there were a number of famous and celebrated actors and actresses on the European continent, in England, and in the United States. In England, when the actor Henry Irving was knighted in 1895, it was felt that actors had finally arrived socially.

In the twentieth century, with the advent of television, and following the great popularity of film, performers became full-fledged celebrities. Every blip on the radar screen of their lives was featured in fan magazines, on television, and on websites on the Internet.

In Asian theater, performers for many centuries were primarily men, though a curious phenomenon occurred at the beginning of kabuki in Japan. It began in the early seventeenth century with all-women troupes. Social disruptions arose, however, because of feuds over the sexual services of the women, and in 1629 the shogun forbade performances of women's kabuki. Thereafter the performers were all boys, but eventually it was felt that these young men were becoming the sexual targets of older men in the audience; and so in 1652, boys' kabuki was banned as well. From that point on, kabuki was adult and all-male, as was nō theater and puppet theater, bunraku.

Performing in Classics Today

No one would expect an actress or actor today to perform a classical role as it was originally presented. Although we don't know exactly how such a performance would have looked or sounded, it seems clear from what we do know that the effect today would be ludicrous. At the same time, it should also be clear that any modern performer who is appearing in a play from the past must develop a special set of skills and must be able to respond successfully to a number of challenges.

Consider an actor undertaking the role of Hamlet. To begin with, the actor must have a sense of the physical and vocal qualities that a character like Hamlet would have. How would Hamlet walk? How would he handle a sword? How would he greet a friend like Horatio? What movements and gestures would he use? And how would he speak? What vocal range and speech patterns would he use?

The actor must have athletic ability and control of his body. If the stage setting has ramps and platforms, he must be able to navigate these with ease; and in a scene near the end of the play, he must engage in a sword fight with Laertes, which means that he must have mastered certain techniques of fencing.

Moreover, an actor playing Hamlet must be able to speak Shakespeare's lines clearly and intelligently. This is particularly true of Hamlet's soliloquies—the speeches he delivers while alone onstage. Because much

of the language of Shakespeare's plays is poetry, the actor must have breath control and an ability to project his voice. To achieve beauty of sound, he should also have a resonant voice; and to convey the meaning of a speech, he must have a full understanding of the words.

In addition to all this, the actor must be able to convey the numerous and often contradictory emotions the character is experiencing: that Hamlet is aware of the betrayal and treachery taking place around him; that he is saddened by the recent death of his father and the hasty marriage of his mother to his uncle; that he wants to murder his uncle once he learns that his uncle has murdered his father, but has difficulty bringing himself to do so; that he berates himself for not being more decisive; that he loves Ophelia but is repelled by the web of circumstances of which she, perhaps unwittingly, is a part.

To prepare for a role like Hamlet, one of the actor's first tasks is to study the script carefully and analyze the role. Many choices must be made regarding interpretation, emphasis, and the like; and it will be impossible for the actor to make these choices intelligently unless he has a firm understanding of the play and his part.

In Chapter 6 we will turn to performers' training today. How does a young actor prepare himself to play a classical role like Hamlet or the many modern characters he might be called on to undertake? How does a young actress equip herself to undertake the variety of roles she will be asked to play?

SUMMARY

1. All human beings engage in certain forms of acting; imitation and role playing are excellent examples of acting in everyday life.

2. Acting onstage differs from acting in everyday life—for several reasons, including the fact that a stage actor or actress is always being observed by an audience, and the fact that acting for the stage involves playing roles with which the performer has no direct experience in life.

3. Historically, stage performances have required exceptional physical and vocal skills: the ability to move with agility and grace and to engage in such things as sword fights and death scenes; the ability to deal with poetic devices (meter, imagery, alliteration, etc.); the skill to project the voice to the furthest reaches of the theater space.

4. Acting is a difficult, demanding profession. Despite its glamour, it calls for arduous training and preparation. Looking at what is called for in a role like Hamlet gives some idea of the challenges involved.

EXPLORING THEATER ON THE WEB

Acting: Offstage and in the Past

Acting is an integral part of our everyday lives, whether it be through role playing or through imitation. As familiar as acting is, however, most actors must go through rigorous training in preparation for the stage. Historically, classical training for actors has included both physical and vocal preparation.

Several classical acting groups on the web include:

Royal Shakespeare Company
http://www.rsc.org.uk

African-American Shakespeare Company
http://www.african-americanshakes.org

Exercises

1. The Juilliard School of Drama (http://www.juilliard.edu/college/drama.html) offers both graduate and undergraduate degrees in fine arts through its Drama Division. Its mission statement reads, in part: "We are trying to form an actor equipped with all possible means of dramatic production, capable of meeting the demands of today's and tomorrow's ever-changing theater. . . . For in the final analysis . . . everything ultimately depends on the human being—the actor." Do you agree?

   Visit the Juilliard site and answer the following questions: How many candidates typically audition for the twenty spots in each year's freshman class? What is the curriculum like during the first year of the program? Why, if acting is so much a part of our lives, do you think such intense training is necessary for theater?

2. The African-American Shakespeare Company performs European classical works within the perspective and cultural dynamics of African American culture. Compare its season with that of the Royal Shakespeare Company. Are there any plays that both companies are producing? How do you think these productions will differ?

3. Visit http://www.actorsmeanbusiness.co.uk/roleplay.htm, the Actors Mean Business webpage, addressing "Role Play and Industrial Theatre." In what ways are role playing, theater, and industry or business connected? Is role playing similarly connected to other fields outside the performing arts? How so? Give examples.

CHAPTER SIX

Stage Acting Today

For most people, the primary exposure to acting is on film and television; they see many more performances in movie houses and on their television screens than they see onstage. As a result, both audiences and aspiring performers make some unconscious, mistaken assumptions about acting in the theater.

For example, it is often assumed that acting is essentially a simulation of everyday life, which a camera will record. Because of this, beginning acting students, when preparing their first scene for an acting class, frequently take up a position only a few feet away from the observing students. They have not learned an essential difference between television and stage acting: on television, the camera comes to the actress or actor; onstage, the performer must reach out to the audience. A camera may be only a few feet away from the performers, but in the theater the closest a performer is likely to be to any audience member is 10 feet; in many cases the distance will be 40 feet or more. This requires a different way of looking at performing and at the preparation required for performing.

To give a clearer idea of stage acting today, this chapter will examine several aspects of modern performance.

◀ THE CHALLENGE OF ACTING FOR THE THEATER

To play a character convincingly, an actor or actress must develop both outer techniques and inner emotional resources. The scene shown here is from A Streetcar Named Desire *by Tennessee Williams. In this production at the Royal National Theatre in London, Glenn Close played Blanche and Iain Glen played Stanley. These two, the protagonist and antagonist of the play, are locked in a fierce psychological and personal battle. Blanche, a sensitive woman desperately in need of support and sexual reassurance, is a threat to the brutish Stanley whom she constantly accuses, indirectly if not directly, of being little more than an animal. For both performers, but especially the actress, the characters demand depth of feeling, contradictory emotions, and a wide range of actions and reactions.* (© Donald Cooper/PhotoSTAGE)

THE ACTING EXPERIENCE

To understand what is involved in the career of a stage actress or actor, let us look at a typical sequence that begins before a performer is cast in a role and continues to his or her opening-night performance before an audience. We'll imagine that our performer is an actress named Jennifer.

The first step for Jennifer is hearing about a forthcoming production. This might be a presentation by a theater department at a college or university, or by an amateur community theater, or by a professional regional theater; it might even be a large-scale Broadway production. In each case, the procedure will be similar. Jennifer must ***audition.*** This means that she must appear before the director and others (perhaps the producer, and in the case of a new play, the playwright) to be interviewed and probably to present one or more scenes she has prepared. These may be scenes from the play being presented, or scenes she has prepared from other plays to demonstrate her abilities. After a first audition, Jennifer may be called back to read again by herself, or perhaps with other performers who are being considered for parts with which her character would interact.

Auditions, like almost every aspect of performing, can be nerve-racking. Each of us wants to be approved of by others and each of us fears rejection, even in the most casual relationships. In an audition—as in performance before an audience—the reaction is public and pronounced. A performer who does not get a part has been openly turned down, just as a performer attacked by a critic in print has been publicly judged. Those who wish to enter theater as a career must learn to deal with the disappointment of being turned down for a role or being criticized publicly.

Let us assume, though, that this time Jennifer is one of the fortunate ones: she is selected for the production. The next step will be several weeks of intensive rehearsal. If Jennifer has had previous experience in performing, she will know that there is a difference between the work of an actress at an audition and in rehearsal for a production. In an audition, she must work for *results:* that is, in a short period of time she must project her personality and the skills that she hopes will get her the part. In the rehearsal period, on the other hand, she will be *exploring* a character, searching for specifics and an overall curve to her performance; she will be interacting with other performers. The emphasis will be on process, rather than immediate results.

During this period, she must memorize her part in the script, which could be difficult. Her role may be long, or her lines may be poetry, or she may have to speak in dialect—a British or southern accent, for instance. During the rehearsal period, Jennifer must work closely with the director, learning, among other things, where, when, and how to move onstage. Her movements might come from a combination of ideas from the director and her own ideas—such as an impulse she may have to sit, stand, or cross the stage at a certain moment.

Also, Jennifer must work closely with the other performers, learning to adjust to their rhythms, reacting to the dynamics of their characterizations, and the like. Inevitably there will be difficult moments: she and another performer may not be clicking; she may not be able to summon up an emotion that is called for—such as different levels of anger, joy, or frustration. She may have to bend every effort to find and portray the required emotion. After working first on individual scenes and sections of the script, she will discover when the play is put together that she must make further adjustments. She may be too emotional in an early segment, leaving herself no room to reach a higher pitch later on; or perhaps the pace is too slow and the play drags, so that she and the other performers must find ways to accelerate the action without losing sincerity and conviction.

Just before the public performances, at the time of the first technical rehearsals, new ingredients are added. The performers are in costume for the first time; the lights are changing; scenery is shifted; and the actresses and actors are temporarily in a foreign land. Away from the safe, protected rehearsal hall with which they have become comfortable, they must now contend with stagehands, lighting technicians, real furniture, doors that open differently—in short, a host of new conditions.

After overcoming the initial shock of these new elements, the production will settle into the level of a complete, full presentation, but soon another component is added: the audience. For the first time, usually at a preview or dress rehearsal, strange people are sitting out front watching and listening. Does a scene that must be emotionally gripping actually hold the audience's attention? Does a comic scene evoke laughter? For Jennifer and her fellow performers, such uncertainties can be terrifying. The other side of the coin, of course, is that if they succeed, they will have the thrill not only of a great accomplishment, but of a kind of contact with the public that most people rarely experience.

One objective of a performance is to look natural and easy—to suggest to the audience that playing the role is effortless, just as a juggler attempts to look as casual and carefree as possible. One reason why it is important for acting to look effortless is to relax the audience members and let them believe in the character rather than concentrate on the performer's lengthy and arduous preparation.

During the first few performances before an audience, adjustments are made in the acting and in other elements such as lighting and sound. Rough spots are made smoother; the pace is speeded up or slowed down; awkward moments are dealt with. Finally, opening night comes: the night when the production is ready to be seen and judged by audiences and critics. This is another potentially traumatic moment for Jennifer and her fellow performers. Will they forget their lines? Will a lighting miscue leave them in the dark?

A thousand and one fears come to the surface, but once Jennifer is onstage, she is carried along with the moment; all her preparation has given her enough knowledge, experience, and command of the stage to instill security

THE SPECIAL DEMANDS OF ACTING

At times performing makes exceedingly strong demands on performers, requiring them to convey a range and depth of emotions, or to transform themselves in terms of age, mood, and the like. A good example is the play The Elephant Man *by Bernard Pomerance. The title character is a badly deformed man whose body and face are twisted by a terrible disease. The actor must create this deformity while still carrying out all other demands of acting the part—speech, movement, emotional reactions. Seen here is actor Billy Crudup in the part.* (© Joan Marcus)

and confidence. When she hears laughter in the audience, or when a hush falls, she knows that she and her colleagues have succeeded, and their many hours of hard work, uncertainty, and fear of failure are washed away in a sense of accomplishment and in the satisfaction of bringing to reality their dream of performing onstage.

Before reaching the point of being prepared to undertake a role, however, a performer like Jennifer must undergo extensive training. The following sections discuss techniques that must be acquired, skills that must be honed, and studies that must be undertaken in preparing to become a performer.

CHALLENGES OF ACTING TODAY

In today's theater an actress like Jennifer might be called on to perform many different kinds of roles, using a variety of techniques and approaches. For instance, she will probably be called on to play characters in modern realistic plays: Nina in Chekhov's *The Sea Gull,* for example, or Laura in Tennessee Williams's *The Glass Menagerie,* or a young woman leaving prison in *Getting Out* by Marsha Norman (1947–   ). She will also be asked to undertake roles in the classics: Juliet or Ophelia in Shakespeare, Antigone or Electra in Sophocles, or one of the ingenues in a play by Molière. If she wants to appear in musical theater, she will have to master singing and dancing as well as acting. And there are also experimental and avant-garde theater events, which often call for special skills such as mime and acrobatics.

In order to be prepared for these various challenges, today's performers have to be proficient in a wide range of techniques and disciplines. On the one hand, they must acquire the many special skills—both physical and vocal—of stage performance: the *craft* of acting. Moreover, in addition to theater exercises per se, a performer might train in tai chi or in circus techniques like juggling or trapeze work. On the other hand, performers must learn how to portray believable characters. This requires not only a careful analysis of the script and the character, but a number of techniques developed by the Russian director Constantin Stanislavski (1863–1938) and his successors. Included in this process are such things as integration and "centering."

(Sara Krulwich/The New York Times)

(© Joan Marcus)

Performers Play Diverse Roles Performers are often called on to play a wide range of parts, from different historical eras and with quite different emotional and personality demands. An example would be the various characters portrayed by the actor Brian Stokes Mitchell. Depicted here is Mitchell in four different roles: Don Quixote in the musical *Man of La Mancha* (*top left*), an ordinary man (*on the left*), claiming to be nobility in *King Hedley II,* Sweeney Todd, the demon barber of Fleet Street in the musical by that name set in the mid-nineteenth century (*above*), and the Petruchio figure (*below*), in the musical *Kiss Me, Kate.* Each character has a different dynamic and a different personality, and Mitchell shaped his performance differently in each play or musical to convey these varied characters.

(© Joan Marcus)

(© Joan Marcus)

These two facets of acting, special skills and credible characterization, have sometimes been referred to, respectively, as the *outer* and *inner*, or the *external* and *internal*, aspects of acting. There have been times in history when a strong emphasis was put on the physical and vocal skills of performance—a powerful speaking voice or dancelike movements. At other times, the inner life of the character—sincerity and conviction—has been more highly valued. These are extremes, however, and the terms *outer* and *inner* oversimplify the two aspects, suggesting a sharper division than generally exists. Great performers have always combined both aspects.

The Development of Realistic Acting

From the mid-seventeenth century on, serious attempts were made to define the craft or technique of credible, natural acting, the most noteworthy being those of Denis Diderot (1713–1784) in the eighteenth century and François Delsarte (1811–1871) in the nineteenth century. Diderot endorsed, for example, the use of more realistic prose dialogue rather than verse, though he had only a minimum of success. Delsarte in the next century devised a system of expression in which the performers' thoughts and emotions were reduced to a specific series of fixed poses and attitudes accomplished through a selective use of body and voice. For instance, anguish might be expressed by a carefully prescribed move of the hand to the brow; a broken heart might be indicated by pressing a hand to the breast. In time, Delsarte's system became mechanistic and unworkable, but it is worth noting that the American Academy of Dramatic Art, founded in 1884, was based on his principles.

A believable, realistic approach to acting became more important than ever at the end of the nineteenth century, when drama began to depict characters and situations close to everyday life. As discussed in Chapter 1, three playwrights—Henrik Ibsen of Norway, August Strindberg of Sweden, and Anton Chekhov of Russia—perfected the type of drama which came to be known as *realism*. This drama was called *realistic* because it closely resembled what people could identify with and verify from their own experience. In performing plays by these dramatists, not only the spirit of the individual dramatic characters but also the details of their behavior had to conform to what people saw of life around them. This placed great demands on actors and actresses to avoid any hint of fakery or superficiality.

The Stanislavski System: A Technique for Realistic Acting Before the realistic drama of the late 1800s, no one had devised a method for achieving the kind of believability these plays required. Through their own talent and genius, individual actresses and actors had achieved it, but no one had developed a system whereby it could be taught to others and passed on to future generations. The person who eventually did this most successfully was the Russian actor and director Constantin Stanislavski.

A cofounder of the Moscow Art Theater in Russia and the director of Anton Chekhov's most important plays, Stanislavski was also an actor. He was involved in both traditional theater—using stylized, nonrealistic techniques—and the emergence of the modern realistic approach. By closely observing the work of great performers of his day, such as Tommaso Salvini, Eleonora Duse, and Fyodor Chaliapin, and by drawing on his own acting experience, Stanislavski identified and described what these gifted performers did naturally and intuitively. From his observations he compiled and then codified a series of principles and techniques which today are regarded as fundamental to both the training and the performance of actors who want to create believable characters onstage.

We might assume that believable acting is simply a matter of being natural; but Stanislavski discovered first of all that acting realistically onstage is extremely difficult. He wrote:

> All of our acts, even the simplest, which are so familiar to us in everyday life, become strained when we appear behind the foot lights [sic] before a public of a thousand people. That is why it is necessary to correct ourselves and learn again how to walk, sit, or lie down. It is essential to reeducate ourselves to look and see, on the stage, to listen and to hear.[1]

To achieve this "reeducation," Stanislavski said, "the actor must first of all believe in everything that takes place onstage, and most of all, he must believe what he himself is doing. And one can only believe in the truth." To give substance to his ideas, Stanislavski studied how people acted in every-day life and how they communicated feelings and emotions; and then he found ways to accomplish the same things onstage. These observations resulted in a series of exercises and techniques for the actor, which had the following broad aims:

1. To make the outward behavior of the performer—gestures, voice, and rhythm of movements—natural and convincing.

2. To have the actor or actress convey the goals and objectives—the inner needs—of a character. Even if all the visible manifestations of a character are mastered, a performance will appear superficial and mechanical without a deep sense of conviction and belief.

3. To make the life of the character onstage not only dynamic but continuous. Some performers tend to emphasize only the high points of a part; in between, the life of the character stops. In real life, however, people do not stop living.

4. To develop a strong sense of *ensemble* playing with other performers in a scene.

Let us now look in some detail at Stanislavski's techniques.

Relaxation When he observed the great actors and actresses of his day, Stanislavski noticed how fluid and lifelike their movements were. They seemed to be in a state of complete freedom and relaxation, letting the behavior of the character come through effortlessly. He concluded that unwanted tension has to be eliminated and that the performer must at all times attain a state of physical and vocal *relaxation.*

Concentration and Observation Stanislavski also discovered that gifted performers always appeared fully concentrated on some object, person, or event while onstage. Stanislavski referred to the extent or range of concentration as a ***circle of attention.*** This circle of attention can be compared to a circle of light on a darkened stage. The performer should begin with the idea that it is a small, tight circle including only himself or herself and perhaps one other person or one piece of furniture. When the performer has established a strong circle of attention, he or she can enlarge the circle outward to include the entire stage area. In this way performers will stop worrying about the audience and lose their self-consciousness.

Importance of Specifics One of Stanislavski's techniques was an emphasis on concrete details. A performer should never try to act *in general,* he said, and should never try to convey a feeling such as fear or love in some vague, amorphous way. In life, Stanislavski said, we express emotions in terms of specifics: an anxious woman twists a handkerchief, an angry boy throws a rock at a trash can, a nervous businessman jangles his keys. Performers must

TECHNIQUES OF ACTING:

THE IMPORTANCE OF SPECIFICS

Constantin Stanislavski believed that performers should concentrate on specifics. In his play The Glass Menagerie, *the playwright Tennessee Williams has provided the character Laura with a collection of glass animals that preoccupies her. Kali Rocha as Laura shows a glass unicorn to the Gentleman Caller (Jay Snyder) in a production at the Yale Repertory Theatre.* (© T. Charles Erickson)

find similar *concrete* activities. Stanislavski points out how Shakespeare has Lady Macbeth in her sleepwalking scene—at the height of her guilt and emotional upheaval—try to rub blood off her hands.

The performer must also conceive of the situation in which a character exists—what Stanislavski referred to as the *given circumstances*—in terms of specifics. In what kind of space does an event take place: formal, informal, public, domestic? How does it feel? What is the temperature? The lighting? What has gone on just before? What is expected in the moments ahead? Again, these questions must be answered in concrete terms.

Inner Truth   An innovative aspect of Stanislavski's work has to do with **inner truth,** which deals with the internal or subjective world of characters—that is, their thoughts and emotions. The early phases of Stanislavski's research took place while he was also directing the major dramas of Anton Chekhov. Plays like *The Three Sisters* and *The Cherry Orchard* have less to do with external action or what the characters say than with what the characters are feeling and thinking but often do not verbalize. It becomes apparent that Stanislavski's approach would be very beneficial in realizing the inner life of such characters. (A synopsis of *The Three Sisters* appears at the end of Part 2.)

Stanislavski had several ideas about how to achieve a sense of inner truth, one being the **"magic if."** The word *if* can transform our thoughts in such a way that we can imagine ourselves in virtually any situation. "*If* I suddenly became wealthy . . ." "*If* I were vacationing on a Caribbean island . . ." "*If* I had great talent . . ." "*If* that person who insulted me comes near me again . . ." The word *if* becomes a powerful lever for the mind; it can lift us out of ourselves and give us a sense of absolute certainty about imaginary circumstances.

Action Onstage: What? Why? How?   Another important principle of Stanislavski's system is that every action onstage must have a purpose. This means that the performer's attention must always be focused on a series of physical actions (also called *psychophysical actions;* see page 129) linked by the circumstances of the play. Stanislavski determined these actions by asking three essential questions: What? Why? How? An action is performed, such as opening a letter (*what*). The letter is opened because someone has said that it contains extremely damaging information about the character (*why*). The letter is opened anxiously, fearfully (*how*), because of the calamitous effect it might have on the character. These physical actions, which occur from moment to moment in a performance, are in turn governed by the character's overall objective in the play.

Through Line of a Role   According to Stanislavski, in order to develop continuity in a part, the actor or actress should find the character's **superobjective.** What is it, above all else, that the character wants during the course of the play? What is the character's driving force? If a goal can be established toward which the character strives, it will give the performer an overall objective. From this objective can be developed a ***through line*** which can be grasped, as a skier on a ski lift grabs a towline and is carried to the top. Another term for *through line* is **spine.**

To help develop the through line, Stanislavski urged performers to divide scenes into units (sometimes called *beats*). In each unit there is an objective, and the intermediate objectives running through a play lead ultimately to the overall objective.

Ensemble Playing   Except in one-person shows, performers do not act alone; they interact with other people. Stanislavski was aware that many performers tend to "stop acting," or lose their concentration, when they are not the main characters in a scene or when someone else is talking. This tendency destroys the through line and causes the performer to move into and out of a role. That, in turn, weakens the sense of ensemble—the playing together of all the performers.

ENSEMBLE PLAYING

Good actors are aware of the importance of ensemble playing. Performers coordinate their work by listening carefully to each other, sensing each other's actions and moods, and responding alertly. Ensemble playing is especially important in plays where interaction between characters is crucial. Anton Chekhov's plays call for an emphasis on ensemble acting. One example is his play The Seagull, *a scene from which is seen here. This was a production of the New York Shakespeare Festival/ Public Theater in New York's Central Park. The two figures kissing are Madame Arkardina and her lover Trigorin, played by Meryl Streep and Kevin Kline.* (© Michal Daniel)

Part 2   The Performers and the Director

STANISLAVSKI AND PSYCHOPHYSICAL ACTION

In the latter part of his career, Stanislavski emphasized the importance of psychophysical action, pointing out that the selection and reenactment of the properly selected physical action would be the most direct route to the character's emotions. Shown here is actress Alyssa Bresnahan portraying the young actress Nina in a play within a play in Chekhov's The Seagull. *She has obviously chosen a quite theatrical gesture to show the dramatic drive and choices of the aspiring actress.* (© T. Charles Erickson/PlayMakers Repertory Company)

Stanislavski and Psychophysical Action Stanislavski began to develop his technique in the early part of the twentieth century, and at first he emphasized the *inner* aspects of training: for example, various ways of getting in touch with the performer's unconscious. Beginning around 1917, however, he began to look more and more at purposeful action, or what he called *psychophysical action.* A student at one of his lectures in 1917 took note of the change: "Whereas action previously had been taught as the expression of a previously-established 'emotional state,' it is now action itself which predominates and is the key to the psychological."[2]

Rather than seeing emotions as leading to action, Stanislavski came to believe that it was the other way around: he held that purposeful action undertaken to fulfill a character's goals was the most direct route to the emotions. When an action is performed as a result of the given circumstances in a play to bring about a change in the dramatic situation, emotion will follow. Because psychophysical or purposeful action is the key, a well-trained, well-developed, responsive body and voice are indispensable. This is stressed in Stanislavski's last two books to be translated into English, *Building a Character* and *Creating a Role.* Body and voice are developed by means of techniques and exercises discussed below.

Later Interpretations of Stanislavski's Approach Stanislavski had a profound influence on the training of performers throughout the twentieth century.

An actor who began working with Stanislavski but then broke away to develop his own approach to training actors was Michael Chekhov (1891–1955), a nephew of the playwright Anton Chekhov. Michael Chekhov is best known for the *psychological gesture*—the notion that character can be successfully projected by the creation of notable, telling gestures that sum up inner feelings, desires, and emotions. For example, a character facing death wants to confess to another man that he has cheated him. In playing this role, Chekhov kept digging his hands into the area of the other man's heart, as though he wanted to become one with the other man.

In the United States, several people who were performers or directors with the Group Theater in the 1930s went on to become important teachers of acting. These included Sanford Meisner, Stella Adler, Robert Lewis, Lee

Strasberg, and Uta Hagen. Strasberg for many years headed the Actors Studio in New York, where a number of prominent film and stage stars studied, including Marlon Brando, James Dean, Paul Newman, Marilyn Monroe, and Al Pacino. Uta Hagen, a well-known actress as well as a teacher, has written two books, *Respect for Acting* and *A Challenge for the Actor*, which are required reading in many actor training programs.

The interpretation of Stanislavski's approach in the United States has been the cause of considerable controversy. A number of experts, for example, feel that Strasberg mistakenly emphasized only the inner or emotional side of Stanislavski's technique—the early work—and neglected the importance of physical action, the voice, and the body. Strasberg particularly emphasized a technique which Stanislavski in his earlier writings called ***emotional recall.*** This is a tool intended to help the performer achieve a sense of emotional truth onstage; it consists of remembering a past experience in the performer's life that is similar to one in a play. By recalling sensory impressions of an experience in the past (such as what a room looked like, any prevalent odors, and any contact with objects), emotions associated with that experience are aroused and can be used as the basis of feelings called for in the play.

This technique has a place in actors' training, but as we have seen, Stanislavski himself moved away from an emphasis on inner, emotional qualities toward the psychophysical; and teachers like Adler, Lewis, and Meisner felt that Strasberg's approach was too one-sided.

The important thing, though, is that regardless of the emphases of his various interpreters—some of whom may have distorted or misread his ideas—Stanislavski's principles have remained the basis of an ever-evolving system of training. There have been changes, modifications, and reinterpretations, but his ideas have provided the springboard from which others have taken off.

Performers' Training Today

Body and Voice Training   One aspect of contemporary training of performers is developing skills in the areas Stanislavski articulated: relaxation, concentration, inner truth, given circumstances, attention to specifics, goals and objectives, and the like. As we have seen, however, to meet the requirements of acting in the classics—such as Shakespeare, Molière, and Greek tragedies—body and voice training are also indispensable.

Let us consider the voice, for example. A primary requirement for performers is to make certain that the lines they speak are heard clearly by the audience. To be heard throughout a theater seating 1,000 or more people, a performer must ***project,*** that is, throw the voice into the audience so that it penetrates to the uttermost reaches of the theater. In modern realistic plays this task is made more difficult by the necessity of maintaining believability. For example, in real life the words of a man and a woman in an intimate love scene would be barely audible even to people only a few feet away; in a theater, however, every word must be heard by the entire audience. A performer needs to strike a balance, therefore, between credibility and the necessity of being heard.

In order to develop projection and to achieve the kind of balance just described, performers must train and rehearse extensively. For example, an actor or actress might use breathing exercises, controlling the breath from the diaphragm rather than the throat so that vocal reproduction will have power and can be sustained. These exercises are often quite similar to those used by opera singers. Also, head, neck, and shoulder exercises can be used to relax the muscles in those areas, thus freeing the throat for ease of projection.

For the development of the body and the voice, a series of exercises and programs have been created. The box on the next page shows a set of warm-up exercises. It should be emphasized, though, that these exercises represent only a small fraction of the kinds of exercises performers must undertake in developing acting skills. There are more specific, advanced exercises for such things as fencing, dancing, and rapid movements up and down stairs or platforms. Also, there are specific vocal exercises for the delivery of poetry, for vocal projection, and so forth.

Beyond exercises, there are other areas of training. For example, vocal training includes learning to coordinate the meaning and understanding of lines of poetry with their proper delivery. Physical training includes developing the skills necessary to deal with the peculiarities of a given historical period, such as the curtsy and bow for plays involving kings and queens.

As a part of body and voice training, many acting teachers emphasize ***centering.*** This is a way of bringing everything together and allowing the performer to eliminate any blocks that impede either the body or the voice. Centering involves locating the place—roughly in the middle of the torso—where all the lines of force of the body come together. It is the "point of convergence of the muscular, emotional and intellectual impulses within our bodies."[3] When performers are able to "center" themselves, they achieve a balance, a freedom, and a flexibility they could rarely find otherwise.

Training Techniques from Other Disciplines In modern training of actors and actresses, teachers borrow from other disciplines. A good example is Asian theater. Stylization and symbolism characterize the acting of the classical theaters of India, China, and Japan. To achieve the absolute control, the concentration, and the mastery of body and nerves necessary to carry out stylized movements, performers in the various classical Asian theaters train for years under the supervision of master teachers. Every movement of these performers is prescribed and carefully controlled, combining elements of formal ballet, pantomime, and sign language. Each gesture tells a story and means something quite specific—a true symbolism of physical movement.

Warm-Up Exercises for Body and Voice

To give an indication of the types of exercises performers must undertake during their years of training—and during their careers as professionals—it is interesting to look at some samples of warm-up exercises. The exercises here are designed to relax the body and the voice.

The following are typical warm-up exercises for body movement:

1. Lie on your back; beginning with the feet, tense and relax each part of the body—knees, thighs, abdomen, chest, neck—moving up to the face. Note the difference in the relaxation of various muscles and of the body generally after the exercise is completed.

2. Stand with feet parallel, approximately as far apart as the width of the shoulders. Lift one foot off the ground and loosen all the joints in the foot, ankle, and knee. Repeat with the other foot off the ground. Put the feet down and move to the hip, spine, arms, neck, etc., loosening all joints.

3. Stand with feet parallel. Allow all tension to drain out of the body through the feet. In the process, bend the knees, straighten the pelvis, and release the lower back.

4. Begin walking in a circle; walk on the outside of the feet, then on the inside, then on the toes, and then on the heels. Notice what this does to the rest of the body. Try changing other parts of the body in a similar fashion and observe the effect on feelings and reactions.

5. Imagine the body filled with either helium or lead. Notice the effect of each of these sensations, both while standing in place and while walking. Do the same with one body part at a time—each arm, each leg, the head, etc.

The following *vocal exercises* free the throat and vocal cords:

1. Standing, begin a lazy, unhurried stretch. Reach with your arms to the ceiling, meanwhile lengthening and widening the whole of your back. Yawn as you take in a deep breath and hum on an exhalation. Release your torso so that it rests down toward your legs. Yawn on another deep breath and hum on an exhalation. On an inhalation, roll up the spine until you are standing with your arms at your sides. Look at something on the ceiling and then at something on the floor; then let your head return to a balance point, so that the neck and shoulder muscles are relaxed.

2. Put your hands on your ribs, take a deep breath, and hum a short tune. Repeat several times. Hum an *m* or *n* up and down the scale. Drop your arms; lift the shoulders an inch and drop them, releasing all tension.

3. Take a deep breath and with the palm of your hand push gently down on your stomach as you exhale. Do this several times. Exhale on sighs and then on vowels.

4. Standing, yawn with your throat and mouth open and be aware of vibrations in the front of your mouth, just behind your front teeth, as you vocalize on the vowels *ee, ei,* and *o.* Take these up and down the scales. Sing a simple song and then say it, and see if you have just as much vibration in your mouth when you are speaking as when you are singing.

5. Using a light, quick tempo, shift to a tongue twister (such as *Peter Piper picked a peck of pickled peppers*). Feel a lively touch of the tongue on the gum ridge on the *t*'s and *d*'s, and a bounce of the back of the tongue on the *k*'s and *g*'s. Feel the bouncing action on the lips on the *p*'s and *b*'s.

Source: Provided by Professor John Sipes of the Oregon Shakespeare Festival and Professor Barbara F. Acker of Arizona State University.

FINGER LANGUAGE: A PART OF INDIAN ACTING AND DANCING

The precise gestures of this Indian art—the graceful, symbolic movements—require extensive training and discipline to perfect. In the finger language shown here, the numbers indicate the following states or emotions: (1) separation or death, (2) meditation, (3) determination, (4) joy, (5) concentration, (6) rejection, (7) veneration, (8) proposal, (9) vexation, and (10) love. (From Margaret Berthold. A History of World Theater, copyright 1972 by Frederick Ungar Publishing Co., Inc.)

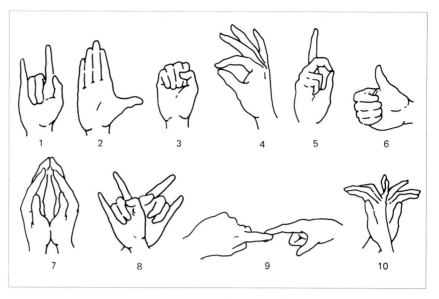

One Asian discipline, not from theater but from martial arts, which modern acting teachers have found helpful is tai chi chuan, commonly called *tai chi.* Unlike some martial arts, tai chi is not aggressive: it is a graceful, gentle exercise regimen performed widely by men, women, and children in China. It has spread to other countries, where it is sometimes practiced in conjunction with meditation or body awareness. The movements of tai chi are stylized and often seem to be carried out in slow motion. Among other things, tai chi requires concentration and control, both valuable qualities for a performer.

Another field to which people involved in training actors and actresses have turned is the circus. Juggling, for instance, teaches both coordination and concentration. Acrobatics make the body limber, and other activities call for teamwork of a very high order.

Training for Special Forms of Theater Certain types of theater and theater events require special discipline or training. For example, musical theater obviously requires talent in singing and dancing. Coordination is also important in musical theater: the members of a chorus must frequently sing and dance in unison.

Pantomime is another demanding category of performance: without words or props, a performer must indicate everything by physical suggestion, convincingly lifting an imaginary box or walking against an imaginary wind.

Various forms of modern avant-garde and experimental theater also require special techniques. A good example is Eugène Ionesco's play *Rhinoceros.* During the course of this play, one of the two chief characters turns into

(© Dean Conger/CORBIS)

THE FORMAL GESTURES OF ASIAN THEATER

In most Asian theater, acting requires careful, precise, formal gestures. Years of training are required to perform correctly in Japanese kabuki theater and in the classic theaters of China and India. Shown here are two examples. In the first, performers are in a scene from The Monkey King, *a piece from Beijing or Peking Opera in China. The second shows the Hindu Chief Dance in a performance of the Kathakali in India. Note in both cases the poses, the physical requirements, the dexterity that is required, as well as the wearing of elaborate costumes, heavy make-up, and striking head pieces.*

(© Charles & Josette Lenars/CORBIS)

Emilio Mercado

ACTING TRAINING FROM OTHER DISCIPLINES

Actor training today often involves exercises and other activities from related disciplines such as circus routines, juggling, acrobatics, and Asian martial arts. A good example is Tai Chi, a refined form of martial arts from China, being practiced in a park by the individuals shown here. (© Emilio Mercado/Index Stock Imagery)

a rhinoceros. The actor playing this part does not actually put on horns or a leathery hide. Rather, he must physically transform himself by means of his posture, voice, and general demeanor. The critic Walter Kerr described how the actor Zero Mostel (1915–1977) did this in the original Broadway production:

> Now the rhinoceros beneath the skin begins to bulge a little at the eyes. The Kaiser Wilhelm mustache that has earlier adorned the supposed Mr. Mostel loses its spiky endpoints, droops, disintegrates into a tangle that makes it second cousin to a walrus. The voice starts to change. "I hate people—and I'll r-r-run them down!" comes out of a larynx that has stiffened, gone hollow as a 1915 gramophone record, and is ready to produce a trumpet-sound that would empty all of Africa. The shoulders lift, the head juts forward, one foot begins to beat the earth with such native majesty that dust—real dust—begins to rise like the afterveil that seems to accompany a safari. The transformation is on, the secret is out, evolution has reversed itself before your horrified, but nevertheless delighted, eyes.[4]

Chapter 6 Stage Acting Today

TRAINING FOR MUSICAL THEATER

Along with the classics and various types of theater from other nations, the American musical with its physical and vocal demands requires extensive training. A prime example is the dancing in many musicals, none more so in recent years than the musical Movin' Out, *which was staged by the choreographer Twyla Tharp and is based on the songs of Billy Joel. In many athletic numbers, the performers create dances that embody ideas about growing up at the time of Vietnam War, all taken from the texts of Joel's songs.* (© Joan Marcus)

In another avant-garde play, Samuel Beckett's *Happy Days*, an actress is buried onstage in a mound of earth up to her waist in the first act, and up to her neck in the second. She must perform through the entire play while virtually immobile.

In some types of avant-garde theater, the performers become acrobats, make human pyramids, or are used like pieces of furniture. In *Suitcase*, by the Japanese playwright Kobo Abe (1924–1993), the actor who plays the suitcase must move as if he is being carried like a piece of luggage. In another play by Abe, *The Man Who Turned into a Stick*, an actor must play the part of a stick.

In the theater of Robert Wilson (1944–) and of Mabou Mines and similar groups, story, character, and text are minimized or even eliminated. The stress, rather than being on a narrative or on exploring recognizable characters, is on the visual and ritualistic aspects of theater. The overall effect is sometimes like a series of tableaux or a moving collage. Because of the em-

Part 2 The Performers and the Director

UNIQUE ACTING DEMANDS OF AVANT-GARDE THEATER

Avant-garde theater often requires special training and techniques—acrobatics, tumbling, mime, and special control of voice, facial muscles, and body. The scene here is from Masurca Fogo, *a theater/dance piece by the German experimental director Pina Bausch whose troupe goes by the name Wuppertaler Tanztheater.*

phasis on the visual picture formed onstage, there is an affinity between this kind of theater and painting. Stage movement in performance art is often closely related to dance; thus the performers must have the same discipline, training, and control as dancers.

In Wilson's work, performers are frequently called on either to move constantly or to remain perfectly still. In an early Wilson piece, *A Letter to Queen Victoria,* two performers turn continuously in circles like dervishes for long periods of time—perhaps 30 or 40 minutes. In other works by Wilson, performers must remain frozen like statues.

Synthesis and Integration

The demands made on performers by experimental and avant-garde theaters are only the most recent example of the rigorous, intensive training which acting generally requires. The goal of all this training—both internal

Chapter 6 Stage Acting Today   133

and external—is to create for the performer an instrument that is flexible, resourceful, and disciplined.

When a performer is approaching a role in a play, the first task is to read and analyze the script. The actress or actor must discover the superobjective of the character she or he is playing and put together not only the spine of the role but the many smaller moments, each with its own objective and given circumstances.

The next challenge is to begin specific work on the role. In taking this step, some performers begin with the outer aspects of the character—with a walk, or posture, or a peculiar vocal delivery. They get a sense of how the character looks in terms of makeup and other characteristics, such as a mustache or a hairstyle. They consider the clothes the character wears and any idiosyncrasies of speech or movement, such as a limp or a swagger. Only then will they move on to the inner aspects of the character: how the character feels; how the character reacts to people and events; what disturbs the character's emotional equilibrium; what fears, hopes, and dreams the character has.

Other performers, by contrast, begin with the internal aspects: with the feelings and emotions of the character. These performers delve deeply into the psyche of the character to try to understand and duplicate what the character feels inside. Only after that will they go on to develop the outer characteristics. Still other actors work on both aspects—inner and outer—simultaneously.

What is important to remember is that whatever the starting point, the end result must be a synthesis of these two aspects. The various aspects of the craft of acting must be blended into a seamless whole to create the total persona of a character: the inner emotions and feelings and the outer physical and vocal characteristics become one. Only then will the character be forcefully and convincingly portrayed. This process is called *integration.*

Finally, we must realize that although a competent, well-trained performer may become a successful actress or actor, another ingredient is required in order to electrify an audience, as truly memorable stage artists do. This results from intangibles—qualities that cannot be taught in acting schools—which distinguish an acceptable, accomplished actor or actress from one who ignites the stage. *Presence, charisma, personality, star quality:* these are among the terms used to describe a performer who communicates directly and kinetically with the audience. Whatever term one uses, the electricity and excitement of theater are enhanced immeasurably by performers who possess this indefinable attribute.

JUDGING PERFORMANCES

As observers, we study the techniques and problems of acting so that we will be able to understand and judge the performances we see. If a performer is unconvincing in a part, we know that he or she has not mastered a technique for truthful acting, such as the system developed by Stanislavski and his successors. We recognize that a performer who moves awkwardly or cannot be heard clearly has not been properly trained in body movement or vocal projection. We learn to notice how well performers play together: whether they listen to one another and respond appropriately. We also observe how well performers establish and maintain contact with the audience.

Earlier, we saw that a performer must project his or her voice into the audience. In fact, the performer must project his or her total personality, because (as has frequently been noted) it is the contact between performer and audience which forms the basic encounter of theater. This is true even in the many types of theater where performers appear to act as if the audience did not exist; from the audience's standpoint, the performer-audience relationship is very intense, because audience members focus exclusively on the stage. Their involvement is so intense that a cough or whisper, which would be unnoticed in an ordinary room, is magnified a hundredfold. The performers are also conscious of this relationship. They may concentrate on an object onstage, or on one another, but a part of them constantly senses the audience and monitors its reaction.

In short, when we consider all the aspects of acting, we see that there is great variation in the intensity and honesty of performers. If they are absorbed in a life-and-death struggle onstage, the audience will be absorbed too, like bystanders at a street fight. If they are listless and uninvolved, the audience will lose interest.

Before leaving the subject of the performer, we should note that actors and actresses have always held a fascination for audiences. In some cases this is because they portray larger-than-life characters; it can also result from the exceptional talent they bring to their performances. Also, of course, some performers have personal charisma or appeal. Theater audiences have often responded to stars onstage in the same way that people tend to respond to a rock star or a film star. There is something in these personalities that audiences find immensely attractive or intriguing. Moreover, the personal lives of actors are often of great interest to the public, and some people find it difficult to separate a stage character from the offstage woman or man.

In Chapter 7, we turn to the person who works most closely with actresses and actors and who helps them shape their performances—the director.

SUMMARY

1. From the end of the nineteenth century to the present day, many plays have been written in a very realistic, lifelike style. The characters in these plays resemble ordinary people in their dialogue, behavior, etc. Presenting them requires that performers make the characters they portray believable and convincing.

2. A Russian director, Constantin Stanislavski, developed a system or method of acting to enable performers to believe in the "truth" of what they say and do. His suggestions included applying techniques of relaxation and concentration; dealing with specific objects and feelings (a handkerchief, a glass of water, etc.); using the power of fantasy or imagination (the "magic if") to achieve a sense of inner truth in a role; using psychophysical action; developing a *spine*, or *through line*, which runs through a role from the beginning to the end of a play; and playing together as an ensemble.

3. Exercises and tasks have been developed to train performers. These include numerous physical and vocal exercises and techniques taken from other disciplines such as tai chi and the circus. "Centering" is often emphasized as part of body and voice training.

4. Avant-garde theater and some other theaters make additional demands on the performer with regard to voice and body training. The voice is sometimes used to emit odd sounds—screams, grunts, and the like. The body must perform feats of acrobatics and gymnastics. (In Ionesco's *Rhinoceros*, for example, the actor must suggest a physical transformation.)

5. The end result must be a synthesis or integration of the inner and outer aspects of acting.

6. Audience members should familiarize themselves with the problems and techniques of acting in order to judge performances properly.

EXPLORING THEATER ON THE WEB

Stage Acting Today

There are many acting-related links on the World Wide Web, from training seminars, to awards (such as the Obies and the Tonys), to labor unions like Actors' Equity. (http://www.actorsequity.org).

One theater company based in Saint Louis, TheatrGROUP, hosts a website dedicated to the training of actors: at http://www.theatrgroup.com. The purpose of this company is to train actors (beginning to advanced) in the approach to the actor's art known as the "Method." It then uses this specifically trained ensemble in TheatrGROUP productions.

Exercises:

1. Go to the free Method workshop at http://www.theatrgroup.com/Method. Scroll down and see the Method acting procedures. Click on the "sense memory" link and try the exercise.

   How did you feel after doing the assignment? Why do you think Method actors have to learn to call on sense memory rather than "just pretending"?

   Cite some examples of "real" acting you have seen onstage or in the movies. Can you contrast those examples with a more stylized performance you have seen?

2. Visit the "Acting Workshop On-Line" homepage (http://www.redbirdstudio.com/AWOL/acting2.html) to explore the various resources and techniques available to today's actor. Topics range from Acting in Theatre and Film to Headshots to Agents to Auditioning. Visit the "AWOL Q&A Page" where you will find discussion and answers to nuts-and-bolts questions regarding the field of acting that you can gain only from experience and mentorship. What issues did you find interesting that affect the acting industry? Bring this insight to an open class discussion and Q&A session.

3. Before the twentieth century, actors were often exploited. Actors Equity Association was founded in 1913 to represent actors and stage managers to negotiate wages, working conditions, and contracts. There are currently about 40,000 active Equity members.

   - Visit the Actors Equity Association homepage at http://www.actorsequity.org to read about how actors are represented by their union. Why do you think performers still need union protection? What working conditions might be dangerous? How must a performer protect his or her instrument?

   - Read about the history of Actors Equity by clicking on the "History" link in the "About Equity" section. What conditions prompted the formation of this union in 1913? Why were the Broadway theaters closed for 13 days in 1960? Check the FAQ page to read about contracts required by theater companies hiring Equity actors. How have things changed since the strike of 1960?

CHAPTER SEVEN

The Director and the Producer

When we see a theater performance, our most immediate connection is with the actresses and actors onstage. We begin to identify with the characters they play and absorb the situations in which they find themselves. Behind the performances, however, is the work of another creative person—the **director.** He or she is the person who rehearses the performers and coordinates their work with that of others, such as the designers, to make certain that the event is performed appropriately, intelligently, and in an exciting manner. In this chapter, we will look at the role of the director, and also at the role of the producer or manager—the person who is responsible for the management and business aspects of theater.

THE THEATER DIRECTOR

The director works most closely with performers in the theater, guiding them in shaping their performances. When a new play is being presented, the director also works closely with the playwright. The director is responsible, as well, for coordinating other aspects of the production, such as the work of the scene, costume, lighting, and sound designers.

◀ THE DIRECTOR GUIDES THE PERFORMERS

The director develops a production concept, explains it to the performers, helps the performers with their roles, and shapes ensemble playing. Shown here is director George C. Wolfe (on the left) *demonstrating a stage movement to actress Queen Esther, during a rehearsal of the revue* Harlem Song, *at the Apollo Theater. In addition to casting the performers and guiding them in rehearsal, the director helps the designers shape the look and the sound of a production.* (Tyler Hicks/The New York Times)

For many audience members, the director's work on a production is one of the least obvious components. Other elements—performers, scenery, and costumes—are onstage and are immediately visible to spectators, and the words of the playwright are heard throughout the performance; but audiences are often not aware that the way performers speak and move, the way the scenery looks, and the way the lights change colors and intensity often originate with the director.

After the playwright, the director is usually the first person to become involved in the creative process of a production, and the choices made by the director at every phase along the way have a great deal to do with determining whether the ultimate experience will be satisfactory for the spectators.

In Chapter 8 we will see that the playwright incorporates in his or her script a point of view toward the material being dramatized. It may be a tragedy, for example, or a comedy. It is crucial for the director to understand this point of view and translate it into production terms, making it clear to the performers, designers, and other artists and technicians involved. Although they work together, these artists and technicians must of necessity work on segments of the production rather than the entire enterprise. During rehearsals, for instance, the performers are much too busy working on their own roles and their interactions with each other to worry much about scenery. To take another example, a performer who appears only in the first act of a three-act play has no control over what happens in the second and third acts. The one person who does have an overall perspective is the director.

Directors get their training in a variety of ways. Many of them begin as actors and actresses and find that they have a talent for working with other people and for coordinating the work of designers as well as performers. Others train in the many academic institutions that have specific programs for directors. These include large universities with theater as part of a liberal arts focus as well as special conservatories and institutes.

Evolution of the Director: A Historical Perspective

It is sometimes argued that the theater director did not exist before 1874, when a German nobleman, George II (1826–1914), duke of Saxe-Meiningen, began to supervise every element of the productions in the theater in his realm. This supervision included rehearsals, scenic elements, and other aspects—which he coordinated into an integrated whole. It is true that beginning with Saxe-Meiningen, the director emerged as a full-fledged, indispensable member of the theatrical team, taking a place alongside the playwright, the performers, and the designers. Although the title may have been new, however, the *function* of the director had always been present in one way or another.

We know, for example, that the Greek playwright Aeschylus directed his own plays and that the chorus in a Greek play would rehearse under the supervision of a leader for many weeks before a performance. At various times in theater history, the leading performer or playwright of a company served as a director, though without the title. Molière, for instance, not only was the playwright and the chief actor of his company but functioned as the director also. We know from Molière's short play *The Impromptu of Versailles* that he had definite ideas about the way actors and actresses should perform; no doubt the same advice he offered in that play was frequently given to his performers in rehearsal. When Hamlet gives instructions and advice to the players who perform the play-within-the-play in *Hamlet,* he is functioning as a director. In England after the time of Shakespeare—from the seventeenth century through the nineteenth—there was a long line of **actor-managers** who gave strong leadership to individual theater companies and performed many of the functions of a director, although they were still not given that title. Among the most famous were Thomas Betterton (1635–1710), David Garrick, Charles Kemble (1775–1854), William Charles Macready (1793–1873), and Henry Irving (1838–1905).

Toward the end of the nineteenth century the term *director* came into common usage and the clearly defined role of the director was first recognized. Perhaps significantly, the emergence of the director as a separate creative figure coincided with important changes which began to take place in society during the nineteenth century. First, there was a breakdown in established social, religious, and political concepts, resulting in part from the influence of Freud, Darwin, and Marx. Second, there was a marked increase in communication. With the advent of the telegraph, the telephone, photography, motion pictures, and—later—television, various cultures which had remained remote from or unknown to one another were suddenly made aware of each other. The effect of these two changes was to alter the monolithic, ordered view of the world which individual societies had maintained earlier.

Before these developments, consistency of style in theater had been easier to achieve. Within a given society, writers, performers, and spectators were on common ground. For example, the comedies of the English playwrights William Wycherley (1640–1716) and William Congreve (1670–1729), written at the end of the seventeenth century, were aimed at a specific audience—the elite upper class, which relished gossip, clever remarks, and well-turned phrases. The code of social behavior was well understood by performers and audiences alike; and questions of style in a production hardly arose, because a common approach to style was already present in the fabric of society. The way a man took a pinch of snuff or a lady flung open her fan was so clearly delineated in daily behavior that performers had only to refine and perfect these actions for the stage. Today, however, because style, unity, and a cohesive view of society are so elusive, the director's task is more important.

(© T. Charles Erickson)

(Kenneth Lambert/AP/Wide World Photos)

(Fred Jewell/AP/Wide World Photos)

The Director at Work The director does most of his or her work in conferences with designers and in rehearsals with performers. Shown here are four different directors working with collaborators and guiding actors and actresses. First, we see director Lisa Peterson (*upper left*) directing her cast in a rehearsal of *Mrs. Warren's Profession* at the Guthrie Theater in Minneapolis. (The actors, left to right, are Paul O'Brien, Leo Kittay, and Michael Booth.) Next is director Chuck Smith (*above*) instructing actress Irma P. Hall and actor Harry Lennix in a rehearsal of a scene from *A Raisin in the Sun* at the Goodman Theatre in Chicago. Director Christopher Ashley (*bottom left*) is talking to the cast in an early rehearsal of *Sweeney Todd* at the Kennedy Center. Last is the Swedish director Ingmar Bergman working (*right*) closely with performers Jan Malmsjö and Virpi Pahkinen in a rehearsal of *The Ghost Sonata* at the Royal Dramatic Theatre in Stockholm.

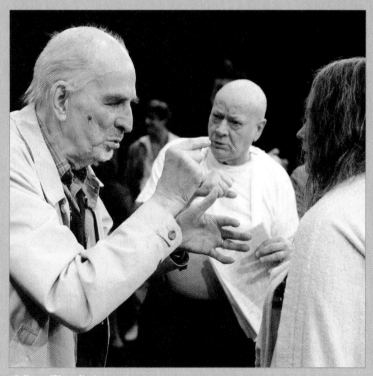

(© Bengt Wanselius)

The Director and the Script

For the most part, spectators experience theater as a unified event; but, as pointed out before, theater is a complex art involving not one or two elements but many simultaneously: script, performance, costumes, scenery, lighting, and point of view. These diverse elements—a mixture of the tangible and intangible—must be brought together into an organic whole, and that is the responsibility of the director. The following are aspects of the director's preparation of a production.

Choosing a Script   Frequently, the director chooses the script to be produced. Generally it is a play to which the director is attracted or for which he or she feels a special affinity. If the director does not actually choose the script but is asked to direct it by a playwright or a producer, he or she must still understand and appreciate the material. The director's attraction to the script and basic understanding of it are important in launching a production. Once the script is chosen, the actual work on the production begins.

If the play is new and has never been tested in production, the director may see problems in the script which must be corrected before rehearsals begin; the director will have a series of meetings with the playwright to iron out the difficulties ahead of time. The director may feel, for example, that the leading character is not clearly defined, or that a clash of personalities between two characters never reaches a climax. If the playwright agrees with the director's assessment, he or she will revise the manuscript. Generally there is considerable give-and-take between the director and the playwright in these preliminary sessions, as well as during the rehearsal period. Ideally, there should be a spirit of cooperation, compromise, and mutual respect in this relationship.

Once the script is selected, the director begins analyzing it and preparing a production. There is no one way a director should go about this: individual directors adopt their own personal approach. To illustrate one method of undertaking this task, the following paragraphs outline the method followed by one of the best-known twentieth-century American directors, Harold Clurman (1901–1980).

The "Spine" of the Play   One of the first steps for a director in preparing a production is to discover the ***spine*** of the play. In his book *On Directing*, Harold Clurman says that the director's first task is to find in the script the general action that "motivates the play." The director must determine the "fundamental drama or conflict" of which "the script's plot and people are the instruments."[1]

Clurman calls the fundamental action or conflict the *spine* of the play; it could also be called the *main action*. Clurman says, for example, that the spine for the characters in Eugene O'Neill's *A Touch of the Poet* is "to make a place for themselves."[2] In one way or another, Clurman feels, every character in that play is seeking this same goal.

Finding a spine for a play allows the director to understand the action and provides a nerve center from which to develop it. Different directors may find different spines for the same play. With *Hamlet,* for instance, several spines are possible: much will depend on the period in which the play is produced and on the point of view of the individual director. One spine could be simple revenge; another could be Hamlet's attempt to resolve his inner conflicts; still another could be Hamlet's attempt to locate and expose the duplicity and corruption he senses in Denmark. Clurman says that such varied interpretations are to be expected and are acceptable as long as the spine chosen remains true to the spirit and action of the play.

Clurman warns of the dangers of not finding a main action or spine: "Where a director has not determined on a spine for his production, it will tend to be formless. Each scene follows the next without necessarily adding up to a total dramatic 'statement.' "[3]

The Style of the Production   Once a spine has been found, the second task for a director, according to Clurman, is "to find the manner in which the spine is to be articulated."[4] Clurman is speaking here of the ***style*** of the production.

The concept of style in a theatrical production is difficult to explain. It means the *way* a play is presented. When we speak of a "casual style" of clothing, we mean that the clothing is loose and informal; when we speak of a "1960s" style, we mean that it has the look and feel of clothing worn in the 1960s. In theater, one way to consider style is in terms of realism and nonrealism. The differences between these two types were discussed in Chapter 1, but they can be further subdivided.

For example, there are several types of realism. At one extreme is ***naturalism,*** a kind of superrealism. The term *naturalism* was originated by several nineteenth-century French writers who wanted a theater that would show human beings—often in wretched circumstances—as products of heredity and environment. In addition to this special use, the term *naturalism* refers more broadly to attempts to put onstage as exact a copy of life as possible, down to the smallest detail. In a naturalistic stage set of a kitchen, for instance, a performer can actually cook a meal on the stove, the toaster makes toast, the faucet produces water, and the light in the refrigerator goes on when the door opens. Characters speak and act as if they had been caught unobserved by a sound camera. In this sense, naturalism is supposed to resemble an undoctored documentary film. Naturalism is sometimes called *slice-of-life* drama, suggesting that a section has been taken from life and transferred to the stage.

At the other extreme of realism is ***heightened realism,*** sometimes referred to as ***selective realism.*** Here the characters and their activities are intended to resemble life, but a certain license is allowed. The scenery, for example, might be skeletal—that is, incomplete and in outline—although the words and actions of the characters are realistic. Or perhaps a character is allowed a modern version of a soliloquy in an otherwise realistic play.

THE DIRECTOR AND THE STYLE OF A PRODUCTION

One of the crucial decisions for a director is to determine the style of a production, based largely on the script, but at times on other considerations as well. Then the director must see to it that all the elements of a production—acting, movement, design—conform to that style. Shown here is a scene from a comedy of manners, Noel Coward's Private Lives, *which calls for "high style" in the gestures and delivery of lines by the performers. The director was Howard Davies who made certain that the sets and costumes had the right quality of sophistication and that his British cast coveyed the proper air of urbanity and savoir faire. The performers, from the left, are Lindsay Duncan, Alan Rickman, Adam Godley, and Emma Fielding.* (© **Joan Marcus**)

All art calls for selectivity, and heightened realism recognizes the necessity for the artist to make choices and to inject creativity into the process.

Realism itself occupies the middle ground between naturalism and heightened, or selective, realism; but when it is used as a broad umbrella term, it includes the extremes at each end.

Nonrealism can also be divided into types which might include such forms as fantasy, poetic drama, musical theater, absurdist theater, and symbolism. Examples of two well-known types of nonrealism are *allegory* and *expressionism*.

Allegory is the representation of an abstract theme or subject through symbolic characters, actions, or other elements of a production, such as scenery. Good examples are the medieval morality plays, in which characters personify ideas in order to teach an intellectual or moral lesson. In *Everyman,* performers play the parts of Good Deeds, Fellowship, Worldly Goods, and so on. In less direct forms of allegory, a relatively realistic story serves as a parable or lesson. *The Crucible* by Arthur Miller is about the witch-hunts in Salem, Massachusetts, in the late seventeenth century; but it can also be regarded as dealing with specific investigations by the United States Congress in the early 1950s that Miller and others considered modern "witch-hunts."

Expressionism was at its height in art, literature, and theater during the first quarter of the twentieth century, but traces of it are still found today, and contemporary plays using its techniques are called *expressionistic*. In simple terms, expressionism gives outward expression to inner feelings. In Elmer Rice's *The Adding Machine,* the feelings of Mr. Zero when he is fired from his job are conveyed by having the room spin around in a circle amid a cacophony of shrill sounds, such as loud sirens and whistles.

Deciding on a directorial style for a production involves giving a signature and an imprint to an entire production: the look of the scenery and lights, and the way performers speak and handle their costumes and props. It also involves the rhythm and pace at which the play moves, a subject that is taken up below.

When a director arrives at a style for a production, two things are essential: (1) the style should be appropriate for the play, and (2) it should be consistent throughout every aspect of the production.

The Directorial Concept   One way for the director to embody the spine in a production and to implement style is to develop a ***directorial concept***. Such a concept derives from a controlling idea, vision, or point of view which the director feels is appropriate to the play. The concept should also create a unified theatrical experience for the spectators.

Concept and Period   To indicate what is involved for the director in developing a concept, let us begin with *period*. Shakespeare's *Troilus and Cressida* was written in the Elizabethan period but is set at the time of the Trojan War, when the ancient Greeks were fighting the Trojans. In presenting the play today, a director has several choices as to the period in which to set the production.

One director might choose to stick to the period indicated in the script and set the play in Troy, with Trojans and Greeks wearing armor, tunics, and the like. Another might set the play in the time when Shakespeare wrote it; in this case the director and the designers would devise court and military costumes like those of Shakespeare's day.

Another option for the director would be to modernize the play in the hope of making it more relevant to the audience. There have been a number of modern productions of *Troilus and Cressida* in recent years. Shakespeare's words are retained, since many of the play's antiwar sentiments and statements about the corruption of love in the face of war are quite relevant today; but the play is transferred to a more recent period by means of costumes, settings, and behavior. For example, in 1956 the British director Tyrone Guthrie (1900–1971) presented a version set in England in the period just before 1914—that is, just before World War I. The play was shifted to drawing rooms and other localities conveying a clear impression of England in the early twentieth century. The uniforms were those of English soldiers of the period, and the women wore dresses typical of that era. The set had grand pianos, the men drank cocktails, and the women used cigarette

THE DIRECTORIAL CONCEPT

Seen here are two examples of directorial concept, in which the director chooses an idea or a device to convey his or her view of a play. Above we see a scene from Metamorphoses, *a drama developed by author/director Mary Zimmerman from the tales of Ovid. One striking notion was to have much of the action take place in or around a shallow pool of water that Zimmerman saw as a natural element for the environment of the play. The actors shown are, left to right, Anjali Bhimani, Louise Lamson, and Mariann Mayberry. A second example was a production of* King Oedipus *by Sophocles mounted at the Hartford Stage. Director Jonathan Wilson presented the play with an African American cast and underscored the elements that reflect the African American experience, as well as the African roots of many African Americans. Shown at right is Reg Flowers in the title role.* (© Joan Marcus)

holders—all this was intended to portray a sophisticated urban environment. A successful production of *Troilus and Cressida* by the Royal Shakespeare Company in 1986 shifted the time of the play to the Crimean war in the middle of the nineteenth century.

This kind of transposition has been carried out frequently with Greek plays, Elizabethan plays, seventeenth-century French plays, and other dramatic classics.

Concept and Central Image Another way to implement a directorial concept is to find a *central*, or *controlling*, *image* or *metaphor* for a theatrical production.

An example would be a production of *Hamlet* that envisioned the play in terms of a vast net or spiderweb in which Hamlet is caught. The motif of a net or spiderweb could be carried out on several levels: in the design of

(© T. Charles Erickson)

the stage set, in the ways in which the performers relate to one another, and in a host of details relating to the central image. There might be a huge rope net hanging over the entire stage, for instance, and certain characters could play string games with their fingers. In short, the metaphor of Hamlet's being caught in a net would be emphasized and reinforced on every level.

Concept and Purpose   The directorial concept should serve the play; the best concept is one that remains true to the spirit and meaning of the script. A director who can translate that spirit and meaning into stage terms in an inspired way will create an exciting theater experience; but a director who

Zelda Fichandler: Director and Artistic Director

Zelda Fichandler was a cofounder of the Arena Stage in Washington, D.C., one of the leading American regional theaters. She was its producing director from 1951 to 1990. She has also served as head of the graduate acting program at New York University and artistic director of the Actors Company.

What would you say to a young director striving to get into the profession? It's very hard to get into this field. You have to make your own opportunities at the very beginning. You have to do something somewhere, get some people in a room, just to see whether *you* like it. There's too much concentration on getting other people to like your work. Young directors have to find out whether *they* really like their work, or if they want to change it before they start showing it. You have to find out whether you have a work method and whether you have something that's ready for you to feel good about. These are practical considerations. "If I show this work, will it be seen as good?" Directors can work in any city. You don't have to work in New York. Any place there are people, there is an audience. You simply have to start anywhere you can, under any circumstances. It becomes a matter of persisting until you find a play that reveals your work as special—defined by your personality, your insights, and your personal set of images. The price of being a director is high. It's a life of enormous concentration, but of great rewards. . . .

Source: Zelda Fichandler, from *The Director's Voice: Twenty-One Interviews* by Arthur Bartow. Copyright 1998 by Arthur Bartow. By permission of Theatre Communications Group.

is too intent on displaying his or her own originality may distort or violate the integrity of the script. For instance, a director might decide to make *Macbeth* into a cowboy play, with Duncan as a sheriff and Macbeth as a deputy who wants to kill the sheriff in order to take the job himself. In this version, Lady Macbeth would be the deputy's wife, whom he had met in a saloon. *Macbeth* could be done this way, but it might also come across as simply a gimmick—a means of calling attention to the director rather than to the script.

In most instances the best directorial concept is a straightforward one deriving from the play itself, not a scheme superimposed from the outside.

The Director and the Dramaturg *Dramaturg* comes from a German word for "dramatic adviser." In Europe, the practice of having a dramaturg, or *literary manager*, attached to a theater goes back well over a century. In the United States, the role of the dramaturg is relatively new; in recent years, however, many regional professional groups and other not-for-profit theaters have engaged full-time dramaturgs.

In making the decisions outlined above, a dramaturg can often be extremely helpful to a director. Among the duties frequently undertaken by dramaturgs are discovering and reading promising new plays, working with playwrights on the development of new scripts, identifying significant plays from the past that may have been overlooked, conducting research on previous productions of classic plays, preparing reports on the history of plays, researching criticism and interpretations of plays from the past, and writing articles for the programs that are distributed when plays are produced.

In looking at the work of the dramaturg or literary manager, it is easy to see how she or he can be helpful to a director. The dramaturg can locate new material and identify important plays from the past; help the director arrive at decisions regarding style, approach, and concept; and make the director aware of how directors have approached plays in the past.

The Auteur Director *Auteur* is a French word meaning "author." Just after World War II, French critics began using this term to describe certain film directors, who, they said, were really the authors of the films they made. In these films the point of view and the implementation of that point of view came almost entirely from the director, not from a writer. The term has since been applied to a type of stage director as well. I am not speaking here of directors who alter the time or place in which the action occurs but retain the original script—the playwright's words, the sequence of scenes, and so forth. I am speaking rather of directors who make more drastic alterations or transformations in the material, taking responsibility for shaping *every* element in the production, including the script.

Interestingly, one of the first and most important auteur directors began his work with Stanislavski and then went out on his own. He was Vsevolod Meyerhold (1874–1940), and he developed a type of theater in which he controlled all the elements. The script was only one of many aspects that Meyerhold used for his own purposes. He would rewrite or eliminate text in order to present his own vision of the material. Performers, too, were subject to his overall ideas. Often they were called on to perform like circus acrobats or robots. The finished product was frequently exciting and almost always innovative, but it reflected Meyerhold's point of view, strongly imposed on all the elements, not the viewpoint of a writer or anyone else.

Following in Meyerhold's footsteps, many avant-garde directors, such as Jerzi Grotowski (1933–1999) and Robert Wilson, can also be classified as auteur directors in the sense of demanding that a text serve their purposes, not the other way around. In some cases, such as many of Wilson's pieces, the text is only fragmentary and is one of the least important elements. In the former Soviet Union and eastern Europe, before the political changes of the early 1990s, certain directors, who had not been allowed to deal with material that questioned the government hierarchy, drastically reworked established texts in order to make a political comment. These directors, too, imposed their own vision, rather than that of the playwright, on the material.

Among women artists, three highly regarded auteur directors are JoAnne Akalaitis (1937–), Anne Bogart (1951–), and Julie Taymor (1952–).

The Director and the Production

The Physical Production At the same time that he or she is developing a conceptual approach to the play, the director is also working with the designers on the physical production. At the outset—once the director's concept is established—the director confers with the costume, scene, and lighting design-

(© Jack Vartoogian)

THE AUTEUR DIRECTOR

Robert Wilson is one of the foremost of the modern directors who create their own theater pieces, serving not only as director but also playwright, and in the case of Wilson, designer as well. Auteur directors control every aspect of the production; it represents their vision, not that of a playwright. Shown above is a scene from one of his productions, White Raven. *Note the abstract, pictorial quality of the scene. Shown at right is Wilson in his workshop at the Watermill Center on Long Island where he conceives many of his productions.*

ers to give visual shape and substance to the concept. It is the responsibility of designers to provide images and impressions which will carry out the style and ideas of the production. (See Chapters 16, 17, and 18.)

During the preproduction and rehearsal period, the director meets with the designers to make certain that their work is on schedule and keeping pace with the rehearsals. Obviously, the preparation of these elements must begin long before the actual performance, just as rehearsals must, so that everything will be ready by the time the performance itself takes place. Any number of problems can arise with the physical elements of a production. For example, the appropriate props may not be available, a costume may not fit a performer, or scene changes may be too slow. Early planning will allow time to solve these problems.

Casting   Now we come to the director's work with the performers. Along with choosing and developing a script and settling questions of concept, style, and the physical production, the director also casts the play.

In theater, the word ***casting*** means fitting performers into roles; it is obviously derived from the phrase "casting a mold." Generally speaking, directors attempt to put performers into the roles for which their personalities and physical characteristics are best suited. A young actress will play Juliet in *Romeo and Juliet,* a middle-aged or elderly actor with a deep voice will play King Lear, and so on. When a performer closely resembles in real life the

(© Nicole Bengiveno, New York Times)

character to be enacted, this is known as ***typecasting.*** There are times, however, when a director will deliberately put someone in a role who does not appear to be right for the part. This is frequently done for comic or satiric purposes and is called *casting against type.* For example, a sinister-looking actor might be called on to play an angelic part.

In modern American theater, performers frequently *audition* for parts in a play, and the director casts from those performers who audition. (Auditioning is described in Chapter 6.) In an audition, actors and actresses read scenes from a play or perform portions of the script to give the director an indication of how they talk and move and how they would interpret a part. From this the director determines whether or not a performer is right for a given role.

Historically, casting was rarely done by audition, because theatrical companies were more permanent. In Shakespeare's time, and in Molière's, certain people in a theatrical troupe always played certain parts: one person would play heroic roles, for example, while another always played clowns. Under these conditions, when a play was selected, casting was simply a matter of assigning roles to the performers who were on hand; auditioning might take place only when a new member was being chosen for the company. Modern counterparts of these earlier theatrical companies are today's repertory companies in Europe and Great Britain, where theater organizations like the Royal National Theater and the Royal Shakespeare Company have a permanent group of actors and actresses.

From the audience's standpoint, it is important to be aware of casting and the difference it can make to the effectiveness of a production. Perhaps an actor or actress is just right for the part he or she is playing. On the other hand, sometimes the wrong performer is chosen for a part: the voice may not be right, or the gestures or facial expressions may be inappropriate for the character. One way to test the appropriateness of casting is to imagine a different kind of actor or actress in a part while watching a performance.

Rehearsals   Once a play is cast, the director supervises all the rehearsals. He or she listens to and watches the performers as they go through their lines and begin to move about the stage.

Different directors work in different ways during the early phases of rehearsal. Some directors *block* a play in advance, giving precise instructions to the performers. (The term ***blocking*** means deciding when and where performers move and position themselves on the stage.) Other directors let the actors and actresses find their own movements, their own vocal interpretations, and their own relationships. And of course there are directors who do a bit of both.

During the rehearsal period, the director must make certain that the actors and actresses are realizing the intention of the playwright—that they are making sense of the script and bringing out its meaning. Also, the director must ensure that the performers are working well together—that they are listening to one another and beginning to play as an ensemble. The director must be aware of performers' needs, knowing when to encourage them and when to challenge or criticize them. The director must understand their personal problems and help them overcome such obstacles as insecurity about a role or fear of failure.

The Director as the Audience's Eye One could say that there are two people in theater who stand in for the audience, serving as surrogate or substitute spectators. One, the critic (discussed in Chapter 3), does his or her work after the event; the other, the director, does his or her work before it.

In preparing a theatrical production, the director acts as the eye of the audience. During rehearsals, only the director sees the production from the spectator's point of view. For this reason, the director must help the performers to show the audience exactly what they intend to show. If one performer hides another at an important moment, if a crucial gesture is not visible, if an actor makes an awkward movement, if an actress cannot be heard when she delivers an emotional speech, the director points it out.

Also, the director underscores the meaning of specific scenes through *visual composition* and *stage pictures,* that is, through the physical arrangement of performers onstage. The spatial relationships of performers convey information about characters. For example, important characters are frequently placed on a level above other characters—on a platform, say, or a flight of stairs. Another spatial device is to place an important character alone in one area of the stage while grouping other characters in another area; this causes the spectator's eye to give special attention to the character standing alone. Also, if two characters are opposed to each other, they should be placed in positions of physical confrontation onstage. Visual composition is more crucial in a play with a large cast, such as Shakespearean productions, than in a play with only two or three characters.

Certain areas onstage can assume special significance: a fireplace, with its implication of warmth, can become an area to which a character returns for comfort and reassurance. A door opening onto a garden can serve as a place where characters go when they want to renew their spirits or relieve a hemmed-in feeling. By guiding performers to make the best use of stage space, the director helps them communicate important visual images to the audience—images consistent with the overall meaning of the play.

It is important to note, too, that directors must adjust their notions of blocking and visual composition to different types of stages: the arena

THE STAGE MANAGER'S PROMPT BOOK

Shown here are the first two pages of a prompt book prepared by Roy Harris for the Broadway production of The Sisters Rozensweig *by Wendy Wasserstein. The first page deals with cues and setups just before the curtain rises. For example, the first entry (at the upper left) is "Warn: House to 1/2"; a warning that the lights in the auditorium will be taken to half strength. LQ stands for "light cue" and SD for "sound." In the middle of the first page of dialogue, "SB, LQ 5" means, "Stand by for light cue 5." Then, near the bottom of the page, light cue 5 is executed. When the stage manager "runs" a show, he or she stands just offstage, near the proscenium opening, and issues orders for light, sound, and other cues; all of this is written down in the prompt book. (Courtesy of Professor Paul Antonie Distler)*

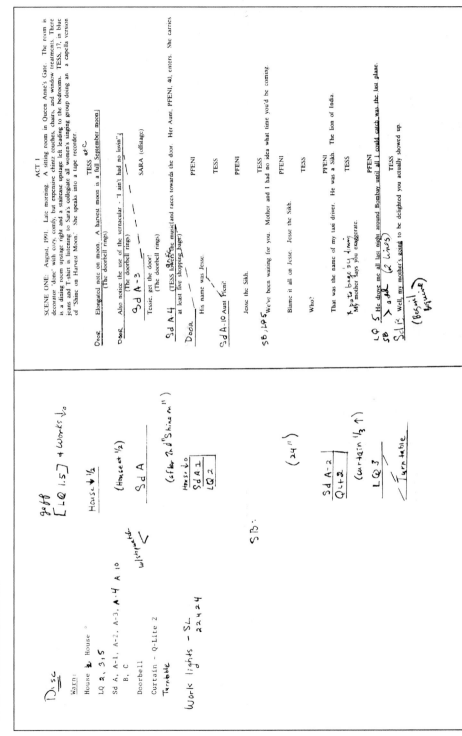

USING STAGE AREAS PROPERLY

One responsibility of the director is to make appropriate use of stage areas to create balance, emphasis, and striking visual effects. Notice the arrangement of the performers in this scene from Federico Garcia Lorca's The House of Bernarda Alba: *The three sisters seated on the left side, the mother in the center, standing, the space between her and the fourth sister seated at the far right. The spatial arrangement is not only attractive but speaks volumes about the relationships of the people involved. The production, directed by Elizabeth Huddle, was at the Madison Repertory Theatre. The performers, left to right, are Jamie England, Monica Lyons, Elisabeth Adwin, Margaret Ingraham, and Diane Robinson.* (Zane Williams)

stage, the thrust stage, and the proscenium stage (discussed in Chapter 4) call for different approaches to the performers' movements and the audience's sight lines.

Movement, Pace, and Rhythm   The director gives shape and structure to a play in two ways: in *space*, as was just described, and in time. Since a production occurs through time, it is important for the director to see that the ***movement, pace***, and ***rhythm*** of the play are appropriate. If a play moves too quickly, if we miss words and do not understand what is going on, that is usually the director's fault. The director must determine whether there is too little or too much time between speeches or whether a performer moves across the stage too slowly or too quickly. The director must attempt to control the pace and rhythm within a scene and the rhythm between scenes.

One of the most common faults of directors is not establishing a clear rhythm in a production. An audience at a performance is impatient to see what is coming next, and the director must see to it that the movement from moment to moment and scene to scene has enough thrust and drive to maintain our interest. Variety is also important. If a play moves ahead at only one pace, whether slow or fast, the audience will become fatigued simply by the monotony of that pace. Rhythm within scenes and between scenes works on audience members subliminally, but its effects are very real. It enters our psyche as we watch a performance and thus contributes to our overall response.

It must be borne in mind as well that although pace, rhythm, and overall effect are initially the responsibility of the director, ultimately they become the performers' responsibility. Once a performance begins, the actors and actresses are onstage and the director is not. In cinema, pace and rhythm can be determined in the editing room; in theater, by contrast, they are in the hands of the performers. Then, too, the audience's reaction will vary from night to night, and that will also alter pace and rhythm. The director must therefore instill and implant in the performers such a strong sense of inner rhythm that they develop an internal clock which tells them how they should play.

Technical Rehearsal   Just before public performances begin, a ***technical rehearsal*** is held. The performers are onstage in their costumes with the scenery and lighting for the first time, and there is a ***run-through*** of the show from beginning to end, with all the props and scene changes. The stagehands move scenery, the crew handles props, and the lighting technicians control the dimming and raising of lights. The backstage crew must coordinate its work with that of the performers.

Let us say that one scene ends in a garden, and the next scene opens in a library. When the performers leave the garden set, the lighting fades, the scenery is removed, and the garden furniture is taken offstage. Then, the scenery for the library must be brought onstage by stagehands and the books and other props put in place. Next, the performers for the new scene in the library take their places as the lighting comes up. Extensive rehearsals are required to ensure that the lighting comes up at just the moment when the scenery is prepared and the performers are in place. Any mishap on the part of the stage crew, lighting crew, prop crew, or performers would affect the illusion and destroy the aesthetic effect of the scene change. The importance of the technical rehearsal is therefore considerable.

Because the technical rehearsal is held primarily to deal with all the mechanical and physical aspects of a production, the performers usually do not attempt to act convincingly or to convey deep emotion. Sometimes they are even told not to say all their lines but simply to jump "from cue to cue."

Dress Rehearsal   Just after the technical rehearsal, but before the first preview or tryout with an audience, the director will hold a ***dress rehearsal***. The purpose of the dress rehearsal is to put all the elements together: the full involvement of the performers as well as the technical components. The dress rehearsal is a full-scale run-through of the production. It is performed as if an audience were present, with no stops or interruptions and with full lights,

scenery, costumes, and sound. Sometimes a few people are invited—friends of the director or cast members—to provide some sense of an audience.

One function of the dress rehearsal is to give everyone concerned—cast, crew, and director—a sense of what the performance will be like. The dress rehearsal also allows for any last-minute changes before the first performance in front of a full audience.

Previews   Once the technical rehearsals and the dress rehearsal are completed and any problems are solved, the next step is a performance in front of an audience. I have stressed from the beginning the importance of performer-audience interaction and the fact that no play is complete until it is actually enacted for an audience. It is crucial, therefore, for a production to be tried out before a group of spectators. What has gone before, in terms of rehearsals and other elements, must now meet the test of combining harmoniously in front of an audience.

For this purpose there is a period of ***previews***—also called ***tryouts***—when the director and the performers discover which parts of the play are successful and which are not. Frequently, for example, the director and performers find that one part of the play is moving too slowly; they know this because the audience members become restless and begin to cough or stir. Sometimes, in a comedy, there is a great deal of laughter where little was expected, and the performers and the director must adjust to this. The audiences

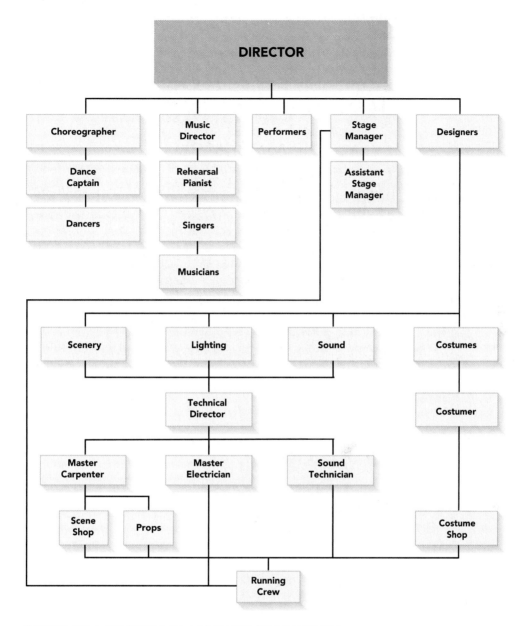

DUTIES OF A DIRECTOR IN A THEATER PRODUCTION

Once a director has decided on a script (and worked with the playwright, if it is a new play), he or she must organize the entire artistic side of the production. This chart indicates the many people that the director must work with and the many elements that must be coordinated.

Putting a Production Together   The director has the overall responsibility for coordinating all the elements that must come together to create a production. This includes not only casting the roles and rehearsing the actors, but also conferring with scenic, lighting, costume, and sound designers, and overseeing technical and dress rehearsals. Shown here are some of the component parts that the director must coordinate. The director was Karen Kessler, and the production was Shakespeare's *Taming of the Shrew* at the Illinois Shakespeare Festival. In the first photograph (*above*), Kessler (*foreground*) is with the assembled performers at the theater. The second photo (*left*) shows Jennifer Snyder building part of the set that had been decided on by Kessler and the designer Peter Beudert. In the third photo (*next page top left*) Abigail Wurster is sewing a costume, designed by Kathryn Rohe in consultation with Kessler. The fourth photo (*next page top right*) shows technician Jim Juhl operating light and sound boards during a dress rehearsal. The final photo (*right*) is Kessler's finished production being performed in front of an audience. (Photos: Peter Guither)

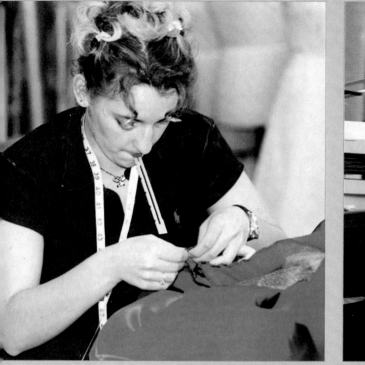

in this preview period become genuine collaborators in shaping the play. After several performances in front of an audience, the director and the performers get the "feel" of the audience and know whether or not the play is ready.

For an idea of the director's full range of responsibilities, see the chart on page 159.

The Director's Power and Responsibility

Any artistic event must have a unity not encountered in real life. We expect the parts to be brought together so that the total effect will enlighten us, move us, or amuse us.

In the theater, the director—who has a voice in so many areas of a production—is in a unique position to bring this about. This power, however, is a double-edged sword. If a director gets too carried away with one idea, for example, or lets the scene designer create scenery which overpowers the performers, the experience for the audience will be unsatisfactory or incomplete. If, on the other hand, the director has a strong point of view—one which is appropriate for the theater piece and illuminates the script—and if all the parts fit and are consistent with one another, the experience will be meaningful and exciting, and at times even unforgettable.

THE PRODUCER OR MANAGER

A theater audience naturally focuses on the event onstage rather than on what happens behind the scenes. But no production would ever be performed for the public without a business component. Here, too, the coordination of elements is crucial, and the person chiefly responsible, known as the **producer** or **manager,** is the behind-the-scenes counterpart of the director.

The Commercial Producer

In a commercial theater venture, the producer has many responsibilities. (See the chart on page 163.) In general, the producer oversees the entire business and publicity side of the production and has the following duties:

1. Raising money to finance the production
2. Securing rights to the script
3. Dealing with the agents for the playwright, director, and performers
4. Hiring the director, performers, designers, and stage crews
5. Dealing with theatrical unions
6. Renting the theater space
7. Supervising the work of those running the theater: in the box office, auditorium, and business office
8. Supervising the advertising

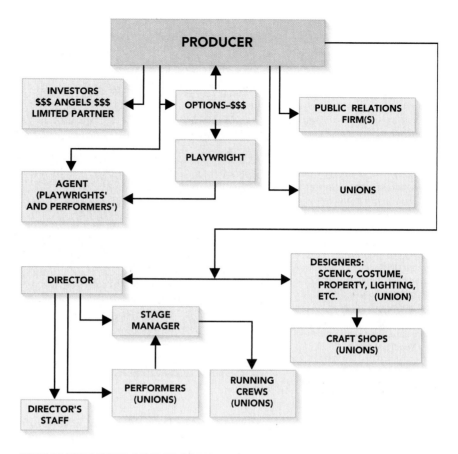

RESPONSIBILITIES OF THE COMMERCIAL THEATER PRODUCER

When a commercial theater production is mounted, the person responsible for organizing the full range of nonartistic activities is the producer. This chart, which shows the producer at the top, indicates the people the producer must deal with and the numerous elements he or she must coordinate.

9. Overseeing the budget and the week-to-week financial management of the production

It is clear that the responsibilities of the commercial producer range far and wide. They require business acumen, organizational ability, aesthetic judgment, marketing know-how, and an ability to work with people. The producer in commercial theater must have the artistic sensibility to choose the right script and hire the right director, but at the same time must be able to raise capital as well as oversee all financial and business operations in a production.

Noncommercial Theaters

In a nonprofit theater the person with many of the same responsibilities as the producer is called the *executive director* or *managing director*.

THE PRODUCER

The person who puts a production together is the producer, or in the case of a not-for-profit company, the Artistic Director. He or she selects the play or musical to be done, and then must decide who will carry out each function: direction, design, and all other elements. In the case of a commercial production, the producer must also raise the funds to make the production possible and decide on a number of other factors such as advertising, marketing, ticket prices, and the like. Though some productions have several producers, there is one person usually known as the lead producer In the case of the musical Hairspray, *that person was Margo Lion, shown here in the center between stars of the show, Harvey Fierstein, as the mother on the left, and Marissa Jaret Winokur as the daughter.* (Sarah Krulwich/The New York Times)

Administrative Organization of a Nonprofit Theater   Most nonprofit theaters—including theaters in smaller urban centers as well as the large noncommercial theaters in major cities like New York, Chicago, and Los Angeles—are organized with a board of directors, an artistic director, and an executive or managing director. The board is responsible for selecting both the artistic and the managing director. The board is also responsible for overseeing the financial affairs of the theater, for fund-raising, for long-range planning, and the like. To carry out some of these tasks, the board frequently delegates authority to an executive committee.

The artistic director is responsible for all creative and artistic activities. He or she selects the plays that will constitute the season and chooses directors, designers, and other creative personnel. Frequently, the artistic director also directs one or more plays during the season.

Responsibilities of a Noncommercial Producer or Manager   The managing director in a noncommercial theater is, in many respects, the counterpart of a producer in commercial theater. In both a commercial production and the running of a nonprofit theater organization, the tasks of the person in charge of administration are many and complex.

The producer or manager is responsible for the maintenance of the theater building, including the dressing rooms, the public facilities, and the lobby.

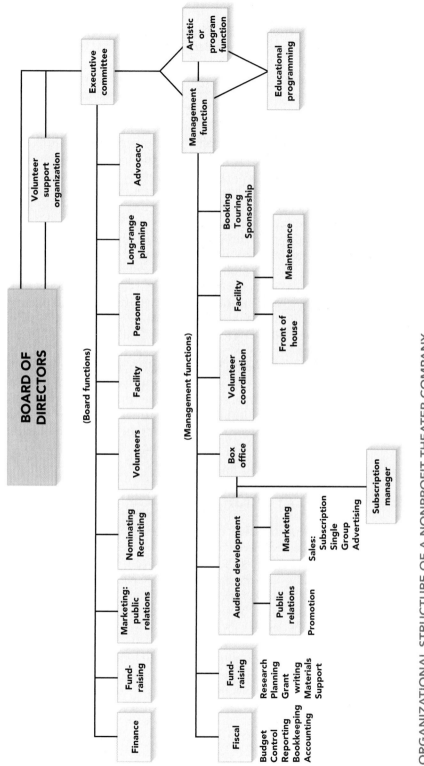

ORGANIZATIONAL STRUCTURE OF A NONPROFIT THEATER COMPANY

A nonprofit theater is a complex institution with many facets. This chart shows the various activities that must be organized for the successful management of such a theater.

Board of Directors

BOARD OF DIRECTORS

Volunteer support organization

Executive committee

(Board functions)

Finance

Fund-raising

Marketing: public relations

Nominating Recruiting

Volunteers

Facility

Personnel

Long-range planning

Advocacy

Artistic or program function

Management function

Educational programming

(Management functions)

Fiscal

Budget
Control
Reporting
Bookkeeping
Accounting

Fund-raising

Research
Planning
Grant writing
Materials
Support

Audience development

Public relations

Promotion

Marketing

Sales:
Subscription
Single
Group
Advertising

Subscription manager

Box office

Volunteer coordination

Facility

Front of house

Maintenance

Booking Touring Sponsorship

The producer or manager is also responsible for the budget, making certain that the production stays within established limits. The budget includes salaries for the director, designers, performers, and stage crews, and expenditures for scenery, costumes, and music. Again, an artistic element enters the picture; some artistic decisions—such as whether a costume needs to be replaced or scenery needs to be altered—affect costs. The producer or manager must find additional sources of money or must determine that a change is important enough artistically to justify taking funds away from another item in the budget. In other words, the producer or manager must work very closely with the director and the designers in balancing artistic and financial needs.

The producer or manager is also responsible for publicity. The audience would never get to the theater if it did not know when and where a play was being presented. The producer or manager must advertise the production and decide whether the advertisements should be placed in daily newspapers, on radio, on television, in student newspapers, in magazines, or elsewhere.

A host of other problems come under the supervision of the producer or manager: tickets must be ordered, the box office must be maintained, and plans must be made ahead of time for how tickets are to be sold. Securing ushers, printing programs, and maintaining the auditorium—usually called the ***front of the house***—are also the responsibility of the producer or manager.

Once again, plans must be made well in advance. In many theater organizations, an entire season—the plays that will be produced, the personnel who will be in charge, and the supplies that will be required—is planned a year ahead of time. It should be clear that coordination and cooperation are as important in this area as they are for the production onstage. (For the organization of a nonprofit theater company, see the chart on page 165.)

COMPLETING THE PICTURE: PLAYWRIGHT, DIRECTOR, AND PRODUCER

A theater presentation can be compared to a mosaic consisting of many brightly colored pieces of stone that fit together to form a complete picture. The playwright puts the words and ideas together; the performers bring them to life; the director integrates the artistic elements; the producer or manager coordinates the business side of a production. The separate pieces in the mosaic must become parts of an artistic whole, providing a complete theater experience.

In Part 3 we turn from the audience and the performers and director to the type of theater being performed. Is it intended merely to entertain, or does it have a more serious purpose? Does it take a tragic or sad view of people and events, or a basically comic view?

SUMMARY

1. The term *director* did not come into general use until the end of the nineteenth century. Certain functions of the director, however—organizing the production, instilling discipline in the performers, and setting a tone for the production—have been carried out since the beginning of theater by someone in authority.

2. The director's duties became more crucial in the twentieth century. Because of the fragmentation of society and the many styles and cultures that now exist side by side, it is necessary for someone to impose a point of view and a single vision on individual productions.

3. The director has many responsibilities:

   Working with the playwright if the script is a new work

   Evolving a concept or approach to the script

   Developing the visual side of the production with the designers

   Holding auditions and casting roles

   Working with the performers to develop their individual roles in rehearsals

   Ensuring that stage action communicates the meaning of the play

   Establishing appropriate pace and rhythm in the movement of the scenes

   Establishing the dynamics of the production as a whole

   Supervising the technical and preview rehearsals

4. *Auteur* directors demand that a text serve their own purposes, rather than shaping their purposes to serve the text.

5. Because the director has such wide-ranging power and responsibilities, he or she can distort a production and create an imbalance of elements or an inappropriate emphasis. The director is responsible for a sense of proportion and order in the production.

6. The producer or manager of a production is responsible for the business aspects: maintaining the theater, arranging publicity, handling finances, and managing ticket sales, budgets, ushers, etc.

EXPLORING THEATER
ON
THE
WEB

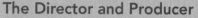

The Director and Producer

Now in its fifth year, the Lincoln Center Theater Directors Lab (http://www.lct.org/dirlab.html) is a developmental program for nurturing stage directors from around the country and around the world. Initiated in 1994, the Directors Lab, according to the website, was "designed as an interactive forum to engage emerging directors in an interactive forum in an intensive study of their craft and to foster collaborative relationships among a community of artists."

Exercises:

1. After you have been to the site and examined the productions that were directed last season, check out the Directors Lab Directory at http://www.lct.org/dlsurvey.html to see which young directors are participating in this program.

   What survey questions were asked of these young directors? Why are those specific questions significant?

   Search the survey results using your home state. Read about a few directors. What are their backgrounds? What kind of theater would they like to make?

   Search in another state in a different region of the country from your own. How are the directors there similar to those in your state? How are they different?

2. National Public Radio's online site, http://www.npr.org, is a useful place to look for archived stories about trends in producing theater. A search using the word "theater" on the homepage yields many archived stories about theater production. One such story is Bob Edwards's report from the radio program *Morning Edition* about a new model for producing musicals in New York. Go to the NPR archives (http://www.npr.org/archives) and search for the June 18, 1997, "Broadway Business" segment. Listen to Bob Edwards's interview with Peter Marks and answer the following questions. (Note: You must have REALPlayer™ installed on your computer to hear this broadcast.)

   If large corporations take over the traditional roles of the producer, what effect might this have on the types of plays produced on Broadway?

   What does Peter Marks mean when he speculates that productions driven by the "bottom line" may not be as "artistically challenging" as "difficult" productions, such as a Sondheim musical?

3. The Ranters Theatre Company from the Victorian College of the Arts in Melbourne, Australia, offers a unique website at http://www.ranterstheatre.com/html/ranters.html. Follow the links to "Directors Notes," where you will find featured several of its current and past directors offering insight into their directing processes and philosophy. Select any two directors and compare and contrast their perspectives on the process of directing. What common threads do you notice from one to the next? Does role prioritization play a role in the director's philosophy? How does the director's philosophy reflect on the process of mounting a production?

DEATH OF A SALESMAN (1949)

Arthur Miller (1915-)

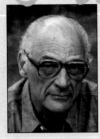

Arthur Miller (1915-)
(©Inge Morath/Magnum Photos)

Chief Characters

Willy Loman
Linda, *his wife*
Biff, *his older son*
Happy, *his younger son*
Bernard, *Biff's friend*
The Woman, *Willy's mistress*
Charley, *next-door neighbor,*
    Bernard's father
Uncle Ben, *Willy's brother*

Setting

Willy Loman's house in New York, and various other locations in New York and Boston.

Time

Late 1940s and flashbacks to the past.

Background

Willy is an older traveling salesman who doesn't produce much business anymore. Many of Willy's friends and business contacts are dead, and he has a tendency to daydream, drifting off into a time when things were better. His sons, Happy and Biff, are not as successful as Willy expected them to be—Biff, for example, was a football star but was not a good student and did not graduate from high school. Linda is a devoted wife and mother, trying desperately to keep the family, and Willy, from falling apart.

Act I: Willy arrives home unexpectedly, having cut short a sales trip. He tells Linda that he kept driving off the road. Linda tells Willy that he should persuade the company to let him work in New York, not on the road. Willy expresses disappointment about his son Biff, who has just returned home after being a drifter in the west. Meanwhile, in their upstairs bedroom, Biff and Happy discuss their concern about their father. Biff is frustrated because of his inability to find a career, and they discuss an old dream of starting their own business.

Downstairs, Willy moves into a scene from the past in which he brags to young Biff about what a great salesman he is and the important people he knows. Bernard, a neighbor who is the same age as Biff, is a good student. Because he idolizes the athletic Biff, Bernard wants to help Biff study so that he can pass his exams. Willy puts Bernard down as the "studious type" and tells Biff that personality will get him further than studying.

Willy, in a different flashback, is shown in Boston with the Woman, with whom he is having an affair. Back in the present, Willy and his neighbor Charley have a minor confrontation during which Willy speaks out loud to his brother Ben's ghost. In Willy's fantasy, Ben was a successful self-made man who once, years ago, offered Willy a chance to go with him, a chance which Willy refused.

Linda defends Willy to the boys and asks Biff to try to get along better with Willy. Linda confesses to the boys that she thinks Willy is trying to kill himself. Willy confronts Biff about Biff's career and is rude to Linda while Biff

Brian Dennehy as Willy Loman.
(Sara Krulwich/The New York Times)

stands up for her. Before they retire to bed, they make amends. Later, Biff finds, attached to a gas line in the basement, some rubber tubing that Willy had planned to use to kill himself.

Act II: The next morning. Willy seems optimistic about the future: Biff represents Willy's final chance to prove that he has not been a total failure, and Willy believes that Biff's former boss will give Biff a job. Also, Linda thinks that Willy has taken the rubber hose away and is no longer contemplating suicide, but later she finds out that it was Biff who removed it.

The scene shifts to Willy's office, where Willy meets with his boss, Howard Wagner, to ask for an assignment to the New York office. Willy is aggressive but becomes desperate when Howard refuses to give him a New York job and then fires him. Willy leaves in despair and vents his frustration on Ben's ghost.

The scene moves to Charley's office, where Willy and Charley's son, Bernard, now a successful lawyer, discuss the time when Biff failed mathematics. Willy blames Biff's failures on that one incident. Bernard says that he always wondered why Biff didn't go to summer school, as he had planned, after he failed. Willy is evasive. Willy asks Charley for a loan; but when Charley offers him a job, as he has often done, Willy turns it down out of pride.

The scene shifts to a restaurant where Biff and Happy are waiting for Willy. Happy is flirting with a young woman at a nearby table. Biff arrives and tells Happy that he had an unsuccessful meeting with his ex-boss; but Willy, when he arrives, won't let Biff tell the real story—Willy wants to hear only a manufactured, upbeat account. Willy admits to the boys that he has been fired and recalls the time when Biff failed math.

Elizabeth Franz as Linda Loman and Brian Dennehy as Willy Loman. (© Eric Y. Exit/The Goodman Theatre)

The scene shifts to the past and a hotel room in Boston where Willy is with the Woman; the young Biff shows up unannounced and finds them together. Biff feels that everything Willy stands for is false and returns home beaten. Back in the present, Happy and Biff leave Willy alone in the restaurant, distraught and fantasizing.

At home, a bitter Linda accuses the sons of deserting Willy in his hour of need when they left him at the restaurant. Willy, still caught up in fantasies, has returned home to plant a garden at night. He tells an imaginary Ben about his insurance policy—the $20,000 would help Biff get on his feet. Back in the present, Willy accuses Biff of blaming him for his own failure, though Biff denies it. Biff tells Willy that he has finally come to realize the truth about himself and tries desperately to make Willy see the truth about

his own failures. Although Willy cannot, there is a momentary reconciliation between him and Biff. Linda is still afraid for Willy and wants him to come to bed. Alone, he gets into his car, drives off, and kills himself in an automobile accident. In the final scene, at his funeral, Linda expresses her sorrow and confusion.

Discussion Questions
- Relate the actions of the characters in *Death of a Salesman* to role playing in everyday life.
- Was Willy Loman a man who fooled himself all his life, or was he a victim of a system?
- Could Linda have done more to change the family situation? Could Biff?
- Is the action of the play confusing, moving, as it does, in and out of the past?

Play Synopsis

THE THREE SISTERS (1900)
Anton Chekhov (1860-1904)

Chief Characters

Andrei Sergeevich Prozoroff
Natalia Ivanovna, *his fiancée, later his wife*
Olga, *his sister*
Masha, *his sister*
Irina, *his sister*
Kulygin (Fyodor Ilyich), *a high school teacher, husband of Masha*
Vershinin (Alexander Ignatievich), *lieutenant colonel, a battery commander*
Tusenbach (Nikolai Lvovich), *baron, lieutenant*
Solyony (Vasili Vasilievich), *staff captain*
Tchebutykin (Ivan Romanovich), *an army doctor*
Ferapont, porter of district board, *an old man*
Anfisa, the nurse, *an eighty-year-old woman*

Background

Three sisters—Olga, a schoolteacher; Masha, who is married to a teacher; and Irina, the youngest—are living in a provincial Russian town. They have moved there from Moscow, because their father, an important military figure, had died one year before the play opens. The sisters live in a house with their brother, Andrei, who is likable but weak. He is considering marriage with Natalia, a local woman who has not had the same upbringing as the sisters.

Act I: The play opens on Irina's birthday; the scene is the drawing room of the Prozoroff home. The three sisters are together. They speak of their father and how they miss Moscow. Three army men—Tusenbach, Tchebutykin, and Solyony—enter; they are stationed at a nearby army post. Tusenbach, a baron, is attracted to Irina; he and Irina speak of the importance of work, though neither of them engages in serious work. Lieutenant

Colonel Vershinin arrives. He and the unhappy Masha, who always dresses in black, are attracted to each other. Andrei, the brother of the three sisters, enters. He has been courting Natalia, whom the sisters criticize for the garish way she dresses. Natalia arrives, wearing an outfit of which they disapprove. Everyone goes in to eat dinner, but Natalia is embarrassed, angry, and unhappy at the way she has been treated. Andrei consoles her as the act ends.

Act II: It is a year or so later. Natalia and Andrei have gotten married, and she has had a baby. Furthermore, Natalia has begun to assert herself. There is to be a party, but she puts a stop to it. Also, she wants to make Olga and Irina share a room so that she can have a separate room for her son. Masha and Vershinin, each of whom is married to someone else, have a scene together. Solyony—a difficult, iconoclastic character—declares his attraction to Irina. Natalia, who has stopped the party in which the three sisters were to take part, herself goes out for an evening with a local official whom she is seeing—leaving her husband and child behind.

Act III: The scene is the room now shared by Olga and Irina. There has been a fire in town, and the sisters plan to send clothes to help the victims. They note that Natalia is too self-centered to think of such a thing; in addition, Natalia mistreats the servants, especially Anfisa, an elderly maid who has been with the family many years. Masha explains to her husband Kulygin that her brother Andrei has mortgaged the house (in which the sisters share ownership) in order to pay his gambling debts; Natalia has the remainder of the money he has borrowed. Irina weeps in

disappointment at the failure of the brother from whom so much had been expected. Irina is now working in the town council offices, but she is no happier; she realizes that she will probably never return to Moscow. Masha confesses to her sisters that she loves Vershinin: "It is all awful," she says, and she asks, "How are we going to live through our lives? What is to become of us?" The sisters want to confront Andrei about his and his wife's behavior; but before they do, he accuses himself. As the act ends, Irina agrees to marry Tusenbach, although her heart is not really in it. What all three sisters want most is to return to Moscow.

Act IV: The scene is an old garden outside the Prozoroff house. Symbolically, the three sisters have been put out of their own house. Olga has become headmistress of the school where she teaches and has moved there, taking the maid Anfisa with her. Irina is frightened of the future. Tchebutykin, an old family friend, tries to be optimistic and cheerful. Tusenbach says good-bye to Irina, as if he is just leaving with his regiment, which is due to depart. Olga says good-bye to Vershinin; though Vershinin and Masha have been drawn together, it appears as if Olga has also silently been attracted to him. Masha and Vershinin also part; Vershinin tries to be philosophical. Andrei speaks of how his life has been wasted and asks what went wrong. A band plays in this distance—the departure of the regiment. But Tchebutykin comes with the sad news that Tusenbach, who has been challenged to a duel, has been killed in the duel. The three sisters huddle together in grief. Masha says: "They are leaving us. . . . We remain alone, to begin our life over again. We must live. . . . We must live." Irina, her head on Olga's

bosom, proclaims: "There will come a time when everybody will know why, for what purpose, there is all this suffering. But now we must live, we must work. Tomorrow, I will go away alone, and I'll teach and give my whole life to those who need it." Olga muses on the fact that a band is playing, and she tries to cheer up her sisters, but they know the sad truth: everyone is leaving, and the three sisters have been dispossessed.

Discussion Questions

- Suggest performers from theater, film, or television who might successfully play Olga, Masha, Irina, Andrei, Natalia.
- What acting technique seems most appropriate for *The Three Sisters?* Explain your choice.
- If you were an actress playing Irina, what type of research would you undertake, and what questions would you ask about your character?

Left to right: René Augesen as Masha, Sanaa Lathan as Irina, Greer Goodman as Olga. (© T. Charles Erickson/Yale School of Drama)

Part 3

The Play

Types of Theater

There are many types of theater, serving different purposes, and sometimes more than one purpose: to entertain, to challenge, to inspire, to instruct. ✤ One reason for different types of plays is that they are written from different points of view: serious, comic, or some combination of the two. The drawing by Al Hirschfeld depicts a scene from Eugene O'Neill's *A Moon for the Misbegotten*. O'Neill wrote several plays that could be called modern tragedies. ✤ The play represented here is a modern, domestic drama, obviously written in a serious vein.

CHAPTER EIGHT

The Text: Subject, Purpose, and Perspective

Performers and directors, considered in Part Two, do not create theater by themselves; actresses and actors must have something to perform, and directors must have material to prepare for presentation. Historically, in both western and Asian theater, this has been a **text or script,** usually prepared by a *playwright,* also known as a *dramatist.*

There are times in theater history when groups of performers create theater pieces. One example is **commedia dell'arte,** the improvisatory theater of the Italian Renaissance; another example is found in improvisatory experimental theater groups in the United States in recent years. A third example is performance art, a type of theatrical presentation that came to the forefront in the 1980s and 1990s. In performance art, one or more individuals develop a stage work. The work could consist of storytelling—a form made popular by the writer and performer Spalding Gray (1941–)—or it might be a one-woman theatrical presentation such as *Fires in the Mirror* or *Twilight: Los Angeles, 1992,* by Anna Deveare Smith (1950–), about life in urban ghettos.

◀ THE PLAYWRIGHT'S PURPOSE

Those who create a theater piece have a responsibility to make clear to the audience its purpose and point of view. The intention may be to entertain, to raise timeless questions, as is often the case in tragedy, or to make a political or social comment. In his play Doctor Faustus, *Christopher Marlowe's purpose was to write a tragedy that would inspire both awe and fear in his audience. It presented the story of a man who sold his soul to the devil in return for earthly power over people, including beautiful women. The language was elevated, iambic pentameter, and the characters larger than life, giving the play scope and importance. Shown here is Jude Law in the title role in a recent production at the Young Vic Theatre in London.* (© Donald Cooper/PhotoSTAGE)

In the twentieth century, as we have seen, the director sometimes functioned as the person creating a theater piece. In such cases, a director might take a text—either a play or some other form of writing such as a novel, a biography, or a work of history—and combine that with other material (visual, musical, improvised) to develop a new work. It is important to remember, however, that when actors or a director create a theatrical event, the function of the playwright has not been eliminated; it has simply been taken over by others. The need for a guiding scenario or script remains. Most often, though, it has been the *playwright* who has created a dramatic script, and in Part 4 we will discuss how the playwright develops dramatic structure and creates dramatic characters.

Meanwhile, in Part 3 we will focus on the script itself. Whether established by a playwright, a director, or a performance artist, every theater piece reflects choices as to subject matter, the focus of the work, and the worldview expressed (tragic, comic, and so forth).

SUBJECT

As noted in the Introduction, the subject matter of theater is human beings. But clearly a play cannot simply be about "human beings" or "people" or even about "people's concerns," and the first task of the person or persons creating a theater piece is to decide what aspect of people and their concerns to present.

Will the work be based on history—for example, an episode or incident from the American Civil War, from World War II, or from the Vietnamese War? Perhaps it will be based on biography—on the life of Abraham Lincoln, Eleanor Roosevelt, or Martin Luther King, Jr. Perhaps it will be an exploration of the creator's own life: the problems of growing up or facing a personal crisis as an adult. Still another possibility would be an imaginary story, either resembling everyday life or based on a fantasy or a nightmare.

FOCUS AND EMPHASIS

Along with the subject to be dramatized, there is also the question of determining who and what to focus on. For example, a playwright can emphasize a particular character trait in one play and its opposite in another. This is what Henrik Ibsen often did. In his *Brand,* the leading character is a stark, uncompromising figure who will sacrifice everything—family, friends, love—for his principles. In contrast to this, the leading character in Ibsen's *Peer Gynt* is always compromising, always running away.

In carrying out the purpose of a theater piece, those creating it determine how to interpret the characters or story. A playwright, for instance, may change the order of events. A good example is the way the myth of Electra was treated by three prominent tragic dramatists in Greece in the fifth century B.C.E. The story concerns Electra's revenge on her mother, Clytemnestra, and her stepfather, Aegisthus, for having murdered her natural father, Agamemnon. In carrying out her revenge, Electra enlists the help of Orestes, her brother, who has just returned from exile. In the versions by Aeschylus and Euripides, the stepfather is murdered first, and the mother, Clytemnestra, is murdered last. This puts emphasis on the terror of murdering one's own mother. But Sophocles saw the story differently. He wanted to emphasize that Electra and her brother were acting honorably and to play down the mother's murder. And so he reversed the order of the murders: he had the mother killed first; then he built up to the righteous murder of the stepfather as the final deed. The change made by Sophocles indicates the latitude writers, directors, and performance artists have in altering events to suit their artistic purposes.

ESTABLISHING FOCUS
AND POINT OF VIEW

Playwrights establish a point of view about their subjects and their characters which may vary markedly from one writer to another. An interesting example is the way three Greek tragic dramatists—Aeschylus, Sophocles, and Euripides—treated the story of Electra. Electra and her brother Orestes conspire to kill their mother, Clytemnestra, who has killed their father, Agamemnon. Aeschylus, the first dramatist to tell the story, presented the murder of the mother as a terrible act. Sophocles saw the murder as a noble deed, carrying out the will of the gods. Euripides reduced Electra almost to the level of a peasant and in his version the murder of Clytemnestra is a cowardly act. The scene here shows Electra, as performed by Zoë Wanamaker, in the Sophoclean version of the play at the McCarter Theatre in Princeton. (© T. Charles Erickson)

PURPOSE

An artwork can serve any one of a number of purposes. Let us take painting as an example. One painter may simply want to reproduce a landscape; another may want to create a portrait that captures the essence of a person; a third might paint a picture that makes a political statement.

Similarly, every theater event is intended to serve some purpose. It may be casual, much as someone says, "Let's go to the movies tonight," or "Let's watch television." Consciously or unconsciously, the purpose here is entertainment or "escape." The purpose may also be more conscious and deliberate. In Chapter 2, it is noted that various types of contemporary theater are presented for a specific purpose: feminist theater, Hispanic theater, African American theater, and so on. In theater of this kind, both those who create the event and members of the audience have a definite purpose in mind.

Historically, the creators of theater—playwrights, directors, performers, and others—have intended it to serve a range of purposes. There have been times, for example, when the purpose of a theater event was religious. In the medieval period, when very few people could read or write, theater performances were used to teach religious precepts and stories from the Bible. At times theater serves a civic function. For example, a pageant may be arranged to present the history of a community. This kind of play is frequently given on important civic anniversaries.

In England in the seventeenth century, plays were frequently written for the purpose of entertaining royalty as part of a celebration. In France, Molière wrote several of his plays as part of an entertainment at a château, or for presentation before King Louis XIV at Versailles. Such a play would be only one of several activities—perhaps including a banquet, a dance, and fireworks—arranged for an evening, or for a celebration of several days' duration.

Sometimes, in present-day theater, a playwright or director may begin work on a theater piece without knowing its exact purpose—which may emerge only as it goes through several revisions. Before a piece goes into production, however, those creating it should have determined where it is headed.

Once the purpose is clear, a primary task of those developing a production is to make certain that everyone concerned is moving toward the same goal—otherwise, various elements will be in conflict. If, for instance, a playwright intends his or her work to be serious and the performers make fun of it, they are at cross-purposes.

VIEWPOINT

What Is Point of View?

Closely related to purpose is *point of view,* which expresses the way we look at things.

People and events can always be interpreted in widely different ways. How we perceive them depends on our point of view. There is a familiar story of two people looking at a bottle half-filled with wine; the optimist will say that the bottle is half-full, the pessimist that it is half-empty.

Anyone familiar with the presentation of evidence in a courtroom—in a trial involving an automobile accident, for instance—knows that different witnesses, each of whom may be honest and straightforward, will describe the same incident differently. One will say that she saw a minivan go through a stoplight and hit a blue car; another will say that he remembers clearly that the blue car pulled out before the light had changed and blocked the path of the van. The same variation in viewpoint affects our assessment of politicians and other public figures. To some people, a certain politician will be a dedicated, sincere public servant, interested only in what is best for the people. But to others, the same politician will be a hypocrite and a charlatan.

Point of view is particularly important in the arts. Under ordinary circumstances, those who attempt to influence our point of view, such as advertisers and politicians, frequently disguise their motives. They use subtle

Suzan-Lori Parks: Playwright

A recipient of a 2001 MacArthur Foundation "genius" Award, Ms. Parks is the author of more than fifteen plays, including The America Play, Venus, In the Blood, *and* Topdog/Underdog, *which won the 2002 Pulitzer Prize for drama.*

. . . Some people start from a love for theatre and go on from there. But I was a short-story writer in a class with James Baldwin when I was a student at Mount Holyoke College. He was teaching creative writing at Hampshire College and I took a class with him. We had to read our stories out loud for the class and I loved reading aloud. So he said, "You should try playwriting," and I said, "I'll try it." That's how I got into it. So the love of theatre and interest in theatre came after, came through the writing. . . .

The first real time I spent in the theatre at Mount Holyoke was when I went up there in March [1997] to direct *Devotees in the Garden of Love* [1991]. I studied some theatre at Hampshire College because you could take courses there. I remember I read *for colored girls* and directed it in college—but not in the theatre. We just brought some people together and put on a show. . . . I remember a teacher of mine in the English Department at Mount Holyoke. I was walking down the hall one day and she saw me coming and ran in her office and came back out with a book and kind of held it out like I was a train and she had the mailbag and I just took it and kept walking, and I got to the end of the hall and it was *Funnyhouse of a Negro* [by Adrienne Kennedy]. So I read it and reread it and reread it and reread it. It also had a hand in shaping what I do. . . .

I graduated in '85 and went to London for a year and studied acting because I thought I was going to be a writer. . . . I said if I'm going to do this playwriting thing which I enjoy, I should study acting. I didn't want to study writing because I didn't think it was going to help me.

Source: Suzan-Lori Parks from Playwright's Voice by David Savran, Copyright 1999. By permission of Theater Communications Group.

and indirect techniques to convince us that they are not trying to impose their views on us, though people who understand the process know that this is exactly what an advertiser or a politician is trying to do. In the arts, on the other hand, the imposition of a point of view is direct and deliberate. The artist makes it clear that he or she is looking at the world from a highly personal and perhaps unusual angle, possibly even turning the world upside down.

A good example can be found in films, where we have become familiar with the various points of view, angles of vision, and perspectives which the camera selects for us. In a close-up, we do not see an entire room or even an entire person; we see one small detail: hands on a computer keyboard or a finger on the trigger of a gun. In a medium shot we see more—a couple embracing, perhaps—but still only part of the scene. In an exterior scene we might have a panorama of the Grand Canyon or a military parade. The camera also predetermines the angle from which we see the action. In a scene emphasizing the strength of a figure, the camera might look up from below to show a person looming from the top of a flight of stairs. In another scene we might look down on the action. In still other instances the camera might be tilted so that a scene looks off balance; a scene might be shot out of focus so that it is hazy or blurred, or it might be filmed through a special filter.

In everyday life we resist having someone tell us how to look at things, and so we greet an advertisement or a political speech with skepticism; but in the arts our reaction is just the opposite. We value art precisely because it presents its own point of view, giving us a fresh look at ourselves and the world around us. The viewpoint of the theater artist tells us how to interpret the words and actions of the characters we see onstage; it provides a key to understanding the entire experience.

The Dramatist's Point of View

"There is nothing either good or bad, but thinking makes it so," Shakespeare wrote in *Hamlet*. To this could be added a parallel statement: "There is nothing either funny or sad, but thinking makes it so." One's point of view determines whether one takes a subject seriously or laughs at it, whether it is an object of pity or of ridicule.

Horace Walpole (1717–1797), an eighteenth-century English author, wrote: "This world is a comedy to those that think, a tragedy to those that feel." Walpole's epigram underlines the fact that people see the world differently; it is difficult to say just why some people look at the world and weep while others look at it and laugh, but there is no question that they do.

Once adopted, a point of view is transmitted to others in innumerable ways. In everyday life, for instance, we telegraph to those around us the relative seriousness of a situation by the way we behave. Anyone coming onto a scene where a person has been hurt in an accident will immediately sense that the situation is no laughing matter. The people looking on will have concerned expressions on their faces, and their voices and actions will reflect tension and urgency. In contrast, a person coming into a group where a joke is being told will notice an air of pleasurable expectancy among the spectators and a teasing, conspiratorial tone on the part of the storyteller.

Something similar happens in theater. Point of view begins when a dramatist, a director, or a performance artist takes a strong personal view of a subject, deciding that it is grave, heroic, or humorous. In theater, as in other art forms, opportunities for selectivity are greater than in everyday life; hence a point of view can be adopted in drama consciously and deliberately.

In the case of a playwright, point of view is incorporated in the script itself, with characters being given words to speak and actions to perform which convey a certain attitude. In a serious work the writer will choose language and actions suggesting sobriety and sincerity.

Take the lines spoken by Shakespeare's Othello:

Oh, now for ever
Farewell the tranquil mind! Farewell content!
Farewell the plumed troop and the big wars
That make ambition virtue!

These words express unmistakably Othello's profound sense of loss.

Language, actions, and other elements in a script indicate point of view. In Shakespeare's Othello, *for example, the language is the language of tragedy, especially at moments like the one shown here just after Othello (Ray Fearon) has strangled Desdemona (Zoe Walters). The production is by the Royal Shakespeare Company.*
(© Donald Cooper/PhotoSTAGE)

Another writer might take what is ordinarily a serious subject and treat it humorously. A good example is Arthur Kopit (1937–), who, in his play *Oh, Dad. Poor Dad. Mama's Hung You in the Closet, and I'm Feelin' So Sad,* gave a comic twist to a dead body. The title itself, with its mocking tone and its unusual length, makes it clear from the beginning that Kopit wants us to laugh at his subject.

Once the playwright's intentions are known, the director and the performers transmit them to the audience. The actor playing Othello, for example, must deliver his lines in a straightforward manner and move with dignity, that is, without the exaggerations or excesses of comedy. When the gestures, vocal inflections, and actions of performers are combined with the words and ideas of the dramatist, a special world is created. It might be a

A CLIMATE FOR TRAGEDY

The worldview of a society is one factor that determines whether it will embrace and encourage tragedy. Some cultures, such as Athens in the fifth century B.C.E. and Elizabethan England, have an atmosphere in which tragic drama can develop. In the Jacobean period, immediately following the Elizabethan, tragedy remained a mainstay of drama, even though it became more melodramatic and violent. A good example is The White Devil *by John Webster, a revenge tragedy filled with intrigue and bloody retribution. Shown here in a production from the Sydney Theatre Company of Australia are Marcus Graham and Angie Milliken.* (© Richard Termine)

sad world, a bittersweet world, or a pleasurable world. If it is fully and properly created, however, the audience becomes aware of it instantly.

Society's Point of View

In discussing point of view, we cannot overlook the role that society plays in the viewpoint adopted by an artist such as a playwright. As discussed in Chapter 2, there is a close relationship between theater and society. This relationship manifests itself particularly in the point of view artists adopt toward their subject matter.

Tragedy, for example, generally occurs in periods when society as a whole assumes a certain attitude toward people and the universe in which they live. Two periods conducive to the creation of tragedy were the golden age of Greece in the fifth century B.C.E. and the Renaissance in Europe. Both periods incorporated two ideas essential to tragic drama: on the one hand, a concept of human beings as capable of extraordinary accomplishments; and on the other, the notion that the world is potentially cruel and unjust. A closer look at these two periods will demonstrate how they reflect these two viewpoints.

In both the fifth century B.C.E. in Greece and the Renaissance (the fourteenth through the sixteenth centuries) in continental Europe and England, human beings were exalted above everything else; the gods and nature were given a much less prominent place in the scheme of things. The men and women of those periods considered the horizons of human achievement unlimited. In the fifth century B.C.E., Greece was enjoying its golden age in commerce, politics, science, and art; nothing seemed impossible in the way of architecture, mathematics, trade, or philosophy. The same was true in Europe and England during the centuries of the Renaissance. Columbus had reached the New World in 1492, and the possibilities for trade and exploration appeared infinite. Science and the arts were on the threshold of a new day as well.

In sculpture during the two periods, the human figure was glorified as it rarely had been before or has been since. Fifth-century Greece abounded in statues—on friezes, in temples, in public buildings—of heroes, goddesses, athletes, and warriors. And during the Renaissance, Michelangelo was only one of many artists who gave inimitable grace and distinction to the human form.

The celebration of the individual was apparent in all the arts, including drama. The Greek dramatist Sophocles exclaimed:

Numberless are the world's wonders, but none
More wonderful than man

And in the Renaissance, Shakespeare has Hamlet say:

What a piece of work is man! How noble in reason! How infinite in faculty! In form, in moving, how express and admirable! In action how like an angel! In apprehension how like a god!

The credo of both ages was expressed by Protagoras, a Greek philosopher of the fifth century B.C.E.:

Man is the measure of all things.

But there is another side to the tragic coin. Along with this optimistic, humanistic view, there was a faculty for admitting, unflinchingly, that life can be—and frequently is—cruel, unjust, and even meaningless.

Shakespeare put it this way in *King Lear:*

As flies to wanton boys, are we to the gods;
They kill us for their sport.

In *Macbeth,* he expressed it in these words:

Out, out brief candle!
Life's but a walking shadow, a poor player
That struts and frets his hour upon the stage
And then is heard no more; it is a tale
Told by an idiot, full of sound and fury,
Signifying nothing.

These periods of history—the Greek golden age and the Renaissance— were expansive enough to encompass both strains: the greatness of human beings on the one hand, and the cruelty of life on the other.

To clarify the distinction between the tragic point of view and other points of view, we need only examine periods in history when one or both of the attitudes forming the tragic equation were absent or were expressed quite differently. In continental Europe and Great Britain, the eighteenth century was known as the *age of enlightenment,* and the nineteenth century as the *century of progress.* The French and American revolutions were a part of this, as was the industrial revolution; the merchant class and the middle class were in the ascendant. Individual men and women—alone and un- afraid—were not glorified so much as the groups, or masses, that were be- ginning to stir and throw off the yoke of the past. Enlightenment and progress: together they express the philosophy that men and women can analyze any problem—poverty, violence, disease, injustice—and, by apply- ing their intelligence, solve it. An age of unbounded optimism in which no problem is thought insurmountable, and a sense of moral justice runs strong, is not one in which tragedy can easily emerge.

This is borne out by art. For example, in 1681 a man named Nahum Tate (1652–1715) rewrote the ending of Shakespeare's *King Lear* so that Lear's daughter Cordelia remains alive rather than dying as she does in the original play. Tate's version, which softens the tragic effect, was performed in England throughout the eighteenth century and much of the nineteenth. In times such as the eighteenth and nineteenth centuries in Europe, it is difficult for any dramatist, no matter what his or her personal inclinations, to produce tragedy.

When such an optimistic attitude prevails, the outlook of society, however, serves only as the background in creating theater. In the foreground stands the point of view of the individual artist. Proof of this is the variation among playwrights within the same era. At the same time that Euripides was writing tragedies in ancient Greece, Aristophanes was writing satirical farces. In France in the seventeenth century, Molière was writing comedies when Jean Racine (1639–1679) was writing tragedies. In the modern period particularly, we have a multiplicity of individual viewpoints expressed in drama.

Viewpoint and Genre

Plays that share a particular point of view are frequently considered as forming a group, referred to as a ***genre,*** after a French word meaning "category" or "type." Genres—which include tragedy and comedy—are discussed in Chapters 9 and 10.

Viewpoint as a Collaborative Effort In certain arts, point of view is established largely by a single device—the brush strokes of the artist in painting, or the use of the camera in films. In theater, on the other hand, point of view results from a collaborative effort of many artists. The creation of a viewpoint in theater is the responsibility of all the artists involved in a production, who must add to and reinforce the original concept.

As an example, let us take a production of *M. Butterfly* by David Henry Hwang. The play is based on a true story of a French diplomat stationed in Beijing, China, who fell in love with a singer in Chinese opera, not realizing, he claimed, that the singer was a man in woman's clothing (the custom in Chinese opera) and also a communist spy.

Hwang's play incorporates many elements of Asian theater, not only in the costumes but also in the scenery and in stylized devices like the use of stagehands who, by convention, are considered "invisible." All those connected with a production of this play—the director, the performers, the designers—must be aware of this and must incorporate it in their contributions. The designers, in their use of colors, fabrics, scenery, and lighting, must convey an Asian sensibility. The director and the performers must develop ges-

(© Richard Feldman)   (© Donald Cooper/PhotoSTAGE)

INDIVIDUAL POINT OF VIEW

In addition to social and cultural climate, the individual artist's outlook determines whether a work will be serious or comic. Even two people writing in the same country at the same time will view the world differently. A good example is seventeenth-century France. Racine wrote mostly tragedies, such as Phedra. *Shown above left is a production at the American Repertory Theatre featuring Randy Danson in the title role, on the floor, with Karen MacDonald, standing, as the nurse. Racine's contemporary Moliére, however, wrote comedies like* The Misanthrope, *shown above right in a production at the Young Vic in London. Elizabeth McGovern (standing) is Jennifer, and Jo Stone-Fewings is Julian.*

tures, movements, and vocal characteristics that capture the world of the play. There are a number of memory scenes and quick transitions: the designers and the director must establish a flow and a fluid movement that will make these effective. Above all, the various aspects of the production must be consistent with one another and with an overall vision that reflects the world Hwang has created. (A synopsis of *M. Butterfly* appears at the end of Part 3.)

A Cautionary Word about Genre Before we turn to an examination of specific genres, I should express a word of caution about genres—or categories—of drama. The attempt to separate and organize plays according to categories can be a hindrance in developing a free and open understanding of theater. Shakespeare makes fun of this problem in Hamlet when he has Polonius announce that the players who have come to court can perform anything: "tragedy, comedy, history, pastoral, pastoral-comical, historical-pastoral, tragical-historical, tragical-comical-historical-pastoral." In spite of such absurdities, there are those who continue to try to pigeonhole or label every play that comes along.

Plays do not always fit neatly into categories. At times individual dramas intersect and overlap: some are pure tragedy, but others mix serious and comic elements; some combine a sense of fun with political comment. Preoccupation with establishing categories diverts our attention from the main purpose of theater: *to experience the play in performance.*

Having heard this warning, however, we will find that it is still helpful to understand the various genres into which stage works can fall. A play which aims at a purely melodramatic effect, for instance, should be looked at differently from one which aspires to tragedy. A lighthearted comedy should not be judged by the same standards as a philosophical play. It is to understand these differences that we study dramatic genres.

The category we will examine in Chapter 9 is serious drama. In Chapter 10, we will consider comedy and tragicomedy.

SUMMARY

1. Drama is written and produced for different purposes: to move us, to involve us, to amuse us, to entertain us, to inform us, to shock us, to raise our awareness, to inspire us. Audiences, too, go to the theater for different purposes.

2. Point of view is the way we look at things: the perspective, or angle of vision, from which we view people, places, and events.

3. In the arts, the establishment of a point of view is direct and deliberate; it is an integral part of a performance or work of art, giving the audience a clue about how to interpret and understand what is being seen and heard.

4. Whether a theater piece is serious, comic, or some combination of the two depends on the point of view of the artists who create it.

5. The viewpoint of society also affects the outlook of individual artists in terms of tragedy, comedy, etc.

6. Ideally, a clear point of view should inform and permeate every aspect of a theatrical production. It should create in each play a world which the spectators can enter and inhabit. Point of view tells the spectators how to approach what they are seeing and how to assess its meaning.

7. In studying various types of drama—tragedy, comedy, farce—an overemphasis on labels and categories must be avoided; otherwise, theater is robbed of its immediacy and spontaneity.

EXPLORING THEATER ON THE WEB

The Text: Subject, Purpose and Perspective

The Dramatic Exchange (http://www.dramex.org) is a Web resource for playwrights, producers, and anyone else interested in plays. Playwrights can make their plays available to readers and potential producers at this site. The plays are indexed by author and genre; most are in text file format and can be downloaded and printed.

Exercises:

1. Use The Dramatic Exchange's search tool (http://www.dramex.org/search.shtml) and choose one play in each category: (1) children's theater, (2) experimental theater, (3) comedies.

   What is the subject of each play?

   What is the purpose of each play?

   What is the point of view of each play?

2. Visit any of the mainstream play services such as those listed below to determine the types and divisions of plays utilized within the theater industry. In what ways do the play services differ in their organization of offerings? How are new and experimental texts handled?

Bakers Plays	http://bakersplays.com
Broadway Play Publishing, Inc.	http://www.broadwayplaypubl.com
Direct Plays	https://www.directplays.com
Dramatic Publishing	http://www.dramaticpublishing.com
Dramatists Play Service	http://www.dramatists.com
Pioneer Play Service	http://www.pioneerdrama.com
Samuel French	http://www.samuelfrench.com

3. Visit the Dramatists Guild of America homepage at http://www.dramaguild.com and follow the internal links to access feature articles by playwrights regarding their own work. Choose one playwright that seems interesting. How does this playwright perceive his or her plays? From what viewpoint does the playwright prefer to write? What influences his or her writing process?

CHAPTER NINE

Tragedy and Other Serious Drama

Serious drama takes a thoughtful, sober attitude toward its subject matter. It puts the spectators in a frame of mind to think carefully about what they are seeing and to become involved with the characters onstage: to love what these characters love, fear what they fear, and suffer what they suffer. The best-known form of serious drama, to which we turn first, is *tragedy*. Other forms of serious theater are *heroic drama, domestic drama,* and *melodrama*.

◄ TRAGEDY

Serious drama emphasizes the somber aspects of life, and its highest form is considered to be tragedy. The tragic hero or heroine is usually "larger than life," a person of stature who becomes caught in a web of circumstances from which there is no escape and accepts his or her fate. In Medea *by Euripides, the heroine has been wronged by her husband Jason, and for revenge she sends a poisoned robe to the woman he has turned to. The robe burns the woman to death, and in addition to this, Medea kills the sons she has had with Jason to further punish him. Shown here is British actress Fiona Shaw holding one of the sons she has murdered while Jason (Jonathan Cake) rages.*
(© Donald Cooper/PhotoSTAGE)

TRAGEDY

Tragedy asks very basic questions about human existence. Why are people sometimes so cruel to one another?F Why is the world so unjust? Why are men and women called on to endure such suffering? What are the limits of human suffering and endurance? In the midst of cruelty and despair, what are the possibilities of human achievement? To what heights of courage, strength, generosity, and integrity can human beings rise?

Tragedy assumes that the universe is indifferent to human concerns or—often—cruel and malevolent. Sometimes the innocent appear to suffer while the evil prosper. In the face of this, some humans are capable of despicable deeds, but others can confront and overcome adversity, attaining a nobility which places them "a little lower than the angels."

We can divide tragedy into two basic kinds: traditional and modern. *Traditional tragedy* includes works from several significant periods of the past. *Modern tragedy* generally includes plays from the late nineteenth century to the present day.

Traditional Tragedy

Three noteworthy periods of history in which tragic drama was produced are Greece in the fifth century B.C.E., England in the late sixteenth and early seventeenth centuries, and France in the seventeenth century. Tragedies from these three ages have in common the following characteristics, which help define traditional tragedy.

Tragic Heroes and Heroines   Generally, the hero or heroine of a tragedy is an extraordinary person: a king, a queen, a general, a nobleman or noblewoman—in other words, a person of stature. In Greek drama, Antigone, Electra, Oedipus, Agamemnon, Creon, and Orestes are members of royal families. In the plays of Shakespeare, Hamlet, Claudius, Gertrude, Lear, and Cordelia are also royal; Julius Caesar, Macbeth, and Othello are generals; and others—Ophelia, Romeo, and Juliet—are members of the nobility. Because the heroes and heroines are important, the plays in which they appear have added importance; the characters of tragedy stand not only as individuals but also as symbols for an entire culture or society. This idea is expressed in *Julius Caesar:*

> Great Caesar fell
> Oh! what a fall was there, my countrymen.
> Then I, and you, and all of us fell down. . . .

Tragic Circumstances   The central figures of the play are caught in a series of tragic circumstances: Oedipus, without realizing it, murders his father and marries his mother; Antigone must choose between death and dishonoring her dead brother; Phaedra falls hopelessly and fatally in love

with her stepson, Hippolytus; Othello is completely duped by Iago; and Lear is cast out by the daughters to whom he has given his kingdom. In traditional tragedy, the universe seems determined to trap the hero or heroine in a fateful web.

Tragic Irretrievability The situation becomes irretrievable: there is no turning back. The tragic figures are in a situation from which there is no honorable avenue of escape; they must go forward to meet their fate.

Acceptance of Responsibility The hero or heroine accepts responsibility for his or her actions and also shows willingness to suffer and an immense capacity for suffering. Oedipus puts out his own eyes; Antigone faces death with equanimity; Othello kills himself. King Lear suffers immensely, living through personal humiliation, a raging storm on a heath, temporary insanity, and the death of his daughter, and finally confronts his own death. A statement by Edgar in *King Lear* applies to all tragic figures: "Men must endure their going hence even as their coming hither."

Tragic Verse The language of traditional tragedy is verse. Because it deals with lofty and profound ideas—with men and women at the outer limits of their lives—tragedy soars to the heights and descends to the depths of human experience; and many feel that such thoughts and emotions can best be expressed in poetry. Look at Cleopatra's lament on the death of Mark Antony; the sense of admiration for Antony, and her desolation, could never be conveyed so tellingly in less poetic terms:

> Oh, wither'd is the garland of war,
> The soldier's pole is fall'n! Young boys and girls
> Are level now with men. The odds is gone,
> And there is nothing left remarkable
> Beneath the visiting moon.

These words have even more effect when heard in the theater spoken by an eloquent actress.

The Effect of Tragedy When the elements of traditional tragedy are combined, they appear to produce two contradictory reactions simultaneously. One is pessimistic: the heroes or heroines are "damned if they do and damned if they don't," and the world is a cruel, uncompromising place, a world of despair. When one sees the play *Hamlet,* for instance, one can only conclude that people are avaricious and corrupt and that the world is unjust. Claudius, Gertrude, Polonius, Rosenkrantz, Guildenstern, and even Ophelia are part of a web of deception in which Hamlet is caught. And yet, in the bleakest tragedy—whether *Hamlet, Medea, Macbeth,* or *King Lear—* there is affirmation. One source of this positive feeling is found in the drama itself. Sophocles, Euripides, Shakespeare, and the French dramatist Jean Racine, although telling us that the world is in chaos and utterly lost, at the same time affirmed just the opposite by creating brilliant, carefully shaped works of art. Why bother, if all is hopeless, to create a work of art at all? The answer must be some residual hope surviving in the midst of all the gloom.

There is another positive element, which has to do with the tragic heroes and heroines themselves. They meet their fate with such dignity and such determination that they defy the gods. They say: "Come and get me; throw your worst at me, and I will not only absorb it but fight back. Whatever happens, I will not surrender my individuality or my dignity." In Aeschylus's play *Prometheus,* the title character—who is one of the earliest of the tragic heroes—says: "On me the tempest falls. It does not make me tremble." In defeat, the men and women of tragedy triumph. This paradox gives traditional tragedy much of its resonance and meaning and at the same time explains why we are both devastated and exhilarated by it.

As for the deeper meanings of individual tragedies, there is a vast literature on the subject, and each play has to be looked at and experienced in detail to obtain the full measure of its meaning. Certain tragedies seem to hold so much meaning, to contain so much—in substance and in echoes and reverberations—that one can spend a lifetime studying them.

Modern Tragedy

Tragedies of the modern period—that is, beginning in the late nineteenth century—do not have queens or kings as central figures, and they are written in prose rather than poetry. For these as well as more philosophical reasons, a debate has raged for some time over whether modern tragedies are true tragedies. Small men and women, the argument runs, lack the stature of tragic figures. According to this point of view, a traveling salesman, such as Hickey in *The Iceman Cometh* by O'Neill or Willy Loman in *Death of a Salesman* by Miller; a nymphomaniac schoolteacher like Blanche DuBois in *A Streetcar Named Desire* by Williams; and a housewife who shoots herself, like Hedda Gabler in the play of that name by Ibsen, lack the grandeur of royal or noble characters.

Also, it is argued that the present worldview, in our industrialized, computerized age, often looks on the individual human being as a helpless victim of society. How can a hero or heroine defy the gods when people are not free to act on their own but are controlled by social or mechanical forces?

In answer to these questions, the playwright Arthur Miller argues that it is not necessary to have people of noble birth as tragic heroes and, furthermore, that modern characters do have an element of choice in shaping their lives. In an essay entitled "Tragedy and the Common Man," Miller states: "Insistence upon the rank of the tragic hero, or the so-called nobility of his character, is really but a clinging to the outward form of tragedy." He adds: "I believe that the common man is as apt a subject for tragedy in its highest sense as kings were." Regarding the tragic feeling experienced by the audi-

A MODERN TRAGIC FIGURE

Commentators debate whether modern tragedy is possible. Arthur Miller, who wrote Death of a Salesman, *argues that there can be "tragedy of the common man," and certainly many figures in modern drama bear the marks of tragedy. Shown here is Anthony LaPaglia* (right) *as Eddie Carbone in Arthur Miller's* A View from the Bridge. *Carbone, a Brooklyn longshoreman, falls fatefully in love with his wife's teenage niece. Allison Janney* (left) *plays the wife, and Brittany Murphy* (center) *the niece.* (Sara Krulwich/NYT Pictures)

ence, Miller has this to say: "The tragic feeling is evoked in us when we are in the presence of a character who is ready to lay down his life, if need be, to secure one thing—his sense of personal dignity. . . . Tragedy, then, is the consequence of a man's total compulsion to evaluate himself justly."[1]

In support of Miller's ideas about figures in tragedy, it should be pointed out that today we have no kings or queens—either in a mythology or, except in a few places like Great Britain, in real life. Must this mean that no one can stand for other people or symbolize a group or culture? Do we not have characters today who can stand as symbolic figures for important segments of society? Many would answer that we still do.

Another argument against modern tragedy is that the lofty ideas of tragedy can never be adequately expressed in the language of ordinary conversation. There is no doubt that poetry can convey thoughts and feelings to which prose can never aspire. Some prose, however, approaches the level of poetry; and beyond that, there is nonverbal expression: the structure of the plot, the movements and gestures of performers, the elements of sound and light. These have a way of communicating meanings below the surface of the words themselves.

Speaking about the importance of nonverbal elements in theater, Friedrich Nietzsche (1844–1900), in *The Birth of Tragedy,* wrote:

> The myth by no means finds its adequate objectification in the spoken word. The structure of the scenes and the visible imagery reveal a deeper wisdom than the poet himself is able to put into words and concepts.[2]

The director Constantin Stanislavski, discussed in Chapter 6, stressed what he called the **subtext** of a play, by which he meant emotions, tensions, and thoughts not expressed directly in the text. These often appear much stronger than the surface expressions, and when properly presented they are abundantly clear to the audience.

In attempting to create modern tragedy, the question is not whether we view the human condition in the same way as the French in the seventeenth century or the Greeks in the fifth century B.C.E.—the truth is that those two societies did not view life in the same way either—but whether our age allows for a tragic view on its own terms. The answer seems to be yes. Compared with either the eighteenth or the nineteenth century—ages of enlightenment, progress, and unbounded optimism—our age has its own tragic vision. Modern tragic dramatists probe the same depths and ask the same questions as their predecessors: Why do men and women suffer? Why is there violence and injustice in the world? And perhaps most fundamental of all: What is the meaning of our lives?

On this basis, many commentators would argue that writers like Ibsen, Strindberg, García Lorca, O'Neill, Williams, and Miller can lay claim to writing legitimate modern tragedy. The ultimate test of a play is not whether it meets someone's definition of tragedy but what effect it produces in the theater and how successful it is in standing up to continued scrutiny. Eugene

O'Neill's *Long Day's Journey into Night* takes as bleak a look at the human condition, with, at the same time, as compassionate a view of human striving and dignity, as it seems possible to take in our day.

HEROIC DRAMA

The term **heroic drama** is not used as commonly as *tragedy* or *comedy*, but there is a wide range of plays for which *heroic drama* seems an appropriate description. I use the term specifically to indicate serious drama of any period which incorporates heroic or noble figures and other features of traditional tragedy—dialogue in verse, extreme situations, etc.—but differs from tragedy in important respects. Heroic drama may differ on the one hand in having a happy ending, or on the other in assuming a basically optimistic worldview even when the ending is sad.

Several Greek plays, ordinarily classified as tragedies, are actually closer to heroic drama. In Sophocles's *Electra,* for instance, Electra suffers grievously, but at the end of the play she and her brother Orestes triumph. Another example is *The Cid,* written by Pierre Corneille (1606–1684) in France in the seventeenth century; it has a hero who leads his men to victory in battle but is not killed; in the end, he wins a duel with his rival. In the late seventeenth century in England, a form of drama also called *heroic drama,* or sometimes *heroic tragedy,* was precisely the type about which I am speaking: a serious play with a happy ending for the hero or heroine.

Photo Essay Modern Domestic Drama

Modern Domestic Drama   The problems of families—husbands and wives, parents and children, extended families—are the stuff of domestic drama. For well over a century, this has represented a key segment of theatrical offerings. Here are four examples: *Cat on a Hot Tin Roof,* by Tennessee Williams, (*upper left*) about a Southern family in turmoil; *Hedda Gabler* (*left*) by Henrik Ibsen (with Harris Yulin and Kate Burton) about a woman trapped in an unhappy marriage who feels suppressed by society; *The Goat or Who Is Sylvia?* by Edward Albee (*above*) about a couple facing a crisis because of the husband's attachment to a goat (with Mercedes Ruehl and Bill Pullman); and *The House of Bernarda Alba* (*right*) about a group of young women confined to their home by an overbearing mother. (The actress is Selenis Leiva.)

Many Asian plays—from India, China, and Japan—though resisting the usual classifications and including a great deal of dance and music—bear a close resemblance to heroic drama. Frequently, for example, a hero goes through a series of dangerous adventures, emerging victorious at the end. The vast majority of Asian dramas end happily.

A second type of heroic drama involves the death of the hero or heroine, but neither the events along the way nor the final conclusion can be thought of as tragic. Several of the plays of Johann Wolfgang von Goethe (1749–1832) follow this pattern. Goethe's *Egmont,* for instance, depicts a much-loved count who fights for freedom and justice. He is imprisoned and dies, but not before he sees a vision of a better world to which he is going, where he will be a free man. (Many of Goethe's plays, along with those of his contemporaries in the late eighteenth century and early nineteenth century, form a subdivision of heroic drama referred to as **romantic drama.** *Romanticism,* a literary movement which took hold in Germany at the time, and spread to France and throughout much of Europe, celebrated the spirit of hope, personal freedom, and natural instincts.)

A number of plays in the modern period fall into the category of heroic drama. *Cyrano de Bergerac,* written in 1897 by Edmond Rostand (1868–1918), is a good example. The title character dies at the end, but only after the truth of his love for Roxanne—a love that has been hidden for 15 years—is revealed. He dies a happy man, declaring his opposition to oppression and secure in the knowledge that he has not loved in vain. *Saint Joan,* by George Bernard Shaw, is another example: Although Joan is burned at the stake, her death is actually a form of triumph; and as if that were not enough, Shaw provides an epilogue in which Joan appears alive again.

In the history of theater, the plays I refer to as *heroic drama* occupy a large and important niche, cutting across Asia and western civilization and across periods from the Greek golden age to the present.

BOURGEOIS OR DOMESTIC DRAMA

With the changes in society that resulted from the rise of the middle class and the shift from kings and queens to more democratic governments, we move from classic tragedy to modern tragedy. In the same way, during the past 150 years heroic drama has largely been replaced by *bourgeois* or **domestic drama.** *Bourgeois* refers to people of the middle or lower middle class rather than the aristocracy, and *domestic* means that the plays often deal with problems of the family or the home rather than great affairs of state. In the Greek, Roman, and Renaissance periods, ordinary people served as main characters only in comedies; they rarely appeared as heroes or heroines of serious plays. Beginning in the eighteenth century, however, as society changed, there was a call for serious drama about men and women with whom members of the audience could identify and who were like themselves.

In England in 1731, George Lillo (1693–1739) wrote *The London Merchant,* a story of a merchant's apprentice who is led astray by a prostitute and betrays his good-hearted employer. This play, like others that came after it, dealt with recognizable people from the daily life of Britain, and audiences welcomed it.

From these beginnings, bourgeois or domestic drama developed through the balance of the eighteenth century and the whole of the nineteenth, until it achieved a place of prominence in the works of Ibsen, Strindberg, and more recent writers such as Arthur Miller, Tennessee Williams, Lorraine Hansberry, August Wilson, and Paula Vogel. Problems with society, struggles within a family, dashed hopes, and renewed determination are typical characteristics of domestic drama. When sufficiently penetrating or profound, domestic drama achieves the level of modern tragedy.

In one form or another, bourgeois or domestic drama has become the predominant form of serious drama throughout Europe and the United States during the past hundred years.

MELODRAMA

In melodrama, the emphasis is on suspense and excitement. The good and bad characters are clearly delineated. Sometimes, too, there is a message, a moral, the author wants to convey. This is the case with **The Little Foxes** by Lillian Hellman. Here we see two of the "good people" in the play: the father (Keir Dullea) and the daughter (Nicole Lowrance) in a production at the Shakespeare Theatre in Washington, D.C. (© Carol Rosegg)

MELODRAMA

During the eighteenth and nineteenth centuries, one of the most popular forms of theater was **melodrama.** The word, which comes from Greek, means "music drama" or "song drama." Its modern form was introduced by the French in the late eighteenth century and applied to plays which had background music of the kind we hear in movies: ominous chords underscoring a scene of suspense and lyrical music underscoring a love scene.

Melodrama is exaggerated theater, and it sometimes appears laughable; we have all seen silent movies where a heroine with blond curls, pure as the driven snow, is being pursued by a heartless villain, a man with a sinister moustache and penetrating eyes who will foreclose the

Emily Mann: Playwright-Director

Emily Mann is a writer and director of serious drama. Often, her plays are based on events from real life. She is currently artistic director of the McCarter Theatre in New Jersey, and she has also directed at the Guthrie Theatre, the Brooklyn Academy of Music, and the Actors Theatre of Louisville. She received Obie awards in 1981 for distinguished playwriting and directing for her play Still Life. *Her play* Execution of Justice *won a Drama Desk Award in 1986. In 1994, she adapted and directed* Having Our Say. *Her most recent works include* Meshugah *and* Greensboro (A Requiem).

How did you get interested in theatre? I was in high school, at the University of Chicago Laboratory School, in 1966 and things in my neighborhood were heating up. The Hyde Park area was a seat of political ferment: the Weathermen and SDS, the Panthers ten blocks away. Elijah Muhammad lived three doors down, drugs were coming in, people were getting heavily politicized. When we arrived in 1966 the neighborhood was integrated and absolutely for integration. By '68, with Black Power, the separatist movement had taken hold and there was a lot of heartbreak for everyone.

I was always interested in music, writing, art, and literature, and the theatre became a place where these came together in a very exciting way. You worked in a collaborative fashion and made something beautiful, something positive or critical—but still in a positive way—to say to a community. It felt much better to me than being one in a mass of people marching—not that I didn't march, but I have always distrusted crowds. I don't like that anonymity, being part of a group that can get whipped up. I'm sure it's all my training about Nazi Germany. This rather brilliant guy at the Laboratory high school, Robert Keil, took a lot of emotionally churned up, smart, excited and excitable young people and turned all that energy into an artistic endeavor, making theatre.

I hadn't really had much interest in theatre before that. I remember my first Broadway show was *Fiorello!* about the mayor of New York. We were invited to go because my father, who's a historian, had just written the biography of LaGuardia. I was very excited—I was seven, I think—and I got to go backstage and meet Tom Bosley. But theatre never occurred to me as something you actually did, as a serious person in the world.

Source: Emily Mann from *In Their Own Words: Contemporary American Playwrights* by David Savran, copyright 1988 David Savran. By permission of Theatre Communications Group.

mortgage on the home of the girl and her mother unless the girl will let him have his way with her. This is a caricature, however; true melodrama is an ancient and honorable form of serious drama. It does have a measure of exaggeration, but so does most theater.

Among the effects for which melodrama generally strives is fright or horror. It has been said that melodrama speaks to the paranoia in all of us: the fear that someone is pursuing us or that disaster is about to overtake us. How often do we have a sense that others are ganging up on us or a premonition that we have a deadly disease? Melodrama brings these fears to life; we see people stalked or terrorized, or innocent victims tortured. Murder mysteries and detective stories are almost invariably melodramas because they stress suspense, danger, and close brushes with disaster. This type of melodrama usually ends in one of two ways: either the victims are maimed or murdered (in which case our worst paranoid fears are confirmed); or, after a series of dangerous episodes, they are rescued (in which case the play is like a bad dream from which we awaken to realize that we are safe in bed and everything is all right).

Probably the easiest way to understand melodrama is to look at films and television. In the past century these two forms have taken melodrama away from the stage; before that, the only place audiences could see a cracking-good melodrama was the theater. Movies utilize many forms of melodrama—each with the characteristics of the form:

1. The audience is drawn into the action.
2. The issues are clear-cut, and there is a strong delineation of right and wrong.
3. The characters are clearly recognizable as good or bad.
4. The action is exaggerated, with the main characters always living in danger and on the edge of calamity.
5. There is a strong emphasis on suspense.

Melodrama emphasizes results and will sacrifice reality and logic in order to achieve them. In this, it differs from modern tragedy and domestic drama. In those forms the characters and their problems are credible; thus when something devastating happens—a family disaster, a serious illness, a confrontation between a parent and a child—we are meant to take it seriously. The problems in these plays have substance. In melodrama we identify strongly with the characters, but we do not take their difficulties completely to heart. We know that in the end everything will be all right.

Among the kinds of melodrama we find in movies and on television is the *western,* with its heroes and villains and a shootout on Main Street for the finale, as in *High Noon.* We also find television *soap operas,* with their perpetual crises, complicated love interests, adulterous affairs, sudden turns of fortune, and wicked, insincere villains; *science fiction* epics like *Star Trek, Star Wars,* and *Jurassic Park,* in which once again the good characters oppose the bad and which feature a series of spectacular narrow escapes; *horror films* like *Halloween, Nightmare on Elm Street, Friday the 13th, The Blair Witch Project,* and *The Sixth Sense,* which try to frighten the audience as much as possible; and *detective stories* or *spy mysteries* like the 1940s classic *The Maltese Falcon* or James Bond films and *The Fugitive,* which feature a succession of sensational, dangerous adventures.

Still another form of melodrama argues a political or moral issue. Melodrama invariably shows us the good guys against the bad guys. Therefore, a playwright who wants to make a strong political case will often write a melodrama in which the good characters represent his or her point of view.

Lillian Hellman (1905–1984), in order to depict the predatory nature of greedy southern materialists, wrote a forceful melodrama called *The Little Foxes.* The play takes place around 1900, after the Civil War; the leading character, Regina Giddens, wants to take control of the family cotton mills so that she will be rich and can move to Chicago. She will do anything to obtain her objectives: flirt with a prospective buyer, blackmail her own brothers, and even allow her husband to die. In a horrifying scene, her husband has a heart attack, while she stands by, refusing to get the medicine which would save his life.

A list of significant melodramas would range over most of theater history and would include writers from Euripides through Shakespeare and his contemporaries to dramatists throughout Europe and the Americas in the modern period. Other types of serious drama, tragic and nontragic, frequently have strong melodramatic elements as well.

In this chapter we have examined the genres of serious theater: traditional tragedy, modern tragedy, heroic drama, bourgeois or domestic drama, and melodrama. In Chapter 10, we turn to comedy and tragicomedy.

SUMMARY

1. Tragedy attempts to ask very basic questions about human existence: Why do men and women suffer? Is there justice in the world? What are the limits of human endurance and achievement? Tragedy presupposes an indifferent and sometimes malevolent universe in which the innocent suffer and there is inexplicable cruelty. It also assumes that certain men and women will confront and defy fate, even if they are overcome in the process.

2. Tragedy can be classified as traditional or modern. In traditional tragedy the chief characters are persons of stature—kings, queens, and the nobility. The central figure is caught in a series of tragic circumstances which are irretrievable. The hero or heroine is willing to fight and die for a cause. The language of the play is verse.

3. Modern tragedy involves ordinary people rather than the nobility, and it is generally written in prose rather than verse. In this modern form, the deeper meanings of tragedy are explored by nonverbal elements and by the cumulative or overall effect of events as well as by verbal means.

4. There are several kinds of nontragic serious plays, the most notable being heroic drama, bourgeois or domestic drama, and melodrama.

5. Heroic drama has many of the same elements as traditional tragedy—it frequently deals with highborn characters and is often in verse. In contrast to tragedy, however, it has a happy ending or an ending in which the death of the main character is considered a triumph, not a defeat.

6. Bourgeois or domestic drama deals with ordinary people, always seriously—sometimes tragically, sometimes not. It stresses the problems of the middle and lower classes and has become a particularly prominent form in the twentieth century.

7. Melodrama features exaggerated characters and events arranged to create horror or suspense or to present a didactic argument for some political, moral, or social point of view.

EXPLORING THEATER
ON
THE
WEB

Tragedy and Other Serious Drama

The Internet Classics Archive (http://classics.mit.edu) at the Massachusetts Institute of Technology (MIT) provides full texts of classical literature, links to classical and electronic text resources, and a forum for readers to discuss each archived work. Among the archived holdings are plays by the classical Greek tragic playwrights.

Exercises:

1. On the Internet Classics Archive visit Aristotle's *Poetics* at http://classics.mit.edu/Aristotle/poetics.html. (You can download a text version to print.)

   In Section 1, Aristotle suggests some ways in which tragedy differs from comedy. What are some of these differences?

   In Section 2, Aristotle describes the "perfect" tragedy. What are some of the characteristics of the "perfect" tragedy?

   In Section 3, metaphor is discussed. How does Aristotle define metaphor? Why does he feel metaphor is important for the playwright to use?

2. Visit http://www.hoflink.com/~jimdonahoe/drama.html and read the essay "Modern Tragedy: Fact or Fiction?" discussing the philosophical debate concerning the existence of modern tragedies and their basis according to Aristotle's ideas of tragic structure. Where does your opinion fall on the issue of modern tragedy? Do you side with Aristotle or Arthur Miller? Is any definition all-inclusive? Set up a classroom debate on the topic to foster discussion.

3. Melodrama has rarely been used on the contemporary stage, but it has thrived on the screen. Visit the Internet Movie Database (http://www.imdb.com) to search for some of your favorite films using melodrama as defined in this textbook. What elements of melodrama does your chosen film use?

Comedy and Tragicomedy

Aside from a basically serious point of view, there are two other fundamental approaches to dramatic material. One is *comedy,* with its many forms and variations; the other is a mixture of the serious and the comic, called *tragicomedy.*

COMEDY

People who create ***comedy*** are not necessarily more frivolous or less concerned with important matters than people who create serious works; they may be extremely serious in their own way. Writers of comedy like Aristophanes, Molière, and George Bernard Shaw cared passionately about human affairs and the problems of men and women. But those with a comic view look at the world differently: with a smile or a deep laugh or an arched eyebrow. Writers like these perceive the follies and excesses of human behavior and develop a keen sense of the ridiculous, with the result that they show us things which make us laugh.

◀ COMEDY: MOSTLY FOR FUN

In pure comedy no one gets hurt too seriously, but human foibles are exposed. In farce, more than other comic forms, the emphasis is on laughter. Both the plot and the characters are often extreme, but the results are highly amusing. Shown here are Christopher Fitzgerald and Paxton Whitehead in **Where's Charley?***, a musical based on the classical farce,* **Charley's Aunt.** *Fitzgerald plays the part of Charley, who cross-dresses in the course of the play to portray his aunt. Notice the expressions of the two performers, which indicate comedy—a farcical situation played against the reserved, formal expressions of the performers and the portrait behind them. The production, directed by Nicholas Martin, was at the Williamstown Theatre. (© Richard Feldman)*

Laughter is one of the most elusive of human behaviors. No one has provided a perfect explanation of how it works. One thing most people do agree on, however, is that laughter is quintessentially human. Other creatures express pain or sorrow—emotions we associate with tragedy—but apparently only human beings laugh.

It should also be noted that there are many kinds of laughter. They range all the way from mild amusement at a witty saying or a humorous situation to a belly laugh at some wild physical comedy to cruel, derisive laughter at someone who is different. An example of this last kind would be a group of children mocking a newcomer to the neighborhood who looks different or has some handicap such as a speech impediment. Theater, which reflects life and society, encompasses comedies that display a similar range, from light comedies to outrageous farces.

Characteristics of Comedy

If we cannot fully explain comedy, we can at least understand some of the principles that make it possible.

Suspension of Natural Laws   One characteristic of most comedy is a temporary suspension of the natural laws of probability, cause and effect, and logic. Actions do not have the consequences they do in real life. In comedy, when a haughty man walking down the street steps on a child's skateboard and goes sprawling on the sidewalk, we do not fear for his safety or wonder if he has any bruises. The focus in comedy is on the man's being tripped up and getting his comeuppance.

In burlesque, a comic character can be hit on the backside with a fierce thwack, and we laugh, because we know that it does not hurt anything but his or her pride. At one point in stage history a special stick consisting of two thin slats of wood held closely together was developed to make the sound of hitting even more fearsome. When this stick hits someone, the two pieces of wood slap together, making the whack sound twice as loud as normal. The stick is known as a *slapstick*, a name which came to describe all kinds of raucous, knockabout comedy.

Prime examples of the suspension of natural laws in comedy are silent movies and film cartoons. In animated cartoons, characters are hurled through the air like missiles, are shot full of holes, and are flattened on the sidewalk when they fall from buildings. But they always get up, with little more than a shake of the head. In the audience, there are no thoughts of real injury, of cuts or bruises, because the cause-and-effect chain of everyday life is not operating.

Under these conditions, murder itself can be viewed as comic. In *Arsenic and Old Lace,* by Joseph Kesselring (1902–1967), two sweet elderly women—sisters—thinking they are being helpful, put lonely old men "out of their misery" by giving them arsenic in elderberry wine. The two sisters let their brother, who thinks he is Teddy Roosevelt, bury the bodies in the cellar, where he is digging his own version of the Panama Canal. All together, these innocent-seeming ladies murder twelve men before their scheme is uncovered. But we do not really think of it as murder, and we have none of the feelings one usually has for victims. The idea of suffering and harm has been suspended, and we are free to enjoy the irony and incongruity of the situation.

Contrast between the Social Order and the Individual   Generally, the comic viewpoint stems from a basic assumption about society against which the writer places other factors, such as the characters' behavior or the unusual events of the play. Comedy develops when these two elements—the basic assumption about society and the events of the play—cut against each other like the blades in a pair of scissors. Most traditional comic writers accept the notion of a clear social and moral order—when something goes wrong, it is not the laws of society which are at fault but the defiance of those laws by individuals. The excesses, frauds, hypocrisies, and follies of men and women are laughed at against a background of normality and moderation. This view, we should note, is in contrast to the view of many serious plays, particularly tragedies, which assume that society itself is upside down, or that "the time is out of joint."

TARTUFFE: CONTRAST BETWEEN INDIVIDUAL AND SOCIAL ORDER

A frequent device of comedy is a contrast established between an individual and the social order in which he or she lives. An excellent example is found in the play Tartuffe *by Molière in which a charlatan and hypocrite takes advantage of a gullible head of a household in Paris. The scene shown here is from a production at the Roundabout Theatre with Kathryn Meisle as the wife whom Tartuffe (Henry Goodman) is attempting to seduce. (© Joan Marcus)*

Chapter 10   Comedy and Tragicomedy

In Molière's comedy *Tartuffe,* the chief character is a charlatan and hypocrite who pretends to be pious and holy, going so far as to wear clerical garb. He lives in the house of Orgon, a foolish man who trusts him implicitly. The truth is that Tartuffe is trying to seduce Orgon's wife as well as steal his money; but Orgon, blind to Tartuffe's true nature, is completely taken in by him. The audience and the other members of Orgon's family can see how ludicrous these two characters are, and in the end both Tartuffe's hypocrisy and Orgon's gullibility are exposed. But it is the individual who is held up to ridicule; Molière is not assailing either religion or marriage.

In terms of our image of a pair of scissors, many modern comedies can be said to reverse the positions of the blades: the basic assumption is that the world is not orderly but absurd or ridiculous. Society, rather than providing a moral or social framework, offers only chaos. Against this background, ordinary people are set at odds with the world around them, and the comedy in this case results from normal people's being thrust into an

VERBAL HUMOR

Among the key elements of comedy is verbal wit. No one was more a master of wit than the playwright Oscar Wilde whose epigrams and clever word play are still quoted today. Shown here is an exchange among three elegant ladies (Madeleine Potter, Dulcie Gray, and Anna Carteret) in Wilde's play An Ideal Husband. *(© Joan Marcus)*

Part 3   The Play: Types of Theater

abnormal world. This is especially true of tragicomedy and theater of the absurd, which will be discussed later in this chapter.

The Comic Premise The suspension of natural laws in comedy makes possible the development of a ***comic premise.*** The comic premise is an idea or concept which turns the accepted notion of things upside down and makes this upended notion the basis of a play. The premise can provide thematic and structural unity and can serve as a springboard for comic dialogue, comic characters, and comic situations.

Aristophanes, the Greek satiric dramatist, was a master at developing a comic premise. In *The Clouds,* Aristophanes pictures Socrates as a man who can think only when perched in a basket suspended in midair. In *The Birds,* two ordinary men persuade a chorus of birds to build a city between heaven and earth. The birds comply, calling the place Cloudcuckoo Land, and the two men sprout wings to join them. In another play, *Lysistrata,* Aristophanes has the women of Greece agree to go on a sex strike: they will not make love to their husbands until the husbands stop fighting and sign a peace treaty with their opponents.

Techniques of Comedy

The suspension of natural laws and the establishment of a comic premise in comedy involve exaggeration and incongruity, and the contradictions which result from these show up in three areas—verbal humor, characterization, and comic situations.

Verbal Humor Verbal humor can be anything from a pun to the most sophisticated discourse. A *pun*—usually considered the simplest form of wit—is a humorous use of words with the same sound but different meanings. A man who says he is going to start a bakery if he can "raise the dough" is making a pun.

Close to the pun is the ***malaprop***—a word which sounds like the right word but actually means something quite different. The term comes from Mrs. Malaprop, a character in *The Rivals* by the English playwright Richard Brinsley Sheridan (1751–1816). Mrs. Malaprop wants to impress everyone with her education and erudition but ends up doing just the opposite because she constantly misuses long words. For example, she insists that her daughter is not "illegible" for marriage, meaning that her daughter is not "ineligible." Frequently a character who wants to appear more learned than he or she really is uses a malaprop. In *Juno and the Paycock,* by Sean O'Casey (1880–1964), the self-important chief character, Captain Boyle, complains that the world is "in a state of chassis," when he means "a state of chaos."

A sophisticated form of verbal humor is the *epigram.* Oscar Wilde (1854–1900), a man devoted to verbal humor, often turned accepted values upside down in his epigrams. "I can resist anything except temptation," says one of his characters; and "A man cannot be too careful in the choice of his enemies," says another.

PLOT COMPLICATIONS: A HALLMARK OF FARCE

Frequently used devices of comedy include twists and turns in the plot, mistaken identity, unexpected developments, and a rush of events. A good example is found in the double play House *and* Garden *by Alan Ayckbourn, two plays that take place simultaneously on adjoining stages. The cast must run back and forth behind the scenes to appear first in one play, then the other. Shown here in a farcical scene from* Garden *is John Curless (with his face in a cake), Veanne Cox, and Michael Countryman. The production, directed by John Tillinger, was at the Manhattan Theatre Club.* (Sara Krulwich/The New York Times)

Comedy of Character In comedy of character the discrepancy or incongruity lies in the way characters see themselves or pretend to be, as opposed to the way they actually are. A good example is a person who pretends to be a doctor—using obscure medicines, hypodermic needles, and Latin jargon—but who is actually a fake; such a person is the chief character in Molière's *The Doctor in Spite of Himself.* Another example of incongruity of character is Molière's *The Would-Be Gentleman,* in which the title character, Monsieur Jourdain, a man of wealth, but without taste or refinement, is determined to learn courtly behavior. He hires a fencing master, a dancing master, and a teacher of literature (the last tells him, to his great delight, that he has been speaking prose all his life). In every case Jourdain is made a fool of: he dances and fences awkwardly and even gets involved in a ridiculous courtship with a noblewoman. All along he is blind to what a ridiculous figure he makes, until the end, when his follies and pretenses are exposed. Comedy of character is a basic ingredient of Italian commedia dell'arte and all forms of comedy where stock characters, stereotypes, and characters with dominant traits are emphasized.

Plot Complications Still another way in which the contradictory or the ludicrous manifests itself in comedy is in plot complications, including coincidences and mistaken identity. A time-honored comic plot is Shakespeare's *The Comedy of Errors,* based on *The Menaechmi,* a play of the late third century B.C.E. by the Roman writer Titus Maccius Plautus (c. 254–184 B.C.E.). *The Comedy of Errors* in turn was the basis of a successful American musical comedy, *The Boys from Syracuse,* with songs by Richard Rodgers (1902–1979) and Lorenz Hart (1895–1943).

In *The Comedy of Errors,* identical twins and their identical twin servants were separated when young, with one master and servant growing up in Syracuse and the other master and servant growing up in Ephesus. As the play opens, however, both masters and both servants—unknown to one another—are in Ephesus. The wife and mistress of one master, as well as many other characters, mistake the second master and his servant for their counterparts in a series of comic encounters leading to ever-increasing confusion, until all four principals appear onstage at one time to clear up the situation.

A classic scene of plot complication occurs in Sheridan's *The School for Scandal,* written in 1777. Joseph Surface, the main character in the play, is thought to be an upstanding man but is really a charlatan, whereas Charles, his brother, is mistakenly considered a reprobate. In a scene called the "screen scene," the truth comes out and the accepted images are reversed. As the scene opens, Lady Teazle, a married woman, is visiting Surface secretly. When her husband, Sir Peter Teazle, unexpectedly appears, she quickly hides behind a floor screen, but shortly after Sir Peter's arrival, Surface's brother Charles turns up as well, and in order not to be seen by Charles, Sir Peter starts for the screen. Sir Peter notices a woman's skirts behind the screen, but before he can discover that it is his wife, Surface sends him into a closet. Once Charles enters the room, he learns that Sir Peter is in the closet and flings it open. As if this discovery were not enough, he also throws down the screen and in one climactic moment reveals both the infidelity of Lady Teazle and the treachery of Surface. The double, even triple, comic effect is due to the coincidence of the wrong people being in the wrong place at the wrong time.

A master of the device of characters hiding in closets and under beds was Georges Feydeau (1862–1921), a French dramatist who wrote over sixty farces. Variations of this form—complications and revelations arising from coincidences and mistaken identity—are found in plays from Roman times to the present.

Forms of Comedy

Comedy takes various forms, depending on the dramatist's intent and on the comic techniques emphasized.

Farce   Most plays discussed in the section on plot complications are *farces.* Farce thrives on exaggeration—not only plot complications but also broad physical humor and stereotyped characters. It has no intellectual pretensions but aims rather at entertainment and provoking laughter. In addition to excessive plot complications, its humor results from ridiculous situations as well as pratfalls and horseplay. Farces rely less on verbal wit than the more intellectual forms of comedy do. Mock violence, rapid movement, and accelerating pace are hallmarks of farce. Marriage and sex are the objects of fun in *bedroom farce,* but farce can also poke fun at medicine, law, and business.

FARCE

Farce is an exaggerated type of comedy, emphasizing outrageous characters, extreme plot complications, and verbal wit. One of the finest practitioners of farce of all times was the French writer George Feydeau. The scene here shows Stephen Ouimette as Dr. Moulineaux in Feydeau's A Fitting Confusion, *produced at the Stratford Festival in Canada.* (David Cooper)

(© Carol Rosegg)

(© Carol Rosegg)

Forms of Comedy   Comedy takes a number of forms, depending on whether the emphasis is on verbal wit, plot complications, or character eccentricities, and also the degree of fantasy and exaggeration. Shown here are a variety of types of comedy: comedy of manners (*above*), exemplified by Richard Brinsley Sheridan's 1775 comedy *The Rivals,* which among other outrageous social types features Mrs. Malaprop who uses words improperly to humorous effect; the satire *Forbidden Broadway* (*left*), which makes fun of Broadway shows and performers; the Shakespearean comedy *Twelfth Night* (*bottom right*), as produced by the New York Shakespeare Festival; and the knock-about farce of *Noises Off!,* (*upper right*) by Michael Frayn, with its mistaken identities and comic plot twists.

(Sara Krulwich/The New York Times)

(© Michal Daniel)

Burlesque   *Burlesque* also relies on knockabout physical humor, as well as gross exaggerations and, occasionally, vulgarity. Historically, burlesque was a ludicrous imitation of other forms of drama or of an individual play. In the United States, the term *burlesque* came to describe a type of variety show featuring low comedy skits and attractive women.

Satire   A form related to traditional burlesque, but with more intellectual and moral content, is *satire.* Satire uses wit, irony, and exaggeration to attack or expose evil and foolishness. Satire can attack specific figures; for example, the revue *Forbidden Broadway* makes fun of the more flamboyant or excessive stars in Broadway musicals. It can also be more inclusive, as in the case of Molière's *Tartuffe,* which ridicules religious hypocrisy generally.

Domestic Comedy   The comic equivalent of domestic or bourgeois drama is *domestic comedy.* Usually dealing with family situations, it is found most frequently today in television situation comedies—often called *sitcoms*—which feature members of a family or residents of a neighborhood caught in a series of complicated but amusing situations. Television shows such as *Friends, Everybody Loves Raymond,* and *The Bernie Mac Show* are good examples. This type of comedy was once a staple of theater and can still be found onstage in plays by writers like Neil Simon (1927–).

Comedy of Manners   *Comedy of manners* is concerned with pointing up the foibles and peculiarities of the upper classes. Against a cultivated, sophisticated background, it uses verbal wit to depict the cleverness and expose the social pretensions of its characters. Rather than horseplay, it stresses witty phrases. Pointed barbs are always at a premium in comedy of manners. In England a line of comedies of manners runs from William Wycherley, William Congreve, and Oliver Goldsmith (1730–1774) in the seventeenth and eighteenth centuries to Oscar Wilde in the nineteenth century and Noël Coward (1899–1973) in the twentieth. (A synopsis of Congreve's *The Way of the World* appears at the end of Part 3.)

Comedy of Ideas   Many of George Bernard Shaw's plays could be put under a special heading, *comedy of ideas,* because Shaw used comic techniques to debate intellectual propositions and to further his own moral and social point of view. Though witty and amusing, Shaw's plays frequently included provocative discussions of controversial social issues. *Mrs. Warren's Profession,* about a woman who runs a house of prostitution, deals with hypocrisy in society; *Arms and the Man* is not only an amusing story of a pompous soldier but also a treatise on war and heroism; *Major Barbara* poses difficult questions about philanthropy and the source of funds needed to carry out reforms.

In all its forms, comedy remains a way of looking at the world in which basic values are asserted but natural laws are suspended in order to underline human follies and foolishness—sometimes with a rueful look, sometimes with a wry smile, and sometimes with an uproarious laugh.

TRAGICOMEDY

In twentieth-century theater a new genre came to the forefront—***tragicomedy.*** In this section, we will examine this form that has proved so important in the modern period.

What Is Tragicomedy?

In the past, comedy has usually been set in opposition to tragedy or serious drama: serious drama is sad, comedy is funny; serious drama makes people cry, comedy makes them laugh; serious drama arouses anger, comedy brings a smile. True, the comic view of life differs from the serious view, but the two are not always as clearly separated as this polarity suggests. Many comic dramatists are serious people; "I laugh to keep from crying" applies to many comic writers as well as to certain clowns and comedians.

TRAGICOMEDY: FUNNY AND SAD AT THE SAME TIME

In **The Visit** *by Friedrich Duerrenmatt, serious and comic elements are intertwined. The chief character, the richest woman in the world, demands the death of the leading citizen of a small town, because he wronged her when she was young. This part of the play is completely serious, but at the same time there are also comic, ironic elements. This scene is from a production at the Williamstown Theatre Festival.* (© Richard Feldman)

A great deal of serious drama contains comic elements. Shakespeare, for instance, included comic characters in several of his serious plays. The drunken porter in *Macbeth*, the gravedigger in *Hamlet*, and Falstaff in *Henry IV, Part 1* are examples. In medieval plays, comic scenes are interpolated in the basically religious subject matter. In a play about Noah and the ark, Noah and his wife argue, like a bickering couple on television, with Mrs. Noah refusing to go aboard the ark with all those animals. Finally, when the flood comes, she relents, but only after she has firmly established herself as a shrewish, independent wife.

One of the best known of all medieval plays, *The Second Shepherds' Play*, concerns the visit of the shepherds to the manger of the newborn Christ child. While they stop in a field to spend the night, Mak, a comic character, steals a sheep and takes it to his house, where he and his wife put it in a crib, pretending that it is their baby (a parody of Christ lying in the manger). When the shepherds discover what Mak has done, they toss him in a blanket, and after this horseplay the serious part of the story resumes.

The alternation of serious and comic elements is a practice of long standing, particularly in episodic plays; but *tragicomedy* does not refer to plays which shift from serious to comic and back again. In such cases the plays are predominantly one or the other—comic or serious—and the change from one point of view to the other is clearly delineated. In tragicomedy the point of view is itself mixed: the *overview,* or prevailing attitude, is a synthesis or fusion of the serious and the comic. It is a view in which one eye looks through a comic lens and the other through a serious lens; and the two points of view are so intermingled as to be one, like food which tastes sweet and sour at the same time.

In addition to his basically serious plays and his basically comic plays, Shakespeare wrote others which seem to be a combination of tragedy and comedy, such as *Measure for Measure* and

COMBINING TRAGEDY AND COMEDY

In several of Shakespeare's so-called "problem plays," the comic and serious elements are intermixed. A good example is Measure for Measure, *a scene from which is shown here. Tragicomedy has become more and more prominent in the modern period and has taken its place alongside traditional tragedy, comedy, and other genres as a major form of our time.* (© Michal Daniel)

Nicky Silver: Playwright

In his plays, Nicky Silver mixes high comedy and low comedy, realism and nonrealism, humans and ghosts, wild humor and serious tragedy. The result may be hilariously funny or heart-breaking and provocative. His works include Fat Men in Skirts, Pterodactyls, *and* The Food Chain.

I have no memory of a moment when I was not interested in theatre as a form of playacting. I was not like Katharine Hepburn who put on plays in her backyard and had the Hepburn family playing out different parts. But I think I saw it instinctively as a form of escape. . . . I remember being in school plays, like, in third grade, and I found it very addictive. I think I always knew I wanted to have some career in the theatre. . . . Like most people in the theatre and most people in the arts, I thought it was a safe place in which you could become someone else. Later you find out it's a safe place to vent your spleen, under the guise of literature, and take revenge on those who harmed you. And it was fun—I don't think I was intellectual about it. My initial interest was not.

When I was in junior high school, I spent my summers at a theatre camp. . . . This place was run by a man named Jack Romano. . . . We had classes during the day and were in plays at night. And he had you doing plays like *Follies* or *The House of Bernarda Alba* when you were ten years old. And this was of course far too sophisticated for us and probably scarred us emotionally but it did alter our aesthetic completely.

When I was about ten or eleven my father took me to see *Equus*. I picked the play. It was very thrilling because growing up in the suburbs of Philadelphia, I'd never seen a play in which people talked to the audience. I certainly had never seen naked men on stage. . . . I moved to New York when I was sixteen. I skipped twelfth grade and went early admission to NYU. . . . I think it was just about that time that Christopher Durang and Wendy Wasserstein were emerging at Playwrights Horizons. This was an incredibly exciting time to be going to the theatre in New York City.

Source: Nicky Silver from Playwright's Voice by David Savran, copyright 1999. By permission of Theater Communications Group

All's Well That Ends Well. Because they do not fit neatly into one category or the other, these plays have proved troublesome to critics—so troublesome that they have been officially dubbed *problem plays.* The "problem," however, arises largely because of difficulty in accepting the tragicomic point of view, for these plays have many of the attributes of the fusion of the tragic and the comic. A sense of comedy pervades these plays, the idea that all will end well and that much of what happens is ludicrous or ridiculous; at the same time, the serious effects of a character's actions are not dismissed. Unlike true comedy, in which a fall on the sidewalk or a temporary danger has no serious consequences, the actions in these plays appear quite serious. And so we have tragicomedy.

In *Measure for Measure,* for instance, a man named Angelo—a puritanical, austere creature—condemns young Claudio to death for having made his fiancée pregnant. When Claudio's sister, Isabella, comes to plead for her brother, Angelo is overcome by passion and tries to make her his mistress. Angelo's sentencing of Claudio is deadly serious, but the bitter irony that arises when he proves to be guilty of "sins of the flesh"—even guiltier than Claudio—is comic. The result is that we have tragic and comic situations simultaneously.

Modern Tragicomedy

In the modern period—during the past hundred years or so—tragicomedy has become the primary approach of many of the best playwrights. As suggested in Chapter 2, these writers are not creating in a vacuum; they are part of the world in which they live, and ours is an age which has adopted a tragicomic viewpoint more extensively than most previous ages. As if to keynote this attitude and set the tone, the Danish philosopher Søren Kierkegaard (1813–1855) made the following statement in 1842: "Existence itself, the act of existence, is a striving and is both pathetic and comic in the same degree." The plays of Anton Chekhov, written at the turn of the twentieth century, reflect the spirit described by Kierkegaard. Chekhov called two of his major plays *comedies;* but Stanislavski, who directed them, called them *tragedies,* which is an indication of the confusion arising from Chekhov's mixture of the serious and the comic.

One illustration of Chekhov's approach is a scene in the third act of *The Cherry Orchard* (1904), in which Lyubov Andreyevna, the owner of the orchard, talks to an intense young graduate student about love and truth. She tells him that we should be understanding about people who are in love. The student, however, insists that reason is all and that feelings must be put aside. She retorts that he is not above love but is actually avoiding it, and she insists that, at his age, he should have a mistress. He is incensed and runs offstage. A moment later he is heard falling down a flight of stairs. A crash is heard, women scream, and then, after a pause, they laugh. The women scream because they fear he is hurt—not the spirit of comedy—but once they learn that he is all right, they laugh, realizing that the fall of this pompous lad is extremely comic. Here we have the perfect blend: one part of the scene is deadly serious; another part, genuinely comic.

A comparable, and even more significant, scene occurs at the end of the third act of Chekhov's *Uncle Vanya,* first produced in 1899. Vanya and his niece, Sonya, have worked and sacrificed for years to keep an estate going in order to support her father, a professor. At the worst possible moment, just when Vanya and Sonya have both been rebuffed by people they love, the professor announces that he wants to sell the estate, leaving Vanya and Sonya with nothing. Sonya explains how cruel and thoughtless this is, and a few moments later Vanya comes in to shoot the professor. He waves his pistol in the air like a madman and shoots twice, but he misses both times and then collapses on the floor. In this scene, Vanya and Sonya are condemned to a lifetime of drudgery and despair—a serious fate—but Vanya's behavior with the gun (there is doubt that he honestly means to kill the professor) is wildly comic. Again, serious and comic elements are inextricably joined.

Theater of the absurd is a good example of modern tragicomedy. It probes deeply into human problems and casts a cold eye on the world, and yet it is also imbued with a comic spirit. The plays of Harold Pinter (1930–), a writer associated with theater of the absurd, have been called ***comedies of menace,*** a phrase suggesting the idea of a theater simultaneously terrifying and entertaining.

THEATER OF THE ABSURD

After World War II, a new type of theater emerged in Europe and the United States, which the critic Martin Esslin called ***theater of the absurd.*** Although the dramatists whose work falls into this category do not write in identical styles and are not really a "school" of writers, they do have enough in common to be considered together. Esslin took the name for this form of theater from a quotation in *The Myth of Sisyphus* by the French writer, dramatist, and philosopher Albert Camus (1913–1960). Camus maintained that in the modern age we have lost the comfort and security of being able to explain the world by reason and logic: one cannot explain the injustice, inconsistency, and malevolence of today's world in terms of the moral yardsticks of the past. In *The Myth of Sisyphus,* Camus says that there is a separation between "man and his life, the actor and his setting," and that this separation "constitutes the feeling of Absurdity."[1]

Plays falling into the category of absurdism convey humanity's sense of alienation and its loss of bearings in an illogical, unjust, and ridiculous world. Although serious, this viewpoint is generally depicted in plays with considerable humor; an ironic note runs through much of theater of the absurd.

A prime example of theater of the absurd is Beckett's *Waiting for Godot.* In this play Beckett has given us one of the most telling expressions of loneliness and futility ever written. There is nothing bleaker or more desolate than two tramps on a barren plain waiting every day for a supreme being called "Godot," who they think will come but who never does. But they themselves are comic. They wear baggy pants like burlesque comedians, and they engage in any number of vaudeville routines, including one in which they grab each other's hats in an exchange where the confusion becomes increasingly comical. Also, the characters frequently say one thing and do just the opposite. One says to the other, "Well, shall we go?" and the other says, "Yes, let's go." But having said this, they don't move.

Absurdist plays suggest the idea of absurdity both in what they say—that is, their content—and in the way they say it, their form. Their structure, therefore, is a departure from dramatic structures of the past.

Absurdist Plots: Illogicality

Traditional plots in drama proceed in a logical way from a beginning through the development of the plot to a conclusion, an arrangement that suggests an ordered universe. In contrast, many absurdist plays not only proclaim absurdity but also embody it.

An example is *The Bald Soprano* by Eugène Ionesco. The very title of the play turns out to be nonsense; a bald soprano is mentioned once in the play, but with no explanation, and it is clear that the bald soprano has nothing whatever to do with the play as a whole. The absurdity of the piece is manifest the moment the curtain goes up. A typical English couple is sitting in a living room when the clock on the mantle strikes seventeen times; the wife's first words are, "There, it's nine o'clock."

The American dramatist Edward Albee has also written absurdist plays. *The American Dream,* a study of the banality and insensitivity of American family life, introduces a handsome young man of around 20 as the embodiment of the "American dream." The Mommy and Daddy of the play want to adopt him because he seems perfect to them. We learn, however, that he is only half a person: all appearance and no feeling. He is the other half of a child Mommy and Daddy mutilated and destroyed years before when it began to have feelings. Obviously Mommy and Daddy care more for appearance than for true human emotions.

Absurdist Language: Nonsense and Non Sequitur

Events and characters are frequently illogical in theater of the absurd, and so too is language. *Non sequitur* is a Latin term meaning "it does not follow"; it implies that something does not follow from what has gone before, and it perfectly describes the method of theater of the absurd. Sentences do not follow in sequence, and words do not mean what we expect them to mean.

An example of the irrationality or debasement of language is found in Beckett's *Waiting for Godot.* The character Lucky does not speak for most of his time onstage, but at the end of the first act he delivers a long speech consisting of incoherent religious and legalistic jargon. The opening lines offer a small sample.

> Given the existence as uttered forth in the public works of Puncher and Wattmann of a personal God quaquaquaqua with white beard quaquaquaqua outside time without extension who from the heights of divine apathia divine athambia divine aphasia loves us dearly with some exceptions for reasons unknown but time will tell. . . .[2]

Numerous examples of such language appear not only in the plays of Ionesco and Beckett but in those of many other absurdist writers.

Absurdist Characters: Existential Beings

A significant feature of absurdist plays is the handling of characters. Not only is there an element of the ridiculous in the characters' actions, but they frequently exemplify an **existential** point of view. According to this viewpoint, existence precedes essence; a person creates himself or herself in the process of living. Beginning with nothing, the person develops a self in taking action and making choices.

In theater, existentialism suggests that characters have no personal history and therefore no specific causes for their actions. The two main characters in *Waiting for Godot,* for example, are devoid of biography and personal motivation; we know nothing of their family life or their occupations. They meet every day at a crossroads to wait for Godot, but how long they have been coming there, or what they do when they are not there, remains a mystery.

In addition to the plays of the absurdists, other modern plays also incorporate the tragicomic spirit. A good example is *The Visit,* by Friedrich Durrenmatt (1921–), a Swiss dramatist. In this play a wealthy woman returns to her birthplace, a small, poverty-stricken village. She offers a huge sum of money to the village on the condition that the citizens murder a storekeeper who wronged her when she was young. The townspeople express horror at the idea, but at the same time they begin buying expensive items on credit—some from the man's own store. There is a comic quality to these scenes: the shopkeeper's wife, for instance, shows up in a flashy fur coat. The conclusion, however, is not funny, for the man is eventually murdered by his greedy neighbors.

In tragicomedy, a smile is frequently cynical, a chuckle may be tinged with a threat, and laughter is sometimes bitter. In the past, the attitude which produced these combinations was the exception rather than the rule; in our day, it seems far more prevalent, not to say relevant. As a result, tragicomedy has taken its place as a major form alongside the more traditional approaches.

In Chapters 9 and 10 we have looked at the purpose a theater experience is intended to serve: to provide an escape from daily cares, to make us laugh, to make us think, to make us feel deeply. We have also examined the point of view—tragic, comic, tragicomic—that informs the experience. In Chapter 11 we turn to a theatrical form which can incorporate these points of view in a special way: musical theater.

SUMMARY

1. Comedy takes a different approach from serious forms of drama. It sees the humor and incongruity in people and situations. Comic dramatists accept a social and moral order and suspend natural laws (a man falls flat on his face but does not really hurt himself).

2. Comedy is developed by means of several techniques. *Verbal humor* turns words upside down and creates puns, malapropisms, and inversions of meaning. *Comedy of character* creates men and women who take extreme positions, make fools of themselves, or contradict themselves. *Plot complications* create mistaken identity, coincidences, and people who turn up unexpectedly in the wrong house or the wrong bedroom. There are also physical aspects to comedy: slapstick and horseplay.

3. From these techniques, the dramatist fashions various kinds of comedy. For instance, depending on the degree of exaggeration, a comedy can be *farce* or *comedy of manners;* farce features strong physical humor, while comedy of manners relies more on verbal wit.

4. Another type of comedy is *domestic comedy,* which deals with ordinary people in familiar situations. Depending on its intent, comedy can be designed to entertain, as with *farce* or *burlesque,* or to correct vices, in which case it becomes *satire.* Many of Shaw's plays represent *comedy of ideas.*

5. Serious and comic elements can be mixed in theater. Many tragedies have comic relief—humorous scenes and characters interspersed in serious material.

6. Authentic tragicomedy fuses, or synthesizes, two elements—one serious, the other comic. We laugh and cry at the same time. Plays by Chekhov, Beckett, Durrenmatt, and writers of theater of the absurd use tragicomedy. Some commentators feel that this is the form most truly characteristic of our time.

EXPLORING THEATER ON THE WEB

Comedy and Tragicomedy

Comedy has always influenced popular culture. Comedies written by Molière and Shakespeare are often performed by regional theater companies and are still popular with theater audiences. Consider the popularity of the film versions of *Much Ado about Nothing* and *A Midsummer's Night's Dream,* and the adaptation of *The Taming of the Shrew* into *Ten Things I Hate about You.* On the Web, sites such as Comedy Central (http://www.comedycentral.com) provide inside information on contemporary forms of comedy found on television (such as the situation comedy, or sitcom).

The Italian tradition of commedia dell'arte was extremely influential in shaping modern comedy and vice versa. To read more about commedia dell'arte, visit this website dedicated to the history of theater (http://www.theatrehistory.com) and follow the links, starting at "Italian Theatre to *Commedia dell' Arte.*"

Exercises:

1. Examine the four main character types as described on the "Commedia dell' Arte" page. Identify a contemporary sitcom character that could replace each of the stock characters in your own sitcom commedia troupe. What stock character, for example, is Homer Simpson most like? Which of the many wise servants on television would you choose to play Scapino?

2. Go to http://www.shakespeare.com and search for Shakespeare's play *The Taming of the Shrew.* Do you see any similarities to commedia in the list of characters? Download the play. Do you think Shakespeare was influenced by commedia? Why or why not?

3. Search online for a definition of tragicomedy. What are the components of this textual style? Identify at least five plays that adhere to your definition. Defend your research and choices through course discussion. A website to help you begin this search can be found at the University of Victoria at http://web.uvic.ca/wguide/Pages/LTTragicomedy.html.

CHAPTER ELEVEN

Musical Theater

A significant type of theater, which has its own rules and its own fascination, is musical theater. It can be presented as any one of the several genres discussed in Part 3: comic, tragic, melodramatic, and so forth. The following pages offer a brief history of musical theater and a discussion of its special qualities.

BACKGROUND

Drama and Music

Throughout theater history, drama has been closely associated with music and dance. In ancient Greek tragedy, choral sections were performed to the accompaniment of music and dance. Opera, which began in Italy around 1600, was originated by men who thought that they were imitating Greek drama. Shakespeare, who wrote at about the same time opera began, included songs as an important part of his comedies. The nineteenth-century term *melodrama* came from "song dramas" in which music accompanied the action onstage. In other forms of nineteenth-century theatrical entertainment, such as vaudeville and burlesque, singing and dancing were an important element.

◀ MUSICAL THEATER

During the twentieth century, American artists have been important in developing musical theater as a distinct art form, in terms of both music itself and its integration with dramatic structure. In addition, the production of musicals has become more and more sophisticated. Director Baz Luhrmann employed the techniques of American musical theater production to give new life to Puccini's opera La Bohème, *which took its place alongside traditional Broadway musicals. In the center is Chlöe Wright as Musetta.* (Photo by Sue Adler, courtesy of Boneau/Bryan-Brown)

225

It was in the twentieth century, however, that the form of musical theater with which we are most familiar reached its highest development—for example, in *Oklahoma! West Side Story, My Fair Lady, Fiddler on the Roof, A Chorus Line,* and Stephen Sondheim's musicals. Moreover, these musicals represent a form that came to full flower in the United States. Every other type of drama at which American playwrights and performers have excelled —such as modern tragedy, domestic drama, and farce—traces its origins to another time and another country. Though modern musical theater has antecedents in forms such as European operetta, it is largely a product of American talent and creativity. Proof of its significance and universal appeal is the fact that it is imitated and performed throughout the western world and in numerous other countries.

The Appeal of Music and Dance

Before we look more closely at musical theater, it will be helpful to consider the special appeal that music and dance have as part of theater.

It is not difficult to understand why singing and dancing have frequently been combined with dramatic productions. To begin with, all three are performing arts, and so there is a natural affinity among them. In the second place, singing and dancing have wide popular appeal. People enjoy listening to music at home as well as in the theater. They respond to rhythms and to the emotional pull of a memorable melody, especially when it is performed by a singer with a captivating voice and personality. Dancing can also be immensely appealing. The grace and agility of a talented, expertly trained solo dancer or ensemble and the precision of a group of dancers moving in unison provide entertainment of a high order.

Beyond their value as entertainment, singing and dancing possess an unmatched ability to capture the beauty of sound and movement and to communicate a wide range of emotions. In language there are thoughts and feelings which cannot be adequately expressed in everyday prose, and for these we turn to poetry. In the same way, there are expressions of beauty, anguish, and spirituality which can best be conveyed in vocal and instrumental music and in dance.

Types of Musical Theater

To understand modern *musical theater,* it is necessary to define certain terms—*opera, operetta, musical comedy, musical,* and *revue.*

Opera is a drama set entirely to music. Every part of the performance is sung, including not only the arias but also the transitional sections between them, known as *recitatives.* As a result, opera is usually considered a branch of music. It could just as easily be argued that opera is a blend of drama and

music and should be counted as both; but for our purposes, we will treat it
in the traditional manner and consider it a part of music.

Unlike opera, an **operetta** is not entirely set to music; certain portions
are spoken by the performers, as in a regular drama. Operetta generally features a romantic story set in some far-off locale. An air of unreality and
make-believe makes most operettas remote from everyday life. But the best
ones have beautiful, soaring melodies and a plot that tells a complete story,
however fanciful. Operetta features solos, duets, and trios as well as stirring
choral numbers.

Musical comedy is a form of musical entertainment which emerged
in the United States in the 1920s and which features a light, comic story
interspersed with popular music. Originally, the story was often silly or
far-fetched, but it did relate to contemporary people and events, and thus
musical comedy was closer to everyday life than operetta.

The **musical**, also called *musical theater,* evolved out of operetta and
musical comedy. Examples of this form—*Showboat, Porgy and Bess, Oklahoma!* and *My Fair Lady*—will be discussed in the pages that follow.

To round out the range of musical entertainment, we should note the
revue (also discussed in Chapter 13), in which sketches and vignettes alternate with musical numbers. The important thing to remember about the revue is that there is no single story that carries through from beginning to
end; the scenes and songs stand alone and may have very little relationship
to each other, although they often have a common theme.

A BRIEF HISTORY OF THE AMERICAN MUSICAL

Antecedents

The modern American musical had a number of antecedents in the theater of the nineteenth and early twentieth centuries. One of these was operetta; two others were *vaudeville* and *burlesque*. Though burlesque eventually became synonymous with vulgar sketches and "girlie shows," for most of the nineteenth century it featured dramatic sketches and songs that satirized or made fun of other theatrical forms. Vaudeville was a series of variety acts—music, sketches, juggling, animal acts—that made up an evening's entertainment. Another form of musical production that flourished in the nineteenth century was the *minstrel show,* a variety show that featured white performers wearing blackface.

A production that many historians consider a significant forerunner of the modern musical happened by accident. In 1866, a far-fetched melodrama called *The Black Crook* was scheduled to open in New York at about the same time that a French ballet troupe was to appear there. However, the theater in which the ballet was to perform burned down. The producer of *The Black Crook* had so little faith in his melodrama that he hired the dispossessed ballet company to perform as part of the production. The combination proved wildly successful, and the show toured the country and returned to New York over and over again.

Another milestone was reached in the early twentieth century with the musical shows of George M. Cohan (1878–1942), who was a performer as well as a writer and composer. Rather than imitating European models, as most American composers did, Cohan—in songs like "Yankee Doodle Dandy" and "Give My Regards to Broadway"—introduced a strong American strain. Also, Cohan made his dialogue more realistic and down-to-earth than was common in musicals of the time, and he moved his shows more toward the *book musical.* This is a term referring to a show that has a story, or "book," which traces the fortunes of the main characters through a series of adventures with a beginning, middle, and end. (The book of a musical is sometimes referred to as the *libretto,* and the person who writes it as the *librettist;* the person who writes the lyrics to a musical score is called a *lyricist.*)

By the early twentieth century, with burlesque and vaudeville, Cohan's musicals, and American imitations of European operettas, the seeds of American musical comedy had been sown.

The 1920s and 1930s: Musical Comedies

Around the time of World War I (1914–1918), a truly native American musical began to emerge. The story was often frivolous and silly, though at least it was a story rather than a series of patched-together blackout sketches, as in earlier attempts at musical shows. More important than the story—or book—was the music. A group of exceptional composers and lyricists wrote the songs for these shows. These songs from the musical comedies of the 1920s and 1930s became known as *standards;* that is, they were so popular that they were played over and over again, and many of them are still played on radio and television and are available to the public through recordings.

Among the composers were Irving Berlin (1888–1989), Jerome Kern (1885–1945), George Gershwin (1898–1937), Cole Porter (1893–1964), and Richard Rodgers. The work of these men was fresh and innovative. Their melodies ranged from the sprightly to the haunting and featured surprising modulations and developments in the melodic line. Matching the inventiveness of the composers were the words of the lyricists. Ira Gershwin (1896–1983) wrote lyrics for many of his brother George's tunes, and Lorenz Hart teamed up with Richard Rodgers. Irving Berlin and Cole Porter wrote their own lyrics.

The lyrics were generally witty and clever, and they reflected a high order of intelligence; the rhymes were resourceful and often unexpected. For example, in "You're the Top" Cole Porter compares the singer's beloved to a wide range of superlative objects, stating that the person is the Colosseum and the Louvre Museum, comparing the loved one to a Bendel bonnet and a Shakespeare sonnet, then rhyming the Tower of Pisa with the smile on the Mona Lisa.

The 1920s and 1930s: Advances in Musicals

While composers and lyricists were perfecting the art of their songs, a few shows were steps forward for the form of the musical itself. Among the first were a group of productions with music by Jerome Kern known as *Princess musicals,* presented between 1915 and 1918 at the small Princess Theater in New York. Some artists developed native musicals; others adapted European operetta to American purposes—one of the most successful composers in the latter category was Sigmund Romberg (1887–1951).

Romberg's collaborator on *The Desert Song,* Oscar Hammerstein II (1895–1960), was able to combine some of the best features of operetta with native musical comedy in the landmark musical *Showboat,* which opened in 1927. Hammerstein wrote the book and lyrics for *Showboat,* and Jerome Kern composed the music. It represented an advance over previous musicals in several respects.

Showboat was based on a novel by Edna Ferber about life on a Mississippi riverboat. Thus the story itself was thoroughly American, not an exotic romantic fable of the kind that was generally found in operetta. But it was a serious story, and this set *Showboat* apart from lighthearted musical comedies. The story concerns Magnolia Hawks and Gaylord Ravenal, who meet, fall in love, perform on the showboat, later lose their money because of Gaylord's gambling, and eventually separate. Meanwhile, a subplot—a

SHOWBOAT: A LANDMARK MUSICAL

When Showboat *opened in 1927, it began a new chapter in the history of the American musical. The chorus line was eliminated; a romance between a white man and a black woman was treated onstage for the first time; and some of the problems facing African Americans were touched on. Also, it had a glorious musical score by Jerome Kern and Oscar Hammerstein II. Shown here is a scene from a revival directed by Harold Prince.* (Michael Cooper/Live Entertainment of Canada Inc.)

second romance, between the characters Julie and Steve—represented a first for the American musical: it was the love story of a black woman and a white man. At the time, nothing like this had been shown onstage. There was further daring and realism in the depiction of the lives of black workers on the levees of the Mississippi, as exemplified in the song "Ol' Man River."

The score of *Showboat* included songs that would achieve lasting fame, such as "Why Do I Love You?" "Make Believe," and "Bill." Moreover, these songs were more carefully integrated into the plot than had previously been the case. Another innovation in *Showboat* was the elimination of a line of chorus girls, which had always been considered indispensable.

Another milestone for the American musical was passed in 1931, when *Of Thee I Sing* was awarded the Pulitzer Prize, the first time that a musical had been so honored and a sign that the form was beginning to be taken more seriously. With music and lyrics by George and Ira Gershwin, *Of Thee I Sing* was a satire on political and cultural institutions such as presidential elections and Miss America contests.

In 1935, eight years after *Showboat,* another important musical opened. This was *Porgy and Bess,* with music by George Gershwin, book by DuBose Heyward (1885–1940), and lyrics by Heyward and Ira Gershwin. Once again, the story was powerful and realistic—even more so than in *Showboat.* And the score by George Gershwin, which included "Summertime," "It Ain't Necessarily So," and "Bess, You Is My Woman Now," represented some of the finest compositions written for musical theater.

Porgy and Bess is set in a black community of Charleston, South Carolina, known as "Catfish Row," and deals with Porgy, a crippled man who falls in love with Bess, who has been the woman of a man named Crown. So forceful and complete is the musicalization of the story that there is some debate over whether *Porgy and Bess* should be considered musical theater or opera. It has been performed in both theaters and opera houses, including the Metropolitan Opera in New York.

Meanwhile, other steps were being taken that advanced the musical. A musical of 1936 called *On Your Toes* was about a Russian ballet company being persuaded to present a modern ballet. The musical score was by Rodgers and Hart, and the coauthor of the book was George Abbott (1887–1995). In addition to writing a number of the musicals of this period, Abbott was the best-known director of musicals, and he was recognized for the energy, ebullience, and fast pace of his productions. The innovative aspect of *On Your Toes* was its introduction of a serious dance into musical comedy: a ballet called "Slaughter on Tenth Avenue."

In another Rodgers and Hart musical, *Pal Joey* (1940), the hero is a heel: a nightclub singer who takes advantage of women to get ahead. The presentation of an antihero as a leading character was a further step in the development of American musical theater—which emerged full-blown in the 1940s and 1950s.

Musical Theater of the 1940s and 1950s

In 1943 a musical opened that was to herald the golden era of American book musicals. This was *Oklahoma!*—which brought together for the first time the team of Richard Rodgers and Oscar Hammerstein II. Both had been involved in musical theater since the 1920s, but they had never collaborated before.

Oklahoma! is sometimes hailed as more revolutionary than it really was; many of the innovations it is credited with had actually appeared in earlier musicals. Set against the background of the founding of the state of Oklahoma, it tells the love story of Curly and Laurey, who are thwarted by a character named Jud. During the course of the action, Curly kills Jud onstage. This was considered extremely daring, but several years earlier, Porgy had

THE GOLDEN AGE BEGINS: OKLAHOMA!

In 1943, Oklahoma! *inaugurated a quarter-century in which there was an outpouring of musicals that set a standard throughout the world.* Oklahoma!—*written by Rodgers and Hammerstein—was set during the founding of the state of Oklahoma; it featured ballet as an important element and songs that were fully integrated with the story. The scene shown here is from a successful revival by the Royal National Theatre in London.* (© Donald Cooper/PhotoSTAGE)

killed Crown onstage in *Porgy and Bess. Oklahoma!* was also praised for integrating the songs with the story, but this too had happened previously.

Even so, *Oklahoma!* in many respects offers a prime example of how complete and effective a musical can be. An important achievement was its inclusion, for the first time, of ballet as a crucial element throughout the piece. Agnes de Mille (1905–1995), a choreographer with classical training, created several dances that carried the story forward and became an indispensable part of the fabric of the musical. What's more, the entire piece—story, music, lyrics, dances—fit together in tone, mood, and intention to present a seamless whole. From *Oklahoma!* on, American musicals could tackle any subject, serious as well as frivolous, and present it as an integrated art form with acting, dancing, and singing masterfully intertwined. For Rodgers and Hammerstein, *Oklahoma!* was the first in a long line of successful musicals that included *Carousel* (1945), *South Pacific* (1949), *The King and I* (1951), and *The Sound of Music* (1959).

Choreography, which became such an integral part of musical theater in the decades to follow, encompassed a number of dance forms, from the classical lifts and turns of Agnes de Mille's work to the energetic athleticism favored by Jerome Robbins (1918–1999) to the sharp, angular, eccentric moves created by Bob Fosse (1927–1987). In order to execute the many kinds of steps required, dancers became highly trained and enormously versatile, and they were able to perform everything from classical pirouettes to muscular leaps and rapid-fire tap dancing.

The outpouring of first-rate musicals in the 1940s and 1950s remains unparalleled today. Several writers who had been involved in musicals in previous decades did their best work in this period. These include Irving Berlin, with *Annie Get Your Gun* (1946), a musical version of the life of Annie Oakley; and Cole Porter, with *Kiss Me, Kate* (1948), the story of a theater company putting on a version of Shakespeare's *Taming of the Shrew*.

In addition, a number of new composers, lyricists, and writers appeared on the scene and produced memorable musicals: Frank Loesser (1910–1969), who wrote the words and music for *Guys and Dolls* (1950); Alan Jay Lerner (1918–1986) and Frederick Loewe (1904–1988), who wrote *My Fair Lady* (1956), a musical version of George Bernard Shaw's *Pygmalion;* and the composer Leonard Bernstein (1918–1990) and lyricist Stephen Sondheim (1930–), who created *West Side Story* (1957), a modern version of Romeo and Juliet.

The two decades of the 1940s and 1950s were remarkable not only for the number of outstanding musicals produced but for the range and depth of those musicals. They covered a wide variety of subjects, and the quality was impressive not only in the better-known shows but in many shows in the second rank as well. Along with composers and writers, performers, directors, designers, and choreographers were all working at the top of their form.

Musicals from the 1960s through the 1990s

Fiddler on the Roof, which opened in 1964, is believed by many to mark the end of the golden era of book musicals. *Fiddler on the Roof,* with music by Jerry Bock (1928–), lyrics by Sheldon Harnick (1924–), and a book by Joseph Stein (1912–), tells of a Jewish family whose father tries to uphold the traditions of the past in a small village in Russia, where the Jewish community faces persecution and a pogrom. It was directed and choreographed by Jerome Robbins, who gave it an overall style and point of view that represented the best of the American musical.

(© Joan Marcus)

Diverse American Musicals The modern American musical has covered a wide range of subjects, some light-hearted, but others quite serious. Shown here are examples of the diversity of American musicals. *Man of La Mancha* (*above*) with Brian Stokes Mitchell (*center*) is based on Don Quixote by Cervantes; *South Pacific* by Richard Rodgers and Oscar Hammerstein II it is based on the stories, *Tales of the South Pacific*, and tackles serious subjects such as an interracial love affair (shown below are Brad Anderson and Liz Paw); *Cabaret*, (*next page, bottom*) with a score by John Kander and Fred Ebb (*bottom right*), is set in Berlin in the 1930s and depicts the decadent life there on the eve of World War II. *Hairspray*, (*next page, top*) based on the movie of the same name, is an escapist musical about an overweight girl who finds happiness.

(© Scott Suchman/Arena Stage)

(© Carol Rosegg)

AMERICAN MUSICALS FROM THE 1970'S THROUGH THE 1990'S

Though not considered the enduring classics of previous decades, the American musicals of the last forty years of the twentieth century nevertheless displayed great diversity and vitality. Two examples are Chicago *(above), based on a gangster story, with a score by Kander and Ebb, and* Bring in Da' Noise, Bring in Da' Funk *(next page), a musical created largely by Savion Glover that told the story of African American struggles and triumphs primarily in terms of tap dancing.*

One indication of changes in the musical was the opening in 1967 of *Hair,* a celebration of the informal, antiestablishment lifestyle of young people in the 1960s. *Hair,* written by Galt MacDermot (1928–) and Gerome Ragni (1942–), had no real story line and represented a radical departure from the book musicals that had dominated the scene for the past 25 years.

After *Hair,* musical theater became increasingly fragmented. In the 1970s and 1980s, fewer and fewer book musicals were written, though some successful ones continued to appear. In place of book musicals there were other approaches, one being the *concept musical,* in which a production is built around an idea rather than a story. Two examples, both composed by Stephen Sondheim and directed by Harold Prince (1928–), are *Company*

(© Michal Daniel/The Joseph Papp Public Theater)

(1970), which centers on the life of a New York bachelor, and *Follies* (1971), about former stars of the Ziegfeld Follies who look back at their lives.

Occasionally a musical came up with a variation on old formulas and appeared to break fresh ground. Such a musical was *A Chorus Line,* which presents a group of aspiring dancers auditioning for a Broadway show. *A Chorus Line,* which was directed by Michael Bennett (1943–1987), opened in 1975 and ran until 1990.

A Chorus Line symbolized the ascendancy of dancers and choreographers in the musical. Beginning with Jerome Robbins, the "vision" of musicals was furnished more and more by choreographers who had become directors. In addition to Robbins and Bennett, these included Gower Champion (1920–1980), who was responsible for *Hello Dolly!* (1964) and *42nd Street* (1980); and Bob Fosse, who directed *Sweet Charity* (1966) and *Pippin* (1972).

In recent years, choreographer-directors have often not worked with a solid book or with inspired scores, and as a result, they have emphasized the outward aspects of their productions, stressing the look and style. The result in many cases has been a substitution of style for substance.

Still another trend of the 1970s and 1980s was the emergence of British composers and lyricists in the creation of musicals. The composer Andrew Lloyd Webber (1948–) and the lyricist Tim Rice (1944–) wrote *Jesus Christ Superstar* (1971) and *Evita* (1979), the story of Eva Perón of Argentina; and Webber wrote the music for *Cats* (1982), *Phantom of the Opera* (1987), and *Sunset Boulevard* (1993). Two other large-scale British musicals of the period were *Les Misérables* (1986) and *Miss Saigon* (1989).

Along with British imports, there has also been a trend toward revivals of earlier musicals—indicating that there is not the same output of new work today as in earlier years, but also confirming that these shows form part of an important heritage and that they have lasting value. In other words, despite the fact that in the past two decades top-flight American musicals were not being produced in profusion, the genre remains full of vitality, as illus-

BRITISH MUSICALS

During the past two decades, musicals originating in Britain have become popular worldwide. Building on American musicals, they feature serious stories and the music is often continuous throughout. An example is Les Misérables, *written by two Frenchmen, but produced by Cameron Macintosh, who was also responsible for producing* Cats, Phantom of the Opera, *and* Miss Saigon. *All feature lush music and extremely elaborate scenic effects.* (© Joan Marcus)

trated by such musicals as *Rent* (1996)—which won numerous awards, including the Pulitzer Prize and the Tony Award for best musical of the year—and *The Lion King* (1998), winner of many awards as well.

At the beginning of the twenty-first century, several trends were evident in musical theater. One was that revivals of musicals from the past, mentioned above, seemed to be happening more and more. A second was the occasional appearance of offbeat contemporary shows following in the path of *Rent*. Such a musical was *Urinetown,* a somewhat irreverent show that satirized former musical forms at the same time that it offered a skeptical view of current business practices. A third trend was musicals based on films. This list would include *The Producers,* a big hit of the 2001 season; *The Full Monty; Thoroughly Modern Millie; Hairspray;* and musicals presented by the Disney organization.

In this chapter we have looked at a form that offers a special kind of theater experience—the musical. In Chapter 12 we turn to a variety of types that make up today's rich theater of diversity.

SUMMARY

1. At many points in theater history, music and dance have been combined with drama.

2. Types of musical theater include *opera,* a drama set entirely to music; *operetta,* scenes of spoken dialogue alternating with songs; *musical comedy,* a light, comic story interspersed with popular music; the *musical,* also known as *musical theater,* which evolved from musical comedy; and the *revue,* a series of individual, independent songs and comic sketches.

3. The modern musical is largely an American creation—the only theatrical form developed primarily in the United States.

4. There were many forerunners of the modern musical in the nineteenth and early twentieth centuries, including operetta, vaudeville, burlesque, and the minstrel show.

5. The American musical began to take shape in the early twentieth century, in works such as those written by George M. Cohan.

6. During the 1920s and 1930s, musical comedy emerged: comic, sometimes silly stories that had glorious music with intelligent, witty lyrics, written by people like Irving Berlin, Jerome Kern, Cole Porter, Richard Rodgers, and Lorenz Hart.

7. The period from the early 1940s to the late 1960s was the golden age of the American musical, with a profusion of successful shows, many of them modern classics. These musicals integrated dancing and singing to form an overall structure that had great variety as well as unity.

8. In the past three decades, musical theater has become fragmented: fewer book musicals are being produced; choreographer-directors rather than writers or directors have been responsible for the total vision of the show; experiments are being made with other forms, such as the concept musical; and more musicals are being imported from Great Britain.

240

EXPLORING THEATER ON THE WEB

Musical Theater

A general search for "musical theater" on the Internet yields a number of personal pages dedicated to a wide range of musical productions. Most of the sites post amateur reviews, trivia about Broadway, and current touring musicals. One professional musical theater organization is the Rodgers & Hammerstein Organization (http://www.rnh.com). Although this is a commercial site, it is full of historical information about Rodgers and Hammerstein productions. There is an extensive database, which includes composers' biographies, background information on specific musical theater productions, and bibliographies for all historical information.

Exercises:

1. Click on the "Biographies" link on www.rnh.com and use the drop-down menu to go to the Irving Berlin page. What "phenomenally successful" Broadway musical composed by Berlin won the Tony for Best Musical Revival in 1999? (Hint: Follow the links from Berlin's biography.) Once you have found the famous musical, follow the "Bull's Eye" link at the bottom of the page. What famous singer was cast as the lead in the premier production?

2. Use any generic search engine such as http://www.ask.com or http://www.google.com to research the following list of major figures in musical theater, matching them with a list of their respective musicals. Place them on a timeline and notice that the timeline becomes a web as composers and lyricists work in collaboration with one another. Can you notice influences transcending these collaborations? Contributors:

Lorenz Hart	Jonathan Larsen
Stephen Sondheim	Jerome Robbins
Bob Fosse	George Gershwin
Irving Berlin	Richard Rodgers
Frank Loesser	Andrew Lloyd Webber
Ira Gershwin	Sigmund Romberg
Oscar Hammerstein II	Cole Porter
George M. Cohan	Richard O'Brien
Agnes de Mille	Jerry Bock
Tim Rice	Jeanine Tesori
Tommy Tune	Dale Wasserman

3. Visit http://memory.loc.gov/ammem/vshtml/vsforms.html, the American Variety Stage homepage, to explore the evolution of musical theater forms from the early variety/vaudeville shows to the musical comedy. Create a timeline showing the chronological and contextual changes in the musical form. How does this fit in with cultural developments of the various periods? Does it mirror life? The times? Trends within the arts? With musicals such as *Mamma Mia!* (based on the work of the 1970s pop group ABBA), Billy Joel's *Movin' Out,* and the composite musical *Contact,* what influence is popular music likely to have on the future of the musical theater form?

CHAPTER TWELVE

Theater of Diversity

In Part Three we have been discussing types of theater. In no area is this topic more important than in a development of recent years referred to in Chapter 2, the emergence of *theater of diversity,* especially multicultural, multiethnic, and gender theaters. In this chapter we will examine those theaters, as well as performance art—and postmodernism, a viewpoint with which they are sometimes associated. Many of these theaters reflect the perspectives of groups or artists who in the past felt marginalized or disenfranchised because of their race, gender, sexual preference, or political or artistic point of view.

Each of the theater movements covered in this chapter has antecedents— in other countries, in past centuries, or both; in addition, earlier in the twentieth century significant Italian, Jewish, and German theater traditions developed in the United States. This chapter, however, will focus on the theater movements that came to the forefront in the second half of the twentieth century: African American theater, Asian American theater, Hispanic theater, Native American theater, feminist theater, gay and lesbian theater, and performance art.

◀ DIVERSITY IN TODAY'S THEATER

In recent decades there has been a marked trend toward the writing and producing of plays by, about, and for specific audiences: minority groups; feminist, lesbian and gay groups; politically active groups. Also, other forms of theater, such as performance art, have come to the forefront. A prime example of multicultural performance art is the work of John Leguizamo, who in pieces such as Sexaholic . . . A Love Story, *presents a one-man show of autobiographical material about his life as a Hispanic living in the America of today.* (Sara Krulwich/The New York Times)

These theater movements have a number of things in common. Most emerged in the 1960s and 1970s—a period characterized by social and political protest and by a growing awareness of the rights of minorities. This was the era of protests against the Vietnamese war; of civil rights marches; of the women's movement; of Native American advocacy. In this atmosphere, theaters began to appear that expressed the anger and aspirations of special populations.

After the initial surge of the 1960s and 1970s, the 1980s saw a consolidation of various movements. In the 1990s, some groups became less active while others continued and expanded. In certain cases there was a split between the more uncompromising, militant exponents of a political or social ideal and those who, while retaining their interest in a minority agenda, entered the mainstream of theater. It is against this background that we consider specific culturally diverse theaters.

TOPDOG/UNDERDOG

A recent example of an African American work is the play Topdog/Underdog *by playwright Suzan Lori Parks. Shown here are Don Cheadle and Jeffrey Wright in the production that originated at the Joseph Papp Public Theater in New York and was directed by George C. Wolfe. The play, which was awarded the Pulitzer Prize, is about two brothers, both losers, trying to make their way in life but meeting a series of obstacles. It also chronicles their relationship as brothers.* (©Michal Daniel)

AFRICAN AMERICAN THEATER

African American theater—also referred to as *black theater*—is theater written by and for black Americans or performed by black Americans. It is a prime example of an ethnic theater which reflects the diversity of American culture as well as the contribution of a particular group to that culture.

Background of African American Theater

African American theater partakes of two important traditions. One is western theater, in which actors like Paul Robeson (1898–1976) and writers like Lorraine Hansberry made significant contributions. The other tradition traces its origin to theater in Africa and the Caribbean.

In American drama of the eighteenth and nineteenth centuries, comic black servants were

*Two significant productions in
the history of African American
theater were musicals by the
team of Bert Williams and George
Walker:* In Dahomey *and* Abyssinia.
*The productions featured African
American performers who were
not wearing burnt-cork makeup,
who were not speaking in dialect,
and who wore high fashion
outfits. They were among the first
Broadway productions by and
with African Americans. Shown
here are Mr. and Mrs. Bert
Williams appearing in* Abyssinia.
(White Studio/Billy Rose Theatre
Collection/The New York Public
Library for the Performing Arts,
Astor, Lenox and Tilden
Foundations)

popular characters, but these roles were performed by white actors wearing blackface; it was rare to see African American performers on the American stage in the nineteenth century. A popular nineteenth-century form caricaturing blacks was the minstrel show, which comprised comic and sentimental songs, skits, jigs, and shuffle dances. While the vast majority of minstrel performers were white, there were a few black minstrel companies, some of which, ironically, also performed in blackface.

A theater which did feature African American performers was the African Grove Theater, founded in New York during the 1820–1821 season by an African American, William Brown, and the West Indian actor James Hewlett. The company was particularly noted for presenting Shakespearean plays. Hewlett was the first black to play *Othello,* and the renowned actor Ira Aldridge (c. 1806–1867) made his stage debut with the company. Here, too, the drama *King Shotaway*—believed to be the first play written and performed by African Americans—was presented. The African Grove closed in 1827 after attacks by white audience members.

African American performers in the nineteenth century were faced with the choice of abandoning their profession, accepting roles as stupid servants, or going to Europe, where racism against blacks was not so virulent. Ira Aldridge, for instance, chose to move to Europe, where he performed in England, Russia, and Poland in the plays of Shakespeare, receiving great acclaim.

At the beginning of the twentieth century, the popular syncopated rhythms of ragtime had a strong influence on the emerging musical theater and served as a bridge to mainstream theater for a number of talented African Americans. Bob Cole (1864–1912) and William Johnson (1873–1954) conceived, wrote, produced, and directed the first black musical comedy, *A Trip to Coontown* (1898). The comedians Bert Williams (1876–1922) and George Walker (?–1909) and their wives joined composers and writers to produce musicals and operettas such as *In Dahomey* (1902) and *Abyssinia* (1906). These were productions in which Americans for the first time saw

AFRICAN AMERICAN THEATER

A landmark production in the recent history of African American theater is For Colored Girls Who Have Considered Suicide/When the Rainbow Is Enuff *by the poet, novelist, and playwright Ntozake Shange. The play, which features dialogue, song, and dance, tells the story of a group of black women and the many hardships they face. Shown here are performers in the twentieth anniversary production.* (© Tom Brazil)

blacks on the Broadway stage without burnt-cork makeup, speaking without dialect, and costumed in high fashion.

The early twentieth century also saw the formation of African American stock companies, of which the most significant was the Lafayette Players, founded by Anita Bush (1894–1938). By the time it closed in 1932, it had presented over 250 productions and employed a number of black stars. African American performers and writers were also making inroads into commercial theater in the 1920s. Twenty plays with black themes were presented on Broadway in this decade, five of them written by African Americans, including *Shuffle Along* (1921), with lyrics and music by Noble Sissle (1889–1975) and Eubie Blake (1883–1983). Some black performers also achieved recognition in serious drama, among them Charles Gilpin (1878–1930), Paul Robeson, and Ethel Waters (1896–1977).

African American Theater in the Middle and Late Twentieth Century

Possibly the most significant occurrence for black theater during the 1930s was the founding of the Federal Theater Project, intended to help theater artists through the Depression. African American units of the Federal Theater were formed in twenty-two cities, where they mounted plays by black and white authors and employed thousands of African American writers,

August Wilson: Playwright

August Wilson is currently the best-known African American playwright. He won Pulitzer Prizes for Fences *in 1987 and* The Piano Lesson *in 1990. His other well-known works include* Ma Rainey's Black Bottom, Joe Turner's Come and Gone, Two Trains Running, *and* Seven Guitars. *Two new plays emerged in 1999–2000:* Jitney *and* King Hedley II.

What were your early experiences in theatre? I was a participant in the Black Power movement in the early sixties and I wrote poetry and short fiction. I was interested in art and literature and I felt that I could alter the relationship between blacks and society through the arts. There was an explosion of black theatre in the late sixties—theatre was a way of politicizing the community and raising the consciousness of the people. So with my friend, Rob Penny, I started the Black Horizons Theatre of Pittsburgh in 1968.

I knew nothing about theatre. I had never seen a play before. I started directing but I didn't have any idea how to do this stuff, although I did find great information in the library. We started doing Baraka's plays and virtually anything else out there. I remember the *Drama Review* printed a black issue, somewhere around '69, and we did every play in the book. I tried to write a play but it was disastrous. I couldn't write dialogue. Doing community theatre was very difficult—rehearsing two hours a night after people got off work, not knowing if the actors were going to show up. In '71, because of having to rely so much on other people, I said "I don't need this," and I concentrated on writing poetry and short stories.

Then in 1976 a friend of mine from Pittsburgh, Claude Purdy, was living in L.A. He came back to Pittsburgh and came to a reading of a series of poems I'd written about a character, Black Bart, a kind of Western satire. He said, "You should turn this into a play." He kept after me and eventually I sat down and wrote a play and gave it to him. He went to St. Paul to direct a show and said, "Why don't you come out and rewrite the play?" He sent me a ticket and I thought, "A free trip to St. Paul, what the hell?" So I went out and did a quick rewrite of the play. That was in November '77. In January '78, the Inner City Theatre in Los Angeles did a staged reading of it.

Source: August Wilson from *In Their Own Words: Contemporary American Playwrights* by David Savran, copyright 1988 David Savran. By permission of Theatre Communications Group.

performers, and technicians. The Federal Theater Project created a new generation of African American theater artists who would develop the theater of the 1940s and 1950s.

The 1940s saw a stage adaptation based on the controversial novel *Native Son* (1941) by Richard Wright (1908–1960), directed by Orson Welles for his Mercury Theater. *Native Son* showed the effects of racism on a young black man—a daring theme at the time. Other important Broadway ventures included Paul Robeson's record run of 296 performances in *Othello* (1943), and *Anna Lucasta* (1944) by Philip Yordan. The 1950s saw the first phases of the explosion in black theater that occurred in the next four decades. *Take a Giant Step* by Louis Petterson (1922–), a play about growing up in an integrated neighborhood, premiered in 1953. In 1954, the playwright-director Owen Dodson (1914–1983) staged *Amen Corner* by James Baldwin (1924–1987) at Howard University.

Possibly the most important production of the postwar era was *A Raisin in the Sun* (1959) by Lorraine Hansberry. It tells the story of the Youngers, a black family in Chicago, held together by a God-fearing mother. The Youngers plan to move into a predominantly white neighborhood where they are unwelcome; the son loses money in a get-rich-quick scheme but later assumes responsibility for the family. (For a synopsis of the play, see the end of Part 1.) *A Raisin in the Sun* was directed by Lloyd Richards (1922–   ), the first black director on Broadway. Richards later became the head of the Yale School of Drama, where in the 1980s he nurtured the talents of the black playwright August Wilson, author of *Ma Rainey's Black Bottom* (1984), *Fences* (1987), *Joe Turner's Come and Gone* (1988), *The Piano Lesson* (1990), *Two Trains Running* (1993), *Seven Guitars* (1996), and *King Hedley II* (2001). (A synopsis of *Fences* appears at the end of Part 3.)

From 1960 to the 1990s, there was an outpouring of African American theater, much of it reflecting the battle for civil rights. Amiri Baraka (1934–   ) came to theatergoers' attention in 1964 with *Dutchman,* a verbal and sexual showdown between an assimilated black man and a white temptress, set in a New York subway. His plays *The Slave* (1965), *The Toilet* (1965), *Baptism* (1967), and *Slave Ship* (1970) also deal with the political, sociological, and psychological dilemmas confronting blacks. Among the other significant plays of these two decades were *Ceremonies in Dark Old Men* (1969) by Lonne Elder (1932–1996); *No Place to Be Somebody* (1969), winner of the Pulitzer Prize, by Charles Gordone (1925–1995); *Day of Absence* (1970) by Douglas Turner Ward (1930–   ); and *A Soldier's Play* (1981) by Charles Fuller (1939–   ), which also won the Pulitzer Prize for drama.

In 1970 the Black Theater Alliance listed over 125 producing groups in the United States. Although only a few of these survived the decade, many had a significant impact. In addition to the emergence of these producing organizations, another major change after the 1970s was the presence of a larger black audience in Broadway theater, which accounted for a significant number of commercial African American productions, such as *Don't Bother Me, I Can't Cope* (1972); *The Wiz* (1975); *Bubbling Brown Sugar* (1976); *Black and Blue* (1989); *Jelly's Last Jam* (1992); and *Bring in 'Da Noise, Bring in 'Da Funk* (1996). The last two of these were directed by George C. Wolfe (1955–   ), who also serves as artistic director of the Joseph Papp Public Theater in New York City. A more recent play directed by Wolfe was *Topdog/Underdog* by the African American playwright Suzan-Lori Parks. It won the Pulitzer Prize in 2002.

The National Black Arts Festival, which features theater, among the other arts, was founded in 1987. During the 1990s it had difficulty finding a permanent home and establishing a regular schedule. But as of the summer of 2002, under the leadership of Stephanie Hughley, it seems to have found its footing as a permanent, annual festival in Atlanta.

ASIAN AMERICAN THEATER

Asian American theater should be seen against its background: the long, important heritage of the theaters of Asia. The three great Asian theater traditions—Indian, Chinese, and Japanese—all reached a high point of artistic excellence at a time when religion and philosophy were central in each culture; and this has kept the focus of traditional theater allied to these realms, even though the societies themselves have modernized and changed. In addition, these three cultures created and sustained a form of theater in which many facets of theatrical art—acting, mime, dancing, music, and text—were combined.

BEIJING OPERA
One of the most popular forms of entertainment in Chinese theater is Beijing Opera (formerly called Peking Opera). It combines music, theater, dance, and acrobatics. It also employs the colorful, highly stylized costumes that are hallmarks of much of Asian theater. Seen here are two performers in a Beijing Opera production. (© Forrest Anderson/Getty Images)

Background of Asian Theater

India In India, Hindu culture entered its golden age around 320 C.E., and during the next centuries a number of great dramas were written and performed. What remains from the tradition of this golden age is a group of plays written in Sanskrit, the language of the noble classes. These were performed in various court circles, and they draw on themes from Indian epic literature. The most celebrated playwright of the classic period is Kalidasa (373?–415 C.E.), whose play *Shakuntala* is a lengthy love idyll on various classic themes.

Along with playwriting, dramatic criticism also reached a peak during the high point of *Sanskrit theater*. The best-known work of criticism is the *Natyasastra,* probably written sometime between 200 B.C.E. and 100 C.E.; in addition to discussing Sanskrit drama, the *Natyasastra* also serves as a dictionary of theatrical practices.

By the end of the ninth century, the golden age of Hindu culture had faded; however, folk dramas and dance dramas, based on epic materials from Sanskrit drama and Indian myths, remained popular. In more recent times, *kathakali,* a heightened form of Sanskrit drama which presents violence and death onstage in dance and pantomime, has been prominent in southwestern India. The stories of kathakali revolve around clashes between good and evil, with good always winning; a language of 500 or more gestural signs has been developed to tell the stories.

China The early development of theater in China, like that of many other forms of Chinese art, was linked to the patronage of the imperial court. Records of court entertainments go back as far as the fifth century B.C.E., and ancient chronicles mention other theatrical activities such as skits, pantomimes, juggling, singing, and dancing. The court of the emperors during the Tang period (618–906 C.E.) was one of the high points of world culture. It included a training institute for theatrical performers—referred to as the *Pear Garden*—which firmly established a tradition of training.

A synthesis of art and the popular tradition in the Yuan period (1271–1368) resulted in plays such as *The Romance of the Western Chamber,* a drama cycle by Wang Shifu (fl. late thirteenth century). These plays chronicle the trials of two lovers—a handsome young student and a lovely girl from a good family—who became the models for thousands of imitations down to the present century. A new dramatic form, which expanded the structure of Yuan drama, emerged in the Ming period (1368–1644). One of the best-known plays of this type was *Lute Song* by Gao Ming (c. 1301–1370), which dealt with questions of family loyalty in a woman abandoned by her husband.

In the nineteenth century, elements of folk theater and other genres popular among ordinary people formed the basis for a new popular theater called *Peking,* or *Beijing, opera.* Unlike the grand opera we know in the west, Beijing opera combines music, theater, dance, and even acrobatics.

The theater space traditionally used for Beijing opera is reminiscent of a modern dinner theater, with audience members seated at tables and eating and drinking during performances. In its staging, Bejing opera stresses the symbolic. The only furniture onstage is usually a table and several chairs, but these few items can symbolize a number of elements: dining halls, courts of justice, clouds, mountains, and so forth.

Japan The first important period in the history of Japanese theater occurred in the fourteenth century. This was not long after similar developments in China. The sudden and remarkable development of *nō* theater, which is one of three great traditional forms of Japanese theater, came about when popular stage traditions and advanced learning joined forces. The person given chief credit for perfecting nō theater is Zeami Motokiyo (1363–1443), who

JAPANESE KABUKI
One of the three ancient forms of theater in Japan is Kabuki; the other two are nō and bunraku, the puppet theater. Kabuki is quite stylized: the stories have many symbolic, imaginative elements, and the performers, such as the one seen here, Uzaemon Ichimura in the Kabuki play Shibaraku, *wear extremely elaborate costumes and makeup. The performers are always male and train from childhood to master the dance-like movements and gestures that are essential to Kabuki.* (AP/Wide World Photos)

headed a theatrical troupe under the patronage of the shogun of Japan. The elegance, mystery, and beauty of nō have fascinated the Japanese since the time of Zeami; and the tradition, passed on from teacher to disciple, has been carried on to the present day.

The stories on which nō plays were based often came from literary or historical sources. One notable source was a famous novel of Heian court life, Lady Murasaki's *The Tale of Genji,* written around 1000. (The Heian period in Japan was 794–1195.)

Nō actors (all performers in nō were male) move in a highly stylized fashion that involves important elements of both dance and pantomime. During the performance of a nō text, the actors alternate sections of chanting with a heightened speech that might best be compared to recitative in western opera. The costumes are usually of great elegance, and the masks worn by the chief character are among the most beautiful, subtle, and effective ever created for any theater.

Nō remained the most popular theatrical form during Japan's long medieval period. Civil wars and other disturbances, however, caused political disarray until in 1600 a general, Tokugawa Ieyasu, unified the country. The first of the new popular forms of theater to flourish in the years that followed was a puppet theater known as *bunraku,* which features musicians and a chanter who tells the story and creates the voices of all the characters. The puppets enacting the drama are approximately two-thirds of human size and are operated by men dressed in black who move the puppets' head, arms, and body; the fact that the men are in black means that to the audience they are considered invisible. The first and undoubtedly the best of the writers for bunraku, Chikamatsu Monzaemon (1653–1725), contributed enormously to the transformation of this popular theater into a true art form.

Shortly after bunraku, a new form of theater developed in the early and middle seventeenth century: *kabuki.* According to legend, kabuki was originated by a woman performer named Okuni, but by 1652 kabuki was presented by all-male acting companies. Drawing its material from the plays written for bunraku and nō, kabuki quickly established itself as a tremendously popular form of theater. Kabuki actors are trained from childhood in singing, dancing, acting, and feats of physical dexterity, and the male actors who play women's parts are particularly skillful in imitating feminine characters through stylized gestures and attitudes.

Contemporary Asian American Theater

It is against the backdrop of these ancient traditions that contemporary Asian American theater developed. As early as the 1850s, puppet shows, acrobatic acts, and traditional operas were imported from China to California. For most of the nineteenth century and the first half of the twentieth century, however, Asians appeared in dramatic offerings strictly as stereotypes. In films, for instance, Asian Americans played such menial parts as cooks,

ASIAN AMERICAN THEATER

One of the major playwrights in the emergence of a strong Asian American theater is David Henry Hwang. Hwang turned his sensibilities to a Rodgers and Hammerstein musical, Flower Drum Song, *completely reworking the original libretto to give the piece a strong Asian American point of view. Shown here is Sandra Allen and the chorus. In other plays of his such as* M. Butterfly *and* Golden Child, *Hwang has given full reign to his point of view as an Asian American playwright.* (© Joan Marcus)

spies, and vamps. Leading parts—even Asian characters—were played by whites in makeup.

With the coming of cultural and ethnic awareness in the 1960s and 1970s, things began to change. In 1965 several Asian American performers and directors founded the East West Players in Los Angeles. In 1973, two more groups were formed—the Asian Exclusion Act in Seattle and the Asian American Theatre Workshop in San Francisco—and in 1977 the director-actor Tisa Chang (1945?–) founded the Pan Asian Repertory Theatre in New York. These groups employed Asian American performers, produced dramas from the Asian cultural heritage, and emphasized new plays written by and for Asian Americans.

A number of plays by Asian American writers were produced in the 1970s and 1980s, including a memory play by Philip Kan Gotanda (1950–   ) called *Song for a Nisea Fisherman* (1980). A playwright who came to prominence in the 1980s was David Henry Hwang, the son of first-generation Americans who had immigrated to California from China. Hwang wrote several plays that won wide recognition: *FOB*, produced in 1980, which took place in the back room of a Chinese restaurant in California, was about the conflict between Americanization and traditions among Chinese immigrants; *The Dance and the Railroad*, produced in 1981, concerned Chinese labor employed to build western railroads. Later in the decade, in 1988, Hwang's *M. Butterfly* opened successfully on Broadway. Based on a true story, the play dealt with a French diplomat who meets and falls in love with a Chinese opera singer who he thinks is a woman but turns out to be a man—and a spy. (A synopsis of *M. Butterfly* appears in Chapter 7.) Another play by Hwang, *Golden Child*, opened in the 1996–1997 theater season.

There has also been a movement to have more Asian Americans employed as performers in appropriate roles. Hwang and the actor B. D. Wong, who played the Chinese opera singer in the original production of *M. Butterfly* led a vigorous protest against the hiring of an English actor to play the leading role in the musical *Miss Saigon*. That battle was lost; but by 1996, when a revival of *The King and I* opened on Broadway, it had a large proportion of Asian American performers. In 2001, David Henry Hwang wrote a revised version of Rodgers and Hammerstein's *Flower Drum Song*.

HISPANIC THEATER

There is a strong theatrical tradition in Spain that includes such significant seventeenth-century playwrights as Lope de Vega (1562–1635) and Calderón de la Barca (1600–1681). Also, various Spanish-speaking groups coming to the United States—in the southwest, for instance—brought with them theater from their home countries. One example is the Mexican-influenced Spanish-language theater produced in Texas in the nineteenth century. In this chapter, however, we are exploring Hispanic theater of the past century that involves playwrights, directors, and performers with roots in South America, Central America, Cuba, Mexico, and Puerto Rico as well as Spain.

Contemporary Hispanic theater can be divided into several groups which include Chicano theater, Cuban American theater, Puerto Rican theater, and Nuyorican theater. All these address the experiences of Hispanics living in the United States. The plays are sometimes written in Spanish but are usually in English.

Chicano theater, which originated primarily in the west and southwest, came to prominence at the same time as the civil rights movements of the 1960s. The theater troupe known as El Teatro Campesino ("farmworkers' theater") grew out of the work of Luis Valdéz (1940–   ), who joined César Chávez in organizing farmworkers in California. Valdéz wrote *actos,* short

agitprop pieces dramatizing the lives of workers. (The term **agitprop** means "agitation propaganda"; it was applied in the 1930s to plays with a strong political or social agenda.)

El Teatro Campesino became the prototype of other groups such as Teatro de la Gente ("people's theater"), founded in 1967; and Teatro de la Esperanza ("theater of hope"), begun in 1971 in Santa Barbara, California. Also in 1971, a network of these theaters across the country was established. In the 1990s a well-known theater, Teatro Vista, performed for Mexican and Hispanic communities in Chicago.

In 1978 Valdéz's play *Zoot Suit,* about racial violence in Los Angeles in 1943, opened to considerable acclaim; it later moved to Broadway. Other plays about the Chicano experience followed, one of the most notable being *Roosters* (1987) by Milcha Sanchez-Scott (1955–), in which cockfighting is a metaphor used to explore Chicano concerns and family conflicts. Among other writers who have dealt with Chicano as well as wider themes is Arthur Giron (1937–), an American writer from Guatemala.

Cuban American theater developed chiefly in Florida. The Federal Theater Project of the 1930s resulted in fourteen Cuban American productions in 1936 and 1937. In 1966 in New York City, Max Ferra founded Intar, a Cuban American theater. A highly regarded Cuban American dramatist whose works began to be produced in the 1970s was Maria Irene Fornes; her play *Fefu and Her Friends* is discussed in Chapter 3. Among the current generation of Cuban American writers who have emerged in the past quarter-century are Manuel Martín, Mario Peña, Dolores Prida, Iván Acosta, and Omar Torres. (Torres's work is centered in Miami and New York.) *Anna in the Tropics* by Nilo Gruz won the 2003 Pulitzer Prize.

A LANDMARK HISPANIC MUSICAL

An important milestone in the history of Hispanic theater in America was the production of the musical Zoot Suit, *first in Los Angeles in the late 1970s, and later on Broadway, as well as in a revival at the Goodman Theatre in Chicago in 2000. The scene here is from the Goodman production. The story deals in terms of song and dance with racial violence in Los Angeles in 1943. In this scene, El Pachucho (Marco Rodriguez) stands as Henry Reyna (Andrew Navarro) holds a knife to Rafa's throat (Joel Maisonet).* (© Liz Lauren)

Nuyorican is a term that refers to Puerto Rican culture, mostly in New York, but elsewhere as well. The Nuyorican Poets' Café presented plays by a number of Hispanic writers, including an ex-convict, Miguel Piñero (1947–1988), whose *Short Eyes,* a harshly realistic portrait of prison life, proved to be very successful and won a number of awards in the 1973–1974 season. Nuyorican theater sometimes mixes English and Spanish in the same work. Another Puerto Rican theater, The Puerto Rican Travelling Theater, founded by Miriam Colon, presents plays by Puerto Rican writers strictly in Spanish, or in English. Another important Puerto Rican theater, which began producing plays by native writers in the 1960s and 1970s, at the same time as the Travelling Theater, is the Teatro Repertorio Español, founded by Gilberto Zaldivar and Rene Buch. Today a new group of Puerto Rican playwrights has come to prominence, including Yvette Ramirez, Cándido Tirado, Edward Gallardo, Juan Shamsul Alam, Carmen Rivera, and Oscar A. Colon.

NATIVE AMERICAN THEATER

No group has suffered more from stereotyping onstage and in film than Native Americans. In films they were long depicted as either subhuman (bloodthirsty savages) or superhuman (healers and noble primitives). When they appeared as characters in plays, it was usually the same.

Native American theater tradition, which stressed ancient rituals and communal celebrations, differed from western theater in several respects. For one thing, it was infused with cosmic significance; for another, there was no audience as such: those observing were considered participants just as much as the principal performers. Much of this theater legacy was wiped out during the nineteenth century, along with much of Native American life itself. In recent years, though, there have been attempts to recapture lost rituals and traditions from among the 3 million native peoples and their 500 tribal cultures.

As for Native American life onstage, a movement began at somewhat the same time as other minority-oriented theaters to establish a true Native American theater. Two examples of groups that emerged in the late 1960s and early 1970s are the Red Earth Theatre in Seattle, Washington, and the Native American Theatre Ensemble in New York, headed by Hanay Geiogamah.

Later, a significant production was *Black Elk Speaks*, presented by the Denver Center Theatre Company in 1993. This was a collaboration between Native Americans and others, including Donovan Marley, the director of the Denver company; it was based on a healing vision experienced by Nicholas Black Elk, a Sioux born in 1863. At age 9, Black Elk fell into a coma lasting twelve days, during which he had a transforming dream: he saw that a sacred hoop, uniting all nations, was broken and had to be repaired. Sixty years later Black Elk related the vision in great detail to others who recorded it in a book; and it was this book which Marley, guided by advice from Native American elders, turned into the play.

NATIVE AMERICAN THEATER
One group that in the past has felt particularly marginalized is Native Americans. In recent years attempts have been made, both by Native Americans and by those interested in their culture and history, to bring their theater into the mainstream. Shown here is actor Lorne Cardinal, a Native American, in the play Black Elk Speaks, *a drama produced by the Denver Center Theatre Company dealing with the events surrounding a figure in Native American history who saw visions.* (Terry Shapiro)

FEMINIST THEATER

Feminist theater is another significant movement that began in the socially active atmosphere of the late 1960s and early 1970s. It developed alongside the more general feminist movement, which stressed consciousness-raising to make people aware of the secondary position women had too often been forced to occupy in social and political structures. Activists in this period attempted to revise cultural value systems and interpersonal relations in

DIVERSITY IN TODAY'S THEATER

In recent decades there has been a marked trend toward the writing and producing of plays by, about, and for specific audiences: minority groups; feminist, lesbian and gay groups, and politically active groups. Also, other forms of theater, such as performance art, have come to the forefront. Eve Ensler's highly personal solo production The Vagina Monologues *includes several of these theatrical approaches: performance art, feminism, lesbianism, political and social theater. Ensler has been praised for her humor as well.* (©Joan Marcus)

terms of an egalitarian ideology. In theater this took the form of groups like the It's Alright to Be a Woman Theatre in New York, one of the first groups to translate consciousness-raising into stage performances.

Feminist theater developed in several directions. For one thing, there was an attempt to make women writers, past and present, more widely acknowledged and recognized. Thus historical figures like Hrosvitha, a nun who wrote plays in her convent at Gandersheim in Germany in the tenth century, and the English playwrights Aphra Behn (1640–1689) and Susanna Centlivre (c. 1670–1723) have been brought to the forefront. In addition, attention was paid to several women playwrights who had made their mark in the early and middle twentieth century, notably Susan Glaspell (1876–1948), Rachel Crothers (1878–1958), Sophie Treadwell (1890–1970), and Lillian Hellman (1905–1984).

In the period after World War II, consciousness of contemporary women playwrights increased. The Susan Smith Blackburn Prize for women playwrights was inaugurated in 1979; and in the 1980s three women in quick succession (all previous winners of the Blackburn Prize) were awarded the Pulitzer Prize: Beth Henley (1952–   ) for *Crimes of the Heart* (1981), Marsha Norman (1942–   ) for *'Night, Mother* (1983), and Wendy Wasserstein (1950–   ) for *The Heidi Chronicles* (1989). An important British writer in the emerging feminist theater (also a winner of the Blackburn Prize) was Caryl Churchill (1938–   ), with such plays as *Cloud Nine* (1979) and Top Girls (1982). A key theoretician of the feminist movement and related movements was Judith Butler (1956–   ) in such works as *Gender as Performance*.

Another direction in which feminist theater developed was militancy and protest. Those who took this route disdained mainstream theater, remaining radical not only politically but also artistically. In the 1960s, a series of trends had led to the idea that the text was no longer sacred; happenings, rituals, and improvisatory work became the basis for theater events. Taking a cue from this development, a number of groups created theater pieces that explored and spoke up for women's issues. Such groups included the Omaha Magic Theater in Nebraska, headed by Megan Terry (1932–   ); the Spiderwoman Collective in New York City; and At the Foot of the Mountain in Minneapolis.

A third direction of feminist theater involved several groups that took a decidedly lesbian point of view. Feminist theater, therefore, split into the divisions that have marked the feminist movement in general: liberal feminists, radical feminists, and lesbian-rights feminists. However, although some groups are definitely in one camp or another, for others there is considerable overlapping.

GAY AND LESBIAN THEATER

Theater by, about, and for gay and lesbian audiences has been coming more and more to the forefront in recent decades. It is also interesting to note that this theater often appeals to a wide variety of audience members, many of whom are not themselves gay or lesbian. Sometimes the material is political and polemical, but just as often it is humorous, satirical, or simply camp. A very successful author and performer is Charles Busch, whose work has been seen on Broadway, and who has also written and acted off-Broadway. He is shown here as Lady Sylvia Allington in a play of his called Shanghai Moon, *a take-off on movie heroines of Asian theme films of the 1930s and 1940s. (© Joan Marcus)*

GAY AND LESBIAN THEATER

Lesbian theater groups can be part of feminist theater, but gay and lesbian theater is also a distinct movement.

A number of plays and performers introduced homosexual and lesbian themes into theater before the 1960s. For example, in the nineteenth century and the early twentieth century there was a considerable amount of cross-dressing in performances: men often appeared in "drag" and women performed in men's clothing, raising questions about sexual and gender roles. Also, plays included material on this subject; one good example is Lillian Hellman's *The Children's Hour* (1934), in which a presumed lesbian relationship between two schoolteachers was presented.

However, the play that first brought gay life to the forefront was *The Boys in the Band* (1968), by Mart Crowley (1935–   ). Crowley depicted a group of men living an openly gay life. Ironically, at the height of its success there was a backlash against *The Boys in the Band*. In 1969, the year after it opened, gay patrons of the Stonewall Inn in New York's Greenwich Village fought against police officers attempting to close the bar. This uprising, considered the beginning of the modern gay rights movement, changed attitudes of gay activists—who now rejected what they considered a stereotype of homosexuals as closeted, narcissistic, and filled with self-hatred. Since several of the key characters in *The Boys in the Band* displayed these characteristics, the play was rejected by a number of influential gays. In 1996, however, when the play was revived in New York City, it received a more balanced reception, and its historical significance was acknowledged.

A key development in lesbian theater was the WOW (Women's One World) festival, which originated in New York City in 1981 and featured lesbian and feminist works. Also of importance were the numerous examples of cross-gender casting that began to appear. For example, several theater companies, including the LA Women's Shakespeare Company, presented all-women's Shakespeare.

In the years that followed, complex gay characters were presented unapologetically. Plays in the 1970s and 1980s included *The Ritz* (1975) by Terrence McNally (1939–   ) and *Torch Song Trilogy* (1983) by Harvey Fierstein (1954–   ). Since then, more and more plays have dealt expressly with gay issues. In these dramas, not only is the lifestyle of gays and lesbians presented forthrightly, but frequently a gay or lesbian agenda is also put forward. In addition to a general concern for gay and lesbian issues, there has been a sense of urgency engendered by the AIDS crisis. This has led to a number of significant dramas, including *The Normal Heart* (1985) by Larry Kramer (1935–   ), *As Is* (1985) by William M. Hoffman (1939–   ), Tony Kushner's two-part play *Angels in America* (1993–1994), and Terrence McNally's *Love! Valor! Compassion!* (1995).

"Gender-bender" groups such as the Cockettes and the Angels of Light in San Francisco and Centola and Hot Peaches in New York are an offshoot of gay and lesbian theater. An important company in New York was the Ridiculous Theatrical Company founded by John Vaccaro, which developed an extraordinary writer and performer—Charles Ludlum (1943–1987). Ludlum rewrote the classics to include a good deal of wild parody and frequent cross-dressing.

Though a number of groups have not survived, individual performers and playwrights in gay and lesbian theater remain very much a part of the theater scene. Current groups presenting lesbian, cross-gender, and related material are the Queer@Here Festival in New York City and the Theatre Offensive in Boston.

PERFORMANCE ART

Performance art, as such, is not a multicultural or gender movement, but it is a way in which many exponents of these movements have expressed their points of view. Performance art has several important antecedents: first, avant-garde experiments of the early twentieth century, such as dada and surrealism, which stressed the irrational and attacked traditional artistic values; second, the theories of Antonin Artaud (1896–1948) and Jerzy Grotowski; third, the influence of action artists such as the painter Jackson Pollock; fourth, the Fluxux movement which featured the work of Yoko Ono and which has been described as part dada, part Bauhaus, and part Zen; fifth, the Happenings, in the 1950s and early 1960s, presented by Allan Kaprow and others.

During the past three decades, the term *performance art* has stood for various things. In its earliest manifestations, performance art was related on the one hand to painting and on the other hand to dance. In the 1970s, one branch of performance art emphasized the body as an art object; some artists suffered self-inflicted pain, and some went through daily routines (such as preparing a meal) in a museum or in a theater setting. Another branch focused on "site-specific" or environmental pieces in which the setting or context was crucial: theater pieces were created for a specific location such as a subway station, a city park, or a waterfront pier.

In an article in *Artweek* in 1990, Jacki Apple explained how the emphasis in performance art shifted in the 1970s and 1980s:

> In the 70's performance art was primarily a time-based visual art form in which text was at the service of image; by the early 80's performance art had shifted to movement-based work, with the performance artist as

choreographer. Interdisciplinary collaboration and "spectacle," influenced by TV and other popular entertainment modes . . . set the tone for the new decade.[1]

In recent years the connotation of the term *performance art* has changed yet again. It is now often associated with individual artists who present autobiographical material onstage. Four such artists became a center of controversy when their work was seized on in 1990 by ultraconservative religious groups and members of Congress as a reason to oppose funding the National Endowment for the Arts. These artists often espouse such causes as civil rights for lesbians and homosexuals For example, one of the "NEA Four," Tim Miller, refers in his pieces to his experiences as a gay man in the age of AIDS, to his sexual encounters, and to memories of his childhood and his friends who have died.

Two artists who began performing solo pieces in alternative spaces but later received commercial productions are Spalding Gray (1941–) and Bill Irwin (1950–). Gray, a monologuist who discusses issues which range from his own personal concerns to politics, is reminiscent of ancient storytellers who created a theatrical environment single-handedly. Irwin's performances are mimelike, and he uses popular slapstick techniques to reflect on the contemporary human condition.

Anna Deavere Smith (1952–), an African American performance artist, won considerable acclaim for pieces dealing with racial unrest in the early 1990s. In her works, she portrays numerous real people she has met and interviewed. Her *Twilight: Los Angeles, 1992* presented people affected by the uprising that followed the acquittals in the first trial of police officers charged with brutalizing Rodney King. Her most recent work is *House Arrest.*

The work of Gray and Smith underlines another shift that performance art has undergone in its various twists and turns. This is a return to language. At certain points in the history of performance art, those involved eschewed the spoken or written word. They were very much opposed to any reliance on language, emphasizing instead gesture, image, and other nonlinguistic components. But in recent years language has come back to a place of prominence among a number of performance artists.

PERFORMANCE ART

Performance art covers a wide range of presentations in today's theater. Some are militantly political, others strongly autobiographical, still others sexually explicit and defiant. An important performance artist of recent years is Anna Deavere Smith, a writer as well as a performer. Typically Smith goes into a situation where a crisis has occurred—in Brooklyn or in Los Angeles, for example, with racial tensions—and interviews a wide range of people. Out of this comes a mosaic in which she enacts segments portraying the various people who were involved, expressing their many points of view. She is known as an extremely accurate observer, as well as a first-rate performer. Here she is in a scene from House Arrest, *a performance piece about the political scene in Washington, D.C. (© Michal Daniel/ The Joseph Papp Public Theater)*

It should be noted that the work of many performance artists active today is strongly political in nature. Among the groups to whom this applies
are the Guerilla Girls, the Poetry Slams, Survival Research Lab, the Zapatist
Movement, and the Electronic Disturbance Theatre. Active individuals
would include Annie Sprinkle and Guillermo Gomez-Peña.

Along with those in the United States, there are also significant performance artists in most major cities around the world.

FRINGE THEATER FESTIVALS

A sign of the vitality of performance art and theater of diversity is the number of festivals featuring a wide variety of offerings outside the mainstream
of large-scale commercial and not-for-profit theaters. Festivals in three
widely diverse cities—New York; Edinburgh, Scotland; and Avignon,
France—indicate the scope of these presentations.

The International Fringe Festival in New York City is now well established. One of its offerings from 1999—the musical *Urinetown*—moved first
to off-Broadway and then to Broadway. In August 2002, the Fringe Festival
presented a total of 195 productions by many widely diverse groups in a variety of conventional and unconventional venues. Moreover, attendance that
year increased greatly over previous years.

In Avignon, France, an event called Festival Off has become an annual
event, again offering a rich variety of theater and dance pieces in more than
20 different locations. In addition, over 500 companies each year, not officially invited to the festival, come at their own expense and perform as well.

One of the oldest and best-established of these events is the Edinburgh
Fringe in Scotland, which each year presents an impressive amount of avant-
garde theater, performance art, and iconoclastic theater.

POSTMODERNISM AND CULTURALLY DIVERSE THEATER

In many cases, recent developments in performance art and culturally diverse theaters are related to a theoretical concept of literature and the arts
known as *postmodernism*. Many theater artists—auteur directors, avant-
garde performing groups, etc.—could be described as postmodernist.

Postmodernism has several facets. For one thing, it reflects issues of
power in art. Postmodernists question the idea of an accepted "canon" of
classics; they also ask why certain artists (such as playwrights) and certain
groups (such as white males) should have held positions of power or "priv-
ilege" throughout theater history.

Accordingly, postmodernists rebel against traditional readings of texts, arguing that a theater production may have a variety of "authors," including the director and even individual audience members: they believe that each audience member creates his or her own unique reading. Postmodernist directors are noted for "deconstructing" classic dramas—that is, taking an original play apart; developing a new, individual conceptualization; and trying to represent onstage the issues of power embedded in the text. When a classic is "deconstructed" in this way, it may serve simply as the scenario for a production.

The term *postmodernism* also suggests that the "modernist" interest in realism, antirealism, and form is no longer central to theater, that artists have now moved beyond being concerned with representing either reality or abstraction. Instead, postmodernists mix abstraction and realism, so that their works cannot be easily classified. Furthermore, the distinction between "high art" and popular art can no longer be clearly defined: postmodernists mix popular concerns and techniques with those of high art.

A number of individuals and groups that can be classified as postmodern are still quite active. Among the directors in this group are Richard Foreman, Robert Wilson, and Anne Bogart. The Wooster Group is a longtime company that can be described as postmodern, as can a number of organizations that are spin-offs from the Wooster Group. These include Builder's Association, Elevator Repair Service, Radiohole, and Collapsible Giraffe.

In Part 3 we have examined the purpose and point of view of a theatrical production, and also the genres into which most dramatic works fall. In addition, we have looked at types of theater that offer a special kind of theater experience: the musical and theater of diversity—multicultural theater, gender theater, and performance art. In Part 4 we turn to an area that is a particular province of the playwright: the creation of dramatic characters and dramatic structure.

SUMMARY

1. Diverse, culturally rich theaters have emerged in recent decades, reflecting the interests of various multicultural, multiethnic, and gender groups.

2. African American theater often blends concerns of black heritage and black life in the United States with western theater traditions.

3. Asian American theater, which deals with problems and issues facing people of Asian descent, builds on a rich tradition of Asian theater, particularly Chinese and Japanese theaters.

4. Hispanic theater can be divided into several branches, including Chicano theater, with a Mexican orientation; Cuban American theater; and Nuyorican theater, which deals largely with Puerto Rican concerns.

5. Native American theater has a background rooted in tribal rituals and traditions, which adapt less easily to western theater than most other multicultural theaters.

6. Feminist theater, a reflection of the feminist movement, takes several forms: (a) advocates of wider recognition of female theatrical figures, past and present; (b) radical, militant groups and playwrights who address specifically feminist issues; and (c) groups and individuals associated with lesbian issues.

7. Gay and lesbian theater deals with questions, problems, and assertions of gay and lesbian lifestyles.

8. Performance art has undergone several transformations since the 1960s; a recent incarnation is the one-person show with an individual expressing a highly personal—often political or idiosyncratic—point of view.

9. Not only performance art but other non-traditional theater forms are the focus of a number of festivals known a Fringe Theater Festivals.

10. Many recent developments in theater are related to a multifaceted theoretical concept called postmodernism.

EXPLORING THEATER ON THE WEB

Theater of Diversity

The online community continues to grow at an ever-expanding rate. The very nature of the World Wide Web makes information about diverse cultures accessible to everyone. As multicultural theater companies develop their online presence, more and more information about diverse theater communities is becoming available. Here is a sampling of sites on the Internet related to multicultural theater:

http://www.townestreet.org

Towne Street Theater: African American Theatre Company, Los Angeles, California

http://www.naatco.org

National Asian-American Theatre Company, Brooklyn, New York

http://www.latinotheater.com

Latino Theatre Company, Los Angeles, California

http://www.logan.com/redhen

Red Hen Productions: Feminist Theatre Company, Cleveland, Ohio

http://www.therhino.org

Theatre Rhinoceros: Gay and Lesbian Theater Company, San Francisco, California

Exercises:

1. Browse the links listed above. Do you recognize similar theater arts groups in your community? How do the plays that are being produced by each of these companies address issues pertinent to that particular community?

2. Do you think it is important to be exposed to other cultures? In what ways might live theater be more powerful than just reading about another culture in a textbook or an online article?

3. Visit http://www.theatrehistory.com and access the "Index of Topics" to locate articles and resources subdivided by cultural or national orientation, or use the internal search engine to locate three resources reflecting theater as seen from diverse orientations. How do the conventions differ? What role does geographic location play in theatrical style? What role does culture play?

Play Synopsis

M. BUTTERFLY (1988)
David Henry Hwang (1957-)

(AP/Wide World Photos)

Chief Characters

Rene Gallimard, *French diplomat stationed in China*

Song Liling, *singer in Chinese opera*

Marc, *high school friend of Gallimard*

Helga, *Gallimard's wife*

Comrade Chin, *Communist agent*

M. Toulon, *French ambassador to China*

Renée, *Danish student in Beijing*

Background

The play is loosely based on a true story of a French diplomat who was tried as a spy along with the Chinese person to whom he was married and whose identity had fooled him for 20 years.

Time and Place

A prison in Paris, 1988; and, in flashbacks, the years 1960–1986 in Beijing, China, and Paris, France.

Act I: Rene Gallimard, a former French diplomat, is in prison in Paris, recalling the bizarre events that put him there. His favorite opera was Puccini's *Madame Butterfly,* and its submissive heroine was his "feminine ideal." As a schoolboy, unlike his friend Marc, he was shy with girls. At age 31 he married Helga, to whom he was faithful until he was posted to the embassy in Beijing, China. It was there that he met Song Liling, a singer in Chinese opera.

When Gallimard sees Liling play the death scene in *Madame Butterfly,* he is reminded of his "feminine ideal." At their first meeting, though, Liling explains to him that she objects to Butterfly

Alec Mapa *(foreground)* and Tony Randall (© Joan Marcus)

Tony Randall (*foreground*) and Alec Mapa (© Joan Marcus)

because this character symbolizes the subjugation of Asian women to western men.

Four weeks after their meeting, Gallimard goes to a club where Liling is performing. Liling engages him in a challenging, flirtatious conversation. That night, as Gallimard sleeps, his boyhood friend Marc appears to him in a dream and encourages him to think that Liling is in love with him. Gallimard is awakened from this dream by an early-morning phone call from Liling, inviting him to a performance a few days hence.

Fifteen weeks go by, in which Gallimard frequently sees Liling perform or meets with Liling, but their meetings are always brief. When Gallimard is finally invited to Liling's apartment, the singer is wearing an elegant black dress; Gallimard makes physical approaches, and Liling seems to be flattered, though flustered. Gallimard is determined to make Liling subservient, like Butterfly, so after this he doesn't get in touch with Liling for five weeks.

Meanwhile, Marc appears in scenes taking place in Gallimard's

imagination. In one of these scenes, Gallimard recalls how Marc arranged for him to have his first sexual experience, with an aggressive girl in high school.

During the sixth week of their separation, Gallimard begins to receive letters from Liling. Finally, he receives the letter he wants: Liling agrees to be totally submissive.

At a reception, the French ambassador tells Gallimard that he is being promoted, one reason being his recently acquired macho attitude and behavior.

In the final scene of Act I, Gallimard is at Liling's apartment and, after much coaxing, gets Liling to be his Butterfly. When he attempts to make love, Liling again pleads extreme shyness. Liling turns off all the lights, promising to make him happy.

Act II: In a flashback from his cell in Paris in 1988, Gallimard returns to 1960 and the apartment he and Liling have rented in Beijing. Liling asks Gallimard for government information which Chin, Liling's contact as a communist spy, has been pressing for. It turns out that Liling is also a spy. Gallimard's wife, Helga, wants a child and has been to a doctor, who says she can have a child; she wants Gallimard to see the doctor also, but later Liling dissuades him.

At a party at the Austrian embassy in 1963, Gallimard meets Renée, a voluptuous Danish student who initiates an affair with him. Though Gallimard neglects Liling, he later longs for Liling's shyness and submissiveness because he has become intimidated by the aggressive, uninhibited Renée.

The French ambassador tells Gallimard that the French government will pursue the policies Gallimard has recommended for Vietnam, but if they fail, it will be Gallimard's fault. Gallimard realizes that he has been set up and betrayed by his superiors, including the ambassador.

Back with Liling, Gallimard asks to see the singer undressed; but when Liling invites him to do the undressing, he withdraws his request. Then, Liling unexpectedly claims to be pregnant. Later Liling tells Chin that the Communist Party must find a baby—a blond baby—to present to Gallimard. Liling does present a baby seven months later, telling Gallimard that it is theirs.

We move forward from 1963 to 1966. Gallimard, in Beijing, explains that China is beginning to change: Mao is growing old; things aren't going as expected in Vietnam. Gallimard is being posted back to Paris, and Liling is sent to a labor camp. In Paris, Gallimard tells Helga he wants a divorce. Liling, released from the camp, pursues Gallimard to Paris, where they get married.

Act III: During the intermission between Acts II and III, Liling sits at a dressing table removing makeup and changing clothes. With the change of clothes, at the beginning of Act III, we see that Liling is actually a man and has deceived Gallimard, who desperately wanted a submissive female. It is 1986 in Paris, and Liling and Gallimard are put on trial, both accused of being spies for the Chinese communists. The revelation that for twenty years Gallimard has been having a love affair with, and has actually married, a man makes him the laughingstock of Paris. Liling flaunts his real identity and humiliates Gallimard.

Finally, in 1988, in his prison cell, Gallimard must face the reality of Liling's identity or hold onto the fantasy he has pursued. He chooses the fantasy, and finding in his cell a costume for the character Madame Butterfly, he slowly puts it on. Then, while music from the opera plays, he commits suicide.

Discussion Questions

- What are the Asian elements in *M. Butterfly*—in dramatic elements? in the story? in the characters?
- Is the story of *M. Butterfly* too unreasonable to be believed? What about the fact that it is based on a true story?
- Are some true stories too fantastic or incredible to be believed, even in a play or a movie?

Play Synopsis

THE WAY OF THE WORLD (1700)
William Congreve (1670-1729)

Chief Characters

Mirabell, *in love with Millamant*
Millamant, *niece of Lady Wishfort*
Lady Wishfort, *enemy of Mirabell*
Fainall, *in love with Mrs. Marwood*
Mrs. Fainall, *wife of Fainall and daughter of Lady Wishfort*
Mrs. Marwood, *friend of Mr. Fainall*
Sir Wilfull Witwoud, *nephew of Lady Wishfort*

Witwoud, *follower of Millamant*
Petulant, *follower of Millamant*
Waitwell, *servant of Mirabell*
Foible, *maid of Lady Wishfort*

Background

The play takes place among members of the upper class in London in the late seventeenth century. The society it depicts is highly artificial and, above everything else, values gossip, intrigue, deception, seduction, and sparkling conversation.

Act I: A chocolate shop. Mirabell complains to Fainall that his attempt to win the love of Millamant is not succeeding because Millamant's aunt and guardian, Lady Wishfort, has turned against him. Lady Wishfort is infatuated with Mirabell, but she feels he has not been attentive enough to her. Witwoud, a follower of Millamant, joins the conversation. As his name suggests, Witwoud thinks that he is extremely clever and witty, when in fact he is a bore. Petulant, another follower of Millamant, then enters. As his name suggests, he is always at the point of being petulant. Both men prove to be foils for Mirabell in conversation.

Act II: In St. James Park, Mrs. Fainall and Mrs. Marwood are talking when Fainall and Mirabell join them. (Mrs. Fainall is Mirabell's mistress, though he really loves Millamant.) When Mirabell and Mrs. Fainall are alone, Mrs. Fainall complains that she detests Fainall, whom Mirabell compelled her to marry. Though disappointed in Mirabell, Mrs. Fainall's passion for him leads her to help in his next scheme, even though it involves her mother, Lady Wishfort. Mirabell wants to marry the beautiful and wealthy Millamant, but her aunt is jealously withholding her consent. With Mrs. Fainall's contrivance, Mirabell arranges to have his servant, Waitwell, in the guise of an uncle called Sir Rowland, pay court to Lady Wishfort. Then, since Mirabell has already accomplished a secret marriage between Waitwell and Lady Wishfort's maid, Foible, he declares his intention to expose the scandal. He will remain silent only if he can have Millamant and her fortune.

Tom Hollander as Sir Wilfull Witwoud

Joan Plowright as Lady Wishfort (left) and Maggie Smith as Mrs. Millamant
(© Donald Cooper/PhotoSTAGE)

Act III: With the scheme perfected, the scene shifts to Lady Wishfort's house. Foible tells Lady Wishfort that a man known as Sir Rowland has seen her picture and is infatuated with her. A meeting is arranged, but their plot is overheard by Mrs. Marwood, another of Mirabell's conquests and herself a crafty schemer. Desiring Mirabell for herself, Mrs. Marwood promptly influences Lady Wishfort to agree that her rival Millamant shall be married to Sir Wilfull, a rich and amiable dunce. Then Mrs. Marwood, to make sure of success, enlists the help of Fainall, who is infatuated with her and jealous of Mirabell. Fainall agrees to Mrs. Marwood's plan; she will write a letter to be delivered to Lady Wishfort when Waitwell, as Sir Rowland, is with her. The letter will expose the fraud, and Mirabell will be ruined. Mrs. Marwood neglects to tell Fainall that she wants to save Mirabell for herself.

Act IV: Lady Wishfort is atwitter as she awaits the bogus Sir Rowland. Meanwhile, Mirabell and Millamant discuss the kind of commonsense "contract" they believe a husband and wife should agree to in order for their marriage to succeed. The action then returns to Lady Wishfort and the arrival of Sir Rowland. He and Lady Wishfort get along famously: he begs for an early marriage, declaring that his nephew, Mirabell, will poison him for his money if he learns of the romance. The jealous Lady Wishfort promptly agrees, suggesting that Sir Rowland starve Mirabell "inch by inch." Then Mrs. Marwood's letter, denouncing Sir Rowland as Waitwell, arrives; but Sir Rowland deftly declares the letter to be the work of his nephew, and he leaves claiming that he must fight a duel.

Act V: Lady Wishfort learns of the deception being practiced on her and turns on Foible. The frightened Foible confesses that Mirabell conceived the whole plot, and Lady Wishfort is planning a dire revenge when more trouble comes: Fainall, her son-in-law, demands that his wife turn over her whole fortune to him, or else he and Mrs. Marwood will reveal to the world that Mrs. Fainall was Mirabell's mistress before her marriage and that she continues to be. Lady Wishfort is reflecting upon this new humiliation when Mirabell comes to ask her forgiveness.

The susceptible Lady Wishfort offers to forgive Mirabell if he will renounce his ideas of marrying Millamant. Mirabell offers a compromise: if Lady Wishfort will permit her niece to marry him, he will contrive to save Mrs. Fainall's reputation and fortune. If he can do this, Lady Wishfort agrees, she will forgive all and consent to anything. Mirabell then tells her: "Well, then, as regards your daughter's reputation, she has nothing to fear from Fainall. For his own reputation is at stake. He and Mrs. Marwood—we have proof of it—have been and still are lovers. . . . And as regards your daughter's fortune, she need have no fear on that score either: acting upon my advice and relying upon my honesty, she has made me the trustee of her entire estate." Cries Fainall: "'Tis outrageous!" Says Mirabell: "'Tis the way of the world."

Discussion Questions

- What makes a comedy of manners different from (a) a domestic comedy; (b) a comedy of ideas; (c) burlesque?
- Does the artificiality of *The Way of the World* make it too remote from contemporary life to be acceptable or relevant to today's audiences?
- Are any of the characters admirable? Are most characters too superficial to be admired?

FENCES (1987)
August Wilson (1945-   )

Characters

Troy Maxon, *53, a sanitation worker*
Jim Bono, *a fellow worker*
Rose Maxon, *43, Troy's wife of 18 years*
Cory Maxon, *17, Troy and Rose's son*
Lyons, *Troy's son by his first wife*
Gabriel, *Troy's younger brother*
Raynell, *Troy's daughter by another woman*

Setting

The backyard and back porch of Troy Maxon's two-story house in a decaying neighborhood in a northern industrial city of the United States.

Act I, Scene 1: A Friday evening, fall 1957. Troy, a large, self-confident man, and Bono, his sidekick of many years, enter the backyard from the

alley that runs alongside the house. It is Friday night, payday, when the two men have a ritual of talking and drinking. They are sanitation workers, and Troy has filed a complaint: all the African Americans lift garbage cans but don't drive trucks. Rose—Troy's wife—appears and tells Troy that their son Cory is being recruited by a college football team. Troy objects strenuously; he himself was a talented baseball player, but because African Americans could not play in the major leagues at that time, he was not allowed to realize his potential. He does not accept the fact that times have changed. Troy describes a time when he was sick and had an encounter with Death, whom he "wrassled" and beat.

Lyons, Troy's older son—who wants to be a jazz musician but has never gotten solid work—comes to borrow money, which he will probably not repay. Troy refuses to give it to him, but when Troy turns over his wages to Rose, as he does every payday, she gives Lyons $10.

Scene 2: The next morning. Troy's brother Gabriel enters; he is 7 years younger than Troy. Gabriel has a metal plate in his head—a result of a wound in World War II. He wears a trumpet around his waist because he thinks he is the angel Gabriel. He has been living with Troy and Rose but

Mary Alice, Ray Aranha, James Earl Jones (© Ron Scherl)

Courtney B. Vance James Earl Jones (© Ron Scherl)

has recently moved to a rooming house. Soon Troy disappears, claiming that he is going to listen to a ball game on the radio.

Scene 3: A few hours later. Cory (Troy and Rose's son) enters and is talking to Rose when Troy arrives. Troy is building a fence around the backyard at Rose's request and wants Cory to help him with it. Troy again expresses strong disapproval of Cory's taking a football scholarship, and they argue. Cory asks why Troy doesn't like him. Troy says he puts food on the table for Cory and a roof over his head. That's enough: "What law is there say I got to like you?"

Scene 4: The following Friday. Troy and Bono enter; Troy has been to the commissioner's office and has finally gotten a job driving. Lyons comes, not to ask for money as Troy assumes, but to repay the $10. Gabriel arrives. Troy tells about his past: his family in the south lived in poverty; he left home at 14 and had to steal to live; he was thrown in jail for 15 years. When he got out of jail, it was too late to star in baseball. Then he met Rose and settled down. Cory arrives, and there is another confrontation between him and Troy.

Act II, **Scene 1**: A Saturday, fall 1957. Bono warns Troy that he shouldn't mess around with Alberta, another woman—Rose is a good woman and doesn't deserve such treatment. When Bono leaves, Troy starts to work on his fence as Rose arrives to say that Gabriel had been picked up by the police and may be committed to an institution again. Troy, with great difficulty, tells Rose that he has made another woman pregnant. Rose cannot believe it. Troy explains how the other woman helps him forget his obligations and troubles. But Rose denounces him, explaining all that she has sacrificed for him.

Scene 2: Friday, Spring 1958. Rose and Troy have not been talking; he stays away from the house except to get his clothes. Rose accuses Troy of signing papers committing Gabriel to an institution, and of taking part of the money that Gabriel will receive as a result of being committed. Troy angrily denies this, but it becomes clear that it is true. The phone rings, and Rose learns that Alberta—Troy's other woman—has had a baby girl but has died in childbirth. Left alone, Troy once more challenges Death to come get him: to cross the fence he is building and fight him.

Scene 3: Three days later. Troy shows up at the house with the baby girl, Raynell—Alberta's daughter—in his arms. He wants Rose to raise her because she is his flesh and blood. At first Rose says no, but then she agrees.

Scene 4: Two months later. Cory has graduated from high school and is job-hunting. Troy and Cory have another confrontation, this one even angrier than previous ones. Troy orders Cory out of the house; Cory says that the house was built partly with money that Gabriel received for his disability but that Troy took. The two fight with a baseball bat. Troy finally gets the bat and could hit Cory, but he stops; then he orders Cory out.

Scene 5: Summer 1965. Troy has died, and it is the morning of his funeral. Cory, now a Marine, is home. Bono and Lyons are organizing the pallbearers. Cory and Rose talk. Cory refuses to go to the funeral: he has to say no to his father, once and for all. Rose says that staying away from his father's funeral is not the way to become his own man. Rose explains how much she compromised and sacrificed to be Troy's wife, but life has given her some compensation: little Raynell, now 7, whom she loves like her own daughter. Raynell comes out, and Cory says that he will go to the funeral. Gabriel comes and attempts to blow his trumpet—unsuccessfully, but he does a dance instead. This is the announcement of Troy's arrival at heaven's gate.

Discussion Questions

- August Wilson has been writing plays about African Americans set in different decades of the twentieth century. Fences is set in the 1950s. Are the issues in the play still relevant? Explain your answer.
- Describe the father-son conflict.
- Give your impressions of the main characters—Troy, Rose, Cory. What is each one's best trait? What is his or her worst trait?

Part 4

The Playwright

Dramatic Characters and Dramatic Structure

The playwright is responsible for creating in his or her script the dramatic characters and the dramatic structure of the play, for developing action, and for writing dialogue. In these drawings by Al Hirschfeld we see important playwrights from the past and the present. On the left is William Shakespeare surrounded by a number of the characters with which he peopled his plays: Antony and Cleopatra, King Henry V, Juliet, Hamlet, Falstaff, and Othello. ❧ On the right are two prominent modern American playwrights: Tennessee Williams and Arthur Miller.

CHAPTER THIRTEEN

Dramatic Characters

We have spoken previously of the primacy in any theater experience of the actor-audience relationship. In relating to the performers, however, it must be remembered that audience members are relating to the character being portrayed, not to the personality of an individual actress or actor. The performer is playing not herself or himself but a personage who comes from the imagination of the dramatist.

Although they often seem like real people, dramatic characters are created by playwrights. By carefully emphasizing certain features of a character's personality while eliminating others, a dramatist can show us in 2 hours the entire history of a person whom it could take us a lifetime to know in the real world. In Tennessee Williams's *A Streetcar Named Desire,* for example, we come to know the leading character, Blanche DuBois, in all her emotional complexity, better than we know people we see every day. The dramatist reveals to us not only Blanche's biography but her soul, and we become intimately acquainted with the workings of her mind.

◀ TRADITIONAL DRAMATIC CHARACTERS: EXCEPTIONAL FIGURES

Heroes and heroines of traditional theater stand apart from ordinary people in position and personality; they are often "larger than life." Kings, queens, generals, dukes, duchesses and the like have great privileges, possessions, authority, and responsibility—they lead other people and make decisions that affect other peoples' lives. Drama, especially drama of the past, frequently deals with such people, who may stand as symbols for all their contemporaries; it also often shows characters who represent the best and worst of humanity. Shown here is Antigone (Aysan Celik) in the play by Sophocles in which the title character on principle stands up to her uncle Creon (Douglas Thompson) even though opposing him leads to her death. The production was at the American Repertory Theatre. (© Richard Feldman)

The playwright has wide latitude in how to present a character and what to emphasize. A stage character can be drawn with a few quick strokes, as a cartoonist sketches a political figure; or given the surface detail and reality of a photograph; or fleshed out with the more interpretive and fully rounded quality of a portrait in oils.

In this chapter we will examine dramatic characters in two ways. We will look first at single characters. In theater there is a wide variety in types of characters, ranging from those who are "larger than life" to those who are mundane and predictable. There is also a marked difference in the way individual characters are treated by dramatists: some are fully rounded and three-dimensional; others are flat and one-dimensional. Second, we will examine the way in which characters relate to one another.

We begin with the major types of characters that have proved effective in theater through the years.

TYPES OF CHARACTERS

Extraordinary Characters

In most important dramatic works of the past, the heroes and heroines are extraordinary in some way; they are larger than life. Historically, major characters have been kings, queens, bishops, members of the nobility, or other figures clearly marked as holding a special place in society. In drama, as in life, a queen is accorded respect because of her authority, power, and grandeur; a high military official is respected because of the position he holds.

Dramatists go one step further, however, in depicting extraordinary characters. In addition to filling prestigious roles, dramatic characters generally represent men and women at their best or worst—at some extreme of human behavior. Lady Macbeth is not only a noblewoman; she is one of the most ambitious women ever depicted on the stage. In virtually every instance, with extraordinary characters we see men and women at the outer limits of human capability and endurance.

Antigone is the epitome of the independent, courageous female, willing to stand up to male authority and suffer whatever consequences she is forced to endure. Prometheus and Oedipus are men willing to face the worst the gods can throw at them, with strength and dignity—like the biblical figure Abraham when God confronts him. Thomas à Becket, archbishop of Canterbury under King Henry II of England—the subject of *Becket* by Jean Anouilh and *Murder in the Cathedral* by T. S. Eliot (1888–1965)—is martyred for his defiance of a king. Among characters who represent men and women at their worst are Medea, who murders her own children; and the brothers of the heroine of *The Duchess of Malfi* by John Webster (1580?–1625?), who forbid their sister to marry so that they can grab her estate, and when they discover that she has married, have her cruelly tortured and strangled.

(© T. Charles Erickson)

(Donald Cooper/PhotoSTAGE)

(©Donald Cooper/PhotoSTAGE)

(© Jennifer W. Lester)

Extraordinary Characters   In dramas of the past, the leading characters are often people who are exceptional in some way. Shown here are a gallery of exceptional characters from a range of dramas: Mirjana Jokivic as *Electra*, (*top left*) the heroine in the play by Sophocles, in a production at the Hartford Stage. Imogen Stubbs as Saint Joan (*top right*) in a London production of the play by Shaw. Nigel Hawthorne as *King Lear* (*middle*) in the play of that name by Shakespeare. The production is by the Royal Shakespeare Company in Britain. John Ortiz in the role of *Segismundo,* (*bottom left*) the chief character in *Calderón's Life Is a Dream,* produced by the Hartford Stage Company.

REPRESENTATIVE OR QUINTESSENTIAL CHARACTERS

The characters depicted in contemporary plays are rarely kings, queens, or saints; instead, they are ordinary people. They can be from the upper, middle, or lower class, but their problems and concerns reflect those of people in everyday life—though they may go to extremes. A typical, traditional housewife is Nora from Henrik Ibsen's A Doll's House, *shown here played by Cynthia Nixon. At the end of the play she rebels against the role into which she has been thrown, and leaves her husband, portrayed by David Lansbury.* (© T. Charles Erickson/The McCarter Theater)

Comic characters can also be extremes. The chief character in *Volpone* by Ben Jonson (1572–1637) is an avaricious miser who gets people to present him with expensive gifts because they think he will remember them in his will.

Characters may also be extraordinary because of their exceptional personalities or achievements. A good example is Joan of Arc, the heroine of George Bernard Shaw's *Saint Joan,* a simple peasant girl who rises to become commander of an army that triumphs in the name of the king of France.

Some characters combine extreme virtue and extreme vice. Faustus, treated by Christopher Marlowe in *Doctor Faustus* and by Johann Wolfgang von Goethe in *Faust,* is a great scholar but becomes so bored with his existence and so ambitious that he makes a compact with the devil, forfeiting his soul in return for unlimited power. Cleopatra, an exceedingly vain, selfish woman, also has "immortal longings." Queen Elizabeth I of England and Mary Queen of Scots, rivals in real life, have made admirable dramatic characters—women of strong virtues and telling weaknesses.

In short, larger-than-life characters become the heroes and heroines of drama not only by virtue of their station in life but also because they possess traits common to us all—ambition, generosity, malevolence, fear, and achievement—in such great abundance.

In the eighteenth century, ordinary people began taking over from royalty and the nobility as the heroes and heroines of drama—a reflection of what was occurring in the real world. For instance, in Lillo's play *The London Merchant,* written in 1731, the chief character is a young apprentice, George Barnwell. But despite this move away from royalty and the nobility, the leading figures of drama continued in many cases to be exceptional men and women at their best and worst.

The heroine of August Strindberg's *Miss Julie* is a neurotic, obsessive woman at the end of her rope. So, too, in her own way is Blanche DuBois in *A Streetcar Named Desire.* In *Mother Courage* by Bertolt Brecht, we see a portrait of a woman who will sacrifice almost anything to survive; she even loses a son by haggling over the price of his release. *The Emperor Jones,* by Eugene O'Neill, shows the downfall of a powerful black man who has made himself the ruler of a Caribbean island.

Among modern characters who stand for destructive people are Joe Keller of *All My Sons* by Arthur Miller and Regina of *The Little Foxes* by

QUINTESSENTIAL CHARACTERS

Certain key characters in drama, especially in modern drama, are not extraordinary or exceptional in the way that royalty or military leaders are, but become important because they embody qualities of an entire group of people. Many of the leading characters of the best-known plays of the past century fit this category. Included in this would be the lead characters in Edward Albee's Who's Afraid of Virginia Woolf? *Martha and George, named after Martha and George Washington, are the epitome of a contemporary warring couple. Shown here in these parts are Patrick Stewart and Mercedes Ruehl in a production at the Guthrie Theater, directed by David Esbjornson. (© Carol Rosegg)*

Lillian Hellman. Keller, in his insatiable desire for profit, manufactures defective airplane parts during World War II, leading to the death of several pilots. Regina, a cunning, avaricious woman, stands by while her dying husband has a heart attack, refusing to get the medicine which would save his life.

Representative or Quintessential Characters

When characters from everyday life replaced kings and queens as the leading figures in drama, a new type of character emerged alongside the extraordinary character. Characters of this new type are in many respects typical or ordinary, but they are significant because they embody an entire group. Rather than being notable as "worst," "best," or some other extreme, they are important as *representative* or *quintessential* characters.

A good example of such a character is Nora Helmer, the heroine of Henrik Ibsen's *A Doll's House.* A spoiled, flighty woman, she has secretly forged a signature to get money for her husband when he was very ill and needed medical attention. All her life, first by her father, then by her husband, she has been treated like a doll or a plaything, not as a mature, responsible woman. In the last act of the play, Nora rebels against this attitude; she makes a declaration of independence to her husband, slams the door on him, and walks out. It has been said that Nora's slamming of the door marks the beginning not only of modern drama but of the emancipation of modern women. Certainly Nora's defiance—her demand to be treated as an equal—has made her typical of all housewives who refuse to be regarded as pets. In one sense, Nora is an ordinary wife and mother—far from Antigone or Lady Macbeth—but she is unusual in the way she sums up an entire group of women. *A Doll's House* was written in 1879; but today, well over a century later, Nora is still a symbol of modern women and the play is revived year after year.

In *Who's Afraid of Virginia Woolf?* by Edward Albee, the main characters are a husband and a wife who are in many ways quite commonplace. He is a somewhat ineffectual college professor; she is the daughter of the college president. They argue and attack each other almost to the point of exhaustion. Another unhappily married couple? Yes. But again, they are quintessential. To Albee, they represent an American type: a bitter, alienated couple, bored with themselves and each other. To underline this point, he names them Martha and George—the same first names as Martha and George Washington, America's "first couple."

Another example is Willy Loman, in Arthur Miller's *Death of a Salesman*, who sums up all salesmen, traveling in their territories on a "smile and a shoeshine." Willy has lived by a false dream: the idea that if he puts up a good front and is "well liked," he will be successful and rich. Still another example is Troy Maxon in *Fences* by August Wilson. Maxon epitomizes the proud, headstrong man who in order to survive in a world of oppression and prejudice has developed firmness and resolution which serve him well but take their toll on his wife and son.

Nora Helmer, Martha and George, Willy Loman, and Troy Maxon: all are examples of characters who stand apart from the crowd, not by standing above it but by summing up in their personalities the essence of a certain type of person.

Stock Characters

The characters we have been describing, whether extraordinary or representative, are generally fully rounded figures. Many leading characters in drama, however, are not complete or three-dimensional; rather, they exem-

STOCK CHARACTERS OF COMMEDIA DELL'ARTE
Italian Renaissance comedy developed stereotyped characters who were always the same: each of them was famous for a certain trait—greed, boastfulness, gullibility, or the like—and always wore the same costume. This etching shows two commedia characters: Riciulina and Metzetin. The male characters (such as the one on the right) wore half-masks and elaborate headdresses. (Victoria and Albert Museum, London)

Riciulina.   Metzetin

plify one particular characteristic to the exclusion of virtually everything else. Frequently they are known by their station in life, their sex, and their occupation along with some tendency of personality: the clever servant, for instance, or the absent-minded professor. They are referred to as *stock* characters, and they appear particularly in comedy and melodrama, though they can be found in almost all kinds of drama.

Some of the most famous examples of stock characters are found in *commedia dell'arte*, a form of popular comedy which flourished in Italy during the sixteenth and seventeenth centuries. In commedia dell'arte, there was no script but rather a scenario which gave an outline of a story. The performers improvised or invented words and actions to fill out the play. The stock characters of commedia were either straight or exaggerated and were divided into servants and members of the ruling class. In every character, however, one particular feature or trait was stressed.

Whenever such a character appeared, he or she would have the same propensities and would wear the same costume. The bragging soldier, called *Capitano,* always boasted of his courage in a series of fictitious military victories. (A forebear of this character had appeared in Roman comedy centuries before.) The young lovers were also fixtures. Older characters included *Pantalone,* an elderly merchant who spoke in clichés and chased girls; and a pompous lawyer called *Dottore,* who spoke in Latin phrases and attempted to impress others with his learning. Among servants, *Harlequin* was the most popular; displaying both cunning and stupidity, he was at the heart of most plot complications. These are but a few of a full range of commedia characters, each with his or her own peculiarities.

As for examples of stock characters in melodrama, we are all familiar with such figures as the innocent young heroine, "pure as the driven snow"; and the villain, lurking in the shadows, twirling his moustache.

In today's television, the familiar figures on weekly situation comedies are good examples of stock or stereotypical characters. Stock characters on television have included Ray Romano in *Everybody Loves Raymond,* standing for the "misunderstood father"; Carrie Bradshaw as the single working woman; Niles Crane as the perennial nerd on *Fraiser;* and Phoebe, the scatterbrained neighbor in *Friends.* As with all stereotypes, their attitudes and actions are always predictable.

CHARACTERS WITH A DOMINANT TRAIT
Many comic plays feature characters with one predominant trait—greed, ambition, self-importance, and so forth. The extremes of the character are one of the elements that create the comic effect. The French playwright Molière often named his plays for such characters. One such character he named The Imaginary Invalid. *A Yale Repertory Theatre production of the play featured Raye Birk (center) in the title role, with Paul Mullins and Susan Marie Brecht on either side.* (© T. Charles Erickson)

Characters with a Dominant Trait

Closely related to stock characters are characters with a single trait or "humor." During the Renaissance, there was a widely held theory that the body was governed by four humors, which must be kept in balance for a person to be healthy. In the sixteenth century this theory was expanded to include psychological traits, and the dramatist Ben Jonson followed it extensively in his plays. In *Every Man in His Humour* and *Every Man Out of His Humour,* for instance, Jonson portrayed characters in whom one humor came to dominate all others, making for an unbalanced, often comic, personality. Jonson often named his characters for their single trait or humor. His play *The Alchemist* includes characters with names like Subtle, Face, Dapper, Surly, Wholesome, and Dame Pliant.

During and after the English Restoration, playwrights continued to give characters names indicating their personalities. In *The Way of the World,* by William Congreve, one character is called Fainall, meaning that he feigns all, or pretends everything. Other characters are named Petulant, Sir Wilful Witwoud, Waitwell, and Lady Wishfort, the last being a contraction of "wish for it." Another play from the English Restoration, *The Country Wife* by William Wycherley, includes Mr. Pinchwife (a man who hides his wife from other men), Sparkish (a man who thinks he sparkles with wit), Sir Jasper Fidget, and Mrs. Squeamish. The French playwright Molière, while generally giving his characters ordinary names, frequently emphasized the dominant trait of the main character in the titles of his plays: *The Miser, The Misanthrope, The Would-Be Gentleman,* and *The Imaginary Invalid.*

THE NARRATOR OR CHORUS

A role in drama in which a performer or a group of performers steps out of character to address the audience directly is a narrator or a chorus. In Thornton Wilder's Our Town, *the character of the Stage Manager is the narrator of the piece, and he also plays small roles such as a druggist and the preacher who marries the young couple. Seen here in the role of the stage manager/narrator is actor Paul Newman, in a production that originated at the Westport Playhouse and moved to Broadway.* (Sara Krulwich/The New York Times)

Minor Characters

Stock characters or characters with a dominant trait are not to be confused with **minor characters**. Minor characters are those—in all types of plays—who play a small part in the overall action. Generally they appear briefly and serve chiefly to further the story or to support more important characters. Typical examples of minor characters are servants, soldiers, and so forth; but even figures such as generals, bishops, judges, dukes, and duchesses are considered minor if they play only a small role in the action. Since we see so little of these characters, the dramatist can usually show only one facet of their personalities; but this is a different case from that of a main character who is deliberately portrayed as one-sided.

A Narrator or Chorus

A special type of character is a narrator or the members of a chorus.

Generally, a **narrator** speaks directly to the audience. He or she may or may not assume a dramatic persona as the other characters do. In Tennessee Williams's *The Glass Menagerie* and Thornton Wilder's *Our Town,* for instance, a performer appears both as a narrator and as one or more characters in the play. Ancient Greek drama had a chorus (usually consisting of fifteen performers) who in song and dance commented on the action of the main plot and reacted to events in the story (the chorus is discussed in Chapter 15). Use of a chorus or narrator creates a *dialectic* or *counterpoint* between a party outside the play and characters in the central action. (*Counterpoint* is a term from music denoting a second melody that accompanies or moves in contrast to the main melody.)

Bertolt Brecht used a narrator, and sometimes singers, in a pointed way: to startle the audience by making a sudden shift from the main story to the

PERFORMERS PLAY NONHUMAN PARTS
Sometimes characters are nonhuman, although they usually have human characteristics. This is a tradition that goes back at least as far as the comedies of the Greek writer Aristophanes in fifth century, B.C. Greece. A modern example is in the play Seascape *by Edward Albee in which two characters are lizards (who also happen to be quite human). Shown here in the parts are Annalee Jeffries and David Patrick Kelly in a production at the Hartford Stage.* (© T. Charles Erickson)

presentation of a moral or political argument. In *The Caucasian Chalk Circle,* for instance, Grusha—an innocent, peace-loving peasant woman—steps out of character at one point to sing a song extolling the virtues of a general who loves war. Grusha, in other words, momentarily becomes a sort of chorus when she is asked to sing a song with a point of view opposite to her own. This wrenching of characters and attitudes is deliberate on Brecht's part: it is meant to make us think about some issue, such as war and the ravages of war.

Nonhuman Characters

In Greece in the fifth century B.C.E., and in many primitive cultures, performers portrayed birds and animals, and this practice has continued to the present. Aristophanes, the Greek comic dramatist, used a chorus of actors to play the title parts in his plays *The Birds* and *The Frogs.* In the modern period, Eugène Ionesco has men turn into animals in *Rhinoceros;* and the

TWO ACTORS PLAY ONE CHARACTER

In the script, the playwright creates the character and has wide latitude in how she or he will do this. In his play Philadelphia, Here I Come, *Brian Friel had two separate actors playing the lead character: one of them was the inner man, whose words could not be heard by the other characters on stage, and the other was the outer man whose words could be heard. Shown here are Milo O'Shea as the father, Pauline Flanagan as the mother, Robert Sean Leonard and Jim True as the outer and inner young man.* (© Carol Rosegg)

Part 4   The Playwright: Dramatic Characters and Dramatic Structure

French playwright Edmond Rostand wrote a poetic fable about a rooster called *Chantecler.*

Occasionally performers are called on to play other nonhuman roles. Karel Capek (1890–1938) wrote a play, *R.U.R.,* in which people enact robots. (The initials in the title stand for "Rossum's Universal Robots," and it is from this play that the word *robot* derives.) In the medieval morality play *Everyman,* characters represent ideas or concepts, such as Fellowship, Good Deeds, Wordly Possession, and Beauty.

Dramatic characters in the guise of animals or robots are the exception rather than the rule, however. When they do occur, it is the human quality of the animal or robot which is being emphasized.

CONTRASTING CHARACTERS

Playwrights often set two characters beside each other, or against each other, who stand in sharp contrast to one another. A good example is found in Henrik Ibsen's Hedda Gabler, *in which the frustrated, volatile, reckless Hedda is juxtaposed to her old friend Mrs. Elvsted, a calmer, wiser, quieter person. Playing Hedda and Elvsted in this scene are Laila Robins and Christina Rouner in a production under the direction of David Esbjornson at the Guthrie Theater in Minneapolis.* (© Michal Daniel)

USING DRAMATIC CHARACTERS EFFECTIVELY: JUXTAPOSITION AND INTERACTION

We turn now from single characters to the way characters interact with and relate to one another.

Juxtaposition of Characters

Since dramatic characters are a creation of the playwright, he or she can use them in combination with other characters to bring out certain qualities.

Protagonist and Antagonist   From Greek theater we have the terms *protagonist* and *antagonist.* The **protagonist** is the main character in a play—Othello, for instance—and the **antagonist** is the main character's chief opponent. In *Othello,* the antagonist is Iago. It is through the contest between these two characters that their individual qualities are developed.

Contrasting Characters   Another way dramatists contrast characters is by setting them side by side rather than in opposition. Sophocles created two exceptionally strong-willed, independent female characters—Antigone and Electra—each one the title character in a play. Both are young women intent on defying an older person and willing to risk death to fight for a principle. But unlike other dramatists who had told the same story, Sophocles gave each of them a sister with a sharply contrasting personality. To Antigone he gave

Characters: Images of Ourselves

Dramatic characters sometimes have an impact that seems "more real than real." In fact, the Italian dramatist Luigi Pirandello argued in *Six Characters in Search of an Author* that dramatic characters are more permanent and less illusory than human beings. Speaking through the character of the Father, he says, "He who has had the luck to be born a character can laugh even at death. He cannot die. The man, the writer, the instrument of the creation will die, but his creation does not die." Arguing with a theater manager in the play, the Father points out that whereas human beings are always changing and are different from one day to the next, characters remain the same. The Manager picks up the argument, with the character of the Father:

The Manager: Then you'll be saying next that you . . . are truer and more real than I am.

The Father: But of course; without doubt! . . .

The Manager: More real than I?

The Father: If your reality can change from one day to another . . .

The Manager: But everyone knows it can change. It is always changing, the same as anyone else's.

The Father: No, sir, not ours! Look here! That is the very difference! Our reality doesn't change; it can't change! It can't be other than what it is, because it is already fixed forever.

Their permanence, however, is not the only feature of dramatic characters. When well drawn, they present us with a vivid, incisive picture of ourselves. We see individuals at their best and at their worst; we see them perform heroic acts of courage, acts we would like to consider ourselves capable of; and we also see deeds of cowardice and violence—acts we fear we might commit in moments of weakness or anger. We see outrageous cases of folly and pretension, which make us laugh uproariously. In short, we see ourselves in the revealing and illuminating mirror theater holds before us.

We have seen that the exchange between performer and spectator is the basic encounter of theater. But the dramatic characters impersonated by the performers are images of ourselves. In truth, therefore, the basic encounter of theater is with ourselves. Sometimes, watching a theater event, we see a part of ourselves on the stage and realize for the first time some truth about our lives. This confrontation is at the heart of the theater experience.

Source of dialogue: Eric Bentley (ed.), *Naked Masks: Five Plays by Luigi Pirandello,* Dutton, New York, 1922, pp. 266–267. Copyright 1922 by E. P. Dutton. Renewal copyright 1950 by Stefano, Fausto, and Lietta Pirandello. Reprinted by permission of the publisher.

Ismene, a docile, compliant sister who argues that Antigone should obey the law and give in to authority. To Electra he gave Chrisothemis, a meek, frightened creature who protests that as women they are powerless to act. Sophocles strengthened and clarified Antigone and Electra by providing them with contrasting characters to set off their own determination and courage.

Frequently a dramatist will introduce secondary characters to serve as foils or counterparts to the main characters. In *Hedda Gabler,* by Henrik Ibsen, the main character, Hedda, is a willful, destructive woman, bent on having her own way. Mrs. Elvsted, another character in the play, is Hedda's opposite in almost every way: a trusting, warm, sincere woman. This technique of setting parallel or contrasting characters beside one another is like putting certain colors next to each other. For instance, dark green looks much darker when seen next to pale green.

Major and Minor Characters

As noted above, minor characters are those who take a small part in the action of a play. The *major characters* are the important figures, the ones about whom a play revolves. In *Hamlet* the major characters include Hamlet, Claudius, Gertrude, Polonius, Laertes, and Ophelia. The minor characters include Marcellus and Bernardo, who are standing watch when the ghost appears; and Reynaldo, a servant to Polonius. Some characters fall halfway between major and minor; examples in *Hamlet* are Rosencrantz and Guildenstern, or the gravedigger. These characters have distinctive personalities and play a quite important though small part in the drama.

Orchestration of Characters

Anton Chekhov, the Russian dramatist, is said to have "orchestrated" his characters. The reference is to a musical composition in which the theme is played first by one section of the orchestra, such as the violins, and then by

ORCHESTRATION OF CHARACTERS
Characters in a play serve as contrasts, counterparts, or complements to each other; sometimes one group of characters is set in opposition to another. Chekhov was a master at combining and contrasting characters. Here we see a scene from The Cherry Orchard *at the Yale School of Drama. (© T. Charles Erickson)*

Chapter 13 Dramatic Characters   287

another, such as the brasses or woodwinds. Not only is the theme taken up by various sections, but it can be played in different ways as well—first in a major key, for instance, and then in a minor key. In each of his plays, Chekhov drew a series of characters with a common problem, and each character represented some aspect of the central theme.

In *Uncle Vanya,* for example, Chekhov's theme of disillusionment and frustration with life is reflected by virtually every character in the play, each of whom longs for a love that cannot be fulfilled. The title character, Vanya, has been working on an estate to help support a professor whom he discovers to be a fraud. In the midst of his disillusionment, Vanya falls in love with the professor's young wife, but she does not return his love. A neighbor, Dr. Astrov, has made sacrifices to be a doctor in a small rural community and then has grown dissatisfied with his life. He too loves the professor's wife, but nothing can come of it. Vanya's niece, a plain woman who works hard for little reward, is in love with Dr. Astrov, but he does not return her love. And so it goes; practically everyone embodies the theme. But all this is done subtly and carefully. The theme is brought out through gradations and shadings of meaning which are interwoven in the characters like threads in a tapestry.

Chekhov was a master at orchestrating his characters, but he was not the only dramatist to use the technique. In one way or another, most dramatists try to arrange their characters so that they produce a cumulative effect. It is not what one character does or says but what all the characters do together that creates the effect.

In this chapter we have looked at the creation of dramatic characters. In chapters 14 and 15, we investigate another creation of the playwright and his or her collaborators—the structure and dynamics of a dramatic work.

SUMMARY

1. Dramatic characters symbolize people and fall into several categories. Frequently the chief characters of theater are extraordinary characters, men and women at the outer limits of human behavior.

2. In modern serious theater we frequently find typical or ordinary characters—complete, fully rounded portraits of people—who embody a whole group or type. An example is Willy Loman, the salesman in *Death of a Salesman*.

3. Some characters are stereotypes. Stock characters, for instance, are predictable, clearly defined types. Other characters have one dominant trait which overshadows all other features.

4. A special type of character in drama of many periods is a narrator or the members of a chorus.

5. Occasionally performers are asked to play nonhuman parts—animals, birds, etc.—but these parts generally have a strong human flavor.

6. Characters are placed together by the playwright in certain combinations to obtain maximum effectiveness. A protagonist may be opposed by an antagonist; minor characters support major characters; and individual characters are orchestrated into a whole.

7. Dramatic characters are symbols of people; therefore, the basic confrontation in theater is with ourselves.

EXPLORING THEATER ON THE WEB

Dramatic Characters

The Northwest Playwrights Guild (NPG) is a forum exchanging information and ideas about playwriting, particularly in the northwestern United States. The site hosts links to resources for the student playwright (http://www.nwpg.org).

Exercises:

1. On the NPG site is a link to "Essays on the Craft of Dramatic Writing" by Bill Johnson. Read the essay on creating dramatic characters (http://www.storyispromise.com/wchar.htm).

   What is the most important aspect of making an audience "believe" in a character?

   What does "agent of the action" mean?

2. Read Bill Johnson's analysis of the structure of *Romeo and Juliet* at this link: http://www.storyispromise.com/rjoutlin.htm.

   How are the characters designed to move the action of the play to its climactic conclusion?

3. Read Bill Johnson's analysis of *The Heidi Chronicles* at: http://www.storyispromise.com/heidi.htm.

   What must Heidi do to become the main character in a chronicle about her life?

   How does Wendy Wasserstein use Heidi's relationships with other characters to advance the action of the play?

   Compare the treatment of Heidi's character relationships with the treatment of character relationships in a television show that chronicles the life of a central character (for example: Eric in *That 70s Show*, Ally in *Ally McBeal*, Kevin in *The Wonder Years*).

4. Visit the website (http://www.abwag.com/protagonist.htm) for *Acting without Agony: An Alternative to the Method* by Don Richardson. Follow the links to compare and contrast the motivations and responses of the protagonist and antagonist. From this knowledge, create a character sketch for two characters interacting as protagonist and antagonist. How does one type of dramatic character influence the other?

CHAPTER FOURTEEN

Conventions of Dramatic Structure

As noted in Chapter 8, there are occasions when a theater event originates with a director, a performance artist, or a group of actresses and actors. Most often, however, the person who provides the blueprint for a stage presentation is the **playwright,** also known as the *dramatist*. This has been the case throughout the history of western theater, beginning with the Greeks, and with Asian theater as well.

When a script originates with a playwright, he or she determines the subject matter; decides on the character or characters who will be the focus of the drama; and makes a choice with regard to the type of play it will be: tragic, comic, tragicomic, or some combination of these. The playwright provides the words the characters speak and the actions they perform. The playwright also decides how the events in a play will unfold: where the action will take place and over how long a period of time, as well as the sequence of episodes in the action. In other words, the playwright must *dramatize* the story—transform it into **action** and conversation, which is called **dialogue.**

◀ PRINCIPLES OF DRAMATIC CREATION

In developing a drama, the playwright is aware of certain conventions that have developed through the centuries. These include how a story is turned into a plot, how characters interact, how action is carried forward, and how the play is resolved. A master at plot and character—and a playwright who set precedents for other playwrights to follow—was the Swedish dramatist, August Strindberg. His play Dance of Death *is a taut drama with very few characters that takes place over a short period of time in a confined space (an isolated lighthouse). A wife (Helen Mirren) and husband (Ian McKlellan) verbally duel with each other to the point of exhaustion.* (Sara Krulwich/The New York Times)

Dramatizing a story entails creating a dramatic **structure.** In this chapter, we will examine how dramatic structure is created; in Chapter 15, we will examine the various forms a structure can take.

Every work of art has some kind of structure, or framework. It may be loosely connected or tightly knit; the important thing is that the framework exists. In a sense, the structure of a play is roughly analogous to the structure of a building. Architects and engineers work together like playwrights and directors. An architect and an engineer plan a skeleton or substructure which will provide the inner strength for a building. They determine the depth of the foundation, the weight of the support beams, and the stress on the side walls. Similarly, a playwright and a director establish a premise for a play which serves as its foundation; they introduce various stresses and strains in the form of conflicts; they establish boundaries and outer limits to contain the play; they calculate the dynamics of the action. In short, they "construct" the play.

ESSENTIALS OF DRAMATIC STRUCTURE

In theater, structure usually takes the form of a **plot,** which is the arrangement of events or the selection and order of scenes in a play. Plot, in turn, is generally based on a **story.**

The Form of Drama: Plot versus Story

Stories—narrative accounts of what people do—are as old as the human race, and they form the substance of daily conversation, of newspapers and television, of novels and films. But every medium presents a story in a different form. In theater, the story must be presented in a limited period of time by living actors and actresses on a stage, and this requires selectivity.

It is important to remember that the plot of a play differs from a story. A **story** is a full account of an event, or series of events, usually told in chronological order. **Plot,** as opposed to story, is a selection and arrangement of scenes taken from a story for presentation onstage. It is what actually happens onstage, not what is talked about. The story of Abraham Lincoln, for example, begins with his birth in a log cabin and continues to the day he was shot at Ford's Theater in Washington. To create a play about Lincoln, a playwright would have to make choices. Would the dramatist include scenes in Springfield, Illinois, where Lincoln worked as a lawyer and held his famous debates with Stephen Douglas? Or would everything take place in Washington after Lincoln became president? Would there be scenes with Lincoln's wife, Mary Todd, or would the other characters be only government and military officials? The plot of a play about Abraham Lincoln and Mary Todd would have scenes

Significance of Structure: The Architecture of Drama

Buildings vary enormously in size and shape: they can be as diverse as a skyscraper, a cathedral, and a small cottage. Buildings can exist in clusters, like the homes in a suburban development or the buildings on a college campus. Engineering requirements will vary according to the needs of individual structures: a gymnasium roof, for instance, must span a vast open area; this calls for a different construction from that of a sixty-story skyscraper, which in turn calls for something different from a ski lodge on a mountainside. Plays, too, vary, but, like a building, each play must have its own internal laws and its own framework, which give it shape, strength, and meaning. Otherwise, a theater event is likely to fall apart, just as a badly constructed building will collapse.

Naturally, structure manifests itself differently in theater and architecture. A play is not a building. Rather than occupying space, a play unfolds through time. It evolves and develops like a living organism, and we become aware of its structure as we sense its underlying pattern and rhythm. The repeated impulses of two characters in conflict or the tension which mounts as the pace quickens—these insinuate themselves into our subconscious like a drumbeat. Moment by moment we see what is happening onstage; but below the surface we sense a substructure, giving the event meaning and purpose.

The significance of structure is underscored by the problems that arise when it is *not* developed satisfactorily. Frequently, we see productions in which most elements—acting, costumes, scenery, words, even the situation—appear correct. But somehow the plays themselves do not seem to progress. They become dull and repetitive; or perhaps they become confusing and diffuse, going off in several directions at once. When this happens, it is likely that the problems are structural. Either no clear structure existed to begin with, or an existing structure was violated along the way.

This points up two principles of dramatic structure. First, every theatrical event must have an underlying pattern or organization. Second, once a pattern or an organization is established, it must remain true to itself—it must be organic and have integrity. A rigid plot which suddenly becomes chaotic two-thirds of the way through the play will cause confusion; a loosely organized play that suddenly takes on a tight structure will seem artificial and contrived.

and characters related primarily to their lives. The plot of a play about the Lincoln-Douglas debates would consist mostly of scenes relating to the debates. Even when a play is based on a fictional story invented by the playwright, the plot must be more restricted and structured than the story itself: characters and scenes must still be selected and the sequence determined.

In creating a plot, the playwright decides at what point in the story the plot will begin, what characters will participate, what scenes will be included, and in what sequence the scenes will occur. Two ingredients are essential: action and conflict.

The Subject and Verb of Drama: People and Action

As is pointed out in the Introduction, the subject of theater is always people—their hopes, their joys, their foibles, their fears. In other words, if we were to construct a "grammar of theater," the *subject* would be people, i.e., dramatic characters. In linguistic grammar, every subject needs a verb; similarly, in the grammar of theater, dramatic characters need a verb—some form of action that defines them.

The terms *to act* and *to perform* are used in theater to denote the impersonation of a character by an actor or an actress, but these words also mean "to do something," or "to be active." The word *drama* derives from a Greek root, the verb *dran,* meaning "to do" or "to act." At its heart, theater involves action.

The Crucible of Drama: Conflict

People are often defined, and often define themselves, by the way they respond to challenges. If they cannot face up to a challenge, that tells us one thing; if they meet a challenge with dignity, even though it defeats them, that tells us something else; if they triumph, that tells us something else again. In our own lives, we come to know our families, our friends, and our enemies by seeing how they respond to us and to other people, and how they meet crises.

CONFLICT: THE CRUCIBLE OF DRAMA

Theater requires conflict: between people, between families, between opposing nations, ideologies, or political agendas. Here we see a strong family conflict unfolding in Federico Garcia Lorca's Blood Wedding *in which a rebellious man kidnaps a woman and takes her away from her husband and her family on her wedding day. In the scene here we see the husband and the kidnapper confronting one another. The actors are Pablo Bracho and Pierre Dubois in a production at Stages Repertory Theatre of Houston.* (© Bruce Bennett)

In life this process of challenge and response can take years. But in the theater we have only a few hours, and the playwright must therefore devise means by which the characters will face and be tested by challenges in a short span of time. The American dramatist Arthur Miller named one of his plays *The Crucible*. Literally, a *crucible* is a vessel in which metal is tested by being exposed to extreme heat. Figuratively, a crucible has come to stand for any severe test of human worth and endurance—a trial by fire. In a sense, every play provides a crucible: a test devised by the playwright to show how the characters behave under conditions of stress. Through this test, the meaning of the play is brought out.

The crucible of a play can vary enormously: it might be a fight for a kingdom, or in modern terms a fight for "turf"; but it can just as easily be a

A PLAY OF IDEAS

In his play The Coast of Utopia: Shipwreck, *dramatist Tom Stoppard developed conflict not only among the characters, who are vying with one another, but also with ideas and points of view, about science, philosophy, and a range of subjects.* The Coast of Utopia *is actually three plays that in total take nine hours to present. The setting is nineteenth century Russia in which a group of dissident aristocrats are opposing the serf-owning society in which they live. In the scene here, Will Keen plays Bellinsky, a critic, and Guy Henry plays the writer, Ivan Turgenev. The production was at the Royal National Theatre in London.* (© Donald Cooper/PhotoSTAGE)

INTELLECTUAL OR CONCEPTUAL CONFLICT

In certain plays the main conflict is not emotional but intellectual. A good example is Pirandello's Six Characters in Search of an Author, *in which the philosophical issues include art versus life and appearance versus reality. The scene shown here is from a production at the Oregon Shakespeare Festival, Portland.* (Rick Adams)

fight over a person. It can be an intellectual or a moral confrontation. There may even be no overt clash at all, as in Samuel Beckett's *Waiting for Godot,* in which two men wait on a barren plain for something or someone named Godot who never comes. But there must be tension of some sort. In *Waiting for Godot,* for instance, there are several sources of tension or conflict: the ever-present question whether the mysterious Godot will or will not come; the friction between the two main characters; the unfolding revelation of men deluding themselves over and over again; and on top of these, a constant probing of religious and philosophical ideas in a series of questions posed by the author. (A synopsis of *Waiting for Godot* appears at the end of Part 4.)

A Note on Intellectual or Conceptual Conflict One special form conflict can take is intellectual debate. A drama whose main conflict or problem is intellectual or conceptual is sometimes called a ***play of ideas.*** It is worth pointing out that a purely intellectual approach to theater can present problems. When carried to extremes, it concentrates entirely on abstruse arguments, neglecting the flesh-and-blood characters that are the essence of theater.

STRUCTURAL CONVENTIONS: THE RULES OF THE GAME

In order to make certain that events onstage will be dynamic and that characters will face a meaningful test, conventions or "ground rules" have evolved for dramatic structure. A good analogy would be the rules in games such as card games, board games, video games, and sports. In each case, rules are developed to ensure a lively contest.

Consider, for example, how theater can be compared with sports. Theater is more varied and complex than most sports events, and theatrical rules are not so clearly defined or so consciously imposed as rules in sports. Nevertheless, there are similarities that point up the ways in which a play makes its impact.

Limited Space

Most sports have a limited playing area. In some cases this consists of a confined space: a boxing ring, a basketball court, a baseball field. The playing area is clearly defined, and invariably there is some kind of "out of bounds."

Theater, of course, is usually limited to a stage; but there is also a limit within the play itself. The action of a play is generally confined to a "world" of its own—that is, to a fictional universe which contains all the characters and events of the play—and none of the characters or actions moves outside the orbit of that world.

Sometimes the world of a play is restricted to a single room. In his play *No Exit,* Jean-Paul Sartre (1905–1980), a French existentialist, confines three characters to one room, from which, as the title suggests, there is no escape. The room is supposed to be hell, and the three characters—a man, Garcin; and two women, Estelle and Inez—are confined there forever. Estelle loves Garcin, Garcin loves Inez, and Inez (a lesbian) loves Estelle. Each one, in short, loves the one who will not reciprocate; and by being confined to a room, they undergo permanent torture. There are numerous modern plays in which the action takes place in a single room, one good example being *'Night, Mother* by Marsha Norman.

Limited Time

Sports events put some limit on the duration of action. In football and basketball, there is a definite time limit. In golf, there is a given number of holes; in tennis, there is a limited number of sets. Theoretically, some sports, such as baseball, are open-ended and could go on forever; but spectators tend to become impatient with this arrangement. Tennis, for instance, was originally open-ended but now has a "sudden death" or tiebreaker playoff when a set reaches six-all. A time limit or score limit ensures that the spectators can see a complete event, with a clear winner and loser and no loose ends.

The time limit in theater can be looked at in two ways: first, as the length of time it takes a performance to be completed; second, as the time limit placed on the characters within the framework of the play itself. Let us look at each of these.

Most theatrical performances last anywhere from 1 to 3 hours. The longest theatrical productions about which we have records are medieval **cycle plays,** and even these were limited. A cycle, or series, of plays usually lasted several days—though one, at Valenciennes in France in 1547, went on for twenty-five days. In the drama festivals of ancient Greece, plays were presented for several days in a row. On a single day there might be a trilogy of three connecting plays followed by a short comic play. Still, even if we count a Greek trilogy as one play, it lasted only the better part of a day. Moreover, these examples are exceptions; most performances have been and still are limited to 2 or 3 hours.

More important than the actual playing time of a performance is the time limit or deadline *within* the play. This means the time that is supposed to elapse during the events of the play, the time covered by those events—a few hours, a few days, or longer. Frequently, we find in a play a fixed period within which the characters must complete an action. For instance, at the end of the second act of Ibsen's *A Doll's House,* the heroine, Nora, is trying desperately to get her husband to put off until the following evening the opening of a letter which she fears will establish her as a forger and will threaten their marriage. When he agrees, Nora says to herself, "Thirty-one hours to live."

Strongly Opposed Forces

Most sports, like many other types of games, involve two opposed teams or individuals. This ensures clear lines of force: the good guys and the bad guys, the home team and the visitors. The musical *West Side Story* (based on Shakespeare's *Romeo and Juliet*) features two opposed gangs, not unlike opposing teams in sports. In the simplest dramatic situations, one character directly opposes another—the **protagonist** against the **antagonist.**

In a manual on playwriting, the critic Kenneth MacGowan emphasized that characters in a play "must be so selected and developed that they include people who are bound to react upon each other, bound to clash."[1] A perfect example of characters bound to clash is the man and woman, Julie and Jean, in Strindberg's *Miss Julie.* Julie, an aristocrat, is the daughter of the owner of an estate. She has had an unhappy engagement and is deeply suspicious of men, but at the same time sexually attracted to them. Jean is a servant, an aggressive man who dreams of escaping his life of servitude and

STRONGLY OPPOSED FORCES

Traditional plot structure calls for strongly opposing forces: the antagonist opposes the protagonist; one group opposes another. In The Crucible by Arthur Miller, about the Salem witch trials in Massachusets, John Proctor (Liam Neeson) opposes the church fathers who give way to hysteria to burn women accused of being witches. He also finds himself opposed by his wife, seen here as played by Laura Linney being restrained in a courtroom. (© Joan Marcus)

owning a hotel. These two experience strong forces of repulsion and attraction and are drawn together on midsummer's eve in a climactic encounter.

A similar confrontation occurs between Blanche DuBois and Stanley Kowalski in Tennessee Williams's play *A Streetcar Named Desire*. Blanche is a faded southern belle trying desperately to hold onto her gentility; she sees the crude, aggressive Stanley as the chief threat to her stability and even to her survival. On his side, Stanley, who is insecure about his coarseness and his lack of education, is provoked almost to the breaking point by Blanche and her superior airs. (A synopsis of *A Streetcar Named Desire* appears at the end of Part 4.)

One device frequently used by dramatists to create friction or tension between forces is restricting the characters to the members of one family. Relatives have built-in rivalries and affinities: parents versus children, sisters versus brothers. Being members of the same family, they have no avenue of escape. Mythology, on which so much drama is based, abounds with familial relationships.

Chapter 14 Conventions of Dramatic Structure

Shakespeare frequently set members of one family against one another: Hamlet opposes his mother; Lear opposes his daughters; Othello kills his wife Desdemona. In modern drama, virtually every writer of note has dealt with close family situations: Ibsen, Strindberg, Chekhov, Williams, Miller, and Edward Albee (1928–   ), to mention a few. The American dramatist Eugene O'Neill wrote what many consider his finest play, *Long Day's Journey into Night,* about the four members of his own family.

A Balance of Forces

In most sports, there are rules designed to ensure that the contest will be as equal as possible without coming to a dead draw. We all want our team to win, but we would rather see a close, exciting contest than a runaway. And so rules are set up, with handicaps or other devices to equalize the forces. In basketball or football, for instance, as soon as one team scores, the other team gets the ball so that it will have an opportunity to even the score.

In theater, a hard-fought and relatively equal contest is implicit in what has been said about opposing forces: Jean stands opposite Julie; Blanche stands opposite Stanley. Even in the somewhat muted, low-key plays of Anton Chekhov, there is a balance of forces among various groups. In *The Cherry Orchard,* the owners of the orchard are set against the man who will acquire it; in *The Three Sisters,* the sisters are opposed in the possession of their home by their acquisitive sister-in-law.

Incentive and Motivation

In sports, as in other kinds of games, a prize is offered to guarantee that the participants will give their best in an intense contest. In professional sports it is money; in amateur sports, a trophy such as a cup. In addition, there is the glory of winning, the accolades of television and the press, and the plaudits of family and friends.

In the same way, good drama never lacks incentive or motivation for its characters: Macbeth wants desperately to be king; Saint Joan wants to save France; Blanche DuBois must find protection and preserve her dignity.

CREATING A DRAMATIC STRUCTURE

Working within these conventions, the playwright sets out to develop a dramatic structure, which begins with the crucial opening scene of the play.

The Opening Scene

The first scene of a drama starts the action and sets the tone and style for everything that follows. It tells us whether we are going to see a serious or a comic play and whether the play will deal with fantasy or with affairs of everyday life. The opening scene is a clue or signal about what lies ahead; it also sets the wheels of action in motion, giving the characters a shove and hurtling them toward their destination.

The playwright poses an initial problem for the characters, establishing an imbalance of forces or a disturbance in their equilibrium which compels them to respond. Generally, this imbalance has occurred just before the play begins or develops immediately after the play opens. In *Antigone,* for example, two brothers have killed one another just before the opening of the play. In *Hamlet,* "something is rotten in the state of Denmark," and early in the play the ghost of Hamlet's father tells Hamlet to seek revenge. At the beginning of *Romeo and Juliet,* the Capulets and the Montagues are at one another's throats in a street fight.

Obstacles and Complications

Having met the initial challenge of the play, the characters then move through a series of steps—alternating between achievement and defeat, between hope and despair. The moment they seem to accomplish one goal, certain factors or events cut across the play to upset the balance and start the characters on another path. In theater these may be **obstacles,** which are impediments put in a character's way; or they may be **complications**— outside forces or new twists in the plot introduced at an opportune moment.

Shakespeare's *Hamlet* provides numerous examples of obstacles and complications. Hamlet stages a "play within the play" in order to confirm that his uncle Claudius has killed his father. Claudius reacts to the play in a manner that makes his guilt obvious. But when Hamlet first tries to kill

THE OPENING SCENE
The first scene of a play is crucial, usually setting the location, establishing mood and tone, introducing characters, themes, and action. A famous opening scene is that in Shakespeare's Romeo and Juliet *in which the Capulet and Montague families confront one another in a street fight. This sets the stage for the enmity between the two families which forms the basis for so much of the conflict in the play. Seen here is the opening scene in a production at the Hartford Stage Company.* (© Jennifer W. Lester)

PLOT COMPLICATIONS IN *HAMLET*

In conventional plot structure, the action is prolonged and tension is increased by a series of problems confronting the characters. The twists and turns in the plot of Shakespeare's Hamlet *are a good example. Shown here is Wallace Acton as Hamlet, preparing to kill King Claudius (Ted van Griethuysen) who he thinks has murdered his father. But there is the complication that Claudius is at prayer, and Hamlet hesitates because he does not want to send Claudius to heaven. The production was at the Shakespeare Theatre in Washington, D.C.* (© Carol Rosegg)

Claudius, he discovers him at prayer. An obstacle has been thrown into Hamlet's path: if Claudius dies while praying, he may go to heaven rather than to hell. Since Hamlet does not want Claudius to go to heaven, he does not kill him.

Later, Hamlet is in his mother's bedroom when he hears a noise behind a curtain. Surely Claudius is lurking there, but when Hamlet thrusts his sword through the curtain, he finds that he has killed Polonius. This provides Claudius with an excuse to send Hamlet to England with Rosencrantz and Guildenstern, who carry with them a letter instructing the king of England to murder Hamlet. Hamlet escapes that trap and returns to Denmark. Now, at last, it seems that he can carry out his revenge. But on his return, he discovers that Ophelia has killed herself while he was away, and her brother, Laertes, is seeking revenge on him. This complicates the situation once again; Hamlet is prevented from meeting Claudius head-on because he must also deal with Laertes. In the end Hamlet does carry out his mission, but only after many interruptions.

Crisis and Climax

As a result of conflicts, obstacles, and complications in a play, characters become involved in a series of ***crises.*** A play usually builds from one crisis to another. The first crisis will be resolved only to have the action lead to a subsequent crisis. The final and most significant crisis is referred to as the ***climax.*** In the final climax the issues of the play are resolved, either happily or, in the case of tragedies, unhappily, often with the death of the hero or heroine.

In this chapter we have been looking at the structure of theater, and particularly at the development of plot, which thrusts characters into action. So far, we have examined general principles; when we look at dramatic construction more closely, we discover that certain forms have recurred throughout theater history. In Chapter 15 we will examine specific forms of dramatic structure.

SUMMARY

1. Every work of art, including theater, has some kind of structure. In theater, structure usually takes the form of a plot.

2. *A* dramatic plot is not the same as a story. A story is a complete account of an episode or a sequence of events, but a plot is what we see onstage. In a plot the events have been selected from a story and arranged in a certain sequence.

3. The action of a play frequently consists of a test, or crucible, for the characters, in which their true nature is defined. This test involves some form of conflict.

4. Dramatic conventions, ensuring a strong plot and continuation of tension, are analogous to rules in sports. In both sports and theater there are limited spaces or playing areas, time limits imposed on the action, strongly opposing forces, evenly matched contestants, and prizes or goals for the participants.

5. A play generally begins with an imbalance of forces or a loss of equilibrium by one of the characters; this propels the characters to action.

6. As a play progresses, the characters encounter a series of obstacles and complications in attempting to fulfill their objectives or realize their goals. These encounters produce the tension and conflict of drama.

EXPLORING THEATER

ON

THE

WEB

Conventions of Dramatic Structure

The Internet is an easy place for playwrights to be connected outside of the theater. Online magazines such as *The Playwright's Forum* (http://users.erols.com/pforum/welcome.htm) are becoming forums for writers of all kinds. *The Playwright's Forum* is a nonprofit organization dedicated to the artistic development of talented playwrights from the Washington, D.C., area.

Another website for playwrights is E-Script (http://www.singlelane.com/escript).

Exercises:

1. This page from Scriptseeker.com gives some helpful tips on dramatic structure. What does the site suggest are the key elements of a script's beginning? Middle? End?

2. A dramaturg specializes in dramatic structure. Visit the Dramaturgy Pages at http://www.dramaturgy.net/dramaturgy to find out: What is a dramaturg? What does he or she do?

3. Visit http://staff.lib.muohio.edu/nawpa, the website for the Native American Women Playwrights Archive at Miami University in Oxford, Ohio. Follow the link to the "Author's Roundtable Discussion." Read the article and reflect on the unique challenges faced by this group in embracing the conventions of dramatic structure. Would similar challenges be posed for other playwrights from diverse cultures? Do these challenges transcend culture to become reflected in historical mainstream drama? Comedy? Musical theater? Children's theater? Puppet theater?

CHAPTER FIFTEEN

Dramatic Structure: Climactic, Episodic, and Other Forms

Throughout theater history, we find basic dramatic forms reappearing. In western civilization, a form adopted in Greece in the fifth century B.C.E. emerges, somewhat altered, in France in the seventeenth century; the same form shows up once more in Norway in the late nineteenth century and is repeated throughout the twentieth century. This form can be referred to as *climactic*. Another, contrasting form, best illustrated by the plays of Shakespeare, can be called *episodic*. Through most of the history of western theater, one or the other of these two forms—or some combination of the two—has predominated.

In addition, there are other forms. An approach in which dramatic episodes are strung together without any apparent connection has emerged in a new guise in recent times. Structure based on a ritual or pattern is both old and new. And musical theater has a structure of its own.

◀ CLIMACTIC STRUCTURE IN *HEDDA GABLER*

In different periods and different countries, various approaches to dramatic structure have been followed. Interestingly, certain forms have repeated themselves (in a slightly altered way) throughout theater history. One form is the episodic, best exemplified in the plays of Shakespeare. Another is the climactic form, initiated by the Greeks and taken up later, in the seventeenth century, by French dramatists, in the late nineteenth century and throughout the twentieth century by modern playwrights. One of the first writers to perfect the form in the modern period was the Norwegian dramatist Henrik Ibsen. His play, Hedda Gabler, *whose title character is shown here, depicts an ambitious, bored woman trapped in an unhappy marriage. The conflicts, the twists in the plot, the portrayal of the characters all represent the best in modern, realistic drama. The actress, in a production that began at the Huntington Theatre and moved to Broadway, is Kate Burton. (© T. Charles Erickson)*

305

The characteristics of the basic types will be clearer when we look at each separately. This chapter begins with climactic form, goes on to examine episodic form, and then takes up additional forms.

CLIMACTIC STRUCTURE

Characteristics of Climactic Structure

The Plot Begins Late in the Story   The first hallmark of climactic drama is that the plot begins quite late in the story. Ibsen's *Ghosts,* written in 1881, is a clear example.

Before *Ghosts* begins, the following events have occurred: Mrs. Alving has married a dissolute man who fathers an illegitimate child by another woman and contracts a venereal disease. When she discovers her husband's infidelity early in their marriage, Mrs. Alving visits the family minister, Pastor Manders, telling him she wishes to end the marriage. Although Manders is attracted to her and she to him—and although he realizes that she is wronged and miserable—he sends her back to her husband. She stays with her husband out of a Victorian sense of duty, though she sends her son, Oswald, away to escape his father's influence. When her husband dies, Mrs. Alving builds an orphanage in his honor to camouflage his true character. At this point—as is typical with climactic plot structure—the play itself has still not begun; it begins later, when the son returns home and the facts of the past are unearthed, precipitating the crisis.

In climactic structure, then, the play begins when all the roads of the past converge at one crucial intersection in the present—in other words, at the climax. The fact that the plot begins so late has at least two important consequences for climactic drama. First, it is frequently necessary to explain what has happened earlier by having one or more characters report the information to others. The technical term for revelation of background information is *exposition.* During the early parts of *Ghosts,* the information about the unhappy marriage of Captain and Mrs. Alving must be conveyed by one character to another. Another form of exposition is a description of something that happens offstage during the course of the play. An example in *Ghosts* would be the account of a fire that destroys the new orphanage between Acts II and III. (A synopsis of *Ghosts* appears at the end of Part 4.)

A second consequence of the fact that the plot begins late in the story is that the time span covered within a climactic play is usually brief: in many cases a matter of a few hours, and at the most a few days. Some playwrights, attempting to push events as near the climax as possible, have stage time (the time we imagine is passing when we are watching a play) coincide with real time (that is, clock time). An example is Tennessee Williams's *Cat on a Hot Tin Roof:* the events depicted in the story last the same time as the play itself—2 hours.

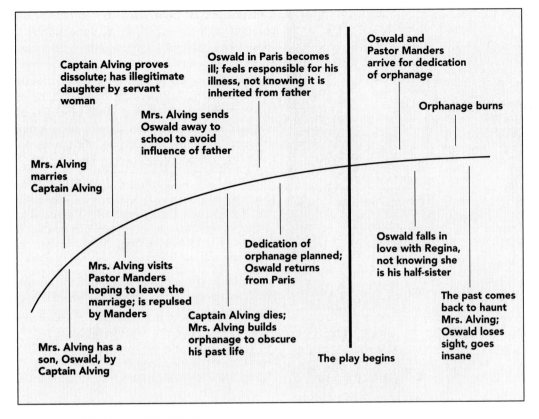

CLIMACTIC STRUCTURE IN GHOSTS

Henrik Ibsen's play follows the climactic form, in which the play begins toward the very end—or climax—of the sequence of events. The parts of the story that occur before the play begins are to the left of the vertical line. Only the events to the right occur in the play; the ones before them must be described in exposition.

Scenes, Locales, and Characters Are Limited Climactic drama typically has a limited number of long segments, or acts. In Greek plays there are generally five episodes separated by choral interludes. The French neoclassicists invariably used five acts. For much of the nineteenth and twentieth centuries, three acts were standard. Today, the norm is two acts, though the long one-act play performed without intermission is also frequently found.

Limiting the scenes in a play usually entails restricting the locale as well. In the discussion of the "rules" of drama in Chapter 14, we saw that the action can be confined to a single room, as in Sartre's *No Exit*. Such close confinement is a hallmark of climactic drama.

Along with restriction of locale, there is a restriction of characters. Greek drama generally has four or five principal characters. Many modern plays have no more than a similar number of main characters.

THE RESTRICTIONS OF CLIMACTIC DRAMA
A climactic play usually has a minimum number of characters, covers a short space of time, and takes place in a limited space—often one room. A good example is Cat on a Hot Tin Roof *by Tennessee Williams. The play deals only with the members of one family and takes place in one room over a period of a few hours. Shown here are Brick (Brendan Fraser) on the left, and his wife Maggie (Frances O'Connor), the cat of the title, on the right in a production at the Lyric Theatre in London.* (© Donald Cooper/PhotoSTAGE)

Construction Is Tight Because it is carefully constructed, a climactic play fits together tightly, with no loose ends. It is like a chain linked in a cause-and-effect relationship. As in a detective story, event A leads to event B; B leads to C, causing D; D leads in turn to E; and so on. Just as the time frame and the restricted space afford no exit, so the chain of events is locked in; once the action begins, there is no stopping it.

Jean Anouilh, in his play *Antigone,* compares tragedy to the workings of a machine.

The spring is wound up tight. It will uncoil of itself. That is what is so convenient in tragedy. The least little turn of the wrist will do the job. . . . The rest is automatic. You don't need to lift a finger. The machine is in perfect order; it has been oiled ever since time began and it runs without friction.[1]

Anouilh applied this notion only to tragedy, but in fact it fits every play in climactic form. In this form the aim is always to make events so inevitable that there is no escape—at least not until the very last moment, when a *deus ex machina* may intervene to untangle the knot. Because climactic dramas are so carefully and tightly constructed, they are frequently referred to as *well-made plays.*

Clearly, the method of climactic drama is compression. All the elements—characters, locale, events—are severely restricted. As if by centripetal motion, everything is forced to the center, in a tighter and tighter nucleus, making the ultimate eruption that much more explosive.

Significant Periods of Climactic Structure

Climactic structure is a popular form for drama. Countries and periods (together with the names of a few well-known playwrights) in which it has been dominant include these:

Greece, fifth century B.C.E.—Aeschylus, Sophocles, Euripides

Rome, third to first centuries B.C.E.—Plautus, Terence
  (c. 185–c. 159 B.C.E.)

France, seventeenth century—Corneille, Racine, Molière

France, nineteenth century—Augustin-Eugène Scribe (1791–1861), Victorien Sardou (1831–1908)

Europe and United States, late nineteenth and twentieth centuries—Ibsen, Strindberg, O'Neill, Williams, Miller, Albee, Wilson, Norman

CLIMACTIC STRUCTURE: THE ACTION IS COMPRESSED

A good example of the compression of climactic drama is Miss Julie *by August Strindberg. All the action takes place in one location, a kitchen, on one night, Midsummer's Eve, and involves two characters with a third minor character. The two main characters are Miss Julie (Rebecca Creskoff), an aristocrat, and Jean (Mark Feuerstein), the servant to whom she is fatally attracted. Theirs is a volatile but doomed love. The production was at the Berkshire Theatre Festival.*
(© Richard Feldman)

EPISODIC STRUCTURE

Characteristics of Episodic Structure

When we turn to examples of episodic structure, we see a sharp contrast. Episodic drama begins relatively early in the story and does not compress the action but expands it; the forces in episodic drama are centrifugal, moving out to embrace additional elements. Also, unlike climactic drama, episodic plays do not necessarily follow a close cause-and-effect development.

People, Places, and Events Proliferate In a typical episodic play the action begins relatively early in the story and covers an extensive period of time—sometimes many years. It also ranges over a number of locations. In one play we can go anywhere: to a small antechamber, a large banquet hall, the open countryside, a mountaintop. Short scenes (some only half a page or so in print) alternate with longer ones. The following examples, giving the number of characters and scenes in each play, indicate the extended nature of episodic drama:

> *Antony and Cleopatra* by Shakespeare has thirty-four characters and forty-plus scenes.
> *The Sheep Well* by Lope de Vega has twenty-six characters and seventeen scenes.
> *The Caucasian Chalk Circle* by Brecht has fifty-plus characters and approximately seventeen scenes.

(© Donald Cooper/PhotoSTAGE)

EPISODIC STRUCTURE: MANY CHARACTERS, PLACES, AND EVENTS

Two good examples of the typically wide-ranging episodic play structure are The Tempest *by William Shakespeare, and* Fuente Ovejuna *by his contemporary, the Spanish playwright, Lope de Vega. The performers in* The Tempest *are Scott Handy (aloft) as Ariel and David Calder (center) as Prospero. The second scene shows several members of the large cast of* Fuente Ovejuna.

(© T. Charles Erickson/Yale School of Drama)

KING LEAR BY WILLIAM SHAKESPEARE

I-1 Lear's Palace. Kent and Gloucester discuss the division of the kingdom and Gloucester's sons. Lear comes. The division of the kingdom: first Goneril and then Regan praise Lear. Cordelia cannot. Kent intercedes and is banished. Gloucester enters with Burgundy and France. Burgundy will not have Cordelia without a dowry. France takes her. Goneril and Regan begin plotting. (305 lines)

I-2 Gloucester's Castle. Edmund's soliloquy and scheme. Letter and plan against Edgar begins. Gloucester leaves, Edgar comes, scheme is furthered. (173 lines)

I-3 Albany's Palace. Goneril and Oswald scheming. (26 lines)

I-4 The same. Kent enters disguised; Lear comes, then Oswald, Kent trips him. Fool enters and talks to Lear. Goneril comes, chides Lear. He curses her and leaves. Goneril, Albany, and Oswald conspire further, then leave. (336 lines)

I-5 In Front of Palace. Lear, Kent, Fool. Lear sends letters to Gloucester, starts to Regan. (46 lines)

II-1 A Court in Gloucester's Castle. Edmund and Curan. Edgar comes, then leaves. Edmund stabs himself; Gloucester comes, Edmund blames Edgar; Gloucester finds letter. Cornwall and Regan enter. (The forces of evil join.) (129 lines)

II-2 Before Gloucester's Castle. Kent confronts Oswald, Cornwall comes; Kent is put in stocks. (163 lines)

II-3 Open Country. Edgar's soliloquy: he will disguise and abase himself. (21 lines)

II-4 Before Gloucester's Castle. Lear comes, sees Kent; confronts Regan. She is stubborn too. Goneril comes. Lear sees a league. Begs; leaves as storm begins. (306 lines)

III-1 A Heath. Kent with a Gentleman. (55 lines)

III-2 Another Part of Heath. Lear comes with Fool. Storm and insanity begin. Kent comes. (95 lines)

III-3 Gloucester's Castle. Gloucester tells Edmund of divisions between dukes and of letter from France. (23 lines)

III-4 The Heath Before a Hovel. Lear, Kent, Fool—storm. Lear's madness and beginning self-realization. Edgar joins them, then Gloucester with a torch. (172 lines)

III-5 Gloucester's Castle. Cornwall and Edmund scheming. (22 lines)

III-6 A Farmhouse Near Gloucester's Castle. The mock trial for Lear. Kent, Gloucester, Fool, Edgar. All leave but Edgar. (112 lines)

III-7 Gloucester's Castle. Cornwall, Regan, Goneril, Edmund. They send for Gloucester (the "traitor"), prepare to blind him. Servant is killed; they pluck out Gloucester's eyes. (106 lines)

IV-1 The Heath. Edgar. Enter Gloucester, blind. Edgar prepares cliff scene. (79 lines)

IV-2 Before Albany's Palace. Goneril and Edmund. Enter Oswald. Intrigue of Goneril and Edmund. Albany comes; Goneril chides him. Servant comes telling of Cornwall's death. (979 lines)

IV-3 French Camp Near Dover. Kent and Gentleman report Lear ashamed to see Cordelia. (55 lines)

IV-4 French Camp. Cordelia and Doctor enter; plan to go to England. (29 lines)

IV-5 Gloucester's Castle. Regan and Oswald. She says Edmund is for her. (40 lines)

IV-6 Country Near Dover. Gloucester and Edgar—jumping scene. Lear comes, mad. The two wronged, mad men together. Gentleman comes, then Oswald attacks him. Edgar kills Oswald, finds letters to Edmund—Goneril is plotting Albany's death in order to marry Edmund. (283 lines)

IV-7 Tent in French Camp. Cordelia and Kent. Lear brought in. The awakening and reconciliation. (96 lines)

V-1 British Camp Near Dover. Edmund, Regan, etc. Goneril comes, also Albany. Edgar enters, leaves. (69 lines)

V-2 A Field Between Camps. Cordelia and Lear cross. Edgar and Gloucester come. (11 lines)

V-3 British Camp. Edmund comes, Lear and Cordelia are prisoners; are sent away. Edmund sends note with guard. Enter Albany, Goneril, and Regan, who quarrel. Edgar comes; challenges Edmund and wounds him. Truth about Goneril's plan comes out; she leaves. Edgar talks. Goneril and Regan are brought in dead. Edmund dies. Lear enters with the dead Cordelia; then he dies. Kent and Albany pronounce the end. (326 lines)

EPISODIC STRUCTURE IN KING LEAR

Shakespeare's play sets up a juxtaposition of scenes. Note how the scenes move from place to place and alternate from one group of characters to another. Note, too, that the scenes move back and forth from intimate scenes to those involving a number of characters (an alternation of public and private scenes) and that the length of the scenes varies, with short scenes followed by longer ones and so forth. This structure gives the play its dynamics, its rhythm, and its meaning.

There May Be a Parallel Plot or Subplot   In place of compression, episodic drama offers other techniques. One is the *parallel plot,* or *subplot.* In *King Lear,* by Shakespeare, Lear has three daughters, two evil and one good. The two evil daughters have convinced their father that they are good and that their sister is wicked. In the subplot—a counterpart of this main plot—the Earl of Gloucester has two sons, one loyal and one disloyal; and the disloyal son has deceived his father into thinking he is the loyal one. Both old men have misunderstood their children's true worth, and in the end both are punished for their mistakes: Lear is bereft of his kingdom and his sanity; Gloucester loses his eyes. The Gloucester plot, with complications and developments of its own, is a parallel and reinforcement of the Lear plot.

Juxtaposition and Contrast Occur   Another technique of episodic drama is *juxtaposition* or *contrast.* Rather than moving in linear fashion, the action alternates between elements:

Short scenes alternate with longer scenes. King Lear begins with a short scene between Kent and Gloucester, goes on to a long scene in which Lear divides his kingdom, and then returns to a brief scene in which Edmund declares his intention to deceive his father.

Public scenes alternate with private scenes. In Brecht's play *The Caucasian Chalk Circle,* the first bustling scene of revolution in the town square contrasts with a quiet scene between the two lovers, Grusha and Simon, which follows immediately.

We move from one group to an opposing group. In Shakespeare's *Othello* we move back and forth from scenes in which Iago develops his plot to arouse Othello's jealousy to scenes with Othello himself. We can view both sides in action as the tragedy unfolds.

Comic scenes alternate with serious scenes. In *Macbeth,* just after Macbeth has murdered King Duncan, there is a knock on the door of the castle. This is one of the most serious moments of the play, but the man who goes to open the door is a comical character, a drunken porter, whose speech is a humorous interlude in the grim business of the play. In *Hamlet,* a gravedigger and his assistant are preparing Ophelia's grave when Hamlet comes onto the scene. The gravediggers are joking about death; but for Hamlet, who soon learns that the grave is Ophelia's, it is a somber moment. This juxtaposition of the comic with the serious may seem incongruous; but properly handled, it can bring out the irony and poignancy of an event in a way rarely achieved by other means.

COMIC SCENES ALTERNATE WITH SERIOUS SCENES

One device possible in episodic drama is the juxtaposition and alternation of serious and comic scenes. Shakespeare often incorporates this technique in his plays. A good example is the gravedigging scene in Hamlet, *in which a comic scene is interspersed with very serious scenes involving the death of Ophelia and other tragic events. Shown here is Denis Quilley, on the left as the gravedigger, and Simon Russell Beale as Hamlet, in a production by the Royal National Theatre in London.*
(© Donald Cooper/PhotoSTAGE)

Comparing Climactic and Episodic Form

Climactic	Episodic
1. Plot begins late in the story, toward the very end or climax.	**1.** Plot begins relatively early in the story and moves through a series of episodes.
2. Covers a short space of time, perhaps a few hours or at most a few days.	**2.** Covers a longer period of time: weeks, months, and sometimes many years.
3. Contains a few solid, extended scenes, such as three acts with each act comprising one long scene.	**3.** Has many short, fragmented scenes; sometimes an alternation of short and long scenes.
4. Occurs in a restricted locale, such as one room or one house.	**4.** May range over an entire city or even several countries.
5. Number of characters is severely limited—usually no more than six or eight.	**5.** Has a profusion of characters, sometimes several dozen.
6. Plot is linear and moves in a single line with few subplots or counterplots.	**6.** Is frequently marked by several threads of action, such as two parallel plots, or scenes of comic relief in a serious play.
7. Line of action proceeds in a cause-and-effect chain. The characters and events are closely linked in a sequence of logical, almost inevitable development.	**7.** Scenes are juxtaposed to one another. An event may result from several causes, or from no apparent cause, but arises in a network or web of circumstances.

The table above outlines the chief characteristics of climactic and episodic forms and illustrates the differences between them. It is clear that the climactic and episodic forms differ from each other in their fundamental approaches. One emphasizes constriction and compression on all fronts; the other takes a far broader view and aims at a cumulative effect, piling up people, places, and events.

There are, of course, other forms of alternation in episodic drama, but these illustrations give an indication of how this technique can be used to create dramatic effects.

The Overall Effect Is Cumulative With regard to cause and effect in episodic drama, the impression created is of events piling up: a tidal wave of circumstances and emotions sweeping over the characters. Rarely does one letter, one telephone call, or one piece of information determine the fate of a character. Time and again, Hamlet has proof that Claudius has killed his father; but it is a rush of events which eventually leads him to kill Claudius, not a single piece of hard evidence.

Significant Periods of Episodic Structure

The countries and periods in which episodic form has predominated include these:

England, late sixteenth and early seventeenth centuries—Shakespeare, Marlowe

Spain, late sixteenth and early seventeenth centuries—Lope de Vega, Calderón de la Barca (1600–1681)

Germany, late eighteenth and early nineteenth centuries—Goethe, Gotthold Lessing (1729–1781), Friedrich von Schiller (1759–1805), Georg Büchner (1813–1837)

Europe and the United States, late nineteenth and twentieth centuries—Ibsen, Brecht, Jean Genet (1910–1986)

In modern theater both climactic form and episodic form have been adopted, sometimes by the same playwright. This is characteristic of the diversity of our age. Ibsen, for example, wrote a number of "well-made" or climactic plays—*Ghosts, Hedda Gabler,* and others—but also several episodic plays, such as *Brand* and *Peer Gynt*.

THE CHORUS: A TIME-HONORED DRAMATIC DEVICE

The Greeks were the first to use a chorus. It extended the range and sweep of their plays, which otherwise adhered closely to climactic form. Shown here is the chorus in a production of The Oedipus Plays *by Sophocles in a version presented by the Royal National Theatre in London. (© Donald Cooper/PhotoStage)*

COMBINATIONS OF CLIMACTIC AND EPISODIC FORM

There is no law requiring a play to be exclusively episodic or exclusively climactic. It is true that during certain periods one form or the other has been predominant; and it is not easy to mix the two forms, because—as we have seen—each has its own laws and its own inner logic. In several periods, however, they have been successfully integrated.

For example, I have described Greek drama as conforming to climactic structure. With regard to the main plot of the play, this is true: in *King Oedipus* by Sophocles, for instance, the plot begins late in the story, the action takes place in one location, and there are very few characters. There is an element in Greek drama, though, that gives it an added dimension—the *chorus*. The Greek chorus stood outside the action, arguing with the main characters, making connections between present events and the past, warning the main characters of impending danger, and drawing conclusions from what had occurred. The choral sections, which alternated with the episodes of the main plot, make Greek drama less rigidly climactic than a play like *Ghosts* or classical French plays like those of Racine. (A synopsis of *King Oedipus* can be found at the end of Part 1.)

COMBINING THE CLIMACTIC AND THE EPISODIC

The plays of Chekhov combine features of both climactic and episodic form: they often occur in one place, but they range over a considerable period of time and involve a number of characters. A good example is The Three Sisters *by Anton Chekhov. The scene here, showing one of the sisters with an army officer and an old friend, is from a production at the McCarter Theatre in Princeton. (© T. Charles Erickson)*

A group of plays that combine elements of the climactic and episodic forms are the comedies of the Restoration period in England (from 1660, when the English monarchy was restored, to 1700). These comedies usually had large casts, a subplot as well as a main plot, and several changes of scene. They did not, however, cover extended periods of time or move rapidly from place to place as the plays of Shakespeare did.

The climactic and episodic forms have frequently been combined successfully in the modern period. Chekhov, who generally wrote about one principal action and set his plays in one household, usually has more characters than is customary in climactic drama—there are fifteen in *The Cherry Orchard,* for instance. Frequently, too, Chekhov's plays cover a period of several months or years.

RITUAL AND PATTERN AS DRAMATIC STRUCTURE

Rituals

Like acting, ritual is a part of everyday life of which we are generally unaware. Basically, *ritual* is a repetition or reenactment of a proceeding or transaction which has acquired special meaning. It may be a simple ritual like singing the national anthem before a sports contest, or a deeply religious ritual such as the Roman Catholic mass or the Jewish kaddish, a prayer for the dead.

All of us develop rituals in our personal or family life: a certain meal we eat with the family once a week, for example, or a routine we go through every time we take an examination in school. Occasions like Thanksgiving, Christmas, and Passover become family rituals, with the same order of events each year, the same menu, and perhaps even the same conversation. Rituals give us continuity, security, and comfort. Often, as in the case of primitive tribes, people assume that if they perform a ritual faithfully, they will be blessed or their wishes will be granted. Conversely, they assume that failure to follow a ritual to the letter will lead to punishment.

In theater, ritual is an activity where the old and new come together. Traditional plays are full of rituals: coronations, weddings, funerals, and other ceremonies. And in modern theater, ritual has been discovered and given new life. Certain avant-garde theater groups, for example, have made a conscious attempt to develop new rituals or revive old ones.

Ritual has structure. Actions are repeated in a set fashion; these actions have a beginning, a middle, and an end; and there is a natural progression of events. Despite this, we might ask: Is ritual not in danger of deteriorating into dull routine or hollow repetition? It can be, of course; but a ritual, though sometimes known by heart, is not static. Remember that it is a reenactment, or reliving, of some episode or occasion, and as such it is active, not passive. Beyond that, ritual has special powers; it carries with it the magic or mystery of a meaningful, almost holy, act.

RITUAL IN MODERN THEATER
Many avant-garde playwrights and groups use ceremonies and rituals. One example is the French dramatist Jean Genet. Genet's
The Balcony *takes place in a brothel where the prostitutes play roles, such as a horse to be ridden by a general, and the men who visit them dress up in exaggerated costumes as bishops, generals, judges, and so forth. The two groups play out elaborate games and rituals as an important part of the action. The scene here is from a production by the Jean Cocteau Repertory Theatre. (© Gerry Goodstein)*

Patterns

Related to ritual is a pattern of events. In Samuel Beckett's *Waiting for Godot,* the characters have no personal history, and the play does not build to a climax in the ordinary way. But if Beckett has sacrificed traditional plot structure, he has replaced it with a repeated sequence of events containing its own order and logic. The play has two acts, and in each act a series of incidents is duplicated. Each act opens with the two chief characters coming together on a lonely crossroads after having been separated. Then, in both acts, a similar sequence of events occurs: they greet each other; they despair of Godot's ever coming; they attempt to entertain themselves.

Two other men, Pozzo and Lucky, appear and, following a long scene, disappear. The first two men are left alone once more. The two acts continue to follow the same sequence: a small Boy comes to tell the men that Godot will not come that day, the Boy leaves, and the men remain together for another night. There are important differences between the two acts, but the identical sequence of events in each act achieves a pattern which takes on a ritualistic quality.

Part 4 The Playwright: Dramatic Characters and Dramatic Structure

SERIAL STRUCTURE

Another kind of structure is a series of acts or episodes—individual theater events—offered as a single presentation. In this case, individual segments are strung together like beads on a necklace. Sometimes a central theme or common thread holds the various parts together; sometimes there is little or no connection between the parts.

The musical *revue* is a case in point. In a revue, short scenes, vignettes, skits, dance numbers, songs, and possibly even vaudeville routines are presented on a single program. There may be an overall theme, such as political satire or the celebration of a past event or period. Sometimes a master of ceremonies provides continuity between the various segments. Also, in today's theater we frequently see a program of short plays. Sometimes there will be a bill of one-act plays by the same author; at other times there will be two or three plays by different authors. On some occasions an attempt is made to relate the separate plays to a central theme; but sometimes the plays are chosen simply to complete an evening's entertainment.

EXPERIMENTAL AND AVANT-GARDE THEATER

Special Structures

During the past few decades a number of theater groups in Europe and the United States have experimented with theatrical forms, including ritual. These have included the Polish Laboratory Theater, headed by Jerzy Grotowski; and the Living Theater, the Open Theater, the Performance Group, and the Wooster Group in the United States. These groups questioned long-held beliefs about theater. They had two things in mind. On one hand, they felt that the theater of the past was no longer relevant to the problems of the present and that new forms had to be found to match the unique challenges and aspirations of the late twentieth century. On the other hand, they wanted to look back beyond the traditions of the past 2,500 years to the beginning of theater, to scrape off the many layers of formality and convention that had accumulated through the centuries, and to rediscover the roots of theater.

In many cases these two impulses led to similar results; and from the experiments of this radical theater movement, several significant departures from traditional theater practice were developed. Among them were the following: (1) emphasis on *nonverbal theater,* that is, theater where gestures, body movements, and sounds without words are stressed rather than logical or intelligible language; (2) reliance on improvisation or a scenario developed by performers and a director to tell the story, rather than a written text; (3) interest in ritual and ceremony; and (4) stress on the importance of the physical environment of theater, including the spatial relationship of the performers to the audience.

The theater groups that developed these ideas are referred to as ***avant-garde,*** a French term that literally means "advance guard in a military formation." The term has come to mean an intellectual or artistic movement in any age that breaks with tradition and therefore seems ahead of its time.

Richard Foreman: Director, Playwright, and Designer

Richard Foreman, a director-designer-playwright, founded the Ontological-Hysteric Theatre in New York City in 1968. He has also coproduced his work with the New York Shakespeare Festival and the Wooster Group. Foreman has directed for the Hartford Stage Company and the New York Shakespeare Festival.

How does a young man born in Staten Island, removed to Scarsdale, who goes to Brown and Yale in the 1950s, and then goes to New York to write Broadway comedies, become a unique revolutionary artist in the theatre? For some reason, from the time that I was very young, I had an attraction for the strangest material. I read *The Skin of Our Teeth* for the first time at about twelve and thought, "It's like a dream, it's so weird, it's wonderful." I remember seeing Elia Kazan's production of *Camino Real*, which I dragged my Scarsdale parents to, and they said, "What's this all about?"

I have always gravitated to things that try to talk to some more spiritually oriented level, rather than realistic discussions and manipulations of the real, practical, empirical world in which we live.

Then the big revelation was discovering Brecht—and especially his saying that you could have a theatre that was not based on empathy. For some reason, even at an early age what I hated in the theatre was a kind of asking for love that I saw manifested on the stage, getting a unified reaction from everybody in the audience. Brecht said it didn't have to be like that, and until I was in my middle twenties, he was the beginning, middle, and end of everything for me. That only changed when I came to New York and encountered the beginnings of the underground film movement, and that reoriented me, because up to that point I had thought of America as being rather unsophisticated, naive and simplistic as compared with the complexities and aggressiveness of European art and thought. Then in America, in the middle 1960s, I discovered people my age were making their own movies, operating on a level that was akin to poetry rather than storytelling. And I thought, "Aha! Why can't the techniques of poetry that operate in film, operate in theatre?" I came to terms with trying to make an American kind of art that exploited and put onstage everything that up till then I had wanted to reject about myself. I gravitated to theatre though I was opened up by filmmakers.

Source: Richard Foreman, from *The Director's Voice: Twenty-One Interviews* by Arthur Bartow, copyright 1988 by Arthur Bartow. By permission of Theatre Communications Group.

Segments and Tableaux as Structure

The experimental theater pieces of the directors Robert Wilson (noted in Chapters 6 and 7) and Richard Foreman (1937–), like other types of avant-garde theater, often stress nonverbal elements. At times they include *non sequitur* as well. In spite of this, their work does have structure. Often the various elements are united by a theme, or at least by a pronounced point of view on the part of the director. Also, the material is organized into units analogous to the frames of film and television, or to the still-life tableaux of painting or the moving tableaux of dance. (In theater, a *tableau*—plural, *tableaux*—is a static scene onstage featuring performers in costume.)

Robert Wilson, in productions such as *A Letter to Queen Victoria, Einstein on the Beach,* and *CiVil WarS: A Tree Is Best Measured When It Is Down,* begins a segment with a visual picture—like a large painting, but three-dimensional. The performers move from this static image into the activities

of the segment. When one segment has concluded, another picture or tableau will be formed to initiate the next segment.

Frequently directors like Foreman and Wilson will use rapid movements—as in silent films—or slow-motion movements. At times several activities will occur simultaneously. All of these, however, relate both to an image and to a tableau or frame.

STRUCTURE IN MUSICAL THEATER

In musical theater, structure often involves alternation and juxtaposition. Musical numbers alternate with spoken scenes; solos and duets alternate with choral numbers; singing alternates with dance numbers; and sometimes comic songs and scenes alternate with serious ones.

A good example of structural principles in musicals is found in *My Fair Lady,* with book and lyrics by Alan Jay Lerner and music by Frederick Loewe. The story is based on George Bernard Shaw's play *Pygmalion*.

My Fair Lady concerns a speech teacher, Henry Higgins, who claims that the English judge people by how they speak. He bets his friend Colonel Pickering that he can take an ordinary cockney flower girl, Eliza Doolittle, and by teaching her correct diction, pass her off as a duchess. The comic subplot of *My Fair Lady* deals with Eliza's father, Alfred P. Doolittle, a ne'er-do-well who doesn't want to achieve middle-class respectability, because if he does he will have to marry the woman he lives with.

The first song in the show is sung by Higgins—"Why Can't the English Learn to Speak?" The next song shifts to Eliza and her dreams of luxury as she sings "Wouldn't It Be Lovely?" She is joined in this number by a cho-

MY FAIR LADY: A MUSICAL WITH A CLEAR DRAMATIC STRUCTURE

Musicals, like other forms of theater, require a definite form and structure. In My Fair Lady *by Lerner and Loewe (based on Shaw's play* Pygmalion*), scenes of dialogue alternate with musical and dance numbers; solos alternate with duets and choral numbers. Here, in a production by the Royal National Theatre in London, we see Freddie (Peter Prentice), Eliza (Joanna Riding), and Freddie's mother (Jill Martin) when the transformed Eliza first appears in public at Ascot.* (© Donald Cooper/PhotoSTAGE)

rus. The action now shifts to the subplot, and Alfred Doolittle is joined by two buddies to sing of how he hopes to avoid working "With a Little Bit of Luck." We then move back to a scene with Higgins, who is pushing Eliza very hard to learn to speak properly. After a song by Higgins, "I'm an Ordinary Man," Eliza vows revenge on him in her next song: "Just You Wait."

The musical proceeds in this manner, moving from one character to another, from a solo to a trio to a dance routine to an ensemble. There is variety in these numbers—some are serious; some are comic; some explain the characters' feelings; some describe a situation. It is on such alternation that structure in musical theater is based. Always, too, it must be remembered, spoken scenes are interspersed with musical numbers, and ballet or modern dance routines with other numbers.

In Part 4 we have examined the creation of dramatic characters and dramatic structure. In Part 5 we turn to the work of another group forming an integral part of the creation of a theatrical event: the designers.

SUMMARY

1. There are several basic types of dramatic structure. *Climactic* form was adopted by the Greeks and has been used frequently ever since. Its characteristics are a plot beginning quite late in the story, a limited number of characters, a limited number of locations and scenes, little or no extraneous material, and tight construction, including a cause-and-effect chain of events.

2. *Episodic* form involves a plot covering an extended span of time, numerous locations, a large cast of characters, diverse events (including mixtures of comic and serious episodes), and parallel plots or subplots. Shakespeare's plays are good examples of episodic form.

3. The climactic and episodic forms can be combined, as they have been in the Restoration period and in the modern period, in the works of Anton Chekhov and others.

4. Ritual or pattern is often used as the basis of dramatic structure. Words, gestures, and events are repeated; they have a symbolic meaning acquired both through repetition and through the significance invested in them from the past.

5. Theater events are sometimes strung together to make a program. Examples are a group of unrelated one-act plays and a group of skits and songs in a revue. In this case, structure is within the individual units themselves; among the units the only structure might be the unfolding of the separate elements; or there can be a common theme uniting them.

6. Avant-garde theater sometimes arranges events in a random way to suggest the random or haphazard manner in which life unfolds in everyday situations.

7. Experimental groups in the modern period have often used radical forms, including nonverbal and improvisational structures.

8. Segments and tableaux have also been used as structure.

9. Structurally, musical theater consists of different elements put together in a sequence, in which solo musical numbers alternate with group numbers and dances and these musical elements alternate with dramatic scenes.

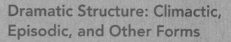

EXPLORING THEATER ON THE WEB

Dramatic Structure: Climactic, Episodic, and Other Forms

There are a growing number of classes and workshops for playwrights on the Internet, including an electronic playwriting textbook on the Web: Richard Toscan's *The Playwriting Seminars* (http://www.vcu.edu/artweb/playwriting/).

Exercises:

1. Visit the "Nine-Act Structure Home Page" at (http://wwwdsigel.com/film/Film_home.html). This site addresses dramatic structure from one methodological perspective as it applies to film and cinema. How does this approach differ from the structural forms noted within this chapter? Is the variance rooted in the difference between film and live theater? Are there similarities that transcend both film and theater? To what extent do you see the crossover? Which form of dramatic structure most closely resembles the "Nine-Act Structure"?

2. Look at the link to the article "The Screenplays of Quentin Tarantino" by Charles Deemer (http://www.creativescreenwriting.com/deemer/deemer01.html). Choose one of Tarantino's scripts to analyze, and compare its structure with the structure of *King Lear.* Can you think of an episodic play that has a nonchronological structure?

3. Visit "Playwriting Links on the Web" (http://www.fortunecity.com/victorian/statue/108/playwriting.html) and choose some links helpful to the playwright. If you were a playwright, which would you use? Why?

Play Synopsis

WAITING FOR GODOT (1954)

Samuel Beckett (1906–1990)

(AP/Wide World Photos)

Chief Characters
Estragon (*also known as Gogo*)
Vladimir (*also known as Didi*)
Lucky
Pozzo
A Boy

Setting
A country road with a tree.

Time
The present.

Background
Estragon and Vladimir have been coming to this same bleak spot every day for some time to wait for an unknown being called Godot. The place is a crossroads, and it is bare except for a small leafless tree in the background. While the men wait, they pass the time discussing the nature of humankind, religion, what they did yesterday, or whatever else happens to be on their minds.

Act I: Estragon is attempting to pull off one of his boots when Vladimir enters. The two men discuss where Estragon spent the night and the fact that he was

Ross Lehman and André de Shields (© Eric Y. Exit/Goodman Theatre)

André de Shields (sitting) and Ross Lehman (© Eric Y. Exit/Goodman Theatre)

beaten again. Vladimir relates the tale of the two thieves who were crucified with Christ and describes how current religious scholars cannot agree on what happened to the thieves. As Estragon paces, the scene is punctuated by pauses which intensify the feeling of waiting. Occasionally the men talk of leaving but then decide that they cannot leave, because they are waiting for Godot. They also consider leaving each other; they argue; they make up. They discuss hanging themselves from the tree but decide that they can't do it, because the limbs are slender and might break.

At the point when they have decided not to do anything, two other men, Pozzo and Lucky, enter. Lucky is carrying heavy baggage and has a rope, held by Pozzo, around his neck. Pozzo jerks occasionally on the rope and barks commands to Lucky, who responds mechanically. Pozzo sits, eats, and smokes his pipe. Estragon asks why Lucky doesn't put down the bags, and Pozzo explains that Lucky wants to impress Pozzo so that Pozzo will keep him. Pozzo says that it would be best to kill Lucky; this makes Lucky cry.

Estragon tries to comfort Lucky, and Lucky kicks him. As the sky changes from day to night, Pozzo tells Lucky to dance, which he does. Pozzo tells Lucky to think, and Lucky, who has been silent until this moment, goes into a long incoherent tirade which agitates the others. When they take off Lucky's "talking hat," he stops talking and collapses in a heap. The men say good-bye, but no one is able to leave. Pozzo finally gets up and exits with Lucky in the lead, still with the rope around his neck.

A Boy enters to tell Vladimir and Estragon that Godot will not be coming today but will surely come tomorrow. After he exits, the moon suddenly rises. Estragon says that he will bring some rope the next day so that they can hang themselves. They talk about parting, but they don't part, as the curtain falls.

Act II: The next day, in the same place. The scene opens with Estragon's boots and Lucky's hat onstage. The small tree that was bare in Act I now has four or five leaves. Vladimir enters in an agitated state, paces back and forth, and begins to sing. Estragon enters, apparently in a foul mood. They embrace, and Estragon says that he was beaten again the night before. Also, Estragon can't remember what happened the day before. They talk about random things so that they will not have to think.

They notice the tree and are amazed that leaves could appear on its limbs overnight. They discover Estragon's boots, which seem to be the wrong color: perhaps someone came along and exchanged boots. They discuss leaving but can't leave, because they are waiting for Godot. Estragon takes a nap, and Vladimir sings a lullaby. Estragon wakes, as if from a nightmare; Vladimir comforts him. They discover Lucky's hat, and they do a comic hat-switching routine. They hear a noise and think that finally Godot is coming. Rather than being pleased, the men are frightened; they rush around excitedly, but nothing happens; no one comes. Once more, they insult each other and then make up.

Pozzo and Lucky enter, and Pozzo is now blind. Lucky stops short, falls, and brings Pozzo down with him. Pozzo calls for help, but Vladimir and Estragon think that finally Godot has arrived. They then discover that it is Pozzo and Lucky. Vladimir and Estragon try to help Pozzo up, but they fall also. Finally, everyone gets up. Estragon goes to Lucky, kicks him, and in the process hurts his own foot. Lucky gets up and gathers his things together, and he and Pozzo exit as before.

Estragon tries in vain to take off his boots and then falls asleep as Vladimir philosophizes. The Boy enters and again tells Vladimir that Godot will not be coming that night but that he will come the next night. The Boy exits. The sun sets, and the moon rises quickly. Vladimir and Estragon discuss leaving but can't go far, because they feel they have to be back the next day to wait for Godot. They talk again of hanging themselves on the tree, but they have no rope. As a substitute, they test the strength of Estragon's belt, but it breaks and his pants fall to the ground. Vladimir tells Estragon to pull up his trousers, and he does. Vladimir says, "Well? Shall we go?" Estragon says, "Yes, let's go." But they do not move. They remain onstage as the play ends.

Discussion Questions

- Is there conflict in *Waiting for Godot*? Between characters? In philosophical arguments?
- Because there is so little action in *Waiting for Godot,* would the play be boring onstage? If not, why not?
- How would the play work with an all-female cast?

Play Synopsis

GHOSTS (1881)

Henrik Ibsen (1828–1906)

(Norwegian Information Center)

Chief Characters

Mrs. Alving, *a widow*
Oswald Alving, *her son, an artist*
Manders, *a pastor*
Engstrand, *a carpenter*
Regina Engstrand, *his daughter*
Mrs. Alving's maid

Setting

The sitting room of Mrs. Alving's house on a large fjord (an inlet of the sea) in western Norway.

Time

The late nineteenth century.

Background

Mr. Alving, a prominent local businessman, was also a womanizer. Because of this, Mrs. Alving once left him and went to seek advice from Pastor Manders. She was attracted to Manders and he to her, but she was persuaded by Manders to return to her "duty." She returned to Alving. Although Alving did not change, Mrs. Alving covered up for him. She sent their son Oswald away to school so that he would not be under his father's influence. One of the women with whom Alving had a liaison was the family's maid Joanna. When Joanna became pregnant, the Alvings married her off to the carpenter Engstrand; the child was a daughter, whom they named Regina. Now, many years later, Joanna has died,

Pamela Payton-Wright and Greg Naughton (Richard Anderson/Center Stage)

Pamela Payton-Wright and James B. Lawless
(Richard Anderson/Center Stage)

and Regina has become a maid in the Alving household.

Act I: Engstrand arrives at the Alving house to try to persuade his "daughter" Regina to leave the Alvings and live with him in a new sailors' home he plans to open in a nearby town. Regina, however, is ambitious and wants to stay with the Alvings, hoping to better herself. She becomes angry and tells Engstrand to leave. Pastor Manders arrives and tries to persuade Regina to go with Engstrand, as a "daughter's duty."

Mrs. Alving is building an orphanage to obliterate the memory of Alving's dissolute life. Manders has come for the dedication of the orphanage; but when Mrs. Alving asks him to stay at her home rather than in town, he refuses, fearing for his reputation. He also advises her not to take out insurance on the new orphanage because people would think that she—and he—had no faith in God's power to protect it. She warns him of a small fire the day before, most likely caused by Engstrand, who is careless, but Manders still insists that there be no insurance. Mrs. Alving also tells him she is against

Regina's moving to the sailors' home Engstrand has planned.

A weary Oswald, who has arrived from Paris the night before, enters. Manders regrets that Oswald never learned what a "well-regulated home" means, but Oswald replies that he has lived with couples who were not married but who were, nevertheless, hardworking and principled. Manders is scandalized, but Mrs. Alving thinks Oswald is right no matter what he does. After Oswald leaves the room, Manders reminds Mrs. Alving that when she left her husband, he made her "do her duty" and return home. She then tells Manders the truth about everything: that her husband died a profligate, that he had a child by her maid, and that it was then that she sent Oswald away to escape his father's influence. She is building the orphanage not really to honor her dead husband but to silence all rumors about him. Meanwhile, Oswald makes advances to Regina in the dining room; when Mrs. Alving hears this, she is agitated because she knows Regina is Oswald's half-sister and she envisions the "ghost" of her husband in Oswald's actions.

Act II: After dinner, Mrs. Alving tells Manders that because Oswald is pursuing Regina, she must find another place for Regina. She also tells him that after Alving got Joanna pregnant, Engstrand married her and took responsibility for the child. Manders is shocked that Engstrand would marry a "fallen woman." Mrs. Alving points out that she was married to a "fallen man." When Engstrand comes to ask Manders to lead the workers at the orphanage in prayer, Manders questions him about his relationship with Regina and tells him that he knows the truth. The clever Engstrand says that he did it for the welfare of Joanna and the baby and convinces Manders that he is repentant.

After Manders leaves, Oswald tells his mother that he fears he is losing his

mind; he has violent headaches, which have been interfering with his work. A doctor has told him that he has inherited a venereal disease: "The sins of the fathers are visited on the children," Oswald says. He has assumed that he must have contracted the disease himself, because he did not think it could have come from his righteous father. Now Oswald sees Regina as his chance for happiness, and he wants to take her to Paris. Mrs. Alving is about to reveal the truth—that his father was dissolute and that Regina is his half-sister—when Manders enters. A moment later, they look out the window and discover that the orphanage is on fire.

Act III: Manders is lamenting the ruined orphanage when Engstrand says that the fire was caused because Manders was careless with a candle. Engstrand plans to blackmail Manders with this untrue accusation, but he tells Manders that he will take the blame if Manders will give him financial help for his sailors' home. Manders is relieved and promises to help him, but Oswald says that the sailors' home will be destroyed also, that nothing will be left in his father's memory. At this point, Mrs. Alving reveals to Regina and Oswald who Regina's true father is.

Mrs. Alving and Oswald talk about the bleak prospects for the future. Oswald is desperate with fear. He had thought that Regina could help him, but she has decided to leave. Mrs. Alving assures him that she will always be there. Oswald makes his mother promise that when he can no longer take care of himself, she will give him some pills so that he can die peacefully. When dawn comes, Oswald has gone blind; the disease has taken over. As the curtain falls, Mrs. Alving is trying to decide whether to help her son take his own life.

Discussion Questions
- Why is *Ghosts* called a climactic play?
- What is the crisis at the end of each act?
- Describe the exact time frame of the play. When does it begin, and when does it end?
- Give several examples of hypocrisy found in the play.

A STREETCAR NAMED DESIRE (1947)

Tennessee Williams (1911-1983)

(Theatre Collection/ Museum of the City of New York)

Chief Characters

Blanche DuBois, *30 years old*
Stella Kowalski, *her sister, 25 years old*
Stanley Kowalski, *Stella's husband, 28 years old*
Harold Mitchell (Mitch), *Stanley's friend*
Eunice Hubbell, *upstairs neighbor*

Setting

A two-story apartment building on a street named Elysian Fields in New Orleans. The section is poor but has a raffish charm.

Scene 1: Blanche DuBois arrives from Laurel, Mississippi, at the apartment of her sister Stella and Stella's husband Stanley in New Orleans. Blanche, who has lost her home and is destitute, is in an anxious state. She expresses disapproval of Stella's "earthy" living conditions.

Scene 2: The next evening. Stanley's friends are coming over for a poker game; before they arrive, Stella takes Blanche out for dinner because Blanche's "sensibilities" would be upset by the men's crudeness. Stanley accuses Blanche of swindling them by selling Belle Reve, the family estate, without giving Stella her share.

Scene 3: The poker night. The women come home late; Blanche flirts with

Mitch, one of the men in the poker game, while Stella dances to music on the radio. Stanley, who is very drunk, gets angry, throws the radio out the window, and attacks Stella. The men subdue him while Blanche takes Stella, who is pregnant, to Eunice's apartment upstairs. Stanley yells for Stella to come home, and she obeys; Mitch sits with the distraught Blanche on the front steps.

Scene 4: The next morning. Blanche is upset and harried, but Stella is happy. Blanche tells Stella she should leave Stanley, whom she calls an "ape," but Stella tells her that she loves him. Stanley overhears Blanche saying that he is "common" and "bestial." He sneaks out and reenters loudly, pretending that he hasn't heard.

Scene 5: Blanche, highly nervous, begins drinking. Stanley asks her if she ever knew a man from a disreputable hotel in Laurel. She denies it, but her reaction makes it obvious that she did know the man. She finds relief in the idea of a forthcoming date with Mitch and admits to

Glenn Close as Blanche DuBois in the National Theatre production in London. (© Donald Cooper/ PhotoSTAGE)

Stella that she is attracted to him.

Scene 6: 2 A.M. that night. Mitch and Blanche come home from their date, go inside, have a drink, and chat awkwardly. Mitch has spoken to his sick mother, with whom he lives, about a possible future with Blanche. Blanche confides to him that her first husband was a homosexual who killed himself.

Scene 7: A late afternoon in mid-September. Stella is preparing for Blanche's birthday party while Blanche is taking a prolonged bath. Stanley tells Stella that he has heard bad stories about Blanche's former life. Stanley admits that he has told Mitch these stories and that Mitch won't be coming to the party. When Blanche comes out of the bathroom, she realizes that something is wrong.

Scene 8: Forty-five minutes later. Mitch has not appeared at the dismal birthday party, and Blanche is miserable. Stanley belligerently presents Blanche with his "present"—a one-way bus ticket back to Laurel. Blanche becomes hysterical and runs into the bathroom; Stella confronts Stanley, becoming so agitated that she goes into labor and is rushed to the hospital.

Scene 9: Later that evening. Blanche is home alone when Mitch arrives, drunk. Mitch says that he has never seen her in full light; he rips the paper lantern off

Iain Glen (Stanley Kowalski), Glenn Close (Blanche DuBois), Essie Davis (Stella Kowalski); National Theatre, London. (© Donald Cooper/PhotoSTAGE)

the lightbulb and turns it on. When he looks at her, she cries out and covers her face. He makes a play for Blanche, but she breaks away and he runs out.

Scene 10: A few hours later. Blanche, who has been drinking, is alone. Stanley returns from the hospital; he has been drinking too. She tells him that a millionaire has invited her to go away. She also makes up a story about Mitch's coming to beg her forgiveness. Stanley knows it is a lie. He puts on the silk pajamas that he "wore on his wedding night." The two of them struggle, and he brutally carries her to bed offstage, where he rapes her.

Scene 11: Several weeks later. Stella is packing Blanche's clothes while the men again play poker: she and Stanley are sending Blanche to a mental hospital. Blanche has told Stella what Stanley did

to her, but Stella won't believe it. When a doctor and matron arrive, Blanche thinks it is her millionaire; when she sees it is not, she runs into the bedroom. The doctor comes in and gently leads Blanche out. Eunice hands the baby to Stella, as she stands crying, and Stanley comforts her.

Discussion Questions
- Drama often presents characters at some extreme point in their lives: at the end of their rope, or facing a last chance. What is Blanche's situation in this regard?
- Describe and analyze each of the four main characters: Blanche, Stanley, Stella, Mitch.
- In what ways are these four characters in conflict with one another?

Part 5

The Designers

Environment, Visual Elements, and Sound

The visual and sound components in a production play a key part in the overall effect of what the audience experiences. Ideally, the visual and aural elements complement, enhance, and blend with the script and the performances. ✤ In some types of productions—modern American musicals, for instance—the design elements are particularly important to the final impact of the end result. ✤ The Al Hirschfeld drawing seen here depicts a scene from the musical *Hairspray* in which costumes, lights, scenery, and sound are all prominent elements.

CHAPTER SIXTEEN

Scenery

The theater experience does not occur in a visual vacuum. Spectators sit in the theater, their eyes open, watching what unfolds before them. Naturally, they focus most keenly on the performers who are speaking and moving about the stage; but always present are the visual images of scenery, costumes, and lighting—transformations of color and shape which add a significant ingredient to the total mixture. Spectators become aware also of the elements of sound that are part of the production. The creation of these effects is the responsibility of designers. A *designer* is a person who creates and organizes one of the visual aspects or aural effects in a theater production.

◀ **SCENE DESIGN SETS THE TONE**

Good scene design sets the tone and style of a production, letting the audience know where and when the action takes place and whether the play is a tragedy, a comedy, or some other type of drama. Also, it harmonizes with other elements of the production—script, acting, and direction—to create a unified whole. Shown here is a scene from the set for the opening scene of Private Lives *by Noel Coward. The setting depicts the adjoining balconies of a hotel on the Riviera and the play concerns the lives of a group of sophisticated, urbane English people. The scenery by designer Tim Hatley captured expertly the elegance and ultra-cosmopolitan quality of the world of the play.* (© Joan Marcus)

The *scene designer* is responsible for the stage set, which can run the gamut from a bare stage with stools or orange crates to the most elaborate large-scale production. No matter how simple, however, every set has a design. Even the absence of scenery constitutes a stage set and can benefit from the ideas of a designer: in the way the furniture is arranged, for example.

On the subject of furniture, it is important to note that the scene designer does not merely create the shape, texture, and outline of the walls or the levels of the set (the outer shell); he or she also deals with all that goes into the stage space: carpets, draperies, furniture, lamps, and so forth.

The *costume designer* is responsible for selecting, and in many cases creating, the outfits and accessories worn by the performers. Costumes help establish individual characters in relationship to the story and the "world" of a play.

Stage lighting, quite simply, includes all forms of illumination on the stage. The *lighting designer* makes decisions in every area of lighting: the color of the lights, the mixture of colors, the number of lights, the intensity and brightness of the lights, the angles at which lights strike performers, and the length of time required for lights to come up or fade out. The lighting designer also adds to or aids in creating a "moment" onstage, in terms of mood and in other ways. Also, movement by means of light changes underscores action and transitions.

A fourth designer might be referred to as the *aural* or *sound designer:* this is the person who arranges the sound components. The sound designer is responsible for sound effects, recorded music, and the placement and synchronization of microphones. He or she must not only plan all the sound but also place microphones appropriately on and around the stage, and on the performers. For the performance itself, the sounds from CDs or tape machines and microphones must be blended properly.

Designers must deal with practical as well as aesthetic considerations. A scene designer must know in which direction a door should open onstage and how high each tread should be on a flight of stairs. A lighting designer must know exactly how many feet above a performer's head a particular light should be placed and whether it requires a 500- or 750-watt bulb. A costume designer must know how much material it takes to make a certain kind of dress and how to "build" clothes so that performers can wear them with confidence and have freedom of movement. A sound designer must know about acoustics, be familiar with echoes, and understand electronic sound systems.

As in other elements of theater, symbols play a large role in design. A single item onstage can suggest an entire room: a bookcase, for instance, suggests a professor's office or a library; a stained-glass window suspended in midair suggests a church or synagogue. A stage filled with a bright yellow-orange glow suggests a cheerful sunny day, whereas a single shaft of pale blue light suggests moonlight or an eerie graveyard at night. How designers deal with the aesthetic and practical requirements of the stage will be clearer when we examine the subject in detail: scene design in this chapter, costumes in Chapter 17, and lighting and sound in Chapter 18.

A BRIEF HISTORY OF STAGE DESIGN

At the beginning of both western and Asian theater there was little of what we now call scene design. The stage itself was the background for action. In Greek theater, for instance, the facade of the stage house usually represented a palace or royal house. There were some scenic elements, however. As noted in the Introduction, a "machine" lowered the gods from the roof of the stage house. There was also a scenic device called the ***periaktoi,*** a vertical three-sided column which could be rotated to present three different scenic pictures.

In medieval theater, "mansions" were set up in town squares. These were small set pieces representing such things as Noah's ark, the whale which swallowed Jonah, and the manger in which Christ was born. The Elizabethan and Spanish theaters of the Renaissance had bare stages in which the facade of the stage house functioned as the background for action, just as it had in Greece. In both of these, set pieces as well as furniture such as thrones were used, but there was still no scenery as we know it.

Actual scenery began to appear along with the proscenium theaters in Italy and later in France and England. These were the theaters (described in Chapter 4) where designers such as the Bibiena family came to the forefront.

Since then, theater has experienced a combination of improved stage machinery—the means by which scenery is shifted—and increasing realism in depicting scenes. This growing realism has been the basis of much modern stage scenery.

"STAGE SETS" IN EVERYDAY LIFE

In stage scenery—as in other areas of theater—there is an analog, or a parallel, between scene design and our experiences in everyday life. Every building or room we enter can actually be regarded as a form of stage set.

Interior decorating, along with architectural design—the creation of a special atmosphere in a home or a public building—constitutes scene design in real life. Good examples are restaurants with a foreign motif—French, Italian, Spanish, "olde English." These restaurants have a form of setting, or "scenery," meant to give the feeling that you are in a different world, when in fact you have simply stepped off the street. A church decorated for a wedding is a form of stage set; so is the posh lobby of a hotel; and so is an apartment interior with flowers, candlelight, and soft music.

In every case the "designer"—the person who created the setting—has selected elements which signal something to the viewer and thus make an

SPECIAL REQUIREMENTS OF STAGE SCENERY

Stage scenery calls for elements not always found in life outside the theater. Realistic scenery looks like the real thing, but often differs in important, though subtle ways. Nonrealistic scenery gives free reign to the designer's imagination. Scenery, too, must meet the requirements of the play and the special demands of the director. In the case of the play Metamorphoses, *based on the stories of* Ovid, *the author/director of the play, Mary Zimmerman, called for a shallow pool of water to occupy the entire central portion of the playing area. The pool was both a visual metaphor and an actual playing area, into which the actors walked and in which they reclined. Shown here is Doug Hara, at the lectern, and Erik Lochtefeld floating on a rubber raft in the pool.* (© Ken Friedman/Berkeley Repertory Theatre)

impression. The combination of colors, fabrics, furniture, and styles tells the viewer exactly where he or she is. These things are often carefully calculated, and a premium is set on an appropriate environment or atmosphere. When we see a library with leather-bound books, attractive wood paneling, comfortable leather chairs, and a beautiful, carved wooden desk, we get a sense of stability, tradition, and comfort. A totally different kind of feeling would come from a modern room in which everything is "hi-tech"—with glass-top tables, furniture of chrome and stainless steel, and track lighting. From this spare, functional look, we get a "modern" feeling. Interior decorators know that appearance is important, that the visual elements of a room can communicate an overall impression to which an observer responds with a set of feelings, attitudes, and assumptions.

SCENERY FOR THE STAGE

We are accustomed to "stage settings" in everyday life; but, as with other elements in theater, there is an important difference between interior decoration in real life and set designs for the stage. For example, the stage designer must deal with scale: the relationship of the performer in the set to his or her surroundings. This must in turn correspond to the scale of settings we experience in the world outside the theater. The scale in a stage set may be different from that of a living room or a courtroom in real life.

Robert Edmond Jones, who is often considered the most outstanding American scene designer of the first half of the twentieth century, put it in these terms:

A good scene should be, not a picture, but an image. Scene-designing is not what most people imagine it is—a branch of interior decorating. There is no more reason for a room on a stage to be a reproduction of an actual room than for an actor who plays the part of Napoleon to be Napoleon or for an actor who plays Death in the old morality play to be dead. Everything that is actual must undergo a strange metamorphosis, a kind of sea-change, before it can become truth in the theater.[1]

A stage set does signal an atmosphere to the viewer in the same way as a room in real life, but the scene designer must go a step further. As has been pointed out many times, the theater is not life: it resembles life. It has,

336   **Part 5**   The Designers: Environment, Visual Elements, and Sound

as Jones suggests, both an opportunity and an obligation to be more than mere reproduction.

The special nature of scenery and other elements of scene design will be clearer when we examine the objectives and functions of scene design.

OBJECTIVES OF SCENE DESIGN

The scene designer has the following objectives:

1. Creating an environment for the performers and for the performance
2. Helping to set the mood and style of the production
3. Helping to distinguish realistic from nonrealistic theater
4. Establishing the locale and period in which the play takes place
5. Evolving a design concept in concert with the director and other designers
6. Where appropriate, providing a central image or visual metaphor for the production
7. Ensuring that the scenery is coordinated with other production elements
8. Solving practical design problems

Objectives 1 through 7 encompass the aesthetic aspects of stage design. Objective 8 encompasses several practical aspects.

AESTHETIC ASPECTS OF STAGE DESIGN

The Scenic Environment

There have been times in the history of theater when scene design was looked on as painting a large picture. In Chapter 4, in discussing the proscenium stage, I noted the temptation to use the proscenium arch as a frame and put a gigantic picture behind it. The tradition of fine scene painting, begun in Italy in the late seventeenth century, continued throughout Europe in the eighteenth and nineteenth centuries. It was still flourishing in Europe and the United States in the early part of the twentieth century, when many famous painters—including Pablo Picasso, Salvador Dalí, and Marc Chagall—undertook to design scenery. This continued later in the century with artists such as Red Grooms, David Hockney, and Louise Nevelson.

Scene painting as an end in itself has not been the only case where the visual side of stage spectacle took precedence over other elements and was featured for its own sake. In the seventeenth century, the elaborate stage effects at the "Hall of Machines" in Paris—clouds descending, rocks opening, turntables rotating—were the main attraction. Throughout the nineteenth century, spectacular effects, such as chariot races and houses burning down onstage, were extremely popular.

SCENERY: AN ENVIRONMENT FOR A PLAY AND A PERFORMANCE

For a production of Oscar Wilde's The Importance of Being Earnest *at the Long Wharf Theatre in New Haven, designer Hugh Landwehr created a formal, elegant setting. Note the curtain swags in the background, the carefully placed furniture, the attractive patterns in the rug and wallpaper. All of this reinforces the highly stylized nature of the play itself.* (© T. Charles Erickson)

In the present day, we can find an example in "performance art," which is allied to painting and dance and puts strong emphasis on visual effects—much more so than on language, character, or story. Also, many modern musicals, such as *Les Misérables, The Phantom of the Opera,* and *The Lion King,* have tended to rely on the visual side of the production fully as much as on other elements such as the book or score.

The person responsible for these visual extravaganzas is the scene designer. He or she is always an important member of the creative team in a theater production, but for an elaborate musical such as *The Lion King* or an avant-garde visual piece, the work of the scene designer becomes a ma-

A BEAUTIFUL STAGE PICTURE

A scene designer must deal with both aesthetic and practical considerations. Where appropriate, a design should have a visual appeal and a beauty all its own; in addition, it should have balance, symmetry, and other elements of good design in general. The set shown here is a striking visual design created by James Noone for a production of the musical Where's Charley? *Note the arches, the brickwork, the green foliage in the foreground and the blue sky in the background, on which the performers are arranged in a striking tableau. The costumes are by Michael Krass, and the production was at the Williamstown Theater Festival in Massachusetts.* (© Richard Feldman)

jor ingredient. A stage picture that constantly engages the attention of the audience and makes a comment all by itself requires inventiveness and imagination of a high order, not to mention a firm grasp of stage effects.

To arrive at a design for a production, the scenic designer looks first at the script and analyzes the world the characters inhabit. How do they speak? How do they move? In what kind of home or office or outdoor setting do they function? What are their goals and objectives? What do they wear? Does their life seem cramped, or does it appear free and open? From the answers to these questions, the designer begins to form visual impressions, sometimes jotting down pencil sketches, sometimes making notes. The object is to absorb the play and the characters and to begin to move toward a concrete manifestation of the visual world of the drama—an environment in which the characters can interact.

Mood and Style

A stage setting can help establish the mood, style, and meaning of a play. Is the play happy or sad, frightening or uplifting? A Roman farce, for example, might call for comic, exaggerated scenery—in the manner of a cartoon, perhaps, with outrageous colors. A satire might call for a comment in the design, like the twist in the lines of a caricature in a political cartoon. A serious play calls for sober, straightforward scenery, even in a nonrealistic piece.

As examples of what is called for in scene design, let us consider two plays by the Spanish playwright Federico García Lorca. His *Blood Wedding* is the story of a young bride-to-be who runs away with a former lover on the day she is to be married. The two flee to a forest, and in the forest the play becomes expressionistic: allegorical figures of the Moon and a Beggar Woman, representing Death, appear and seem to echo the fierce emotional struggle taking place within the characters. It would be quite inappropriate to design a realistic, earthbound set for *Blood Wedding*, particularly for the forest scenes. The setting must have the same sense of mystery, of the unreal, that rules the passions of the characters. We must see this visually in the images of the forest as well as in the figures of the Moon and the Beggar Woman.

MOOD AND STYLE
The designers should establish the mood, tone, and style of a production. This is accomplished with architectural shapes, colors, fabrics, furniture, and other elements. The scene here is from a production in Germany of Goethe's Faust, *directed by Peter Stein. The designer was Ferdinand Wögerbauer. Note the steps that ascend almost the full height of the stage, and the explosions of red color reflected from vapor and mist. The steps allowed director Stein to create fascinating stage compositions with his performers, and the colored effects gave an exciting dimension to a play dealing with "Faustian" compacts with the devil—part of the plot of the play.* (© Ruth Walz)

Scene Design: An Environment for Performers

One element that must never be forgotten in scene design—just as it must never be forgotten when we read a play in book form—is the presence of the performer. Scene design creates an environment: a place for actors and actresses to move and have their being. Robert Edmond Jones spoke forcefully on this point when he said: "Players act in a setting, not against it."

Jones was saying that a stage set is not a complete picture in and of itself; it is an environment with one element missing—the performer. Empty, it has a sense of incompleteness. A stage set is like a giant mobile sculpture, motionless until put into motion by the performers. This, of course, fits with our notion that theater is an experience, an unfolding encounter which moves through time. If the stage picture were complete when we first entered the theater or when the curtain went up, where would the experience lie? Scene design is at its best, therefore, when it underlines and emphasizes the primary values of the play—not competing with the play or overpowering it, but enhancing and supporting it.

Source of quotation: Robert Edmond Jones, *The Dramatic Imagination,* Theatre Arts, New York, 1941, pp. 23–24.

"The Essence of Stage Design"

The designer Robert Edmond Jones explained the difference between decoration of a room in everyday life and the purpose of designing a room as part of a stage set:

> A stage setting holds a curious kind of suspense. Go, for instance, into an ordinary empty drawing-room as it exists normally. There is no particular suspense about this room. It is just—empty. Now imagine the same drawing room arranged and decorated for a particular function—a Christmas party for children, let us say. It is not completed as a room, not until the children are in it. And if we wish to visualize for ourselves how important a part the sense of expectancy plays in such a room, let us imagine that there is a storm and the children cannot come. A scene on the stage is filled with the same expectancy. It is like a mixture of chemical elements held in solution. The actor adds the one element that releases the hidden energy of the whole. Meanwhile, wanting the actor, the various elements which go to make up the setting remain suspended, as it were, in an indefinable tension. To create this suspense, this tension, is the essence of the problem of stage designing.

Source: Reprinted from *The Dramatic Imagination,* Theatre Arts, New York, 1941, pp. 71–72. Copyright 1941 by Robert Edmond Jones, with the permission of the publisher.

Another play of García Lorca's, *The House of Bernarda Alba,* is about a woman and her five daughters. The woman has grown to hate and distrust men, and so she locks up her house, like a convent, preventing her daughters from going out. The action takes place in various rooms of the house and an enclosed patio. From the designer's point of view it is important to convey the closed-in, cloistered feeling of the house in which the women are held as virtual prisoners. The sense of entrapment must be omnipresent. In other words, the setting here stands in sharp contrast to that of *Blood Wedding*.

Occasionally, scenery runs deliberately counter to a play—as a comment on it. For instance, Ionesco's zany absurdist play *The Bald Soprano* (described in Chapter 10) might be set in a realistic family living room as an ironic contrast to its content. This, however, is the exception rather than the rule.

Realistic and Nonrealistic Scenery

The stage designer's role is of special importance in distinguishing between realism and nonrealism. *Realistic theater* calls for settings which look very much like their counterparts in real life. A kitchen resembles a kitchen, a bedroom resembles a bedroom, and so on. One exponent of realism, David Belasco (1854–1931), a producer-director of the early twentieth century, sometimes reproduced onstage an actual kitchen or another room from a house, which included wallpaper and light fixtures.

A complete reproduction, however, is an extreme. Even in realistic theater the stage designer selects items to go onstage, and his or her talent and imagination play an important role. The point is to make the room *resemble,* but not duplicate, its real-life counterpart. It must also support the visual and thematic "world" of the play. A playwright does not simply take a tape recorder into the streets and record conversations; nor does a scene designer reproduce each detail of a room. A set calls for selectivity and editing. In a realistic setting, it is up to the designer to choose those items, or symbols, that will give the appropriate feeling and impression. At times the designer may provide only partial settings for realistic plays. We will see a portion of a room—a cutout with only door frames and windows, but no walls, or walls suggested by an outline. Whether a set is complete or partial, though, the result should convey to us not only the lifestyle but the individual traits of the characters in the play as well.

In *nonrealistic theater,* the designer can give full reign to imagination, and the use of symbol is of special importance. Chinese theater affords a graphic example of the possibilities of symbol in stage design. Chinese theater, during its long history, has developed an elaborate set of conventions in which a single prop or item represents a complete locale or action. An embroidered curtain on a pole stands for a general's tent, an official seal signifies an office, and an incense tripod stands for a palace. A plain table may represent a judge's bench; but when two chairs are placed at each end of the table, it can become a bridge. When performers climb onto the table, it can be a mountain; when they jump over it, a wall. A banner with fish on it represents the sea, a man with a riding crop is riding a horse, and two banners with wheels are a chariot. Interestingly enough, such symbols are thoroughly convincing, even to westerners.

(© Joan Marcus)

(© Jack Vartoogian)

REALISTIC AND NONREALISTIC SCENERY

Generally, realism and nonrealism call for different design elements, underscoring the difference in style between these two types of theater. The top photo shows an extremely realistic set, designed by David Gallo for a production of King Hedley II *by August Wilson, showing the outside of two houses in a run-down neighborhood. The performers are Leslie Uggams, Viola Davis, and Brian Stokes Mitchell. The scene below is a surrealistic landscape designed by the avant-garde director Robert Wilson for an opera by Philip Glass entitled* White Raven. *Note that there are no realistic elements—buildings, trees, or rooms—used as a frame of reference. Rather, the scene is abstract and other worldly.*

Chapter 16 Scenery

Productions in the United States also provide examples of imaginative nonrealistic scenery. For a revival of Sophocles' *Electra,* Ming Cho Lee (1930–) suspended large stone formations on three sides of the stage. This design suggested the three doors of ancient Greek theater; but more important, it conveyed the solidity, dignity, and rough-hewn quality of the play. In contrast, for the musical *Company,* Boris Aronson (1900–1980) designed a sharp, sleek set constructed partly of chrome and Lucite, with straight lines. Actors and actresses moved from one area to another in modern, open elevators which symbolized the chic, antiseptic world of the characters. The set was the epitome of sophisticated urban living.

A more recent example is Richard Hudson's scenic designs for *The Lion King.* In vivid colors, Hudson created trees, grasslands, mountains, and valleys in Africa that were all highly stylized and not in any way intended to duplicate the realistic scenes you would see in, for instance, a documentary film.

Locale and Period

Whether realistic or nonrealistic, a stage set should tell the audience where and when the play takes place. Is the locale a saloon? A bedroom? A courtroom? A palace? A forest? The set should also indicate the time period. A kitchen with old-fashioned utensils and no electric appliances sets the play in the past. An old radio and an icebox might tell us that the time is the 1920s. A spaceship or the landscape of a faraway planet would suggest the future.

In addition to indicating time and place, the setting can tell us what kinds of characters the play is about. For example, the characters may be neat and formal or lazy and sloppy. They may be kings and queens or an ordinary suburban family. The scene design should tell us these things immediately.

The Design Concept

In order to convey information, the scene designer frequently develops a *design concept* similar to the directorial concept discussed in Chapter 7. The design concept is a unifying idea carried out visually. Examples of design concepts would be the claustrophobic setting for *The House of Bernarda Alba* and Ming Cho Lee's Greek-influenced setting for *Electra,* described above.

A strong design concept is particularly important when the time and place of a play are shifted. Modern stage designs for Shakespeare's *A Midsummer Night's Dream* illustrate the point. In most productions it is performed in palace rooms and a forest, as suggested by the script. But for a production by Peter Brook (1925–) in the early 1970s, the designer Sally Jacobs (1932–) fashioned three white, bare walls—like the walls of a gymnasium. Trapezes were lowered onto the stage at various times, and in some scenes the performers actually played their parts suspended in midair.

The concept developed by a scene designer for a stage setting is closely related to the central image or metaphor, discussed next.

A STRIKING DESIGN IMAGE

For a production of Shakespeare's Antony and Cleopatra, *designer Ming Cho Lee created an arresting visual stage picture, consisting of three red panels, over which hovered an oversize Egyptian head which took on different tones as it was illuminated by lights of different colors. There was variety in the tone and look of succeeding scenes, but also the continuity of the central image of the head and the panels. The production was at the Guthrie Theater in Minneapolis.* (© T. Charles Erickson)

The Central Image or Metaphor

Stage design not only must be consistent with the play but also should have its own integrity. The elements of a design—lines, shapes, and colors—should add up to a whole. In many cases, a designer tries to develop a central image or metaphor.

In *Mother Courage* by Bertolt Brecht, the playwright has provided a central image for the designer to work with. This is the wagon which Mother Courage pulls throughout the play and from which she sells wares to support her family. The play takes place during the Thirty Years' War in Europe during the seventeenth century, and Mother Courage is a survivor. She sells goods to all sides in order to keep herself going. The wagon, which she has with her at all times, is a symbol of her transitory life—she is always on the move—and of her need to peddle merchandise. The wagon signifies the whole notion of commerce and its relationship to war. A designer, therefore, must create a wagon which will work onstage and which will embody all the characteristics called for in the script and the character of Mother Courage. It becomes a sort of mobile central image or metaphor around which the scene designer develops his or her entire visual concept. (A synopsis of *Mother Courage* appears at the end of Part 5.)

Coordination of the Whole

Because scenic elements have such strong symbolic value and are so important to the overall effect of a production, the designer has an obligation to provide scenery consistent with the intent of the play and the director's concept. If the script and acting are highly stylized, the setting should not be mundane or drab. If the script and acting are realistic, the setting should not overpower the other elements in the production. It is a question, once again, of how the various parts of a production should contribute to an overall effect.

SCENE DESIGN AND POPULAR ENTERTAINMENT

Before turning to the practical aspects of scene design, we should note a development which parallels a growing tendency not only in design but also in other areas of theater: a crossover between theater on the one hand and film, television, and popular entertainment on the other.

Theater designers have for many years also designed for film and television. But more and more, people involved in other aspects of popular entertainment have turned to scene designers to enhance their presentations. In many cases, these design artists had their training in theater or have a theater background. Examples include figures from the world of rock music: the performer David Bowie, for instance, had a set designed by Mark Raywitz, perhaps the first full-stage rock concert presentation to use a designer in this way. Another artist, Vivien Westwood, designed for the Sex Pistols. Today, an elaborate set, which includes state-of-the-art lights and sound equipment, is a must for concerts by rock stars and many other music stars.

Design has also become increasingly important in theme parks and Las Vegas hotels. Frequently, the background and surroundings in such places are like giant stage sets, creating a fantasy land or perhaps the world of a foreign country. Within theme parks and casino hotels, there is often a stage show—a version of *Cirque de Soleil,* for example—which relies heavily on effective scene design.

In other words, the line between pure theater design and design for other types of entertainment has become less and less clearly defined. Many scenic artists move freely from one area to the other and back again.

PRACTICAL ASPECTS OF SCENE DESIGN

We now move from aesthetic considerations to the practical side of creating a visual environment.

The Physical Layout

The playing area must fit into a certain stage space, and, more important, it must accommodate the performers. In terms of space, a designer cannot plan a gigantic stage setting for a theater where the proscenium opening is only 20 feet wide and the stage is no more than 15 feet deep. By the same token, to design a small room on a 40-foot stage would be ludicrous.

The designer must also take into account the physical layout of the stage space. If a performer must leave by a door on the right side of the stage and a few moments later return by a door on the left, the designer must obviously make allowance for crossing behind the scenery. If performers need to change costumes quickly offstage, the scene designer must make certain that there is room offstage for changing. If there is to be a sword fight, the performers must have space onstage in which to make their turns, to advance and retreat.

GROUND PLAN
To aid the director, performers, and stage technicians, the designer draws a ground plan, or blueprint, of the stage, showing the exact locations of furniture, walls, windows, doors, and other scenic elements.

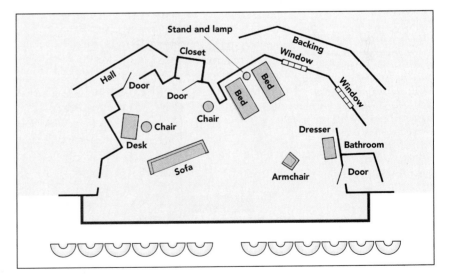

Any physical movement requires a certain amount of space, and the scene designer must allow for this in the ground plan. A *ground plan* is a floor plan, drawn to scale, outlining the various levels on the stage and indicating the placement of scenery, furniture, doors, windows, and so on. It is similar to a map in that the viewer is looking down on the plan from above. Working in conjunction with the director, the designer is chiefly responsible for developing a practical ground plan.

The way doors open and close, the way a sofa is set, the angle at which steps lead to a second floor—all these are the responsibility of the designer and are important to both the cast and the play. If a performer opens a door onstage and is immediately blocked from the view of the audience, this is obviously an error on the part of the scene designer. Also, actresses and actors must have enough space to interact with other performers naturally and convincingly.

To designate areas of the stage, the scene designer uses terminology peculiar to the theater. *Stage right* and *stage left* mean the right and left sides of the stage, respectively, as seen from the performer's position facing the audience. In other words, when the audience looks at the stage, the side to *its* left is stage right, and the side to *its* right is stage left. The area of the

STAGE AREA

Various parts of the stage are given specific designations. Near the audience is downstage; *away from the audience is* upstage. Right *and* left *are from the performers' point of view, not the audience's. Everything out of sight of the audeince is* offstage. *Using this scheme, everyone working on the theater can carefully pinpoint stage areas.*

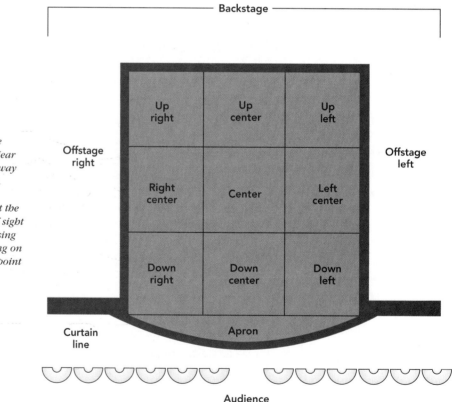

Part 5   The Designers: Environment, Visual Elements, and Sound

stage nearest the audience is known as *downstage,* and the area farthest away from the audience is *upstage.*

The designations *downstage* and *upstage* come from the eighteenth and nineteenth centuries, when the stage was raked—that is, it sloped downward from back to front. As a result of this downward slope, a performer farther away from the audience was higher, or "up," and could be seen better. This is the origin of the expression to *upstage someone.* The term has come to mean that one performer grabs the spotlight from everyone else and calls attention to himself or herself by any means whatever. Originally, however, it meant that one performer was in a better position than the others because he or she was standing farther back on the raked stage and hence was higher.

Materials of Scene Design

In creating a stage set, the designer must be aware of several elements. For example, there is the stage floor itself. Sometimes the stage floor is a *turntable,* that is, a circle set into the floor which can turn electronically or mechanically to bring one set into view as another disappears. At times trapdoors are set in the floor through which performers can enter or leave the stage. For some productions, tracks or slots run across the stage floor, and set pieces or *wagons*—low platforms on wheels—are brought onstage in the tracks and stopped at the proper point. Another device used along the stage floor is a treadmill, which can carry performers, furniture, or props from one side of the stage to the other.

Formerly, pieces of movable equipment—turntables, wagons, treadmills—were moved mechanically or by hand. In recent years, however, these operations are often computerized. Complicated scene changes can be controlled by computer so that they take place efficiently and simultaneously. Computers can also control the turning and shifting of scenic elements. Panels, screens, and scenic flats, for instance, not only can be moved onstage and offstage but also can be turned at angles or even turned 180 degrees by computer. With computerization, one person sitting at a console can control intricate, extremely complicated scene changes. In a matter of seconds, wagons will come onstage or be moved off; panels or screens will fly in from above or be removed; scenic units such as an office, an automobile, or a bedroom will move on- or offstage. These elements will pass each other—turning, twisting, sliding—and finally come to rest at exactly the correct place on- or offstage. In addition, safety features are built into the new computerized equipment. When performers are on moving treadmills, for example, light beams or pressure-sensitive plates can detect a malfunction and shut the system down before anyone is injured.

Instead of coming from the sides, scenery can be dropped from the fly loft—to *fly,* as noted in Chapter 4, is the term used when scenery is raised into the fly loft out of the view of the audience.

SCENIC PROJECTIONS

An increasingly popular scenic resource is projections: rear-screen and front-screen projections, produced on an opaque surface or on a scrim. Projections allow rapid changes of locale, panoramic views, and abstract designs. Shown here are two examples of an effective use of scenic projections. The first is a setting for a production of Horton Foote's play The Carpetbagger's Children *at Lincoln Center. The scenery was by Jeff Cowie and the lighting by Rui Rita. Note that here the projection creates a rural exterior behind the open interior setting in which the action takes place. The projection establishes both place and mood. The second example, from a production at New York's Public Theatre, uses projections to display faces of serious young people behind the dancing and activity of the actors in the foreground. The play was* Dogeaters, *by Jessica Hagedorn; the projections were created by John Woo and the sets were by David Gallo.*

(© T. Charles Erickson)

(© Michal Daniel)

From floor level, ramps and platforms can be built to any height. To create walls or divisions of other kinds, the most common element is the *flat*, so named because it is a single flat unit. In the past, flats consisted of canvas stretched on wood, with the side facing the audience painted to look like a solid wall. Several flats used in conjunction were made to look like a complete room. Today, scene designers and shop technicians often use the *hard flat*, sometimes called a *movie* or *Hollywood* flat; it consists of a firm material called *luan* placed on a wooden or hollow metal frame. A hard flat can be painted; in addition, three-dimensional plastic moldings can be attached to it, creating cornices, chair rails, and other interesting features. The hard flat also has the advantage of not flapping when it is touched. Other vertical units are *cutouts*—small pieces made like flats or cut out of plywood. These too can be painted to look like a solid architectural element.

The scene designer's art comes into play in creating an illusion—with flats and other units—of virtually any type of room or architecture required. To accomplish this, designers not only use traditional materials but also take advantage of a wide range of nonscenic materials. Examples are scaffolding, inflatable scenery, reflective mylar (which can be used for mirror effects), and erosion cloth—the crosshatch material used in highway construction.

A special type of scenery is the *scrim*—a gauze or cloth screen which (like a regular flat) can be painted with thin paint or dye. The wide mesh of the cloth allows light to pass through. When light shines on a scrim from in front—that is, from the audience's point of view—it is reflected off the painted surface, and the scrim appears to be a solid wall. When light comes from behind, the scrim becomes transparent and the spectators can see performers and scenery behind it. The scrim is particularly effective in scenes where ghosts are called for or an eerie effect is desired. Scrims are likewise useful in memory plays or plays with flashbacks: the spectators see the scene in the present in front of the scrim, and then, as lights in the front fade and those behind come up, they see through the gauzelike scrim a scene with a cloudy, translucent quality, indicating a memory, a dream, or a scene in the past.

Another scenic device is *screen projection*. A picture or drawing is projected on a screen either from in front—as in an ordinary movie theater—or from behind. The advantage of projection from behind is that, because the performers will not be in the beam of the light, there will be no shadows or silhouettes. Obviously, projections offer many advantages: pictures can change with the rapidity of cinema, and there is an opportunity to present vast scenes onstage in a way which would hardly be possible otherwise.

In looking at the materials used in scene design, it is important to remember that the designer must have the experience and the know-how to design, paint, build, create drawings and models, engineer, and assemble in a manner that creates an appropriate and exciting "world" for the players and the play to inhabit.

Special Effects

Considering scrims and projections brings us to the subject of *special effects.* These are effects of scenery, lighting, sound, and props that seem unusual or even miraculous. (The term *prop* comes from the word *property.* It refers to any object onstage that is not a permanent part of the scenery or costumes. Props include such things as lamps, ashtrays, water glasses, computers, walking sticks, and umbrellas.)

Special effects include fog, ghosts, knives or swords that appear to stab victims, walls that fall apart, and so on. In the modern era, films and television—because of their technical capabilities—have brought extreme realism to special effects; examples include burning buildings, exploding cars, and scenes in outer space. Special effects onstage, however, are almost as old as theater itself. From the Greeks on, theater has tried to suspend natural laws and create an illusion of miraculous or extraordinary effects.

The see-through scrim and projections (described above) are used to create a number of special effects, such as dream sequences. Fog machines create a cloudy vapor that can be blown across the stage, giving an impression of clouds or fog. In *The Phantom of the Opera,* a huge chandelier falls from the top of the auditorium onto the stage.

Several special lighting effects can be used to create interesting visual pictures. A simple technique is positioning the light source near the stage floor and shining the light on the performers from below. This creates shadows under the eyes and chin and gives the performers a ghostly or horrifying quality. Another special effect is created with ultraviolet light—a dark blue light that causes phosphorus to glow. When the stage is very dark, even black, costumes or scenery that have been painted with a special phosphorus paint will "light up." An effect of slow motion or silent movies, where performers seem to be moving in jerks, can be created by using a *strobe light,* a very powerful, bright gas-discharge light which flashes at rapid intervals.

There are also a number of special sound effects. Sometimes speakers are placed completely around the audience so that the sound can move from side to side. Computerized noises and electronic music can be used to create special sounds for various situations, and tape loops can repeat the same sound over and over for a long time. Echoes can be created by a machine that causes reverberations in sound waves. Applications of light and sound are discussed more fully in Chapter 18.

THE PROCESS OF SCENE DESIGN

Elements of Design

In bringing her or his ideas to fulfillment, the designer makes use of the following elements:

Robin Wagner: Scene Designer

Robin Wagner has been designing sets in New York for more than two decades. His work includes such Broadway shows as A Chorus Line, 42nd Street, The Great White Hope, Saturday Night Fever, Kiss Me, Kate, *and* The Producers.

I'm from San Francisco originally. I had a regular high school education and then two years of art school at the California School of Fine Arts. Aside from little projects in high school, I didn't have any particular theater instruction. I'd never really given much thought to what goes on behind the scenes—as far as I was concerned, theater was just a group of actors who showed up onstage and put on a play. In fact, I was out of high school and an art student before I was exposed to theater. And then when I took a closer look, I discovered that the accumulation of all the work that goes on behind the scenes was even more interesting to me than what was going on in the performance. I realized that it requires so many people to produce a play that I knew there was room for me.

I worked at a number of so-called weekend theaters in San Francisco—the equivalent of off-off-Broadway in New York—where there was no pay but plenty of variety. I started painting scenery and working backstage, but I also had a little design experience. I was fortunate in starting in a city like San Francisco, where at that time there were very few professional designers. Even though I was only an art student just out of high school, I got experience designing that I would never have had if I had had any competition.

I first came to New York in 1958, when the Actors' Workshop production of *Waiting for Godot* that I designed was selected to go to the World's Fair in Brussels. My first real training was in New York, working for three years as an assistant to Oliver Smith, who designed *Hello, Dolly* and *110 in the Shade.* After I worked around the country at a number of regional theaters, I returned to New York and worked off-Broadway until I was asked to design *Hair.* It was 1968, and *Hair* was a breakthrough musical—it had a completely different kind of sound.

1. *Line,* the outline or silhouette of elements onstage: for example, predominantly curved lines versus sharply angular lines.
2. *Mass and composition,* the balance and arrangement of elements: for example, a series of high, heavy platforms or fortress walls versus a bare stage or a stage with one tree on it.
3. *Texture,* the "feel" projected by surfaces and fabrics: for example, the slickness of chrome or glass versus the roughness of brick or burlap.
4. *Color,* the shadings and contrasts of color combinations.
5. *Rhythm,* that is, "visual rhythm"—the repetition of shape, color, and texture in a regular or irregular pattern in a design.
6. *Movement* between scenes and within scenes—the way the action unfolds and the way it progresses from one scene to the next. This may involve rapid scene changes, turntables, and other devices for smooth transitions.

The designer will use these six elements to produce effects in conjunction with the action and other aspects of the production. Sometimes the designer will bring the director rough sketches showing several possible ideas, each emphasizing different elements to achieve different results.

Steps in the Design Process

In meeting the objectives described earlier in this chapter, how does the scene designer proceed? Although every designer has his or her own method, usually a general pattern is followed.

The designer reads the script carefully and begins to form ideas about how the play should come to life visually. Meanwhile, the director reads the script and develops ideas about the scenery. Following that, the director and the designer meet at a preliminary conference. Both have read the script, and they exchange ideas about the design. During these discussions the director and designer will develop and discuss questions of style, a visual concept for the production, the needs of the performers, and so on.

Next, the designer develops rough sketches, sometimes called *thumbnail sketches,* and rough plans to provide the basis for further discussions

THE DESIGN PROCESS

Where possible, the performers and the director in a production prefer to be aware of design elements during the rehearsal process. This can take the form of seeing renderings and models prepared by the designer or, in some cases, seeing the actual props and artifacts. In the case of a production of The Elephant Man, *actor Billy Crudup was able to view a plexiglass representation of a cathedral early in the process. He is shown here, at right, viewing the cathedral beforehand with director Sean Mathias, and, next page, during the finished production.*

(Sara Krulwich/The New York Times)

(© Joan Marcus)

about the scenic elements. As the designer proceeds, he or she attempts to fill out the visual concept with sketches, drawings, models, and the like. Throughout this period there is a good deal of give and take, of tossing ideas back and forth, between the director and the designer. Gradually the director and the designer move toward a mutually agreeable design.

When the designer and the director have decided on an idea and a rough design they like, the designer will make a more complete sketch, often in color, called a *rendering*. If the director approves of this, the designer will make a small-scale three-dimensional *model* which the director can use to help stage the show. There are two types of models. One shows only the location of the platform and walls, with perhaps some light detail drawn in; it is usually all white. The other is a complete finished model: everything is duplicated as fully as possible, including color and perhaps moldings and texture.

Today more and more designers are using computers and computer graphics to develop not only ground plans but also three-dimensional models of what a set will look like. Computerized design, known technically as **computer-assisted design** (CAD), is very flexible: the designer can make instantaneous changes in what appears on the screen and can easily indicate to the director and others alternative plans and features of a stage set. Not only ground plans but also the three-dimensional look of a set can be instantaneously rearranged to let both director and designer see what various configurations would look like. Not only can the scene be shown in three dimensions; it can also be looked at from various perspectives: from the right or left, from above, from the front.

It is important to note that this design process does not necessarily unfold from one step to the next in a predictable fashion. Discussions will be followed by further sketches, which in turn will be subject to consultation with the director and other designers. More than once in creating a production, the designer will feel it necessary to "go back to the drawing board."

The Scene Designer's Collaborators

As with every element of theater, there is a collaborative aspect to scene design: in addition to the director there are a number of other important people with whom the scene designer works.

First, there may be people who help the scene designer draw the architectural plans for platforms, ramps, flats, and other scenery. These require

exact measurements that conform to the stage space and, if it is a proscenium stage, to the proscenium opening. They must be drawn precisely to scale in the manner of a blueprint used by an architect and engineer in constructing a building.

Once the designer and his or her assistants have completed renderings, models, or computer designs—and these have been approved—the project is turned over to the **technical director** of the production. The technical director is also given the necessary ground plans, the designer's elevations, the paint elevations, and the design specifications. (*Paint elevations* indicate colors, shadings, etc., from the point of view of a spectator in the auditorium.) From this material, *scene shops,* also known as *production shops,* create construction drawings. Together with the building and paint crews, the technical director then sees that the scenery, platforms, and other elements are built, painted, and installed onstage. Scenic construction requires a staff of stage carpenters—people who understand materials and methods of construction—to build the platforms, set pieces, flats, and other elements of scenery. During the process of construction, painting, and so forth, the designer frequently visits the shop to make certain the final product will match the original intention.

After the scenery is built, the scene artists must paint it. This requires both talent and technique: to create, for instance, the feeling of rare old wood in a library, or of bricks, or of a glossy, elegant surface in an expensive living room. Along with the painters, there are people who must find fabric for draperies, slipcovers for furniture, and other items that "dress" the stage set.

THE WINTER'S TALE

(Copyright Walt Spangler. Used by special permission of the Designer.)

The Designer Prepares a Production   For a production of Shakespeare's *The Winter's Tale,* directed by Michael Kahn, at the Shakespeare Theater in Washington, D.C., scene designer Walt Spangler created a series of models on which the final sets were based. Shown here is one of the models (*above*) along with a production shot showing the scene as it appeared on stage (*below*).

(Photo by Richard Termine)

Employment Prospects for Young Designers

In today's world it is rare for a young designer, fresh out of graduate design school, to find full-time work in the theater. This is a situation that also exists for other artists in theater: playwrights, directors, and performers. Broadway focuses on large-scale musicals, which tend to play for a number of years; this means that very few new shows open. Off-Broadway offers a limited amount of work and does not always pay handsomely. Positions in important regional theaters are filled by people who stay in those positions for a long time; the artistic directors and the head designers in many regional theaters have been in place for many years and show no sign of moving.

What this means is that young designers—like young playwrights, directors, and performers—who want to work in theater must find a foothold where they can begin. They may start as assistants to established designers; they can also work in low-budget theater productions until they have acquired sufficient experience and credits. In addition, they must attempt to get work in films, television, music videos, or industrial productions to support themselves until the opportunity of working in theater presents itself.

When the time comes for technical rehearsals, dress rehearsals, and the actual performances after the official opening, a production requires stagehands and a stage manager to coordinate scene changes, to actually remove and replace both scenery and furniture, and to see that each setting is correct and is put in place quickly.

Designing a Total Environment

Sometimes a designer goes beyond scenery and special effects, and designs an entire theater space, rearranging the seating for spectators and determining the relationship of the stage area to the audience. For instance, in an open space such as a gymnasium or warehouse, a designer might build an entire theater, including the seats or stands for the audience and the designated acting areas. In this case, the designer considers the size and shape of the space, the texture and nature of the building materials, the atmosphere of the space, and the needs of the play itself. This is also true of multifocus theater.

In this chapter we have examined the work of the scene designer. In Chapter 17, we turn to someone whose work is closely related: the costume designer.

SUMMARY

1. We encounter forms of scene design in everyday life: in the carefully planned decor of a restaurant, in a hotel lobby, or in a decorated apartment.

2. Scene design for the stage differs from interior decorating in that it creates an environment and an atmosphere which are not filled until occupied by performers.

3. In addition to creating an environment, the scene designer has the following objectives: to set tone and style, distinguish realism from nonrealism, establish time and place, develop a design concept, provide a central design metaphor, coordinate scenery with other elements, and deal with practical considerations.

4. As in other aspects of theater, in scene design there has been more and more crossover, and interaction, between theater design and design for many types of popular entertainment.

5. In practical terms the scene designer must deal with the limits of the stage space and the offstage area. For example, ramps must not be inclined too steeply, and platforms must provide an adequate playing area for the performers. In short, the stage designer must know the practical considerations of stage usage and stage carpentry, as well as the materials available, in order to achieve desired effects.

6. In theatrical productions that stress visual elements over the play or the acting, the scene design must constantly engage and entrance the spectator.

7. Special effects are elements of scenery, lighting, costumes, props, or sound that appear highly unusual or miraculous. Technical expertise is required to develop them properly.

8. Elements of design include line, mass, composition, texture, color, rhythm, and movement.

9. The scene designer works closely with the director and other designers and creates a series of drawings (sketches and renderings) and models of what the final stage picture will look like.

10. In dealing with created or found space, the designer must plan the entire environment: the audience area as well as the stage area.

11. The technical director, with his or her staff, supervises the construction of scenery, special effects, and the like, in order to meet the designer's specifications.

EXPLORING THEATER ON THE WEB

Scenery

More and more useful sites for theatrical scene designers appear online. Many of these are commercial sites where one can find traditional stage materials. Others are designer portfolios or period-style research sites that may be of help to a scene designer, props artisan, or scenic artist. The United States Institute of Theater Technology (USITT) is a well-known resource for the theatrical designer. Visit the USITT web page at: http://www.usitt.org

Exercises:

1. On USITT's website, click on the "About USITT" link. What are the seven missions of USITT? When was USITT established? Why is it important to provide a forum for designers and technicians in theater?

2. Browse the "WOW" page (USITT's list of theatrical websites) for links pertaining to theater design and technology: http://www.siue.edu/COSTUMES/WOW/WOW_INDEX.html. The objective of the theatrical designer is to reinforce the tone and style of a production while establishing the locale and period in which the play takes place. How would a student scenic designer use this page to do research for a production of Chekhov's *The Cherry Orchard*?

3. Using a generic search engine, seek out scenic design training programs offered by universities around the globe. How do these programs describe their mission? What components do they include as key to their programs (i.e., what do they view as important to the design process in terms of scenery)? How do the programs differ in their philosophy? One of the most important things for individuals interested in theater scenery to know is how the development of the craft is viewed from within the field. What insight do the programs you visited contribute to this end? Discuss.

CHAPTER SEVENTEEN

Stage Costumes

Because they are actually worn by the performers, costumes are the most personal aspect of the visual elements in theater. To members of the audience, a performer and his or her costume are perceived as one; they merge into a single image onstage. At the same time, costumes have a value of their own, adding color, shape, texture, and symbolism to the overall effect. Other elements or accessories, such as makeup, hairstyles, masks, and personal items like bracelets and necklaces, are an important component of costumes.

◀ STAGE COSTUMES: AESTHETIC, SYMBOLIC, AND SUITED TO THE CHARACTER

In addition to being stylish and beautiful, costumes can convey a wealth of information to the audience. Shown here are two characters in a production of Sheridan's The School for Scandal *at the McCarter Theatre in Princeton. The costume designer, Jess Goldstein, created outfits that suited both the play and the performers who wore them. The play is a comedy of manners, and the characters are members of the upper class and the servants who work for them. The two seen here are Lady Teazle and Sir Peter Teazle. Their costumes indicate the fact that this is a bright, sunny play, not a serious tragedy. The costumes also indicate the period in which the play is set, namely, the eighteenth century.* (© T. Charles Erickson)

COSTUMES IN EVERYDAY LIFE

Aside from theater, most people think of costumes in terms of the outfits people wear in a holiday parade, at a masquerade ball, or in a pageant with historical figures, such as Queen Elizabeth, George Washington, or Abraham Lincoln. Like other aspects of theater, however, costumes play a significant role in daily life. People wear clothing not only for comfort but also for the information they want to convey to others about themselves. If we look around us, we are surrounded by costumes of daily life: the formal, subdued uniform of a police officer; the sparkling outfits of a marching band at a football game; sports gear such as hockey and baseball uniforms; the cap and gown for graduation; a priest's cassock; the dresses worn by bridesmaids at a formal wedding; and brightly colored bathing suits at a swimming pool. In fact, everything we wear, not only special outfits but everyday clothing, is a form of costume.

The power of symbols is discussed in Chapter 1. Nowhere is this power more manifest than in clothing and other personal adornments. Primitive people put on animal skins to give themselves the characteristics of an animal—ferocity or courage, for instance. Feathers and elaborate headdresses were worn to accentuate height; bracelets and belts with charms were worn as sources of power.

Today, we still wear clothes to symbolize different societal qualities. A young person might wear informal clothing as a statement of independence from his or her parents. Adults, on the other hand, might wear conventional clothing in order not to stand out from the crowd, or to avoid criticism by their friends. How one appears to one's peers or to an outside group is a paramount issue with many people, and this is especially noticeable in styles of dress.

Frequently we judge others by their appearance, particularly when we first meet them. If we see a man wearing a dark-blue pinstripe suit and a tie, we may assume that he is middle-class or upper-middle-class; we may assume that he is conservative, and probably a banker or a lawyer. Beyond that, we may make certain assumptions about his politics, his family life, his social attitudes—in fact, his whole psychological profile.

A good example of a symbolic outfit is a judge's robe. Its black color suggests seriousness and dignity; it is draped from the shoulders straight to the ground, covering the whole body, thereby wrapping the judge in the importance and presumed impartiality of the office. The intention is that the robe of a judge invests the wearer with authority and wisdom; and when we see someone in a judicial robe, we are supposed to accept that image. Although individual judges may be foolish or corrupt, it is considered important in our society for the *institution* of the judiciary to be just and incorrupt, and a judge's robe is an important factor in reinforcing that concept.

Clothes have always indicated or signaled a number of things regarding the wearer, including the following:

- Position and status
- Sex

- Occupation
- Relative flamboyance or modesty
- Degree of independence or regimentation
- Whether one is dressed for work or leisure, for a routine event or a special occasion

As soon as we see what clothing people are wearing, we receive messages about them and form impressions of them; we instantaneously relate those messages and impressions to our past experience and our preconceptions, and we make judgments, including value judgments. Even if we have never before laid eyes on someone, we feel we know a great deal when we first see what he or she is wearing.

COSTUMES FOR THE STAGE

In theater, clothes send us signals similar to those in everyday life, but, as with other elements of theater, there are significant differences between the costumes of everyday life and theatrical costumes. Stage costumes communicate the same information as ordinary clothes with regard to sex, position, and occupation; but onstage this information is magnified because every element in theater is in the spotlight. Also, costumes on a stage must meet other requirements not normally imposed in everyday life. These requirements will be clearer after we look at the objectives of costume design.

Objectives of Costume Design

Stage costumes should meet the following seven requirements:

1. Help establish the style of a production

2. Indicate the historical period of a play and the locale in which it occurs

3. Indicate the nature of individual characters or groups in a play: their stations in life, their occupations, their personalities

4. Show relationships among characters: separating major characters from minor ones, contrasting one group with another

5. Where appropriate, symbolically convey the significance of individual characters or the theme of the play

6. Meet the needs of individual performers, making it possible for an actor or actress to move freely in a costume, perhaps to dance or engage in a sword fight, and (when required) to change quickly from one costume to another

7. Be consistent with the production as a whole, especially other visual elements

The Process of Costume Design

In order to achieve these objectives, the costume designer goes through a process similar to that of the scene designer. He or she reads the script, taking particular note of the characters: their age, gender, physical qualities, and special traits, as well as their roles in the play.

Early in the process, the designer also meets with the director and other designers to discuss the "look" that the show will have and how the various elements will be coordinated. The costume designer may make preliminary

Perdita

(Costume design by Catherine Zuber. Copyright Catherine Zuber. Used by special permission of the Designer).

(Photo by Richard Termine)

COSTUME DESIGN: THE PROCESS

Frequently, costume designers will make sketches of costumes before making the actual costume. The sketch will indicate not only shape, outline, and fabric, but also colors. Seen here is a sketch by designer Catherine Zuber for the character of Perdita in Shakespeare's The Winter's Tale. On the left is the design, and on the right is the finished costume as worn by actress Mireille Enos. (The actor with her is Jeremiah Wiggins.) The production was at the Shakespeare Theatre in Washington, D.C.

sketches to show the director and other designers. These may include not only suggestions about style (for example, historical, modern, futuristic) but also ideas for colors and fabrics. Once agreed upon, these designs will move from sketches to renderings of what the costumes will look like in their final form. Swatches of material may be attached to these designs, indicating the texture and color of the fabrics to be used.

As part of this process, the costume designer will meet with the members of the cast, measuring each performer and making certain that the costume will be workable and appropriate for the individual actresses and actors.

The following sections discuss how the various objectives of costume design are realized by the designer in this process.

Indicating Style Along with scenery and lighting, costumes should inform the audience about the style of a play. For a production set in outer space,

COSTUMES INDICATE TONE AND STYLE

For a production of Molière's Tartuffe, *costume designer Jess Goldstein created fanciful period outfits such as those shown here on Dorine (Mary Testa) and Cléante (Wendell Pierce). Note the shape of the costumes, the cut and silhouette, the fabrics, and the colors: all of these go together to create the "look," which is consistent with a comedy and with the period of the play. (© Michal Daniel/The Joseph Papp Public Theater)*

for instance, the costumes would be futuristic. For a Restoration comedy, the costumes would be quite elegant, with elaborate gowns for the women and lace at the men's collars and cuffs. For a tragedy, the clothes would be formal and dignified; seeing them, the audience would know immediately that the play itself was serious.

For the musical *The Phantom of the Opera,* which is set in Paris in 1911, the designer Maria Bjornson fashioned romantic period outfits: the men in

EXAGGERATED AND STYLIZED COSTUMES

In addition to giving information about character, style, and so forth, costumes can be humorous, satirical, and theatrical. Shown here are the elaborate, stylized costumes created by Howard Crabtree for the gay musical revue, Howard Crabtree's When Pigs Fly. *Note the hair pieces, the wide skirts, and the other elements of exaggeration.* (© Gerry Goodstein)

top hats with canes and capes, the women in long dresses with full skirts and elaborate hats and coats. For *The Sisters Rosensweig,* a play by Wendy Wasserstein (1950–) which takes place in the early 1990s in London but concerns three upper-middle-class American women, the costume designer Jane Greenwood (1934–) created clothes reflecting the lifestyles of men and women in that time period and of that socioeconomic status. Angela Wendt, costume designer for the musical *Rent,* clothed the characters in all manner of informal pickup attire appropriate to free-spirited young people living on the Lower East Side in New York City, struggling to make their way.

Indicating Period and Locale Costumes indicate the period and location of a play: whether it is historical or modern, whether it is set in a foreign country or the United States, and so on. A play might take place in ancient Egypt, in seventeenth-century Spain, or in modern Africa. Costumes should tell us when and where the action occurs.

For most historical plays, the director and the costume designer have a range of choices, depending on the directorial concept. For a production of Shakespeare's *Julius Caesar,* for instance, the costumes could indicate the ancient Roman period when Caesar actually lived; in this case, the costumes would include Roman togas and soldiers' helmets. Or the costumes could be Elizabethan; we know that in Shakespeare's day costumes were heightened versions of the English clothes of the time, regardless of the period in which a play was set. As a third option, the designer could create costumes for an entirely different period, including our own day—with the men in business suits, modern military uniforms, and perhaps even tuxedos. Whatever the choice, the historical period should be clearly indicated by the costumes.

Identifying Status and Personality Like clothing in everyday life, costumes can tell us whether people are from the aristocracy or the working class, whether they are blue-collar workers or professionals. But in theater, these signals must be clear and unmistakable. For example, a woman in a long white coat could be a doctor, a laboratory technician, or a hairdresser. A costume onstage must indicate the occupation exactly—by giving the doctor a stethoscope, for instance.

Costumes also tell us about the personalities of characters: a flamboyant person will be dressed in flashy colors; a shy, retiring person will wear subdued clothing.

Costumes also indicate age. This is particularly helpful when an older performer is playing a young person, or vice versa. A young person playing an older character, for instance, can wear padding or a beard.

Showing Relationships among Characters Characters in a play can be set apart by the way they are costumed. Major characters, for example, will be dressed differently from minor characters. Frequently, the costume designer will point up the major characters by dressing them in distinctive colors, in sharp contrast to the other characters. Consider Shaw's *Saint Joan,* a play about Joan of Arc. Obviously, Joan should stand out from the soldiers surrounding her. Therefore, her costume might be bright blue while their costumes are steel gray. In another play of Shaw's, *Caesar and Cleopatra,* Cleopatra should stand out from her servants and soldiers. If she is dressed like them in an Egyptian costume, she should wear an outfit that has brighter colors and is more elegant.

Costumes underline important divisions between groups. In *Romeo and Juliet,* the Montagues wear one color and the Capulets another. In a modern counterpart of *Romeo and Juliet,* the musical *West Side Story,* the two gangs of young men are dressed in contrasting colors: the Jets might be in various shades of pink, purple, and lavender; the Sharks in shades of green, yellow, and lemon.

Creating Symbolic and Nonhuman Characters   In many plays, special costumes are called for to denote abstract ideas or give shape to fantastic creatures. Here the costume designer must develop an outfit which carries with it the appropriate imaginative and symbolic qualities. How does one clothe the witches in *Macbeth* or the ghost of Banquo, for instance? Some way must be found to symbolize the qualities they represent.

To illustrate how costumes can suggest ideas or characteristics, a costume of animal skins can symbolize bestiality; a costume of feathers can indicate a birdlike quality; a costume of a metallic material can suggest a hard, mechanical quality.

In *Peer Gynt* by Ibsen, the main character, Peer, meets a supernatural being called "the Boyg" in the mountains. The Boyg is a symbolic presence urging Peer to compromise in life and go "roundabout." A costume designer might fashion for the Boyg a soft, round outfit with no sharp outlines or edges—a large blob, like a sack of potatoes—to indicate its indecisive, amorphous quality.

The Balcony by the French playwright Jean Genet calls for exaggerated as well as symbolic costumes. The play is set in a house of prostitution where ordinary men act out their fantasies: one man pretends to be a general, another a bishop, and a third a judge. They dress in exaggerated costumes, looking almost like caricatures, with platform shoes, shoulder pads wider than their own shoulders, and high headpieces. The women who serve them also dress fantastically. The woman serving the general is dressed as a horse, and the costume designer has the task of making a costume for her which will bring out her attractiveness as a person but still give her a horse's tail and mane.

For *The Lion King*, the director Julie Taymor, who was also the costume designer, used puppets, masks, and other devices to create outfits for numerous animal characters, such as lions, tigers, giraffes, and elephants.

Meeting Performers' Needs   Virtually every aspect of theater has practical as well as aesthetic requirements, and costume design is no exception. No matter how attractive or how symbolic, stage costumes must work for the performers. A long flowing gown may look beautiful, but if it is too long and the actress wearing it trips every time she walks down a flight of steps, the designer has overlooked an important practical consideration. If actors are required to duel or engage in hand-to-hand combat, their costumes must stand up to this wear and tear, and their arms and legs must have freedom of movement. If performers are to dance, they must be able to turn, leap, and move freely.

Quick costume changes are frequently called for in theater. At the end of the musical *Gypsy*, when an emerging young star sings "Let Me Entertain You," she goes offstage between choruses and reappears a few seconds later

(Kenneth Lambert/AP/Wide World Photos)

(Jack Manning/The New York Times)

The Costume Designer at Work   Shown here are three different aspects of costume designers preparing for a production. In the first photo, designer David Woolard stands in front of the costume sketches he developed for characters in a production of the musical *Sweeney Todd* at the Kennedy Center. At left, designer Jane Greenwood is making adjustments to a costume she designed for a character in a production of *High Society*. On the top of the next page, William Ivey Long exuberantly assists Marissa Jaret Winokur as she tries on a costume he designed for her in *Hairspray*.

(Nicole Bengiveno/The New York Times)

The Costume Designer's Use of Color The costume designer uses fabric, color, line, shape, and silhouette to create the unique look of each costume. An excellent example of the use of color (as well as of line and silhouette) is demonstrated in the scene shown below from a production of Mamet's *Boston Marriage* at New York's Joseph Papp Public Theatre, with costumes designed by Paul Tazewell. Note the yellow of the costume worn by Kate Burton (*left*) contrasted with the blue of the outfit of Martha Plimpton. Both, in turn, stand out against the rose color of the scenery.

(© Michal Daniel)

Jess Goldstein: Costume Designer

Jess Goldstein has designed costumes for Broadway (The Most Happy Fella, A Streetcar Named Desire, Love! Valour! Compassion! and The Rainmaker); for off-Broadway (The Substance of Fire, Other People's Money, and How I Learned to Drive); and for many major regional theaters. He teaches costume design at the Yale Drama School.

Growing up in the New Jersey suburbs right outside New York City, I began seeing Broadway theater at a relatively early age. I think I was always most impressed with the costume and set design, possibly because I had no talent for performing yet seemed to show some aptitude for drawing and painting. But the world of theatrical design, from my naive perspective, seemed far too exotic and unattainable, so I enrolled as a commercial art major at Boston University. But I continued to see a lot of theater in Boston, which in the early 1970s was still an important tryout stopover for Broadway shows.

At B.U. I met students who were majoring in design in the theater school. Somehow, the fact that one could earn a degree in theater design seemed to endow it as a career choice with some validity and security. Well, talk about "naive"! Nevertheless, I switched majors, and really found school and classwork exciting for the first time in my life.

But it was going to the theater and seeing those Hal Prince, Bob Fosse, Gower Champion, and Michael Bennett musicals that really inspired me. The stars of those shows were terrific, but my heroes were Irene Sharaff, Raoul Pene duBois, Patricia Zipprodt, and Florence Klotz. Watching the way colors and shapes might be manipulated in a scene or the way a skirt would move to the choreography was a significant part of my early training.

I soon began seeking out other kinds of theater: plays off-Broadway, the Shakespeare festivals in New York and Stratford, Connecticut, as well as opera and ballet; and by the time the off-off-Broadway theater movement was in full swing in New York in the late 1970s, I had just completed my M.F.A. at the Yale School of Drama and was ready as a designer to be a part of it.

in a different costume. The actress goes through three or four dazzling costume changes in seconds, to the astonishment of the audience. The costumes must be made so that the actress, with the help of dressers offstage, can rapidly shed one outfit and get into another. Tear-away seams and special fasteners are used so that one costume can be ripped off quickly and another put on. For this kind of thing, the fastener Velcro has been of great assistance to present-day costume designers.

Unlike scenery, which stays in place until it is moved, a costume is constantly in motion; it moves as the performer moves. This provides an opportunity for the designer to develop grace and rhythm in the way a costume looks as it moves across the stage, but with that goes the great responsibility of making the costume workable for the performer.

At times it is important for the costume designer to work closely with individual performers. Actresses and actors must know how to use the accessories and costumes provided for them. As an example, the character Sparkish in the Restoration comedy *The Country Wife* by Wycherley is an outrageous fop. Sparkish wears a fancy wig, a hat, and flamboyant breeches. He uses a handkerchief, a snuffbox, and other hand accessories. In creating a costume for Sparkish, the designer must provide an outfit that not only is correct for the style of the production but also suits the physique and appearance of the individual actor. If the actor has never worn a wig or breeches of this kind and has never worked with a handkerchief—which he keeps in the cuff of his jacket—or with a snuffbox, he must learn to use these items, working closely with both the director and the costume designer.

Maintaining Consistency   Finally, costumes must be consistent with the entire production—especially with the various other visual elements. A realistic production set in the home of everyday people calls for down-to-earth costumes. A highly stylized production requires costumes designed with flair and imagination.

The Costume Designer at Work

The Costume Designer's Responsibilities   As noted earlier, the person who puts all these ideas into effect is the costume designer. Every production requires someone who takes responsibility for the costumes. This is true whether the costumes are *pulled* or *built.*

Pulling is a term used when costumes are rented and the designer goes to a costume house or storeroom and selects outfits that are appropriate for the production. The designer must already know about period, style, and the other matters discussed above. He or she must also have the measurements of all the performers for whom costumes are to be pulled.

When costumes are *built,* they are created in a costume shop under the supervision of the designer. They must be sewn, fitted, and completed with accessories such as spangles, brocade, piping, or whatever else is appropriate.

Whether costumes are cut and sewn from scratch or pulled from inventory or a rental house, the costume designer determines how they will look. Obviously, this requires both training and talent. As suggested previously, the costume designer should begin with a thorough knowledge of the play: its subject matter, period, style, and point of view. The costume designer must also have intimate knowledge of the characters in the play. The designer must know each character's personality, idiosyncrasies, relative importance in the play, relationship to other characters, and symbolic value. The designer must be aware, too, of the physical demands of each role: what is called for in terms of sitting, moving from level to level, dancing, falling down, fighting, and so on. Finally, the designer must become thoroughly acquainted with the characteristics of the performers themselves in order to create costumes accommodating their physiques and movement patterns.

The Costume Designer's Resources   Among the elements a costume designer works with are (1) line, shape, and silhouette; (2) color; (3) fabric; and (4) accessories.

THE COSTUME DESIGNER'S MATERIALS

The fabrics and other elements that go to make up a costume are used by the designer to create the visual effect desired. For example, Shakespeare's A Midsummer Night's Dream *takes place in an other worldly, dream-like atmosphere. Depending on the director's vision, the action can be soft or harsh. For a production of the play at the Guthrie Theater in Minneapolis, director Joe Dowling tended to emphasize a harsher quality in certain scenes, and for these costume designer Paul Tazewell developed the costumes seen here. Both Puck (Randy Reyes) on the floor, and Oberon (Shawn Hamilton) are dressed in rough-hewn, metallic fabrics, exaggerated and stylized.* (© Michal Daniel)

Line Of prime importance is the cut or **line** of the clothing. Do the lines of an outfit flow, or are they sharp and jagged? Does the clothing follow the lines of the body, or is there some element of exaggeration, such as shoulder pads for a man or a bustle at the back of a woman's dress? The outline or silhouette of a costume has always been significant. There is a strong visual contrast, for instance, between the line of an Egyptian woman's garment, flowing smoothly from shoulder to floor, and that of an empire gown of the early nineteenth century in France, which featured a horizontal line high above the waist, just below the breasts, with a line flowing from below the bosom to the feet. The silhouettes of these two styles would stand in marked contrast to a woman's outfit in the United States of the early 1930s, a short outfit with a prominent belt or sash cutting horizontally across the hips.

Undergarments are an aspect of costume design often overlooked by audiences. For women's costumes, one example is the hoopskirt. In *The King and I,* a musical of 1951 that was revived on Broadway in 1996, Anna, an English schoolteacher in Siam, wears dresses with hoopskirts several feet in diameter, which were in fashion in England in the mid-nineteenth century, the time of the play.

Other undergarments include bustles, which exaggerate the lines in the rear; and corsets, which can greatly alter a woman's posture and appearance. For example, some corsets pull in the waist and cause the wearer to stand very straight. But in the first decade of the twentieth century, women in society often bent forward because they wore a curved corset that forced them to thrust their shoulders and upper body forward. A costume designer will be aware of the importance of undergarments and will use them to create the appropriate silhouette.

Color A second important resource for costume designers is **color**. Earlier, we saw that leading characters can be dressed in a color which contrasts with the colors worn by other characters, and that characters from one family can be dressed in a different color from those in a rival family. Color also suggests mood: bright, warm colors for a happy mood; dark, somber colors for a more serious mood.

THE COSTUME DESIGNER'S COLLABORATORS
Many people work with designers to bring their ideas to fruition. For costume designers it includes seamstresses, dressers, and others. Shown here is Eleanor Wolfe (kneeling), *a draper fitting a costume on actress Lauren Ward for a production of the musical* Follies. *The costume designer was Theoni V. Aldredge.* (Sara Krulwich/The New York Times)

Beyond these applications, however, color can indicate changes in character and changes in mood. Near the beginning of Eugene O'Neill's *Mourning Becomes Electra*, General Manon, who has recently returned from the Civil War, dies, and his wife and daughter wear dark mourning clothes. Lavinia, the daughter, knows that her mother had something to do with her father's death, and she and her brother conspire to murder the mother. Once they have done so, Lavinia feels a great sense of release. She adopts characteristics of her mother, and as an important symbol of this transformation, she puts on brightly colored clothes of the same shades her mother had worn when she was young.

Fabric Fabric is a third tool of the costume designer. In one sense, this is the costume designer's medium, for it is in fabric that silhouette and color are displayed. Just as important as those qualities are the texture and bulk of the fabric. What is its reflective quality? Does it have a sheen that reflects light? Or is it rough so that it absorbs light? How does it drape the wearer? Does it fall lightly to the floor and outline physical features, or does it hide them? Does it wrinkle naturally, or is it smooth?

Beyond its inherent qualities, fabric has symbolic values. For example, burlap or other roughly textured cloth suggests people of the earth or of modest means. Silks and satins, on the other hand, suggest elegance and refinement—perhaps even royalty.

The connotations of fabrics may change with passing years. Two or three generations ago, blue denim was used only for work clothes, worn by laborers or cowboys who actually rode horseback on a ranch. Today, denim is the fabric of choice in informal clothes for people of all incomes and all ages.

Accessories Ornamentation and accessories can also be used. Fringe, lace, ruffles, feathers, belts, beads, bracelets, earrings—all these add to the attractiveness and individuality of a costume. Also, walking sticks, parasols, purses, and other items carried or worn by performers can give distinction and definition to an outfit.

Using the combined resources of line, color, fabric, and accessories, the costume designer arrives at individual outfits which tell us a great deal about the

MAKEUP: CHANGING A FACE OR CREATING A NEW ONE

Makeup is frequently used so that facial features will not be washed out by bright lights, or to change the appearance of a performer—to make a person look older, for example. At other times, makeup is used to create a kind of mask. This is true of much Asian theater. Here, an actress applies elaborate makeup for a Chinese theater production. (Bruno J. Zehnder/ Peter Arnold, Inc.)

characters who wear them and convey important visual signals about the style and meaning of the play as a whole.

The Costume Designer's Collaborators Once again, it is important to recognize that a number of collaborators aid in the process of costume design. The costume designer works closely with the people who sew and make the costumes, with those who fit them, and with those who care for them and maintain them throughout the run of a show. When a collection of period and other costumes is to be maintained, it must be kept in first-class condition and arranged so that individual costumes can be easily located.

OTHER ELEMENTS

Makeup

A part of costume is *makeup*—the application of cosmetics (paints, powders, and rouges) to the face and body. With regard to age and the special facial features associated with ethnic origins, a key function of makeup is to help the performer personify and embody a character.

Theatrical makeup used to be more popular than it is today. In a modern small theater, performers playing realistic parts will often go without makeup of any consequence. But makeup has a long and important history in the theater, and sometimes it is a necessity—one good example being makeup to highlight facial features which would not otherwise be visible in a large theater. Even in a smaller theater, bright lights tend to wash out cheekbones, eyebrows, and other facial features.

Makeup is often essential because the age of a character differs from that of the performer. Suppose that a 19-year-old performer is playing a 60-year-old character. Through the use of makeup—a little gray in the hair or simulated wrinkles on the face—the appropriate age can be suggested. Another situation calling for makeup to indicate age is a play in which the characters grow older during the course of the action. The musical *I Do, I Do,* with book and lyrics by Tom Jones and music by Harvey Schmidt, is based on the play *The Fourposter* by Jan de Hartog. In the musical, a husband and wife are shown in scenes covering many years in their married life, from the time when they are first married until they are quite old. In order to convey the passing years and their advancing age, the actress and actor must use makeup extensively. Makeup is also a necessity for fantastic or other nonrealistic creatures.

HAIRSTYLES AND WIGS

Hairstyle indicates social status and other facts about a character; it also provides information about when a play is taking place. Shown here is one of the best-known wig makers and hair stylist for innumerable Broadway shows: Paul Huntley. In this photo, Huntley is shaping the hair piece he developed for Sutton Foster for her portrayal of the title character in the musical Thoroughly Modern Millie. (Sara Krulwich/The New York Times)

Douglas Turner Ward (1930–), a black playwright, wrote *Day of Absence* to be performed by black actors in whiteface. The implications of this effect are many, not the least being the reversal of the old minstrel performances in which white actors wore blackface. Ward was not the first to put black actors in whiteface; Genet had part of the cast of his play *The Blacks* wear white masks.

Asian theater frequently relies on heavy makeup. For instance, Japanese kabuki, a highly stylized type of theater, uses completely nonrealistic makeup. The main characters must apply a base of white covering the entire face, over which bold patterns of red, blue, black, and brown are painted. The colors and patterns are symbolic of the character. In Chinese theater, too, the colors of makeup are symbolic: all white suggests treachery, black means fierce integrity, red means loyalty, green indicates demons, yellow stands for hidden cunning, and so forth.

When makeup is used, the human face becomes almost like a canvas for a painting. The features of the face may be heightened or exaggerated; or symbolic aspects of the face may be emphasized. In either case, makeup serves as an additional tool for the performer in creating an image of the character.

Hairstyles and Wigs

Another important component of costume design includes *hairstyles* and *wigs*. In certain periods men have worn wigs: the time of the American Revolution is a good example. In England, judges wear wigs to this day.

For women, hairstyles can denote period and social class. In the middle of the nineteenth century, for example, women often wore ringlets like Scarlett O'Hara's in the film *Gone with the Wind*. A few decades later, in the late 1800s, women wore their hair piled on top of the head in a pompadour; this was referred to as the *Gibson girl look*. In the 1920s, women wore their hair marcelled in waves, sometimes slicked down close to the head. In the modern period, women wear their hair in more natural styles; but again there is tremendous variety. Some women wear short, curly hair; others wear long hair, perhaps even down to the waist.

For men, too, hairstyles are significant and sometimes symbolic. A military brush cut, an Elvis Presley–style pompadour, and a ponytail each point up a certain lifestyle, but each may be interpreted in several ways.

Masks: An Ancient Theatrical Device
Masks have been used in theater almost from its beginning. They can change the appearance of a performer, make the face and head larger than life, and freeze the face into a fixed expression. Here we see four examples: masks (*above left*) by Linda Cho for Jason Butler Harner and Teri Lamm in a production of *Petersburg* at the Yale Repertory Theatre; a half mask designed by Jay Duckworth (*left*) for a production of *Waiting for Tadashi* at the George Street Playhouse (the actress is Sue Jin Song); masks and costumes designed by Daniel Wylie for a production of *The Caucasian Chalk Circle* at the Yale School of Drama; (*opposite top*) and the full-head masks designed by Teresa Snider-Stein for a production of *Drowning* by Maria Irene Fornes (*opposite, bottom*).

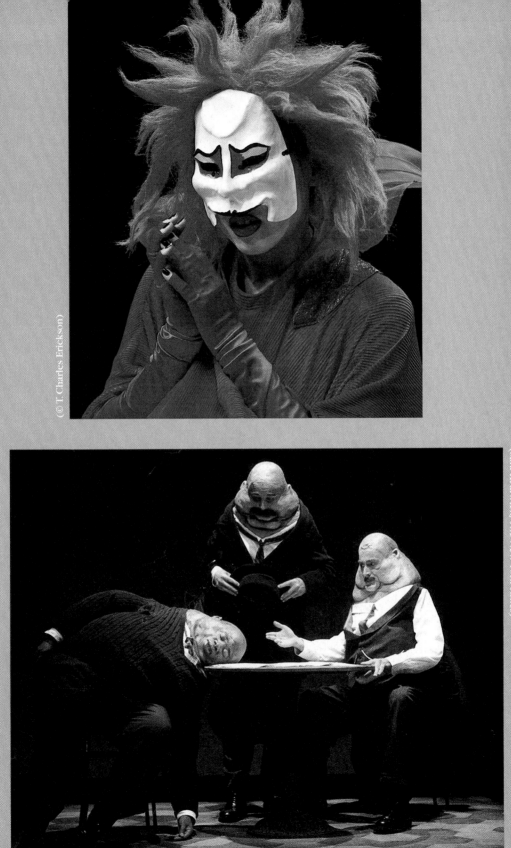

Masks

Masks seem to be as old as theater, having been used in ancient Greek theater and in the drama developed by primitive tribes. In one sense, the mask is an extension of the performer—a face on top of a face. There are several ways to look at masks. They remind us, first of all, that we are in a theater, that the act going on before our eyes is not real in a literal sense but is a symbolic or an artistic presentation. For another thing, masks allow a face to be frozen in one expression: a look of horror, perhaps, which we see throughout a production. Masks can also make a face larger than life, and they can create stereotypes, similar to stock characters (see Chapter 13) in which one particular feature—for example, cunning or haughtiness—is emphasized to the exclusion of everything else.

Masks offer other symbolic possibilities. In his play *The Great God Brown,* Eugene O'Neill calls for the performers at certain times to hold masks in front of their faces. When the masks are in place, the characters present a facade to the public, withholding their true characters. When the masks are down, the characters reveal their inner feelings.

COORDINATION OF THE WHOLE

Actors and actresses would have great difficulty creating a part without costumes and, in some cases, without makeup or a mask as well. These elements help the performer define his or her role and are so closely related to the performer that we sometimes lose sight of them as separate entities. At the same time, costumes, makeup, hairstyles, and masks must be integrated with other aspects of a production.

For example, these elements are essential in carrying out a point of view in a production. Masks, for instance, are clearly nonrealistic and signal to the audience that the character wearing the mask and the play itself are also likely to be nonrealistic. Costumes suggest whether a play is comic or serious, a wild farce or a stark tragedy.

Costumes, makeup, hairstyles, and masks must also be coordinated with scenery and lighting. The wrong kind of lighting can wash out or discolor costumes and makeup. It would be self-defeating, too, if scenery were in one mood or style and the costumes in another. Ideally, these elements should support and reinforce one another, and spectators should be aware of how essential it is for them to work together.

In Chapter 17 we have looked at costume design, and in Chapter 16 at scene design. At this point, it is in order to stress again that the designers do not work in isolation. We have seen that the director confers with designers, and it is important to note that the designers themselves also consult frequently

HATS AND OTHER ACCESSORIES

The accoutrements that are part of costumes are also the result of the costume designer's art. Here we see an array of hats, created by designer Emilio Sosa for a production of Crowns *at the McCarter Theatre in Princeton. One of the chief themes of the play is the important role hats play in the lives and society of African American women of a certain age in particular locations. The hats are a status symbol and also say a great deal about the personalities of the individuals, as well as the statement they wish to make about their roots and about their aspirations in life. (© T. Charles Erickson)*

with one another. In the production process there are regular meetings between two or more designers to coordinate their efforts—not only on such matters as colors and style but also regarding cues and the way various design elements work together. In Chapter 18 we turn to a third visual element, lighting, and to the use of sound in theater.

SUMMARY

1. The clothes we wear in daily life are a form of costume. They indicate station in life, occupation, and a sense of formality or informality.

2. Onstage, costumes—like clothes in real life—convey information about the people wearing them; more than that, these costumes are chosen consciously and are designed to give the audience important information.

3. The objectives of costume design are to set tone and style, indicate time and place, characterize individuals and groups, underline personal relationships, create symbolic outfits when appropriate, meet the practical needs of performers, and coordinate with the total production.

4. The designer works with the following elements: line and shape, color, fabric, and accessories.

5. Makeup and hairstyles are also important to the appearance of the performers and are part of the designer's concern.

6. Where called for, masks, too, are under the direction of the costume designer.

EXPLORING THEATER
ON
THE
WEB

Stage Costumes

Many sites useful to the theatrical costume designer are commercial sites where one can view, and sometimes purchase, traditional costume materials. Others are designer portfolios or period-style research sites that may be of help to a costume designer.

Visit the Costume Society of America website: http://www.costumesocietyamerica.com/. The Costume Society of America is sponsored by the Costume Gallery, (http://www.costumegallery.com), a commercial site that provides research services for costume designers. In addition, there are links to businesses that provide goods and services related to costumes, and links to costume designers' personal websites.

Exercises:

1. The Costume Gallery website has an online library for costume period style and research. Go to the "Study," an area "dedicated to the education and research of costume." In the study, you can visit the online costume library. Imagine that you are designing costumes for a production of Thornton Wilder's *Our Town*. The play is set in Grovers Corners, New Hampshire; the year is 1901. Find and print out images that would aid you in your design research for this play. What sources on this site would be most useful for you? What other research sources could you find?

2. Click on the *Into the Woods* link on the second shelf of the Costume Research Library. The designer states that the "theme for the designs was birds and flowers." Do the sketches of the costumes support this statement? Can you find images of birds and flowers in all the costumes? If the audience doesn't notice this theme, how might it still enhance the production? Imagine that you are designing the costumes for a production of *A Midsummer Night's Dream*. What themes would you use? How would you find research to aid your design process?

3. A significant portion of the costumer's job is connecting to resources needed in the design and realization of costumes. In addition to the aforementioned websites, visit "The Costume Page" at http://users.aol.com/nebula5/costume.html. Make note of the resources needed in the area of costuming. Create a list of the types of resources used by designers and costumers and then use a generic search engine to access information to locate such resources. Hint: There are several costume galleries available online offering assistance with resources.

CHAPTER EIGHTEEN

Lighting and Sound

Like scenery, costumes, and other elements of theater, stage lighting and sound have counterparts in everyday life. For example, in real life the basic function of lighting is, of course, illumination—to allow people to see at night and indoors. But there are also many theatrical uses of light in daily life. Advertising signs often have neon lights or brightly colored bulbs. Restaurants feature soft lights and candles. In homes, people put spotlights on special parts of a room, such as a dining-room table. Also, in homes people frequently use a rheostat so that they can dim lights to create a mood.

◀ THE POWERFUL EFFECTS OF STAGE LIGHTING

Lighting is one of the most versatile and potent visual resources in theater. It can be used to establish focus, to indicate mood, and to create special effects. The effectiveness of lighting in displaying a powerful image is shown in this scene from a production of Goethe's **Faust** *in a production directed by Peter Stein in Berlin, Germany. The silhouette of the figure and the wash of colors in the background are all created by light. The lighting designers were Heinrich Brunke and Vera and Konrad Lindenberg. (© Ruth Walz)*

STAGE LIGHTING

Lighting—historically the last element of visual design to be incorporated in theater production—is perhaps the most advanced in terms of equipment and techniques. Most of these advances have occurred in the past hundred years, and before looking at theater lighting today, it will be helpful to have a short historical view of its development.

A Brief History of Stage Lighting

For the first 2,000 years of its recorded history, theater was held mostly outdoors during the day—a primary reason being the need for illumination. The sun, after all, is an excellent source of light.

Since sophisticated lighting was unavailable, playwrights used imagination—the handiest tool available—to suggest nighttime or shifts in lighting. Performers brought on torches, or a candle, as Lady Macbeth does, to indicate night. Playwrights also used language to indicate lighting. In *The Merchant of Venice,* Shakespeare has Lorenzo say, "How sweet the moonlight sleeps upon this bank"; this is not just a pretty line of poetry but also serves to remind us that it is nighttime. The same is true of the eloquent passage when Romeo tells Juliet that he must leave because dawn is breaking.

> Look, love, what envious streaks
> Do lace the severing clouds in yonder East:
> Night's candles are burnt out, and jocund day
> Stands tiptoe on the misty mountain tops.

Around 1600 C.E., theater began to move indoors. Candles and oil lamps were used for illumination, and the chief refinements were more sophisticated uses of these basic elements, such as those achieved in the 1770s by David Garrick, the actor-manager of the Drury Lane Theater in London, and Philippe Jacques DeLoutherbourg (1740–1812), a French designer whom Garrick brought to the Drury Lane. DeLoutherbourg, for example, installed lighting above the stage and used gauze curtains and silk screens to achieve subtle effects with color. In 1785 an instrument known as the Argand lamp (after its inventor, Aimé Argand of Geneva) was introduced; it made use of a glass chimney and a cylindrical wick to create a steadier, brighter light.

Not until 1803, however, when a theater in London installed gaslights, was there a genuine advance in stage lighting. With gas, which was the principal source of illumination during the nineteenth century, lighting was more easily controlled and managed. Lighting intensity, for example, could be raised or lowered. Its effectiveness, however, remained limited. In addition, the open flames of gas and other earlier lighting systems posed a constant threat of fire. Through the years there were several tragic and costly fires in theaters, both in Europe and in the United States.

In 1879 Thomas Edison invented the incandescent lamp (the electric light bulb), and the era of imaginative lighting for the theater began. Not only are incandescent lamps safe, but they can also be controlled. Brightness or intensity can be increased or decreased: the same lighting instrument will produce the bright light of noonday or the dim light of dusk. Also, by putting a colored film over the light or by other means, color can be controlled.

Beyond the power and versatility of electric light, there have been numerous other advances in controls and equipment over the past fifty years. Lighting instruments have been constantly refined to become more powerful, as well as more subtle, and to throw a more concentrated, more sharply defined beam. Also, lighting has lent itself more successfully than other theater elements to miniaturization and computerization. After all, costumes must still be sewn individually, and scenes on flats or backdrops are still painted by hand. Lighting intensity, however, is controlled by electricity and therefore offers a perfect opportunity to take advantage of advances in electronics. First came resistance dimming systems, then thyratron vacuum tubes, and after that a series of technical innovations with names such as *magnetic amplifiers* and *silicon-controlled rectifiers.*

When applied to lighting, these developments in dimming systems allowed for increasingly complex and sophisticated controls. For a large college theater production, 100 to 200 lighting instruments may be hung around and above the stage; for a large Broadway musical, there may be 800 or more. Each of these instruments can be hooked up to a central computer board, and light settings can be stored in the computer. By pushing a single button, an operator can, in a split second, bring about a shift in literally dozens of instruments. The resulting flexibility and control are remarkable tools for achieving stage effects.

Objectives and Functions of Lighting Design

Adolphe Appia (1862–1928), a Swiss scene designer, was one of the first to see the vast aesthetic, artistic possibilities of light in the theater. He wrote: "Light is to the production what music is to the score: the expressive element in opposition to the literal signs; and, like music, light can express only what belongs to the inner essence of all vision's vision." Norman Bel Geddes (1893–1958), an imaginative American designer who was a follower of Appia, put it in these words: "Good lighting adds space, depth, mood, mystery, parody, contrast, change of emotion, intimacy, fear." Edward Gordon Craig (1872–1966), an innovative British designer, spoke of "painting with light." The lighting designer can indeed paint with light, but far more can be done; on the deepest sensual and symbolic level, the lighting designer can convey something of the feeling, and even the substance, of a play.

The following are the primary functions and objectives of stage lighting:

1. Provide visibility
2. Reveal shapes and forms
3. Provide a focus onstage and create visual compositions

4. Assist in creating mood and reinforcing style
5. Help to establish time and place
6. Establish a rhythm of visual movement
7. Reinforce a central visual image

Visibility   On the practical side, the chief function of lighting is illumination or visibility. We must be able, first and foremost, to see the performers' faces and their actions onstage. Occasionally, lighting designers, carried away with atmospheric possibilities, will make a scene so dark that we can hardly see what is happening. Mood is important, of course, but seeing the performers is obviously even more important. At times a script calls for lights to dim—in a suspense play, for instance, when the lights in a haunted house go out. But these are exceptions. Ordinarily, unless you can see the actors and actresses, the lighting designer has not carried out his or her assignment.

Shape and Form   Any object onstage, whether a performer or a piece of furniture, acquires definition and a three-dimensional quality chiefly because of light. Light—including the angle from which it originates—creates the mass, the depth, and the outline of everything onstage.

Focus and Composition   In photography, the term *focus* means adjustment of the lens of a camera so that the picture recorded on the film is sharp and clear; in theater lighting, *focus* refers to the fact that beams of light are aimed at—focused on—a particular area. Focus in lighting directs our attention to one part of the stage—generally, the part where the important action is occurring— and away from other areas.

In this regard, lights should illuminate the playing area, not the scenery or some area offstage. Most stage scenery is not painted to withstand the harsh glare of direct light and will not be effective if it is too brightly lit. Also, if scenery is lit to the exclusion of everything else, spectators will concentrate on it rather than on the performers. Therefore, the first object of focus is to aim the light in the right place. Designers must be careful to avoid *spill;* that is, they should not allow light from one area to fall into an adjacent area.

By means of focus, light can also create a series of visual compositions onstage. These can vary from turning the stage into one large area to creating small, isolated areas.

Mood and Style   Light, together with scenery and costumes, can help performers create a mood. However, lighting alone can rarely create mood. For example, if the stage is filled with blue light, it might be moonlight—bright and romantic—but it could also be a cold, dark, evil situation. Action, scenery, and words, in conjunction with light, tell us exactly what the mood is. A happy, carefree play calls for bright, warm colors, such as yellow, orange, and pink. A more somber piece will lean toward blue, blue-green, and muted tones.

LIGHTING CREATES MOOD AND STYLE

For a production of La Bohème, *directed by Baz Luhrmann, lighting designer Nigel Levings created a night on a street in Paris in the 1950s. Note the muted but unmistakable background, where light picks up the snow and the snowflakes, and in the foreground, the two young lovers are highlighted and given focus by spotlights. The performers are Lisa Hopkins and Jesús Garcia.* (Photo by Sue Adler, Courtesy of Boneau/Bryan-Brown)

In terms of style, lighting can indicate whether a play is realistic or non-realistic. In a realistic play, the lighting will simulate the effect of ordinary sources—table lamps, say, and outside sunlight. In a nonrealistic production, the designer can be more imaginative: shafts of light can cut through the dark, sculpturing performers onstage; a glowing red light can envelop a scene of damnation; a ghostly green light can cast a spell over a nightmare scene.

Time and Place By its color, shade, and intensity, lighting can suggest the time of day, giving us the pale light of dawn, the bright light of midday, the vivid colors of sunset, or the muted light of evening. Lighting can also indicate the season of the year, because the sun strikes objects at very different angles in winter and summer. Lighting can also suggest place, by showing indoor or outdoor light.

Rhythm   Since changes in light occur on a time continuum, they establish a rhythm running through a production. Abrupt, staccato changes with stark blackouts will convey one rhythm; languid, slow fades and gradual cross-fades will convey another. Lighting changes are coordinated with scene changes; the importance of this synchronization is recognized by directors and designers, who take great care to ensure the proper changes—"choreographing" shifts in light and scenery like dancers' movements.

Reinforcement of the Central Image   Lighting—like scenery, costumes, and all other elements—must be consistent with the overall style and mood of a production. The wrong lighting can distort or even destroy the effect of a play. At the same time, because lighting is the most flexible and the most atmospheric visual element of theater, it can aid enormously in creating the theater experience.

Achieving the Objectives: The Lighting Designer

The person responsible for creating, installing, and setting controls for stage lighting is the lighting designer. It is important for the lighting designer to have a background in the technical and mechanical aspects of lighting as well as a broad, creative visual imagination. The ability to translate words and actions and feelings into color, direction, and intensity comes only after much training and experience.

The Process of Lighting Design   The process a designer uses to light a show can be outlined as follows.

First, the lighting designer reads the script and begins to form some rough ideas and feelings about the play. He or she meets with the director and the scene designer to discuss visual concepts. The lighting designer receives from the set designer copies of all the scenery plans and usually consults with the costume designer to learn the shape and color of the costumes.

The lighting designer initially analyzes the script carefully and completely. He or she will work closely with other designers, especially the scene designer, to arrive at design concepts. These concepts will include both an overall look and specific details. The lighting designer will see one or perhaps several rehearsals to get the feel of the production, to see the exact location of various pieces of furniture and stage business, and to consult with the director about possible effects. Following this, the lighting designer draws a plan of lighting called a *light plot*. This includes the location and color of each lighting instrument. Also indicated is the kind of instrument called for and the area of the stage on which it is focused.

When lighting instruments are moved into the theater and hung (that is, placed on pipes and other supports), the designer supervises the focusing.

Peggy Eisenhauer: Lighting Designer

Peggy Eisenhauer is a lighting de-signer whose credits include concert designs for David Bowie's and Linda Ronstadt's tours, and the Broadway shows Will Rogers Follies, Angels in America, Victor/Victoria, Bring in 'Da Noise, Bring in 'Da Funk *(for which she won a Tony award),* Ragtime, *and* Cabaret.

I grew up in the New York Metro-politan area, the lucky child of parents who exposed me to the thrill and excitement of live perfor-mance. By the time I was 10, I had seen the New York City Ballet, Bill Baird, the Ringling Brothers, and Broadway shows, as well as local concerts and theater. By working in community theater in my high school years, I became familiar with all theatrical crafts and became especially interested in lighting design.

The Broadway production of *Pippin,* with direction by Bob Fosse and lighting by Jules Fisher, was the deciding factor in my choice of career. Jules's unique musicality expressed through lighting design spoke to me, and I tried to see as much of his work as I could. I went on to study lighting design at his alma mater, Carnegie-Mellon University, and met Jules there.

After graduation, and after gaining experience working with other designers on and off Broadway, I saw my dream come true: I assisted Jules on a Broadway project, and we've been working together ever since. Our second production together was Bob Fosse's final musical, *Big Deal,* which opened nearly 10 years to the day after I saw *Pippin.* Our recent joint designs include *Tommy Tune Tonight; Twilight: Los Angeles, 1992;* the *Whitney Houston Bodyguard Tour; A Christmas Carol;* and *Bring in 'Da Noise, Bring in 'Da Funk.*

During technical rehearsals, the lighting designer works with the director to establish light *cues,* that is, instructions about when the lights go on and off. The designer also sets the length of time for light changes and the levels of intensity on the *dimmers.* (The lighting dimmer is a control panel which al-lows lighting intensities to be changed smoothly and at varying rates. It is located offstage, usually in a light booth.)

Properties of Stage Lighting When working on the design for a production, the lighting designer knows what controllable properties of light will achieve the objectives discussed above.

Intensity The first property of light is brightness, or *intensity.* Intensity can be controlled (as noted above) by devices called *dimmers,* which make the lights brighter or darker. A dimmer is an electric or electronic device that can vary the amount of power going to the lights. This makes it possible for a scene at night to take place in very little light and a daylight scene to take place in bright light.

Color The second property of light is *color.* Color is a very powerful part of lighting, and theater lights can very easily be changed to one of several hun-dred colors simply by placing colored material in slots at the front of the light-ing instruments. This material is usually called a *gel*—short for *gelatin,* of which

Chapter 18 Lighting and Sound

(© Joan Marcus)

The Many Uses of Stage Lighting Stage lighting can be used for many purposes: to illuminate, to highlight characters or stage areas, to create mood. Here we see a variety of the effects of stage lighting. The first photo (*above*) is a scene from the musical *Mamma Mia!* Note the lights, designed by Howard Harrison, framing the action on stage. In a production such as this, there will be hundreds of lights—from above, from behind, from the sides—illuminating the performers. Note here, how much light comes from above and behind. On the opposite page, the second photo (*next page, top left*), a scene from *Top Dog/Underdog,* illustrates the way light, by designer Scott Zielinski, can cast shadows and create mood for the performers, Don Cheadle and Jeffrey Wright. The third photo (*next page, bottom*) depicts Oliver Ford-Davies as King Lear in a production in London with lighting designed by Mark Henderson. Note the back-lighting and side lighting that sets the actor in strong relief. The fourth photo (*next page, top right*) illustrates the powerful use of lighting from the side and the back. Lights come through a doorway to strike actress Sarah Agnew playing Ophelia in a production of *Hamlet* with lighting design by Marcus Dilliard.

(© Michal Daniel/Theatre de la Jeune Lune)

(© Michal Daniel/The Joseph Papp Public Theater)

(© Donald Cooper/PhotoSTAGE)

it was originally made. Today, however, these color mediums are generally made of plastic, Mylar, or acetate. Also in recent years, "color scrollers" have been introduced. These devices make it possible to change colors of standard lighting fixtures by remote control from a light board.

Color is mixed so that the strong tones of one shade will not dominate, since that would give an unnatural appearance. Often the lights beamed from one side are *warm* (amber, straw, gold); those from the other side are *cool* (blue, blue-green, lavender). Warms and cools together produce depth and texture, as well as a natural effect. The exception to mixing angles and colors of light would be a scene calling for special effects; we expect stark shadows and strange colors, for example, when Hamlet confronts the ghost of his father.

Direction The third property of light that the lighting designer can use is *direction,* that is, the way a source is placed on or near the stage so that the light comes from a particular direction. In earlier days, *footlights*—a row of lights across the front of the stage—were used, primarily because this provided almost the only location from which to light the front of the performers. Gaslights or oil lights further out in the auditorium would not have reached far enough to illuminate the actors. This light source was below the performers, however, so footlights had the disadvantage of casting ghostly shadows on their faces. Footlights also created a kind of barrier between performers and audience. With the development of more powerful, versatile lights, footlights have been eliminated.

Today, most lighting hits the stage from above, coming from instruments in front of the stage and from the sides. The vertical angle of light beams is typically close to 45 degrees, to approximate the average angle of sunlight. Generally, too, front light on an area of the stage comes from several sources: from at least two lights above a proscenium stage, and from at least four above an arena stage. The lights converge from different sides to avoid the harsh shadows which result when light hits on only one side of the face. Once performers are properly illuminated by lights from the front and above, other lighting is added—*downlighting* from directly overhead and *backlighting* from behind—to give further dimension and depth to the figures onstage.

COLOR IN LIGHTING

One of the prime elements in stage lighting is color. It can alter and transform a stage set or figures on a stage, changing and establishing different moods. Shown here is a scene from Bring in 'Da Noise, Bring in 'Da Funk, *with lighting by Jules Fisher and Peggy Eisenhauer. Note both the shadow of the figure in the background, and in the foreground, the pink color given to the white costume worn by the performer, Thomas Silcott.* (© Michal Daniel/The Joseph Papp Public Theater)

Form The fourth property is the shape, or *form,* in which light comes. This could also be called the "texture" of the lighting. Is it a single shaft of light, like a single beam of moonlight through the trees or a spotlight in a nightclub? Or is the light in a pattern, such as dappled sunlight through the leaves of trees in a forest? Are the edges of the light sharp, or soft and diffused? Light can be shaped by special shutters that close in at the edges—an additional tool for the designer.

Movement The last property of light the designer can work with is *movement.* On one level, the eye is carried from place to place by the shifting focus of lights: follow spots moving from one person or one area to another, automated lights changing directions, a performer carrying a candle or flashlight across the stage. Then there are more general shifts due to **cross-fading.** This occurs when lights go down in one area and come up in another. By crossfading between groups of lights, the designer, with various types of dimmers, can shift the focus from location to location and from color to color. Also, time of day, sunsets, and so on can help provide information for the audience.

For an example of how these properties function, consider the lighting for a production of *Hamlet.* To emphasize the eerie, tragic quality of this play, with its murders and graveyard scene, the lighting would generally be cool rather than warm. As for angles, if the production took place on a proscenium stage, there would be downlighting and backlighting to give the characters a sculptured, occasionally unreal quality. In terms of movement, the lights would change each time there was a shift in locale. This would give a rhythm of movement throughout the play and would also focus the audience's attention on particular areas of the stage.

The Lighting Designer's Resources Among the resources of the lighting designer are various kinds of lighting instruments and other kinds of technical and electronic equipment.

Types of Stage Lights Stage lights include the following:

1. *Soft-edged spotlights.* The most popular soft-edged spotlight is the **fresnel** (pronounced "fruh-NEL"). The lens of the fresnel spotlight produces a soft-edged beam and allows for a variable beam spread. It is especially useful for area lighting where a feathered or undefined edge is desirable. Many lighting designers use this instrument for top- and backlight.

2. *Sharp, concentrated spotlights.* The best-known sharp spotlight is the **ellipsoidal reflector spotlight,** which most lighting designers consider the "workhorse" of contemporary practice. It affords greater control of light than the fresnel and allows for shaping the edges of the beam with shutters. This instrument will also project patterns of light through the use of *templates* or *gobos.* In recent years the standard ellipsoidal spotlight has undergone revisions that have resulted in a brighter unit using nearly 50 percent less energy because of improved reflectors as well as new lens systems. A mobile spotlight, which an operator can shift to follow a performer across the stage, is called a *follow spot.*

3. *Floodlights, "scoops," strip lights,* and *border lights.* These lights bathe a section of the stage or scenery in a smooth, diffused wash of light.

4. *Automated or moving light.* (See below.)

Lighting Controls In terms of technology, lighting is easily the most highly developed aspect of theater; we have already considered some of the advances in this area. Lighting instruments can be hung all over the theater and aimed at every part of the stage; and these many instruments can be controlled by one person sitting at a light board or control console.

Lighting changes—or *cues,* as they are called—usually are arranged ahead of time. Sometimes, in a complicated production (a musical, say, or a Shakespearean play) there will be from 75 to 150 light cues. A cue can range from a **blackout** (where all the lights are shut off at once), to a **fade** (the lights dim slowly, changing the scene from brighter to darker), to a **cross-fade** (one set of lights comes down while another comes up). Moreover, with today's modern equipment, the changes can be timed automatically on a dimmer board so that a cross-fade will take exactly the number of seconds called for; guesswork is eliminated. Cues can be prearranged by computer so that during a performance, the operator at the console pushes a button and an entire change occurs automatically.

For instance, Strindberg's *A Dream Play* has innumerable scene changes—like a dream, as the title implies—in which one scene fades into another before our eyes. At one point in the play, a young woman, called the Daughter, sits at an organ in a church. In Strindberg's words, "The stage darkens as the Daughter rises and approaches the Lawyer. By means of lighting the organ is transformed into a wall of a grotto. The sea seeps in between basal pillars with a harmony of waves and wind." At the light cue for this change, a button is pushed, and all the lights creating the majesty of the church fade as the lights creating the grotto come up.

New Technology in Stage Lighting Stage lighting has benefited from technological advances that were originally developed for rock musicians and others who perform before vast audiences and for whom light and sound are essential elements. Huge banks of lights are focused on the stage; sometimes there are banks of lights behind the performers, forming part of the stage picture.

To achieve maximum flexibility and control, new instruments have been devised. These instruments, known variously as **automated lights** or **moving lights,** are amazingly versatile, allowing a degree of control that was previously impossible for a single instrument. Moreover, not just one element can be controlled, but three: color, direction, and movement. Without a follow-spot operator, these lighting instruments can **pan** (move from side to side) and **tilt** (move up and down) to create movement and change the angle of the beam and therefore the focus onstage. And it is no longer necessary to change color by putting a gel over a beam by hand; instead, by means of dichoric filters these instruments can change to any one of hundreds of colors, shades, and hues.

(Selecon)

(Selecon)

(Selecon)

(Vari*Lite)

Different Lighting Instruments for Different Purposes   Most stage lights have three key elements: a lamp that is the source of the light, a reflector, and a lens through which the beams pass. Shown here are four types of instruments used to light the stage. Upper left is a flood light. Flood lights are employed, singly or in groups, to provide general illumination for the stage or scenery. The light from floods can be blended in acting areas, or used to "tone" settings and costumes. They are also employed to illuminate cycloramas at the rear of the stage, or ground rows along the floor of the stage. Upper right is a small spotlight known as a fresnel (pronounced "fruh-NEL"). The fresnel is a type of spotlight. All spotlights illuminate limited areas of the stage with a concentrated beam of light; they precisely define a particular area to be lighted and leave other areas in darkness. The frenel spotlight has a spherical reflector and a special lens that is flat on one side and has ridges of concentric circles on the other, an arrangement that allows for a thinner, lighter lens that softens the edges of the beam. the fresnel is generally used in positions near the stage—behind the proscenium opening, or mounted close to the action on an area or thrust stage. Lower left is a zoom spotlight. Generally this is an ellipsoidal reflector lighting instrument that is more efficient than a fresnel because it can throw a stronger beam of light much farther. Most spotlights of this type have an ellipsoidal-shaped reflector that partially surrounds the lamp and sends a strong beam through two plano-convex lenses. It is used when the distance between the instrument and the stage area is greatest—for example, from positions outside the proscenium opening in the auditorium. The fourth light *(lower right)* is the newest and most versatile intrument of the group. Sometimes known as an automated light or a moving light, it can do the work that in the past would have had to be carried out by several lighting instruments. Rather than having to change the angle of the light, or its color, or the shape of its beam, this light can carry out all those alterations automatically when commanded from a computer. It can change colors (to any of nearly 1,000 hues or shades), change focus by swiveling in place, and shift beams. All of this is done remotely and has been made possible by advances in the technology of computers, electronics, and other elements. This instrument is particularly useful in elaborate musical productions and is widely used in rock concerts.

The sharpness and width of the beam, as well as the pattern it projects, can be changed instantaneously in each instrument because both the *iris* (which controls the size of the pool of light) and the *gobo* or template (which determines patterns of light) are variable and changeable. All these adjustments are made not manually but remotely, from a central computer panel by an operator pushing a switch or button. Everything is preset on the computer: each movement of the light, each change in color, each alteration in direction or size of the beam. This is done for what are sometimes hundreds of instruments. At a given moment, at the touch of a button by an operator at the central lighting computer, dozens of lights go off, dozens more come on as they swivel in a different direction and change color—and all this occurs simultaneously.

The Lighting Designer's Collaborators   As in every aspect of theater, in lighting too there is collaboration. A number of people work with the lighting designer. These include assistant designers and people who help create the light plot, as well as the technicians who hang and focus the lights (often climbing on catwalks and ladders to remote areas above, behind, and in front of the stage). Lighting technicians also assist in focusing the lights on the proper areas and in making certain that the correct color gels and other lighting devices are in place. Also included are the people who "run" the lights—controlling the light boards, whether manual or computerized, and operating the follow spotlights. These experts who run the lighting boards or computers that control the lights take cues from the stage manager and coordinate their efforts with other technical aspects of the production.

SOUND IN THE THEATER

Scenery, costumes, and lighting can all be described as visual elements of theater. Another design element, sound, is aural. In recent years, it has become an increasingly important aspect of theater, with its own artistry, technology, and designers.

Sound Reproduction: Advantages and Disadvantages

Amplification   In the past few decades, not only has sound reproduction become more prominent in the theater; it has sometimes proved to be controversial as well. At rock concerts, intense amplification has come to be expected, and personal stereos have made listeners expect more pronounced sound reproduction in the theater. As a result, large musicals, whether presented in Broadway houses or in spacious performing arts centers across the country, are now heavily amplified.

The controversy centers on this amplification: Should it be used for singing? If so, how loud should it be? Should speech also be amplified? Critics charge that often amplification is overdone: with the sound too loud, and also too mechanical and artificial. It may be difficult for young people in the early twenty-first century to imagine, but the great American musicals of the 1940s and 1950s—by composers like Rodgers and Hammerstein, Cole Porter, and Irving Berlin—were all produced without any sound amplification whatsoever.

Today, electronic amplification is a way of life in the theater. Nevertheless, the controversy continues and has been extended to opera. In the fall of 1999, for example, there was considerable debate when the New York City Opera announced that it was installing a voice "enhancement" system.

Sound Effects   It should be noted that, aside from the argument about the volume or pervasiveness of amplification systems, sound has always been an important, and necessary, component of theater production. One aspect of this is *sound effects*. In earlier years—for several centuries, in fact—various devices were developed to create such sounds.

The sound of wind, for example, can be produced by a wooden drum made from slats; the drum is usually 2 or 3 feet in diameter and covered with a muslin cloth. When the drum is turned, by means of a handle, it makes a noise like howling wind. For the sound of a door slamming, a miniature door or even a full-size door in a frame can be placed just offstage and opened and shut. Two hinged pieces of wood slammed shut can also simulate the sound of a closing door. This effect sounds like a gunshot as well, or a gunshot sound can be created by firing a gun loaded with blank cartridges. (In some states, blank guns are illegal, and live ammunition should never be used onstage.) Thunder can be simulated by hanging a large, thick metal sheet backstage and gently shaking it. Today, of course, sound effects are far more sophisticated.

The Sound Designer

The person responsible for arranging and orchestrating all the aural aspects of a production is the sound designer. Like his or her counterparts in visual design, the sound designer begins by reading the script, noting all the places where sound might be needed. For a large-scale musical, the designer also decides on the number and type of microphones to be used, the placement of speakers throughout the theater, and all other aspects of sound reproduction.

After reading the script, the sound designer consults with the director to determine the exact nature of the sound requirements, including sound effects and amplification. The designer then sets about preparing the full range of components that constitute sound for a production.

Sound Reproduction and Sound Reinforcement

One way to classify sound design is as *sound reproduction* and *sound reinforcement*. Reproduction is the use of motivated or environmental sounds. *Motivated sounds* would be, for instance, the noise of a car crunching on gravel, a car motor turning off, and a door slamming—a sequence that would announce the arrival of a character at a house where a scene is taking place. Motivated sounds, then, are those called for by the script. *Environmental sounds* are noises of everyday life that help create verisimilitude in a production: street traffic in a city, crickets in the country, loud rock music coming from a stereo in a college dormitory. Such sounds are usually heard as background.

Sound effects, as noted above, are one form of sound reproduction. A sound effect can be defined as any sound produced by mechanical or human means to create for the audience a noise or sound associated with the play. In recent years, most sound effects have been recorded on compact disks. Virtually every sound imaginable—from birds singing to dogs barking to jet planes flying—is available on CDs, not only to expensive professional productions but also to college, university, and community theaters.

Reinforcement is the amplification of sounds produced by a performer or a musical instrument. With the growth of electronics in music, more and more instruments have been amplified. At any rock concert, you can see wires coming out of the basses and guitars. In an orchestra pit in a theater, the quieter acoustic instruments such as the guitar are miked to achieve a balance of sound with the louder instruments. The total sound can overwhelm a singer, especially one who has not been trained—as opera singers are—to project the voice into the farther reaches of a theater. As a result, we have body mikes on the performers.

At first, a body mike was a small microphone attached in some way to the performer's clothing. A wire ran from the mike to a small radio transmitter concealed on the performer; from the transmitter, the sound was sent to an offstage listening device that fed it into a central sound-control system. In today's large musical productions, the microphone worn by a performer is frequently a small instrument, hardly larger than a piece of wire, worn over one ear alongside the temple or placed elsewhere near the performer's head, that carries the sound to the body transmitters. In some musicals, the performers wear a small microphone attached to a headpiece coming around one side of the head, similar to that worn by telephone switchboard operators. Head microphones are used so that they will be as close as possible to the performer's mouth and at a constant distance away.

Sound Technology

Microphones and Loudspeakers In preparing the sound for a production, the designers and engineers not only must assemble all the necessary sounds but also must be certain that the appropriate microphones are used correctly and must place the speakers effectively onstage and in the auditorium.

Part 5 The Designers: Environment, Visual Elements, and Sound

Several types of microphones are used. A *shotgun mike* is highly directional and is aimed from a distance at a specific area. A *general mike* picks up sounds in the general area toward which it is aimed. A *body mike,* as described above, is a wireless microphone attached to a performer's body or clothing. Microphones not worn by performers are placed in various locations. One position is alongside the downstage edge of the stage. Another position is hanging in the air near the lights. Any type of microphone must be hooked up to an amplifier that increases the electronic energy of the sound and sends it through the speakers.

The placement of loudspeakers is both an art and a science. It is necessary to determine the correct speakers for the size and shape of the theater, and to position them so that they carry sound clearly and evenly into the auditorium—to the upper reaches of the balcony, to the side seats, and to areas underneath the balcony as well as the first few rows in the orchestra. Also, live sound from the performers must reach the sides and back of the theater at the same time that it reaches the spectators in front. One problem in this regard is that sound travels much more slowly than light. The speed of sound is only 1,100 feet per second—which means that for a spectator seated at the back of a large theater, sound from a speaker at the rear of the auditorium will be heard before the human voice from the stage. Developments in digital electronics have led to devices that process, sample, and synthesize sound for various effects; and one useful device addresses this problem, delaying the electronic sound so that it arrives through a loudspeaker at the same time as the much slower live sound.

Sound Recordings   The process of assembling sound recordings is similar for professional and nonprofessional productions. First, a list is made of all nonmusical sound effects required. This list is usually developed by the sound designer in consultation with the director, and possibly with a composer: for a show with a great deal of sound or music, there may be both a sound designer and a music composer. Once the list is drawn up, a master recording is made and the sounds are arranged in their order of appearance in the script. This process is called *editing*. When the production moves into the theater, there is a technical rehearsal without performers, during which each sound cue is listened to and the volume is set. When rehearsals with the performers start in the theater, more changes will be made. Depending on the action and the timing of scenes, some cues will be too loud and others too soft; some will have to be made shorter and others made longer.

During an actual performance of a production using sound reinforcement, an operator must sit at a complex sound console "mixing" sound—that is, blending all elements from the many microphones and from the master sound recording—so that there is a smooth, seamless blend of sound. Also, the operator must make certain not only that all sound is in balance but also that sound does not intrude on the performance or call attention to itself, away from the stage and the performers.

New Technologies in Sound   As with lighting, in recent years we have seen frequent advances and breakthroughs in sound equipment and technology. The new body microphones and a device that delays the delivery of electronic sound have already been mentioned. But there are other developments as well.

Analog reel-to-reel tape decks, which were standard only a few years ago, are now giving way to digital technology such as digital audiotape (DAT), recordable compact disks, minidisks, and direct playback from a computer's hard drive. Sound is now recorded and edited at digital audio workstations, based on personal computers. Such stations allow easier editing of sound, more complex effects, and higher-quality sound. Digital playback systems allow very easy and precise cueing of shows, as well as greatly improved sound quality.

It should be clear that sound is rapidly taking its place alongside other design aspects as a key feature of theater productions.

Lighting and sound, like scenery and costumes, are means to an end: they implement the artistic and aesthetic aspects of a production. The colors, shapes, and lines of lighting effects and the qualities of sound interact with other elements of theater and contribute to the overall experience.

SUMMARY

1. Stage lighting, like other elements of theater, has a counterpart in the lighting of homes, restaurants, advertisements, etc.

2. Lighting—historically the last stage visual element to be fully developed—is today the most technically sophisticated. Once the incandescent electric lamp was introduced, it was possible to achieve almost total control of the color, intensity, and timing of lights. Lighting controls have also benefited from computerization, with extensive light shifts being controlled by an operator at a computerized console.

3. Lighting design is intended to provide illumination onstage, to establish time and place, to help set the mood and style of the production, to focus the action, and to establish a rhythm of visual movement.

4. Lighting should be consistent with all other elements.

5. The lighting designer uses a variety of instruments, colored gels, and control dimmers as well as panel control consoles to achieve effects. Electronic developments and computers have greatly increased the flexibility and control of lighting instruments and equipment.

6. Sound is taking its place alongside scenery, costumes, and lighting as a key design element. Rapid advances in technology allow for sophisticated delivery in a theater of both sound and reproduction—sound effects and such—and sound reinforcement, of both musical instruments and the human voice. The sound designer and engineer must (a) prepare the soundtrack, (b) place microphones and speakers appropriately, and (c) mix the recorded and live sounds during the performance to achieve the desired effect.

7. Increasingly in recent years there has been controversy and debate surrounding the use of amplification—is it a good thing or not?

EXPLORING THEATER
ON
THE
WEB

Lighting and Sound

Of the theatrical design disciplines, lighting and sound are the most widely represented on the Internet. Any search on "theater lighting" or "theater sound" will result in a long list of sites devoted to lighting and sound equipment.

The International Alliance of Theatrical Stage Employees, Moving Picture Technicians, Artists, and Allied Crafts (IATSE) is the labor union representing technicians, artisans, and craftspersons in the entertainment industry, including live theater, film, and television production. Visit IATSE's website at http://www.iatse.lm.com/.

Exercises:

1. Go to the "History" link at http://www.iatse.lm.com and click on "One Hundred Years of the IATSE" (http://www.iatse.lm.com/100yrs.html). What conditions affected stagehands in the late nineteenth century? What trend in the early 1900s reduced the need for local New York stage crews? How did the "First Flickers" affect the future of IATSE? How did stage electricians participate in the production and projection of these new films?

2. On the "Crafts of the IATSE" page (http://www.iatse.lm.com/crafts.html) check out the "Stage Technicians" links. Under "Training and Education," look at the Book Lists for Electrics and Sound. What percent of the listed books are about lighting design? About sound design? Look at the Electrics and Sound links. What kinds of links dominate? Why do you think the people who create lighting and sound effects in the film industry are not usually referred to as "designers"?

3. Visit the website of London's Royal National Theatre for this article on its Sound Department: http://www.nationaltheatre.org.uk/backstage/sound.html. What are the "two reasons" for the newly "elevated status" of theatrical sound?

MOTHER COURAGE AND HER CHILDREN (1939-1965)

Bertolt Brecht (1898-1956)

(Courtesy of German
Information Center/IN Press)

Chief Characters

Mother Courage
Kattrin, *her mute daughter*
Eilif, *her elder son*
Swiss Cheese, *her younger son*
Cook
Chaplain
Yvette Pottier, *a prostitute*

Setting

Various army camps in Sweden,
Poland, Bavaria, and Germany.

Time

1624–1636

Background

Mother Courage is a canteen
woman, Anna Fierling, who follows
army camps with her wagon and
sells her wares to soldiers. She has
two sons and a daughter—each
from a different father—who help
pull the wagon.

Scene 1: Spring 1624, on a
highway. A Swedish recruiting
officer complains to a sergeant how
difficult it is to get recruits. Mother
Courage and her children enter,
pulling the wagon from which
Courage sells her goods. The
sergeant distracts Courage while the
recruiting officer persuades her son
Eilif to join the army.

Scene 2: The years 1625 and 1626;
the setting is the kitchen of the
Swedish commander, where the
Cook is arguing with Mother
Courage. The Swedish commander
enters and praises Eilif for his
bravery. Courage has not seen Eilif
since he was taken away to the
army. When she hears Eilif singing
"The Song of the Wise Woman and
the Soldier," she recognizes his
voice and joins in.

Scene 3: Three years later. Mother
Courage, her two children, and
parts of a Finnish regiment are

prisoners. Courage's friend Yvette
Pottier, a prostitute who feels sorry
for herself because her first husband
left her, sings "The Fraternization
Song," about loving a soldier. When
the sound of cannon heralds a
surprise attack by the Catholics,
Courage lends the Chaplain a cloak
to disguise the fact that he is a
Protestant. Her son, Swiss Cheese,
hides the cash box in the wagon,
while Courage rubs ashes onto
Kattrin's face to make her less
attractive to the soldiers. Three days
later, while Courage and the
Chaplain are gone, Swiss Cheese

Elise Stone (second from left) as Mother Courage (© Gerry Goodstein/Jean Cocteau Repertory)

leaves the scene to hide the cash box, and two soldiers, who have been watching, capture him. The soldiers return with Swiss Cheese, but Courage—who has also come back—denies knowing him, even though he is her own son. While the Chaplain sings "The Song of the Hours," about Christ's death, Courage learns that she can free her son if she bribes the sergeant—but she haggles too long, and Swiss Cheese is executed.

Scene 4: Outside an officer's tent. A young soldier enters; he has captured another soldier, who deserted, and is now raging against the captain for taking his reward money. Mother Courage sings "The Song of the Great Capitulation," which persuades them both that there is no use complaining.

Scene 5: Two years later. The Chaplain tells Courage that he needs some linen to help the peasants bind up their wounds; when she refuses, he takes the linen by force. After Kattrin rescues a child, Courage tells her to give it back to the mother.

Scene 6: Bavaria, 1632—the funeral of the fallen commander. The men are getting drunk instead of going to the funeral. When Kattrin is wounded, Courage thinks this is lucky because it will make Kattrin less appealing to the soldiers.

Scene 7: A highway, with the Chaplain, Mother Courage, and Kattrin pulling the supply wagon. Courage sings a song about war being a business proposition.

Scene 8: A camp, 1632. Voices announce that peace is at hand. Courage is distraught: she has just purchased a lot of supplies and will

now be ruined because no one will buy them. Yvette goes with Courage to try to sell the goods. Eilif is arrested for killing some peasants—now that peace has come, such killing is a crime. Courage rushes back in with the news that the war is on again. The Cook and Kattrin pull the wagon while Courage sings.

Scene 9: In front of a half-ruined parsonage, 1634. The Cook tells Courage that his mother has left him an inn that he wants to run with her, but without Kattrin. Kattrin overhears them and is about to leave when Courage stops her; Courage turns the Cook down, and she and Kattrin harness the wagon and march off.

Scene 10: 1635. Courage and Kattrin pull the wagon up to a prosperous farmhouse and hear someone singing about warmth and comfort and safety, conditions that stand in sharp contrast to their own bleak situation.

Scene 11: January 1636; the wagon, in disrepair, stands outside a farmhouse. Soldiers gather up the peasants and pull Kattrin out of the wagon; they ask the way to the town. An old man climbs onto the roof and sees the soldiers getting ready to launch a surprise attack on the sleeping town. Kattrin gets a drum out of the wagon, climbs up on the roof, and beats a warning to save the people in the town. When the lieutenant tries to stop the noise, Kattrin goes on drumming, and the soldiers kill her. Cannon noises and alarm bells announce that Kattrin's warning has been successful—the town is saved.

Molly Pietz as Kattrin. (© Gerry Goodstein/Jean Cocteau Repertory)

Scene 12: Courage sits in front of the wagon, with Kattrin's body, singing a lullaby. The peasants tell Courage that she must leave and that they will bury Kattrin. Courage harnesses up and, this time all alone, pulls the wagon behind a passing regiment.

Discussion Questions
- In what way does the wagon in *Mother Courage* serve as a central image or metaphor?
- Explain how you would design a production of Mother Courage, in terms of: the stage set, the lighting, and the costumes.
- How realistic should the setting be?

Epilogue: Integrating the Elements and Predicting the Future

Theater is a remarkable convergence of artistic and human endeavors: the writing of a play and the planning of a production, which may take weeks, months, or even years; the rehearsal period; the designing and building of scenery and costumes; the technical coordination of light changes, scene shifts, and performers' activities; the adjustments made as a result of responses to previews. All these contribute to the moment when an audience sees the actual performance.

The excitement which comes to a group of performers working together or to a crew working backstage on scenery, lights, and sound is difficult to describe, as with every human endeavor in which a group has trained for weeks or months before having its moment of triumph. Any group working for a common purpose—to win an election or an athletic contest, to make a scientific breakthrough, to organize a neighborhood to make it better—has the same sense of a shared achievement. Each member knows that he or she could not have accomplished the task alone.

Theater is a supreme example of this phenomenon, because, with the possible exception of opera, it is the most complex of the arts. A theater event passes through many hands, and the contribution of each person is essential to its success. When the people creating it work together effectively, they share with one another the deep satisfaction of having collaborated on a difficult but eminently rewarding task. And when the work is performed onstage, the audience senses this achievement and, through its response, becomes a part of the collaboration.

THE AUDIENCE: INTEGRATING THE ELEMENTS

Observation and Assimilation

For audience members, the ultimate integration of a theater event takes place in each person's mind. No matter how closely the people who produce a theater event work together, and no matter how well the director coordinates the various elements, individual audience members must eventually bring the parts together. So many elements make up a theater production that we might wonder how a spectator can combine them. The answer lies in our ability to handle many kinds of information and bring this information together to form a complete picture. Our everyday activities—activities such as driving a car, working at a computer, or cooking a meal—suggest that human beings have a great capacity to absorb data and stimuli, and to integrate them into a single experience.

These powers of assimilation make it possible to form a cohesive whole out of the fragments we see before us onstage: we watch individual performers in action and tune in to their personalities; we observe the costumes, scenery, and lighting effects; we note the progress of the action as characters confront one another; we hear the words of the playwright; and we associate ideas and emotions in the play with our own experiences.

Along the way we relate each present moment with the past. Two kinds of memories contribute to this process. First, we have a lifetime of personal memories—experiences which an event onstage might trigger in our mind—linking our individual past with what is happening onstage. Second, we have the memory of what has just occurred in the play itself. If the audience sees someone hide a gun in a desk drawer in the first act, and a character goes to the drawer in the third act, the audience knows that the gun is about to be used.

Not only do we connect the past with what is happening at each moment in a performance; we also anticipate the future. People have immense curiosity about what lies ahead. Again, this is a human trait which comes into play in theater. We ask ourselves: How will Jason react when he learns that Medea has murdered his children? What will Willy Loman do when his boss fires him? We constantly speculate on the fate of characters and look forward—with both fear and excitement—to their encounters with one another.

Each moment in theater forms a "mini-experience" of its own, resulting from a series of collisions or intersections on many levels: the past meets the present, the present meets the future, performers interact with their roles, ideas combine with emotions, sights fuse with sounds, and so forth. These numerous encounters are pulled together to form a rich, multilayered experience.

Observing the Elements as Parts of a Whole

Throughout this book, we have seen how separate elements contribute to the overall theater experience. By using their powers of perception, spectators can focus on specific areas in a production without losing sight of the total effect. They can also relate individual elements to one another. If members of the audience learn to use these powers to the fullest, their enjoyment and understanding will be enhanced.

We can concentrate for a time on acting, for instance, and ask ourselves whether a performer is interpreting a role appropriately. We can ask, too, how well the performers are playing with one another. Do they look at each other when they speak, and do they listen and respond to the other actors and actresses? As we watch a play unfold, we can also take a moment to observe the visual elements. Do the costumes suit the play? Is the scenery symbolic, and if so, what does it symbolize? Do the colors in the scenery convey a particular mood or feeling?

Although such elements as dramatic structure and point of view are not visible (unlike acting or scenery), it is possible to pause during a performance and consider them as well. As events occur onstage, we can determine what structure is being developed and whether it is maintained. If the structure is climactic, for instance, we can ask whether the events in the play are plausible and whether they follow one another logically.

In looking at separate elements of theater in this way, we need not fear that we will lose sight of the whole. The more we become aware of distinct elements, the more we can fit them into an overall picture. In watching a light comedy, for instance, we can observe how the acting underlines and points up the humor of the script; we can note how the costumes help the performers create comic characters—perhaps through exaggeration—and, at the same time, we can observe how the costumes present a visual image of their own, appropriately bright and lighthearted. We can observe, too, how lighting reinforces the comic spirit of the costumes and the performers. In short, we can see how the various aspects fuse and combine; how they heighten, underscore, and interact with each other to create the final experience.

THE OVERALL EFFECT: WHAT DOES THEATER "MEAN"?

Considering the overall effect of a play raises the question of what a play "means." In a discussion of a play we might hear someone ask: "But what does it mean?" The reply frequently is a catchphrase or brief summary: The meaning of this play is "he who hesitates is lost," or "all's well that ends well." Someone might say, for instance, that the meaning of Shakespeare's *Othello* is that people should not be too quick to believe gossip and should trust those they love. Certainly one can conclude that *Othello* contains ideas which could be interpreted this way. But is this really what *Othello* means? Isn't this a simplistic and incomplete idea of what *Othello* is about? Can we ever summarize the meaning of a play in one sentence?

WHAT DOES THEATER MEAN?

When we are discussing drama, there are two ways to look at meaning. Some plays specifically underscore a meaning in the text. They seem almost to have been written to point toward a moral or to teach a lesson. The title of Lillian Hellman's *The Little Foxes* comes from the "Song of Solomon" in the Bible; the verse reads, "Take us the foxes, the little foxes, that spoil the vines: for our vines have tender grapes." The idea of the quotation is that the foxes are evil because they spoil the vines and ravage and destroy the grapes. Hellman's title, therefore, introduces the theme of plunder and exploitation, and this theme is carried out in the action. At the close of the play the theme is summed up by a young woman, Alexandra, who has come to realize what has been happening in her family. Recognizing that her mother is one of the greediest and most cunning of the foxes, she confronts her. Alexandra says to her mother: "Addie said there were people who ate the earth and other people who stood around and watched them do it. And just now Uncle Ben said the same thing. . . . Well, tell him for me, Mama, I'm not going to stand around and watch you do it. Tell him I'll be fighting as hard as he'll be fighting someplace where people don't just stand around and watch."

PLAYS WITH A SPECIFIC MEANING

The Little Foxes by Lillian Hellman, in a production at the Donmar Warehouse Theatre in London, attempts to embody a specific meaning. By words and actions in the play, including the scene between daughter (Anna Maxwell Martin) and mother (Penelope Wilton) shown here, the audience is told what the playwright wants to convey. The vast majority of plays, however, do not attempt to transmit a single meaning or lesson. Instead, the meaning is the entire experience in its manifold aspects, with all the spoken and unspoken communications, the implications, the various levels of meaning. This is true of most art: it is a metaphor for life, for beauty, for some truth about existence. (© Donald Cooper/PhotoSTAGE)

In a play like *The Little Foxes* the author invites us to find a "meaning" which can be expressed in a few straightforward sentences. Most plays, however, do not contain such direct statements of their meaning. Their substance resides, rather, in their total effect on the spectator.

In the final analysis, a theater event does not "mean"; it *is*—its existence is its meaning. The writer Gertrude Stein (1874–1946) once said, "Rose is a rose is a rose is a rose." On the face of it, this seems to be a simple, repetitive statement of the obvious. As far as art is concerned, though, there is a great truth hidden in Stein's words. She is telling us that a rose is itself, not something else. In any other form it ceases to have its own existence and thus loses its unique quality. The depiction of a rose in a poem, an oil painting, or a color photograph might have a certain beauty and give us a notion of a rose, but none of these can take the place of the real thing. Only in its presence can we see the texture of the petals and smell the fragrance. If our direct experience of a rose is irreplaceable, how much more irreplaceable is our experience of a complex art like theater.

THE MODERN THEATER: DIFFERENT PURPOSES, DIFFERENT EXPERIENCES

Each theater event has its own meaning and impact, but in today's theater these vary widely from one event to another. The elements we have examined in the various sections of this book can be combined in so many different ways that the results offer a variety of experiences. The same play might be performed in a large outdoor theater with nonrealistic acting or in a small indoor theater with realistic acting. By the same token, the same space might serve two quite different productions: a bare stage with no scenery can be the setting for a stark tragedy or an intimate musical comedy. The combination of the play itself with the way it is presented will determine the final outcome.

In the past, in a given historical period or within a given society, the kinds of plays presented and the ways in which they were produced were frequently limited. During the past hundred years, however, there have been marked changes in society and consequently in theater. In the past half-century we have witnessed an acceleration of these changes, with the result that in the post-World War II era we have experienced a rapid shift in morals and social mores. Long-held beliefs and customs—in dress, in attitudes toward women and minority groups, in family structure—were challenged and changed.

This shift of traditional attitudes and customs, along with the introduction of new ideas, has been reflected in theater. No longer is the proscenium stage the chief architectural form. There has been a proliferation of arena and thrust stages, as well as created or found spaces. No longer, either, are episodic and climactic structure the only forms considered by playwrights and directors; other forms have emerged, along with multifocus, unstructured forms and performance art.

The result of these changes has been a multiplicity of theater offerings. It is probably safe to say that never in any culture, at any time in history, has such a diversity of theater events been offered to the public as is available today in metropolitan centers throughout the western world—and this diversity also reaches into areas outside the major cities.

Not only do conditions vary widely in today's theater; the intentions of writers, directors, and producers also vary. Different productions are presented for different purposes. Some plays—farces or light comedies—are intended to entertain us and make us laugh. On the other hand, the intention of serious dramas, like *King Oedipus* or *Long Day's Journey into Night,* is to make us feel deeply about the human condition and identify with people who are suffering. Some plays are presented for the express purpose of giving us information about a person or an event; others have little concern with facts—their purpose is for us to disregard literal truth and simply lose ourselves in the experience, letting sounds and images wash over us. Some plays show us horror and violence—not to celebrate or exploit horror and violence but to make us hate them so much that we will rebel against them

THE CONTEMPORARY THEATER: DIFFERENT PURPOSES, DIFFERENT EXPERIENCES

Theater is eclectic and diversified. Periods, styles, theatrical approaches are often mixed or coexist side by side. Shown here are Robert Cucuzza (left) *and D. J. Mandel* (right) *in a scene from a well known avant-garde theater group, Richard Foreman's Ontological-Hysteric Theater. The production was called* Panic! (How to Be Happy). *It has Foreman's signature mixture of many theatrical elements and styles.* (© Paula Court)

and do everything in our power to prevent them in the future. This kind of theater hopes to shock us into recognition and awareness. Other types of theater—such as melodrama—show us horror or violence mainly for the thrill of it. Still other plays attempt to inspire us or raise our spirits.

In the end, we come to the fact that while there are common denominators in theater—the performer-audience encounter being chief among them—*each theater experience is unique*. It has its own combination of elements and its own particular aim or intention. In turn, audience members have individual responses to each event. With so much variety in contemporary theater, we cannot expect every production to be equally satisfying to every spectator. We can look forward to many kinds of experiences in the theater, some of which bring us a sense of fun and some of which arouse in us thoughts and emotions we never knew were there.

THE FUTURE: WHAT LIES AHEAD?

What of the future? Given the many facets of theater, what can we expect in the years ahead? For one thing, we can expect variety to continue, with plays of all kinds presented under different conditions. Also, the emergence of theatrical events by and for special groups—Hispanic theater, African American theater, Asian American theater, feminist theater, gay and lesbian theater—is a trend we can assume will continue and probably increase.

We can also expect continuing realignments in the institutions which produce plays. The past several decades have seen the development of permanent professional theater companies in major cities throughout the United States. There has also been a marked growth in productions at colleges and universities. Off-Broadway and off-off-Broadway theaters have emerged in New York, and counterparts have emerged all across the country. At the same time, the commercial theaters of Broadway have been presenting fewer and fewer productions—especially, fewer serious new plays. There has thus been a shift from commercial to nonprofit theater and from Broadway to other parts of the country. One problem with the diminution of Broadway is that it becomes more and more difficult to make a living writing plays, and so dramatists are increasingly turning to films and television. How far these trends will extend, no one knows.

With nonprofit theaters coming more to the fore, the question of support for these theaters becomes increasingly important. Such subsidized theaters can never expect to earn all their expenses from ticket sales; thus they depend on grants and subsidies from foundations, corporations, and government agencies. The National Endowment for the Arts, which gave important moral as well as financial support to theaters in the years after its formation, has cut back on aid. State arts agencies have begun to make grants, but most of these are modest. Foundations, which were once generous supporters of theaters, have cut back. Corporations have contributed, but not nearly enough to make up for losses in other areas. Also, the events of September 11, 2001, with the bombing of the World Tade Center, and events surrounding the war in Iraq in 2003 had severe consequences for many arts institutions, including theater. Again, just what will happen in the area of financial support for nonprofit theaters is not clear, but it will vitally affect the future of theater in this country.

No one can predict the exact shape of theater of the future, though experiencing it should be an exciting adventure for everyone concerned—those creating it as well as those watching it. The one thing we do know is that theater will continue; it has already demonstrated this in the way it has met the challenges of film, television, computers, and other electronic innovations. The reason is that when we go to the theater, we become part of a group with a common bond: an audience sharing an experience. In the exchange between performers and audience, we take part in a direct human encounter. From the stage, we hear the dark cry of the soul, we listen to the joyous laughter of the human spirit, and we witness the tragedies and triumphs of the human heart. As long as people wish to join together in a communion of the spirit or share with one another their anguish and suffering, the theater experience will provide them with a unique way of doing so.

SUMMARY

1. Ultimately, the goal in theater is to bring all the elements together to create one integrated whole.

2. Human beings have an enormous capacity to absorb and integrate data. In theater, this allows us to take the images and stimuli we receive and merge them into a single experience. The ultimate integration of a theater event takes place in each spectator's mind.

3. While watching a theater event, we should be aware of the separate elements of a production and of what each contributes to the whole. We must also note how the elements relate to one another and synthesize them in our minds.

4. "Meaning" in theater is sometimes understood to consist of the ideas expressed in a text; some plays stress this aspect of meaning by actually including lines which state the author's position. But in the final analysis, meaning is the sum total of the theater experience. Meaning includes emotional and sensory data as well as intellectual content. Any attempt to summarize the meaning of a play in a few words, or to reduce it to a formula, robs it of its full meaning.

5. Each theater event forms a complete experience; but in today's theater, experiences can vary widely. Different kinds of theater buildings and environments, many performance styles, and variety in the plays themselves ensure a diversity of theater productions.

6. Because of its complexity, and because it is centered on people, theater offers audiences a particularly rare experience—especially when the elements of a production come together successfully.

Technical Terms

Above Upstage or away from the audience.

Acting area One of several areas into which a stage space is divided in order to facilitate blocking and the planning of stage movement.

Ad lib To improvise lines of a speech.

Aesthetic distance Physical or psychological separation or detachment of audience from dramatic action, usually considered necessary for artistic illusion.

Allegory Symbolic representation of abstract themes through characters, action, and other concrete elements of a play.

Amphitheater Large oval, circular, or semicircular outdoor theater with rising tiers of seats around an open playing area; *also,* an exceptionally large indoor auditorium.

Antagonist Opponent of the protagonist in a drama.

Apprentice Young performer training in an Elizabethan acting company.

Apron Stage space in front of the curtain line or proscenium; also called the *forestage.*

Arena Stage entirely surrounded by the audience; also known as *theater-in-the-round.*

Aside In a play, thoughts spoken aloud by one character (often, to the audience) without being noticed by others onstage.

At rise Expression used to describe what is happening onstage at the moment when the curtain first rises or the lights come up.

Automated lights Piece of lighting equipment which can change the direction, focus, color, and shape of the lighting beam by remote control. Made possible by advances in electronics and computerization.

Backdrop Large drapery or painted canvas which provides the rear or upstage masking of a set.

Backstage Stage area behind the front curtain; *also,* the areas beyond the setting, including wings and dressing rooms.

Ballad opera Eighteenth-century English form which burlesqued opera.

Basic situation Specific problem or maladjustment from which a play arises.

Batten Pipe or long pole suspended horizontally above

the stage, upon which scenery, drapery, or lights may be hung.

Beam projector Lighting instrument without a lens which uses a parabolic reflector to project a narrow, nonadjustable beam of light.

Below Opposite of *above;* toward the front of the stage.

Biomechanics Vsevolod Meyerhold's theory that a performer's body should be machinelike and that emotion could be represented externally.

Blackout Total darkening of the stage.

Blocking Pattern and arrangement of performers' movements onstage with respect to each other and to the stage space, usually set by the director.

Book (1) Spoken (as opposed to sung) portion of the text of a musical play. (2) To schedule engagements for artists or productions.

Bookholder Prompter who gave actors their lines in Elizabethan theaters.

Border Strip of drapery or painted canvas hung from a batten or pipe to mask the area above the stage; *also,* a row of lights hung from a batten.

Box Small private compartment for a group of spectators built into the walls of a traditional proscenium-arch theater.

Box set Interior setting using flats to form the back and side walls and often the ceiling of a room.

Business Obvious, detailed physical movement of performers to reveal character, aid action, or establish mood.

Capa y espada ("CAH-pah ee ehs-PAH-dah") Literally, "cape and sword"; Spanish play about intrigue and duels of honor.

Catharsis ("kuh-THAR-sis") Greek word, usually translated as "purgation," which Aristotle used in his definition of tragedy, referring to the vicarious cleansing of emotions in the audience through their representation onstage.

Catwalk Narrow metal platform suspended above the stage to permit ready access to lights and scenery hung from the grid.

Cazuela ("cah-zoo-AY-lah") Gallery above the tavern in the back wall of the theaters of the Spanish golden age; the area where unescorted women sat.

Center stage Stage position in the middle acting area of the stage, or the middle section extended upstage and downstage.

Choregus ("koh-REE-guhs") Wealthy person who financed a playwright's works at an ancient Greek dramatic festival.

Chorus (1) In ancient Greek drama, a group of performers who sang and danced, sometimes participating in the action but usually simply commenting on it. (2) In modern times, performers in a musical play who sing and dance as a group.

City Dionysia ("SIT-ee digh-eh-NIGH-see-uh") The most important Greek festival in honor of the god Dionysus, and the first to include drama. Held in the spring.

Comedia ("koh-MAY-dee-ah") Three-act full-length nonreligious play of the Spanish golden age.

Comedy of manners Form of comic drama that became popular in seventeenth-century France and the English Restoration, emphasizing a cultivated or sophisticated atmosphere and witty dialogue.

Compañias de parte ("cahm-pa-NYEE-ahs day PAHR-teh") Acting troupes in the Spanish golden age, organized according to a sharing system.

Complication Introduction, in a play, of a new force which creates a new balance of power and entails a delay in reaching the climax.

Conflict Tension between two or more characters that leads to crisis or a climax; a fundamental struggle or imbalance—involving ideologies, actions, personalities, etc.—underlying the plot of a play.

Constructivism Post–World War I movement in scene design, in which sets—frequently composed of ramps, platforms, and levels—were nonrealistic and intended to provide greater opportunities for physical action.

Corral Theater of the Spanish golden age, usually located in the courtyard of a series of adjoining buildings.

Counterweight Device for balancing the weight of scenery in a system which allows scenery to be raised above the stage by means of ropes and pulleys.

Crew Backstage team assisting in mounting a production.

Cross Movement by a performer across the stage in a given direction.

Cue Any prearranged signal—such as the last words in a speech, a piece of business, or any action or lighting change—that indicates to a performer or stage manager that it is time to proceed to the next line or action.

Cue sheet Prompt book marked with cues, or a list of cues for the use of technicians, especially the stage manager.

Curtain (1) Rise or fall of the actual curtain, which separates a play into structural parts. (2) Last bit of action preceding the fall of the curtain.

Curtain-raiser In nineteenth-century theater, a short play presented before a full-length drama.

Cyclorama Permanent fixture or curved drop used to mask the rear and sides of a stage, usually representing sky or open space.

Dada Movement in art between the world wars, based on presenting the irrational and attacking traditional artistic values.

Dénouement ("deh-noo-MAHN") Point near the end of a play when suspense is satisfied and "the knot is untied."

Deus ex machina ("DEH-oos eks MAH-kih-nah") Literally, "god from a machine," a resolution device in classic Greek drama; hence, intervention of super-natural forces—usually at the last moment—to save the action from its logical conclusion. In modern drama, an arbitrary and coincidental solution.

Dimmer Device for changing lighting intensity smoothly and at varying rates.

Dim out To turn out lights with a dimmer.

Director In American usage, the person responsible for the overall unity of a production and for coordinating the work of contributing artists. The American director is the equivalent of the British producer and the French *metteur-en-scène* ("meh-TURR ahn SENN").

Dithyramb ("DITH-ih-ramb") Ancient Greek choral song describing the adventures of a god or hero.

Double entendre ("DOO-bluh ahn-TAHN-druh") Word or phrase in comedy that has a double meaning, the second often sexual.

Doubling Term used when a performer plays more than one role in a play.

Downstage Front of the stage, toward the audience.

Drop Large piece of fabric—generally painted canvas—hung from a batten to the stage floor, usually to serve as backing.

Ellipsoidal reflector spotlight Sharp, powerful light used at some distance from the stage.

Emotional recall Stanislavski's exercise which helps the performer to present realistic emotions. The performer feels a character's emotion by thinking of the conditions surrounding an event in his or her own life which led to a similar emotion.

Ensemble playing Acting that stresses the total artistic unity of a group performance rather than individual performances.

Entrance Manner and effectiveness with which a performer comes into a scene, as well as the actual coming onstage; *also,* the way this is prepared for by the playwright.

Epilogue Speech by one of the performers to the audience after the conclusion of a play.

Exit A performer's leaving the stage, as well as the preparation for his or her leaving.

Exposition Imparting of information necessary for an understanding of the story but not covered by the action onstage; events or knowledge from the past, or occurring outside the play, which must be introduced for the audience to understand the characters or plot.

Flat Single piece of flat, rectangular scenery, used with other similar units to create a set.

Flood Lighting instrument without lenses which is used for general or large-area lighting.

Fly loft or flies Space above the stage where scenery may be lifted out of sight by means of ropes and pulleys.

Follow spot Large, powerful spotlight with a sharp focus and narrow beam which is used by an operator to follow principal performers as they move about the stage.

Footlights Row of lights in the floor along the front edge of the stage or apron.

Forestage See *Apron.*

Found space Space not originally intended for theater which is used for theatrical productions. Avant-garde artists often produce in found spaces.

Fourth wall Convention, in a proscenium-arch theater, that the audience is looking into a room through an invisible fourth wall.

Freeze To remain motionless onstage, especially for laughs or in a tableau.

Fresnel ("fruh-NEL") Type of spotlight used over relatively short distances with a soft beam edge which allows the light to blend easily with light from other sources; *also,* the type of lenses used in such spotlights.

Front of the house Portion of a theater reserved for the audience; sometimes called simply the *house.*

Futurism Art movement, begun in Italy about 1905, which idealized mechanization and machinery.

Gallery In traditional proscenium-arch theaters, the undivided seating area cut into the walls of the building.

Gauze See *Scrim.*

Gel Thin, flexible color medium used in lighting instruments to give color to a light beam.

Grid Metal framework above the stage from which lights and scenery are suspended.

Groove system System in which tracks on the stage floor and above the stage allowed for the smooth movement of flat wings on and off the stage; usually there were a series of grooves at each stage position.

Hamartia ("hah-MARH-tee-ah") Ancient Greek term usually translated as "tragic flaw." The term literally translates as "missing the mark," which may suggest that hamartia is not so much a character flaw as an error in judgment.

Hanamichi ("hah-nah-MEE-chee") In kabuki theater, a bridge running from behind the audience (toward the left side of the audience) to the stage. Performers can enter on the hanamichi; important scenes may also be played on it.

Hand props Small props carried on- or offstage by actors and actresses during a performance. See also *Props.*

Hashigakari ("ha-shee-gah-KAH-ree") Bridge in nō theater on which the actors make their entrance from the dressing area to the platform stage.

Hireling Member of an Elizabethan acting troupe who was paid a set salary and was not a shareholder.

House See *Front of the house.*

Hubris ("HEW-brihs") Ancient Greek term usually defined as "excessive pride" and cited as a common tragic flaw.

Inner stage Area at the rear of the stage which can be cut off from the rest by means of curtains or scenery and revealed for special scenes.

Irony A condition the reverse of what we have expected or an expression whose intended implication is the opposite of its literal sense.

Kill To eliminate or suppress; for example, to remove unwanted light or to ruin an effect through improper execution.

Lazzi ("LAHT-zee") Comic pieces of business repeatedly used by characters in Italian commedia dell'arte.

Left stage Left side of the stage from the point of view of a performer facing the audience.

Living newspapers In the United States, the Federal Theater Project's dramatizations of newsworthy events in the 1930s.

Long run Term used in commercial theater when a drama is performed for as long as it is popular.

Magic if Stanislavski's acting exercise which requires the performer to ask, "How would I react *if* I were in this character's position?"

Mask (1) To conceal backstage areas or technical equipment from the audience by means of scenery. (2) Face or head covering for a performer, in the image of the character portrayed.

Masking Scenery or draperies used to hide or cover.

Minstrelsy Type of nineteenth-century production featuring white performers made up in blackface.

Mise-en-scène ("miz-on-SEHN") Arrangement of all the elements in a stage picture at a given moment or throughout a performance.

Multimedia Use of electronic media, such as slides, film, and videotape, in live theatrical presentations.

Multiple setting Form of stage setting, common in the Middle Ages, in which several locations are represented at the same time; also called *simultaneous setting.* Used also in various forms of contemporary theater.

Objective Stanislavski's term for that which is urgently desired and sought by a character, the long-range goal which propels a character to action.

Obstacle That which delays or prevents the achieving of a goal by a character. An obstacle creates complication and conflict.

Offstage Areas of the stage, usually in the wings or backstage, which are not in view of the audience.

Onstage Area of the stage which is in view of the audience.

Open To turn or face more toward the audience.

Orchestra (1) In American usage, ground-floor seating in an auditorium. (2) Circular playing space in ancient Greek theaters.

Pace Rate at which a performance is played; *also,* to perform a scene or play to set its proper speed.

Parabasis ("puh-RAB-uh-sihs") Scene in classical Greek Old Comedy in which the chorus directly addresses the audience members and makes fun of them.

Parados ("PAR-uh-dohs") In classical Greek drama, the scene in which the chorus enters; *also,* the entranceway for the chorus in Greek theater.

Parterre In French neoclassical theater, the pit in which audience members stood.

Patio In theater of the Spanish golden age, the pit area for the audience.

Pensionnaire ("PON-see-oh-NARE") Hireling in a French acting troupe.

Period Term describing any representation onstage of a former age (e.g., *period costume, period play*).

Perspective Illusion of depth in painting, introduced into scene design during the Italian Renaissance.

Pit Floor of the house in a traditional proscenium-arch theater. It was originally a standing area; by the end of the eighteenth century, backless benches were added.

Platform Raised surface on a stage floor serving as an elevation for parts of the stage action and allowing for a multiplicity of stage levels.

Platform stage Elevated stage with no proscenium.

Plot (1) As distinct from story, patterned arrangements of events and characters in a drama, with incidents selected and arranged for maximum dramatic impact. (2) In Elizabethan theaters, an outline of the play posted backstage for the actors.

Point of attack The moment in the story when a play actually begins. The dramatist chooses a point which he or she judges will best start the action and propel it forward.

Pole and chariot Giacomo Torelli's mechanized means of changing sets made up of flat wings.

Preparation (1) Previous arranging of circumstances, pointing of characters, and placing of properties in a production so that the ensuing actions will seem reasonable. (2) Actions taken by an actor or actress in getting ready for a performance.

Private theaters Indoor theaters in Elizabethan England.

Producer In American usage, the person responsible for the business side of a production, including raising the necessary money. (In British usage, a producer is the equivalent of an American director.)

Prologue Introductory speech delivered to the audience by one of the actors or actresses before a play begins.

Prompt To furnish a performer with missed or forgotten lines or cues during a performance.

Prompt book Script of a play indicating performers' movements, light cues, sound cues, etc.

Props Properties; objects that are used by performers onstage or are necessary to complete a set.

Proscenium ("pro-SIN-ee-um") Arch or frame surrounding the stage opening in a box or picture stage.

Protagonist Principal character in a play, the one whom the drama is about.

Public theaters Outdoor theaters in Elizabethan England.

Rake (1) To position scenery on a slant or at an angle other than parallel or perpendicular to the curtain line. (2) An upward slope of the stage floor away from the audience.

Raked stage Stage floor which slopes upward away from the audience toward the back of the stage.

Regional theater (1) Theater whose subject matter is specific to a particular geographic region. (2) Theaters situated in theatrical centers across the country.

Régisseur ("ray-zhee-SUHR") Continental European term for a theater director; it often denotes a dictatorial director.

Rehearsal Preparation by a cast for the performance of a play through repetition and practice.

Repertory or repertoire Acting company which at any time can perform a number of plays alternately; *also,* the plays regularly performed by a company.

Restoration drama English drama after the restoration of the monarchy, from 1660 to 1700.

Reversal Sudden switch of circumstances or revelation of knowledge which leads to a result contrary to expectations; called *peripeteia* ("peh-rih-puh-TEE-uh") or *peripety* ("peh-RIP-uh-tee") in Greek drama.

Revolving stage Large circular turntable in a stage floor on which scenery is placed so that, as it moves, one set is brought into view while another one turns out of sight.

Right stage Right side of the stage from the point of view of a performer facing the audience.

Ritual Ceremonial event, often religious, which takes place in a specific sequence.

Satyr play One of the three types of classical Greek drama, usually a ribald takeoff on Greek mythology and history that included a chorus of satyrs (mythological creatures who were half-man and half-goat).

Scaena ("SKAY-nah") Stagehouse in a Roman theater.

Scene (1) Stage setting. (2) One of a series of structural units into which a play or acts of a play are divided. (3) Location of a play's action.

Scrim Thin, open-weave fabric which is nearly transparent when lit from behind and opaque when lit from the front.

Script Written or printed text—consisting of dialogue, stage directions, character descriptions, and the like.

Set Scenery, taken as a whole, for a scene or an entire production.

Set piece Piece of scenery which stands independently in a scene.

Shareholders In Elizabethan acting troupes, members who received part of the profits as payment.

Sides Script containing only a single actor's lines and cues. Elizabethan actors learned their roles from sides.

Simultaneous setting Medieval tradition of presenting more than one locale onstage at the same time.

Skene ("SKEE-nee") In ancient Greek theater, the scene house behind the orchestra.

Slapstick Type of comedy or comic business which relies on ridiculous physical activity—often vigorous—for its humor.

Soliloquy Speech in which a character who is alone onstage speaks inner thoughts aloud.

Spill Light from stage-lighting instruments which falls outside the area for which it is intended, such as light that falls on the audience.

Spine In the Stanislavski method, a character's dominant desire or motivation; usually thought of as an action and expressed as a verb.

Stage convention An established theatrical technique or practice arbitrarily accepted through custom or usage.

Stage door Outside entrance to dressing rooms and stage areas which is used by performers and technicians.

Stage house Stage floor and the space around it to the side walls, as well as the space above it up to the grid.

Standing room only (SRO) Notice that all seats for a performance have been sold but standees can be accommodated.

Stanislavski method Constantin Stanislavski's techniques and theories about acting, which promote a naturalistic style stressing (among other things) psychophysical action as opposed to conventional theatricality.

Stock set Standard setting for a locale used in every play which requires that environment.

Storm and stress Antineoclassical eighteenth-century German movement which was a forerunner of romanticism; in German, *Sturm und Drang.*

Strike To remove pieces of scenery or props from onstage or to take down an entire set after a final performance.

Subtext Meaning and movement of a play below its surface; that which is not stated but implied.

Summer stock Theater companies which operate outside of major theatrical centers during the summer, often producing a different play every week.

Symbolism Movement of the late nineteenth and early twentieth centuries which sought to express inner truth rather than represent life realistically.

Teaser Short horizontal curtain just beyond the proscenium, used to mask the fly loft and, in effect, to lower the height of the proscenium.

Technical Term referring to functions necessary to the production of a play other than those of the cast and the director, such as functions of the stage crew, carpenters, and lighting crew.

Tetralogy In classical Greek theater, four plays—three tragedies and a satyr play—written by one author for a festival.

Theme Central thought of a play; the idea or ideas with which a play deals and which it expounds.

Thespian Synonym for "performer"; from Thespis (sixth century B.C.E) who is said to have been the first actor in ancient Greek theater.

Thrust stage Stage space that thrusts into the audience space; a stage surrounded on three sides by audience seating.

Tragic flaw The factor which is a character's chief weakness and which makes him or her most vulnerable; it often intensifies in time of stress.

Trap Opening in a stage floor, normally covered, which can be used for special effects or allows for a staircase ostensibly leading to a lower floor.

Treadmill Belt or band, usually 3 feet to 5 feet wide, that moves across the stage, on which scenery, props, or performers can move on- or offstage. Generally moves parallel to the front edge of the stage. Operated electronically today, with safety devices to avoid injuries to performers.

Trilogy In classical Greece, three tragedies written by the same playwright and presented on a single day; they were often connected by a story or thematic elements.

Unities Term referring to the preference that a play occur within one day (unity of time), in one place (unity of place), and with no action irrelevant to the plot (unity of action).

Unity A requirement of art; an element often setting art apart from life. In drama, the term refers to unity of action in structure and story and to the integrity and wholeness of a production.

Upstage At or toward the back of the stage, away from the front edge of the stage.

Wagon stage Low platform mounted on wheels or casters by means of which scenery is moved on- and offstage.

Wings (1) Left and right offstage areas. (2) Narrow standing pieces of scenery, or "legs," more or less parallel to the proscenium, which form the sides of a setting.

Work lights Lights arranged for the convenience of stage technicians, situated either in backstage areas and shaded or over the stage area for use while the curtain is down.

Working lights See *Automated lights*.

Yard Pit, or standing area, in Elizabethan public theaters.

Major Theatrical Forms and Movements

Absurdism See *Theater of the absurd*.

Allegory Representation of an abstract theme or themes through the symbolic use of character, action, and other concrete elements of a play. In its most direct form—for example, in a medieval morality play—allegory uses the device of personification to present characters representing abstract qualities, such as virtues and vices, in action which spells out a moral or intellectual lesson. Less direct forms of allegory may use a relatively realistic story as a guise for a hidden theme. For example, Arthur Miller's *The Crucible* can be regarded as an allegory of the McCarthy congressional investigation in the United States after World War II.

Avant-garde ("ah-vahn-GARD") French term that literally means the "advance guard" in a military formation. It has come to stand for an intellectual, literary, or artistic movement in any age that breaks with tradition and appears to be ahead of its time. Avant-garde works are usually experimental and unorthodox. In twentieth-century theater, such movements as expressionism, surrealism, absurdism, and the theories of Antonin Artaud and Jerzy Grotowski were considered avant-garde.

Bourgeois drama See *Domestic drama*.

Bunraku ("buhn-RAH-koo") Traditional Japanese puppet theater.

Burlesque Ludicrous imitation of a dramatic form or a specific play.

Closely related to satire but usually lacking the moral or intellectual purposes of reform typical of satire; burlesque is content to mock the excesses of other works. Famous examples of burlesque include Beaumont's *The Knight of the Burning Pestle* and, more recently, such burlesques of the theater as *Forbidden Broadway*. In the United States the term has come to be associated with a form of variety show which stresses sex.

Comedy As one of the oldest enduring categories of western drama, comedy has gathered under its heading a large number of different subclassifications. Although the range of comedy is broad, generally it can be said to be a play that is light in tone, is concerned with issues tending not to be serious, has a happy ending, and is designed to amuse and provoke laughter. Historically, comedy has gone through many changes. Aristophanic or Greek *Old Comedy* was farcical, satiric, and nonrealistic. Greek and Roman *New Comedy,* based on domestic situations, was more influential in the development of comedy during the Renaissance. Ben Jonson built his "comedies of humors" on Roman models. In Jonson's plays, ridicule is directed at characters who are dominated to the point of obsession by a single trait, or humor. Comedy of manners was made popular in the late seventeenth century by Molière and the writers of the English Restoration. It tends to have a cultivated or sophisticated milieu, witty dialogue, and characters whose concern with social polish is charming, ludicrous, or both. In the final decades of the nineteenth century, George Bernard Shaw used comedy for the serious discussion of ideas, while Chekhov wrote plays variously interpreted as sentimental and tragicomic. The twentieth century has seen an expansion in the territory covered by comedy as well as a blurring of its boundaries. The horizon of the comic has been expanded by playwrights such as Pirandello and Ionesco, whose comic vision is more serious, thoughtful, and disturbing than that found in most traditional comedies.

Commedia dell'arte Form of comic theater originating in Italy in the sixteenth century, in which dialogue was improvised around a loose scenario calling for a set of stock characters, each with a distinctive costume and traditional name. The best known of these characters are probably the *zanni,* buffoons who usually took the roles of servants and who had at their disposal a large number of slapstick routines, called *lazzi,* which ranged from simple grimaces to acrobatic stunts.

Documentary See *Theater of fact.*

Domestic drama Also known as *bourgeois drama,* domestic drama deals with problems of members of the middle and lower classes, particularly problems of the family and home. Conflicts with society, struggles within a family, dashed hopes, and renewed determination are characteristic of domestic drama. It attempts to depict onstage the lifestyle of ordinary people—in language, in dress, in behavior. Domestic drama first came to the fore during the eighteenth century in Europe and Great Britain, when the merchant and working classes were emerging. Because general audiences could so readily identify with the people and problems of domestic drama, it continued to gain in popularity during the nineteenth and twentieth centuries and remains a major form today.

Environmental theater Term used by Richard Schechner and others to refer to one branch of avant-garde theater. Among its aims are the elimination of the distinction between audience space and acting space, a more flexible approach to the interactions between performers and audience, and the substitution of a multiple focus for the traditional single focus.

Epic theater Form of presentation which has come to be associated with Bertolt Brecht, its chief advocate and theorist. It is aimed at the intellect rather than the emotions, seeking to present evidence regarding social questions in such a way that they may be objectively considered and an intelligent conclusion reached. Brecht felt that emotional involvement by the audience defeated this aim, and he used various devices designed to produce emotional "alienation" of the audience from the action onstage. His plays are episodic, with narrative songs separating the segments and large posters or signs announcing the various scenes.

Existentialism Set of philosophical ideas whose principal modern advocate was Jean-Paul Sartre. The term *existentialist* was applied by Sartre and others to plays which illustrate these views. Sartre's central thesis was that there are no longer any fixed standards or values by which one can live and that each person must create his or her own code of conduct regardless of the conventions imposed by society. Only in this way can one truly "exist" as a responsible, creative human being; otherwise one is merely a robot or an automaton. Sartre's plays typically involve people who are faced with decisions forcing them into an awareness of the choice between living on their own terms and ceasing to exist as individuals.

Expressionism Movement which developed and flourished in Germany during the period immediately preceding and following World War I. Expressionism was characterized by an attempt to dramatize subjective states through the use of distortion; striking, often grotesque images; and lyric, unrealistic dialogue. It was revolutionary in content as well as in form, portraying the institutions of society, particularly the bourgeois family, as grotesque, oppressive, and materialistic. The expressionist hero or heroine was usually a rebel against this mechanistic vision of society. Dramatic conflict tended to be replaced by the development of themes by means of visual images. The movement had great influence because it forcefully demonstrated that dramatic imagination need not be limited to either theatrical conventions or the faithful reproduction of reality. In the United States, expressionism influenced Elmer Rice's *The Adding Machine* and many of O'Neill's early plays. The basic aim of expressionism was to give external expression to inner feelings and ideas; theatrical techniques which adopt this method are frequently referred to as *expressionistic.*

Farce One of the major genres of drama, usually regarded as a subclass of comedy. Farce has few, if any, intellectual pretensions. It aims to entertain, to provoke laughter. Its humor is the result primarily of physical activity and visual effects, and it relies less than so-called higher forms of comedy on language and wit. Violence, rapid movement, and accelerating pace are characteristic of farce. In bedroom farce it is the institution of marriage that is the object of the fun, but medicine, law, and business also provide material for farce.

Happenings Form of theatrical event which was developed out of the experimentation of certain American abstract artists in the 1960s. Happenings are nonliterary, replacing the script with a scenario which provides for chance occurrences. They are performed (often only once) in such places as parks and street corners, with little attempt being made to segregate the action from the audience. Emphasizing the free association of sound and movement, they avoid logical action and rational meaning.

Heroic drama Form of serious drama, written in verse or elevated prose, which features noble or heroic characters caught in extreme situations or undertaking unusual adventures. In spite of the hardships to which its leading figures are subjected, heroic drama—unlike tragedy—has a basically optimistic worldview. It has either a happy ending or, in cases where the hero or heroine dies, a triumphant ending in which the death is not regarded tragically. Plays from all periods, and from Asia as well as the west, fall into this category. During the late seventeenth century in England, plays of this type were referred to specifically as *heroic tragedies.*

History play In the broadest sense, a play set in a historical milieu which deals with historical personages; but the term is usually applied only to plays which deal with vital issues of public welfare and are nationalistic in tone. The form originated in Elizabethan England, which produced more history plays than any comparable place or time. Based

on a religious concept of history, they were influenced by the structure of the morality play. Shakespeare was the major writer of Elizabethan history plays. His style has influenced many later history plays, notably those by the Swedish playwright Strindberg.

Impressionism Style of painting developed in the late nineteenth century which stressed immediate impressions created by objects—particularly those resulting from the effects of light—and which tended to ignore details. As such, its influence on theater was primarily in the area of scenic design, but the term *impressionistic* is sometimes applied to plays like Chekhov's, which rely on a series of impressions and use indirect techniques.

Kabuki The most eclectic and theatrical of the major forms of Japanese theater. It is a more popular form than the aristocratic nō drama and, unlike puppet theater, which is called *bunraku,* it uses live actors. Nevertheless, kabuki has borrowed freely from both of these forms, particularly bunraku. Roles of both sexes are performed by men in a highly theatrical, nonrealistic style. Kabuki combines music, dance, and dramatic scenes with an emphasis on color and movement. The plays are long and episodic, composed of a series of loosely connected dramatic scenes which are often performed separately.

Masque Lavish, spectacular form of private theatrical entertainment which developed in Renaissance Italy and spread rapidly to the courts of France and England. Usually intended for a single performance, a masque combined poetry, music, elaborate costumes, and spectacular effects of stage machinery. It was a social event in which members of the court were both spectators and performers. Loosely constructed, masques were usually written around allegorical or mythological themes.

Medieval drama There is only meager evidence of theatrical activity in Europe between the sixth and tenth centuries, but by the end of the fifteenth century a number of different types of drama had developed. The first of these, known as *liturgical drama,* was sung or chanted in Latin as part of a church service. Plays on religious themes were also written in the vernacular and performed outside of the church. The *mystery plays* (also called *cycle plays*) were based on events taken from the Old and New Testaments. Many such plays were organized into historical cycles which told the story of humanity from the creation to doomsday. The entire performance was quite long, sometimes requiring as much as five days. The plays were produced as a community effort, with different craft guilds usually being responsible for individual segments. Another form of medieval drama was the *morality play*. The morality play was a didactic, allegorical treatment of moral and religious questions, the most famous example being *Everyman*. The medieval period also produced several types of secular plays.

Other than the *folk plays,* which dealt with legendary heroes like Robin Hood, most were farcical and fairly short.

Melodrama Historically, a distinct form of drama popular throughout the nineteenth century which emphasized action and spectacular effects and used music to heighten the dramatic mood. Melodrama had stock characters and clearly defined villains and heroes. More generally, the term is applied to any dramatic play which presents an unambiguous confrontation between good and evil. Characterization is often shallow and stereotypical, and because the moral conflict is externalized, action and violence are prominent, usually culminating in a happy ending meant to demonstrate the eventual triumph of good.

Mime Performance in which the action or story is conveyed through the use of movements and gestures, without words. It depends on the performer's ability to suggest or create his or her surroundings through physical reactions to them and the expressiveness of the entire body.

Musical theater Broad category which includes opera, operetta, musical comedy, and other musical plays (the term *lyric theater* is sometimes used to distinguish it from pure dance). It includes any dramatic entertainment of which music and lyrics (and sometimes dance) form an integral and necessary part. The various types of musical theater often overlap and are best distinguished in terms of their separate historical origins, the

quality of the music, and the range and type of skills demanded of the performance. *Opera* is usually defined as a work in which all parts are sung to musical accompaniment. Such works are part of a separate and much older tradition than the modern musical, which is of relatively recent American origin. The term *musical comedy* is no longer adequate to describe all the musical dramas commonly seen on and off Broadway, but they clearly belong together as part of a tradition that can easily be distinguished from both opera and operetta.

Naturalism A special form of realism. The theory of naturalism came to prominence in France and other parts of Europe in the latter half of the nineteenth century. The French playwright Émile Zola (1840–1902) advocated a theater that would follow the scientific principles of the age, especially those discovered by Charles Darwin. Zola was also impressed by the work of Auguste Comte (1778–1857) and a physician named Claude Bernard (1813–1878). According to Zola's theory of naturalism, drama should look for the causes of disease in society the way a doctor looks for disease in a patient. Theater should therefore expose social infection in all its ugliness. Following Darwin, theater should show human beings as products of heredity and environment. The result would be a drama often depicting the ugly underside of life and expressing a pessimistic point of view. Also, drama was not to be carefully plotted or constructed but was to present a "slice of life": an attempt to look at life as it is. Very few successful plays fulfilled Zola's demands. Some of the works of Strindberg, Gorki, and others came closest to meeting the requirements of naturalism. In the contemporary period the term *naturalism* is generally applied to dramas that are superrealistic, that is, those which conform to observable reality in precise detail. Naturalism attempts to achieve the verisimilitude of a documentary film, to convey the impression that everything about a play—the setting; the way the characters dress, speak, and act—is exactly like everyday life.

Nō Rigidly traditional form of Japanese drama which in its present form dates back to the fourteenth century. Nō plays are short dramas combining music, dance, and lyrics with a highly stylized and ritualistic presentation. Virtually every aspect of the production—including costumes, masks, and a highly symbolic setting—is prescribed by tradition. (Also spelled *noh*.)

Pantomime Originally a Roman entertainment in which a narrative was sung by a chorus while the story was acted out by dancers. Now used loosely to cover any form of presentation which relies on dance, gesture, and physical movement. (See also *Mime*.)

Performance art Type of experimental theater that came to prominence in the 1980s but had its antecedents in previous avant-garde movements of the twentieth century. In its earlier manifestations, it combined elements of dance and the visual arts with theater. At times, video and film were also added. The focus was not a written text, and the playwright, if there was one, was a relatively minor part of the overall scheme. In one type of performance art, the director is the one who supplies the vision for the production and coordinates the various elements. Performers, rather than playing normal characters, usually function as dancers, acrobats, or parts of a *tableau vivant*—they fit into the visual and choreographic scheme along with music, scenery, and the other aspects of the production. The stress is on picturization, ritual, and choreographed movement. More recently, however, performance art has emphasized individual performances. A single artist performs, and often creates, the material presented to an audience. Performance art of this type ranges from the storytelling of Spalding Gray to the one-woman compilations of social and political events by Anna Deavere Smith to the protest performances of Karen Finley.

Play of ideas Play whose principal focus is on the serious treatment of social, moral, or philosophical ideas. The term *problem play* is used to designate those dramas, best exemplified in the work of Ibsen and Shaw, in which several sides of a question are both dramatized and discussed. A play of ideas is sometimes distinguished from the *pièce à thèse*, or thesis play, which makes a more one-sided presentation and uses a character who sums up the "lesson" of the play and serves as the author's voice.

Poor theater Term coined by Jerzy Grotowski to describe his ideal of theater stripped to its barest essentials. According to Grotowski, the lavish sets, lights, and costumes usually associated with theater merely reflect low materialistic values and must be eliminated. If theater is to become rich spiritually and aesthetically, it must first be "poor" in everything that can detract from the performer's relationship with the audience.

Postmodernism Many critics, noting the complexity and diversity of contemporary art and theater, describe a number of contemporary works and artists as *postmodernist*. The term suggests that the "modernist" interest in antirealism is no longer central to art and that artists have moved beyond abstraction. Instead, contemporary playwrights and theater artists today mix abstraction with realism, so that the works they create cannot be easily classified. Furthermore, the distinction between "high" art and popular art can no longer be clearly defined; postmodernists mix popular concerns and techniques with those of high art.

Realism Broadly speaking, realism is an attempt to present onstage people and events corresponding to those observable in everyday life. Examples of realism can be found in western drama—especially in comedies—in the Greek, Roman, medieval, and Renaissance periods. Sections of plays from these periods show people speaking, dressing, and acting in the manner of ordinary people of the time. Certain landmark plays are considered forerunners of modern realism.

These include *Arden of Feversham* (c. 1590), an English play about greed and lust in a middle-class family; *The London Merchant* (1731) by George Lillo (1693–1739), about a young apprentice led astray by a prostitute; *Miss Sara Sampson* (1755), by Gotthold Lessing (1729–1781), a German version of *The London Merchant;* and *The Inspector General* (1836), by Nikolai Gogol (1809–1852), exposing corruption in a provincial Russian town. It was in the latter part of the nineteenth century, however, that realism took hold as a major form of theater. As the middle class came more and more to dominate life in Europe and the United States, and as scientific and psychological discoveries challenged the heroic or romantic viewpoint, drama began to center on the affairs of ordinary people in their natural surroundings. The plays of Ibsen, Strindberg, and Chekhov showed that powerful, effective drama could be written about such people. The degree of realism varies in drama, ranging from *slice-of-life naturalism* to *heightened realism.* In the latter, nonrealistic and symbolic elements are introduced into a basically realistic format. Despite frequent challenges from other forms during the past 100 years, realism remains a major form of contemporary theater. (See also *Naturalism.*)

Restoration drama English drama after the restoration of the monarchy, from 1660 to 1700. Presented for an audience of aristocrats who gathered about the court of Charles II, drama of this period consisted largely of heroic tragedies in the neoclassical style and comedies of manners which reflected a cynical view of human nature.

Romanticism Literary and dramatic movement of the nineteenth century which developed as a reaction to the confining strictures of neoclassicism. Imitating the loose, episodic structure of Shakespeare's plays, the romantics sought to free the writer from all rules and looked to the unfettered inspiration of artistic genius as the source of all creativity. They laid more stress on mood and atmosphere than on content, but one of their favorite themes was the gulf between human beings' spiritual aspirations and their physical limitations.

Satire Dramatic satire uses the techniques of comedy, such as wit, irony, and exaggeration, to attack and expose folly and vice. Satire can attack specific public figures, as does the political satire *Nixon's Nixon,* or it can point its barbs at more general traits which can be found in many of us. Thus Molière's *Tartuffe* ridicules religious hypocrisy, Shaw's *Arms and the Man* exposes the romantic glorification of war, and Wilde's *The Importance of Being Earnest* satirizes the English upper classes.

Street theater Generic term which includes a number of groups that perform in the open and attempt to relate to the needs of a specific community or neighborhood. Many such groups sprang up in the 1960s, partly as a response to social unrest and partly because there was a need for theater which could express the specific concerns of minority and ethnic neighborhoods.

Surrealism Movement attacking formalism in the arts which developed in Europe after World War I. Seeking a deeper and more profound reality than that presented to the rational, conscious mind, the surrealists replaced realistic action with the strange logic of the dream and cultivated such techniques as automatic writing and free association of ideas. Although few plays written by the surrealists are highly regarded, the movement had a great influence on later avant-garde theater—notably theater of the absurd and theater of cruelty.

Symbolism Closely linked to symbolist poetry, symbolist drama was a movement of the late nineteenth and early twentieth centuries which sought to replace realistic representation of life with the expression of an inner truth. Hoping to restore the religious and spiritual significance of theater, symbolism used myth, legend, and symbols in an attempt to reach beyond everyday reality. The plays of Maurice Maeterlinck (1862–1949) are among the best-known symbolist dramas.

Theater of the absurd Term first used by Martin Esslin to describe certain playwrights of the 1950s and 1960s who expressed a similar point of view regarding the absurdity of the human condition. Their plays are dramatizations of the dramatist's inner sense of the absurdity and futility of existence. Rational language is debased and replaced by clichés and trite or irrelevant remarks. Repetitious or meaningless activity is substituted for logical action. Realistic psychological motivation is replaced by automatic behavior which is often absurdly inappropriate to the situation. Although the subject matter is serious, the tone of these plays is usually comic and ironic. Among the best-known absurdists are Beckett, Ionesco, and Albee.

Theater of cruelty Antonin Artaud's visionary concept of a theater based on magic and ritual which would liberate deep, violent, and erotic impulses. He wished to reveal the cruelty which he saw as existing beneath all human action—the pervasiveness of evil and violent sexuality. To do this, he advocated radical changes in the use of theatrical space, the integration of audience and performers, and the full utilization of the affective power of light, color, movement, and language. Although Artaud had little success implementing his theories himself, he had considerable influence on other writers and directors, particularly Peter Brook, Jean-Louis Barrault (1910–1994), and Jerzy Grotowski.

Theater of fact Term encompassing a number of different types of documentary drama that developed during the twentieth century. Methods of presentation differ. The "living newspaper" drama of the 1930s used signs and slide projections to deal with broad social problems; other documentary

dramas have taken a more realistic approach. Contemporary theater of fact, as represented by such plays as *The Deputy* and *The Investigation,* tries to portray actual events with an appearance of authenticity.

Theatricalism Style of production and playwriting which emphasizes theatricality for its own sake. Less a coherent movement than a quality found in the work of many artists rebelling against realism, it frankly admits the artifice of the stage and borrows freely from the circus, the music hall, and similar entertainments.

Tragedy One of the most fundamental dramatic forms in the western tradition, tragedy involves a serious action of universal significance and has important moral and philosophical implications. Following Aristotle, most critics agree that a tragic hero or heroine should be an essentially admirable person whose downfall elicits our sympathy while leaving us with a feeling that there has in some way been a triumph of the moral and cosmic order which transcends the fate of any individual. The disastrous outcome of a tragedy should be seen as the inevitable result of the character and his or her situation, including forces beyond the character's control. Traditionally, tragedy was about the lives and fortunes of kings, queens, and nobles, and there has been a great deal of debate about whether it is possible to have modern tragedy—tragedy about ordinary people. The answers to this question are as

varied as the critics who address it, but most seem to agree that although such plays may be tragedies, they are of a somewhat different order.

Tragicomedy During the Renaissance the word *tragicomedy* was used for plays that had tragic themes and noble characters yet ended happily. Modern tragicomedy combines serious and comic elements. Tragicomedy is, in fact, the form increasingly chosen by "serious" playwrights. Sometimes comic behavior and situations have serious or tragic consequences— as in Dürrenmatt's *The Visit.* At times the ending is indeterminate or ambivalent—as in Beckett's *Waiting for Godot.* In most cases a quality of despair or hopelessness is introduced because human beings are seen as incapable of rising above their circumstances or their own nature; the fact that the situation is also ridiculous serves to make their plight that much more horrible.

Well-made play Type of play popular in the nineteenth and early twentieth centuries which combined apparent plausibility of incident and surface realism with a tightly constructed, contrived plot. Well-made plays typically revolved around the question of social respectability, and the plot often hinged on the manipulation of a piece of incriminating evidence which threatened to destroy the facade of respectability. Although the well-made play is less popular now, many of its techniques continue to be used by modern playwrights.

APPENDIX

Historical Outline

In Chapter 2 and Chapter 8 we spoke of the relationship of theater to society. Theater is always in some manner a reflection of society, either reinforcing the values and ideas of a country at a certain period or challenging those values. Theater also occurs in the sweep of history: events take place on the political, social, and scientific fronts at the same time that they occur in the arts. It is helpful and illuminating to see the connection between developments in theater and in other fields.

The pages that follow present time lines. On one side is a chronological listing of events in the theater—plays that are written; theaters that open; key dates in the lives of playwrights, performers, or other artists; and works of criticism. On the other side are significant events in other fields: politics, social events, scientific discoveries, artistic achievements, and key dates in the lives of important people.

The time lines span every period and country that have had meaningful or memorable achievements in theater: the ancient Greek and Roman periods, Asian theater, the medieval and Renaissance periods, and so forth. In a graphic, vivid format, one can see at a glance what was happening in cities and nations at notable times in history. Placing theater on one side and other categories on the other allows one to see how the two interact and progress alongside each other. Theatrical achievements and the sweep of history unfold clearly and concisely.

Greece
Year, B.C.E.

Theater	Year	Culture and Politics

Theater

Culture and Politics

800 — Age of Homer (800 B.C.E.)

Arion, harpist and poet, develops the dithyramb (c. 600 B.C.E.) —— **600**

—— Thales of Miletus begins natural philosophy (physics) (c. 585 B.C.E.)

575

Thespis, supposedly first "actor" in dithyramb (mid-sixth century) —— **555** —— Peisistratus, tyrant of Athens (560 B.C.E.)

Play contests begin in Athens (534 B.C.E.) ——

525 —— Pythagoras flourishes; Doric temples of southern Italy and Sicily (c. 525 B.C.E.)

—— Athenian democracy (510 B.C.E.)

Comedy introduced to City Dionysia (487 B.C.E.) —— **500** —— Pindar begins to write odes (500 B.C.E.)

Aeschylus introduces second actor (c. 471 B.C.E.) —— Persian Wars (499–478 B.C.E.)
Battle of Marathon (490 B.C.E.)

Sophocles introduces third actor (c. 468 B.C.E.) —— Socrates born (470 B.C.E.)

475 —— Pericles begins rise to power: age of Pericles (462–429 B.C.E.)

Aeschylus' *Oresteia*; introduction of skene (458 B.C.E.) —— Hippocrates born (460 B.C.E.)

Prizes for tragic acting awarded (449 B.C.E.) —— **450** —— Beginning of Parthenon; Herodotus flourishes (447 B.C.E.)

Dramatic activities incorporated into Lenaia (c. 442 B.C.E.) —— Phidias dies (500–435 B.C.E.)

425

Sophocles' *King Oedipus* (c. 430 B.C.E.) —— Peloponnesian Wars (431–404 B.C.E.)

Euripides' *Trojan Women* (415 B.C.E.) —— Athenian fleet destroyed (404 B.C.E.)

—— Spartan hegemony begins (404 B.C.E.)

Aristophanes' *Lysistrata* (411 B.C.E.) —— **400** —— Trial and execution of Socrates (399 B.C.E.)

—— Aristotle born (384–322 B.C.E.)

375 —— Plato's *Republic* (c. 375 B.C.E.)

—— Spartan hegemony ends (404–371 B.C.E.)

Professional actors replace amateurs at City Dionysia (c. 350 B.C.E.) —— **350** —— Theban hegemony ends (371–362 B.C.E.)

Aristotle's *Poetics* (c. 335–323 B.C.E.) —— Philip II, king of Macedonia (352 B.C.E.)

Theater of Dionysus completed (c. 325 B.C.E.) —— **325** —— Alexander succeeds Philip II; in 335 B.C.E. occupies Greece

From this period to c. 100 B.C.E., Greek theaters built throughout Mediterranean (320 B.C.E.) —— Hellenistic culture spreads throughout eastern Mediterranean (c. 320 B.C.E.)

Menander's *Dyskolos* (316 B.C.E.) —— **300**

Artists of Dionysus recognized (277 B.C.E.) ——

275

Rome
Year, B.C.E.-C.E.

Theater		Culture and Politics

750 — Traditional date for the founding of Rome (753 B.C.E.)

250 — First Punic Wars (Greek influence on Roman culture) (264–241 B.C.E.)

Regular comedy and tragedy added to *Ludi Romani* (240 B.C.E.) ——— First Punic Wars...

— Second Punic Wars (218–201 B.C.E.); Hannibal's victories (218–216 B.C.E.)

200

Plautus's *Pseudolus* (191 B.C.E.) ———

— Rome defeats Philip V of Macedonia (200–197 B.C.E.)

Terence's *Phormio* (161 B.C.E.) ———

150

— Censorship of Cato; 1,000 talents spent on sewers (184 B.C.E.)

Vitruvius's *De Architectura* (90 B.C.E.) ———

100 — Roman citizens freed of direct taxation (167 B.C.E.)

First permanent theater in Rome (55 B.C.E.) ———

50 — Rome annexes Macedonia (147 B.C.E.)

Horace's *Art of Poetry* (24 B.C.E.) ———

— First high-level aqueduct in Rome (144 B.C.E.)

0

— Slave revolts in Sicily (135 B.C.E.)

Romans build theaters and amphitheaters throughout the empire (c. 30–200 C.E.) ———

50 — Pompey suppresses piracy (67 B.C.E.)

— Golden age of Roman literature (c. 58–50 B.C.E.)

Seneca (c. 4 B.C.E.–65 C.E.) writes Roman tragedies ———

100 — Caesar's conquest of Gaul (55 B.C.E.)

150 — Jesus crucified (30 C.E.)

— Marcus Aurelius rules (161–180 C.E.)

200

— Severan dynasty; Augustan order disintegrates (193–235 C.E.)

250 — Extensive persecution of Christians (c. 250–300 C.E.)

Theatrical presentations approximately 100 days per year ———

— Constantine rules; empire reunited (324–337 C.E.)

300

— St. Augustine born (354 C.E.)

350 — Julian the Apostate restores paganism (361 C.E.)

— Theodosius I forbids pagan worship (391 C.E.)

Council of Carthage decrees excommunication for those who attend theater rather than church on holy days; actors forbidden sacraments (398 C.E.) ———

400

— Sack of Rome by Visigoths (410 C.E.)

450

— Death of Attila the Hun (453 C.E.)

500 — Fall of western Roman empire (476 C.E.)

Asia
Year, C.E.

Theater		Culture and Politics

Natyasastra, major critical work of Indian Sanskrit drama (c. 200 B.C.E.–100 C.E.)

Sanskrit drama highly developed in India (320–600)

Shakuntala, famous Sanskrit drama by Indian author Kalidasa (fifth century)

The Little Clay Cart, Indian Sanskrit drama attributed to King Shudraka (fifth century)

Academy of the Pear Garden, school for dancers and singers, founded in China (714)

Development of professional theater companies in China (960)

Decline of Sanskrit drama (1150)

Indian dance drama, puppet plays, and folk plays (late twelfth century)

Scholars and artists work in popular theater in China (thirteenth century)

Zeami Motokiyo (1363–1444); development of nō drama

Literary and romantic drama develops during Ming period in China (1368–1664)

In Japan, kabuki first performed in Kyoto (1600–1610)

Nō becomes an aristocratic entertainment and rigidly codified (1650)

Kabuki becomes popular form of theater (1675–1750)

Chikamatsu Monzaemon begins writing for bunraku theater (1684)

Bunraku (puppet theater) formalized in Japan (1685)

Year markers: 300, 500, 700, 900, 1100, 1300, 1500, 1700

Spread of Buddhism in India. In India, trade with China, Egypt, Rome, southeast Asia. Gandhara school of art flourishes. (180 B.C.E.–150 B.C.E.)

Golden age of classical Sanskrit in India (300–500)

Earliest known use of zero and decimals occurs in India (600)

Tang dynasty in China (618–907)

Travels in India of Xuan Zang, Chinese pilgrim and chronicler (630–644)

Song dynasty in China (960–1279); flowering of arts, literature, and scholarship

Civil strife in Japan leads to military government (1100)

Beginning of Muslim rule in India (1192)

Marco Polo visits court of Kublai Kahn, Beijing, China (1271); Polo visits Kayal, southern India (1288)

Yüan dynasty in China (1271–1368)

Rule of Yoshimitsu (r. 1395–1408) in Japan; years of stability followed by civil wars

Ming dynasty in China (1368–1644)

First Europeans visit Japan (1542)

Period of national unification in Japan (1568–1600)

Rule of Shah Jahan in India; construction of great buildings, including Taj Mahal (1628–1657)

Qing (Ching) dynasty in China (1644–1911)

Middle Ages
Year, C.E.

Theater	Year	Culture and Politics
	475	"Dark ages" (476–1000)
Traveling performers (c. 500–925)		
	525	Justinian becomes Byzantine emperor (527)
Byzantine Theater (similar to Roman Theater (fifth through seventh centuries)	575	Mohammed born (c. 570)
	675	
Trulian Synod attempts to end performances in Byzantium (692)	725	Charles Martel defeats Muslims near Poitiers (732)
Traveling performers on European continent (500–975)	775	Charlemagne crowned emperor of Holy Roman Empire (800)
	825	Beginning of Romanesque architecture (c. 830)
	875	
Quem quaeritis trope (c. 925)	925	Earliest European reference to a collar in the harness of a horse which would allow the drawing of heavy loads and plow (920)
Hrosvitha, a nun, writes Christian comedies based on Terence (c. 970)	975	
		Beowulf (1000)
	1025	Norman Conquest (1066)
		First Crusade (1095)
	1075	Beginning of Gothic architecture (1140)
	1125	
	1175	English Magna Carta (1215)
	1225	Oxford University flourishes (c. 1260)
		Roger Bacon's *De Computo Naturali* (1264)
Vernacular religious drama flourishes: Peak of medieval theater (c. 1350–1550)	1275	Black death apparently originates in India (1332)
Second Shepherd's Play (c. 1375)		Boccaccio's *Decameron* (1353)
Pride of Life (c. 1400)	1325	Urban VI in Rome; Clement VII at Avignon (1378)
The Castle of Perseverance (c. 1425)		
Actor playing Judas at Metz almost dies while being hanged (1437)	1375	Peasant revolt in England (1381)
Pierre Patelin (c. 1470)		Chaucer dies (1400)
Hans Sachs born (1494)	1425	Gutenberg invents printing by movable type (c. 1450)
Everyman (c. 1500)		Constantinople falls to the Turks (1453)
Cycle staged at Mons (1510)	1475	Copernicus born (1473)
Jean Bouchet, pageant master, directs cycle at Poitiers (1508)		Martin Luther born (1483)
John Heywood's *Johan Johan* (1533)	1525	Columbus crosses the Atlantic (1492)

Italian Renaissance
Year, C.E.

Theater	Year	Culture and Politics

Theater

Culture and Politics

- 1325 — Death of Dante (1321)
- Antonio Laschis, *Achilles* (c. 1390)
- Manuel Chrysoloras opens Greek classes in Florence; beginning of revival of Greek literature in Italy (1396)
- 1400
- Cosmo de Medicis rules Florence (1432)
- Founding of Platonic Academy in Florence (1440)
- 1425
- Gutenberg invents movable type (c. 1450)

Twelve of Plautus's lost plays rediscovered (1429)

- Leonardo da Vinci born (1452)
- Manuscripts of Greek plays brought to Italy after fall of Constantinople (1453)
- 1450
- Lorenzo de Medicis rules Florence (1469)
- Michelangelo born (1475)
- 1475
- *Birth of Venus* by Botticelli (1484)
- Columbus discovers America; Leonardo da Vinci draws a flying machine (1492)

Vitruvius's *De Architectura* published (1486)

Plays by Aristophanes published by Aldine Press in Venice (1498)

- Italian wars spread Italy's cultural influence; weaken Italy politically (1494)
- 1500

Ariosto's *I Suppositi* (1509)
Machiavelli's comic play *Mandragola* (c.1513)

- Leonardo da Vinci's *Mona Lisa* (1503)
- 1525
- Michelangelo's *David* (c. 1504)

Bibbiena's *La Calandria* (1513)

Beolco begins writing and performing (c. 1520)

- Sistine Chapel (c. 1512)

Serlio's *Architettura* (6 vols.) (1545)

- 1550
- Machiavelli's *The Prince* (1513)

Peak of commedia dell'arte (1550–1650)

- Leonardo da Vinci dies (1519)

First performances of I Gelosi (the Andreinis) (c. 1569)

- Verrazano discovers New York Bay and Hudson River (1524)

Castelvetro requires unities (1570)

- 1575

Teatro Olimpico built (1584)

- Uffizi Museum at Florence founded (1560)

Sabbioneta Theater built (1588)

Peri's *Dafne* (1597)

- Galileo born; Michelangelo dies (1564)

I Gelosi troupe disbands upon the death of Isabella Andreini (1604)

- 1600
- Palladio's *I quattro libri dell'architectura* (1570)

Aleotti uses flat wing (c. 1606)

Teatro Farnese built (1618)

- Catherine de Medicis, queen mother of France, dies (1589)
- 1625
- Mannerism begins to appear in Italy (1600)

Sabbatini's *Manual for Constructing Theatrical Scenes and Machines* (1638)

- Galileo dies (1642)

Torelli's pole-and-chariot system (c. 1645)

- 1650

English Renaissance
Year, C.E.

Theater

Culture and Politics

1450

100 Years' War (1338–1453)

Sackville and Norton's *Gorboduc*: first English tragedy (1561)

1475

War of Roses (1455–1485)

Master of Revels made licenser of plays and companies; James Burbage's Earl of Leicester's Men founded (1574)

The Theater built by James Burbage; first Blackfriars opened (1576)

1500

Henry VIII reigns (1509–1547)

Thomas More's *Utopia* (1516)

Kyd's *Spanish Tragedy* (c. 1587)

Marlowe's *Doctor Faustus* (c. 1588)

1525

Elizabeth I, queen of England, rules (1558–1603)

Sir Walter Raleigh's expedition to Virginia (1584)

Alleyn's Lord Admiral's Men and Burbage's Lord Chamberlain's Men, the major companies in London (1594)

1550

Execution of Mary, Queen of Scots (1587)

Second Blackfriars built by James Burbage (1596)

Defeat of Spanish armada (1588)

James I begins reign (1603)

Globe Theater built (1599)

1575

Jamestown, Virginia, founded (1607)

Shakespeare's *Hamlet* (c. 1600)

Hudson claims part of North America for United Provinces (1609)

Lord Chamberlain's Men become the King's Men (1603)

1600

King James Bible (1611)

Jonson's *Volpone* (1606)

Thirty Years' War begins (1618)

Webster's *Duchess of Malfi* (c. 1613)

Francis Bacon's *Novum Organum* (1620)

Inigo Jones designs masques (c. 1620)

1625

Charles I begins reign (1625)

Jacobean playwrights flourish (c. 1620)

John Ford's *'Tis Pity She's a Whore* (c. 1630)

Charles I dissolves Parliament (1629)

English civil war (1642)

1650

Parliament closes British theaters (1642)

Charles I beheaded (1649)

Spanish Golden Age
Year, C.E.

Theater		Culture and Politics
	1475	Spain united under Ferdinand and Isabella (1469)
		Inquisition established in Spain (1481)
	1500	Jews expelled from Spain; Columbus discovers America; conquest of Granada (1492)
Juan del Encina's *The Eclogue of Placida and Victoriana* (1513)	**1525**	Cortés conquers Aztecs (1519)
Bartolomé de Torres Naharro's *Propalladia* (1517)		Pizzaro takes Peru (1530)
Lope de Rueda, Spain's first popular playwright (c. 1545)	**1550**	Opening of Potosi mines in Bolivia (1545)
City councils assume responsibilities for the staging of autos (c. 1555)		Jesuits begin missionary work in South America (1549)
		Philip II (rules 1556–1598)
Corral de la Cruz; first permanent theater in Spain (1579)	**1575**	Netherlands revolt against Spain (1567)
		Victory of Lepanto against Turks (1571)
Corral del Principe (1583)		El Greco arrives from Greece (1575)
Women licensed to appear onstage (c. 1587)		Philip II annexes Portugal (1580)
	1600	Defeat of Spanish armada (1588)
Strict censorship of plays (1608)		Philip III (rules 1598–1621)
Lope de Vega's *The Sheep Well* (1614)		Cervantes' *Don Quixote*, Part 1 (1605)
Philip IV brings designer Cosme Lotti from Florence (1626)	**1625**	Expulsion of Moors (1609)
Cofradia de la Novena (actors' guild) established (1631)		Philip IV (rules 1621–1665)
Calderón's *Life Is a Dream* (c. 1636)		Velázquez completes painting *Vulcan's Forge* (1630)
Coliseo, court theater with proscenium arch, built (1640)	**1650**	Revolt of Catalans and Portugese (1640)
Public theaters closed (1646–1651)		Defeat of Spanish army by French at Rocroi (1643)
Number of carros for autos increased from two to four (1647)	**1675**	Peace of the Pyrenees; Spain's power declines (1659)
First reference to Spanish designer José Caudi (1662)		Charles II (rules 1665–1700)
		Murillo's *Immaculate Conception* (used this subject thirty times) (1678)
	1750	Publication of Spanish Colonial Code (1680)
		Murillo dies (1617–1682)
Autos sacramentales prohibited (1765)		
	1775	

Neoclassical France
Year, C.E.

Theater	Year	Culture and Politics
	1500	
Confrère de la Passion (founded 1402) given monopoly of Paris theater (1518)	1525	
		Exploration of Gulf of St. Lawrence by Jacques Cartier (1534–1535)
Religious plays prohibited; Hôtel de Bourgogne opens; perspective scenery used for first time at Lyon for performance celebrating marriage of Henri II and Catherine de Medicis (1548)	1550	Henri II (rules 1547–1559)
Alexandre Hardy, first professional playwright, flourishes (1597)		Outbreak of civil war between Protestants and royal troops (1562)
Valleran le Comte (King's Players), first important theatrical manager (1598)	1575	St. Bartholomew's Day massacre; Protestants killed (1572)
		Montaigne's *Essays* (1580)
Farce players, Turlupin, Gaultier-Garguille, Gros-Guillaume popular (1610-1625)		Assassination of Henri III; Henri IV reigns (1589)
	1600	Henri IV abjures Protestantism (1593)
Théâtre du Marais (1634)		Edict of Nantes (1598)
Corneille's *Le Cid* (1636)		
Richelieu's Palais Cardinal opens (later renamed Palais-Royal) (1641)		Permanent French outpost in Quebec (1608)
New Marais with proscenium arch (1644)	1625	Henri IV assassinated; Louis XIII (rules 1610–1643)
Torelli brings Italianate innovations to France (1645)		Richelieu enters royal council (1624)
Bourgogne remodeled (proscenium added) (1647)		Descartes' *Discourse on Method* (1637)
		Richelieu's death (Mazarin's takeover) (1642)
Vigarini comes to France (1659)	1650	Death of Louis XIII; Louis XIV (rules 1643–1715)
Molière's troupe given Palais-Royal (1660)		Civil war (1648–1652)
Molière's *The Miser* (1668)		Louis XIV ("Sun King") personal reign (1661)
Jean-Baptiste Lully given monopoly of musical performances in Paris (1672)	1675	Founding of the French Academy of Science (1666)
After Molière's death, Marais and his company amalgamated by Louis XIV (1673)		Revocation of Edict of Nantes (1685)
Racine's *Phaedra* (1677)		Anglo-Dutch coalition wars against France (1689–1713)
Comédie Française founded (1680)	1700	
Comédie Française gets new theater, to be used until 1770 (1689)		
Paris commedia troupe expelled (1697)		Louis XIV dies (1715)
	1725	

English Restoration
Year, C.E.

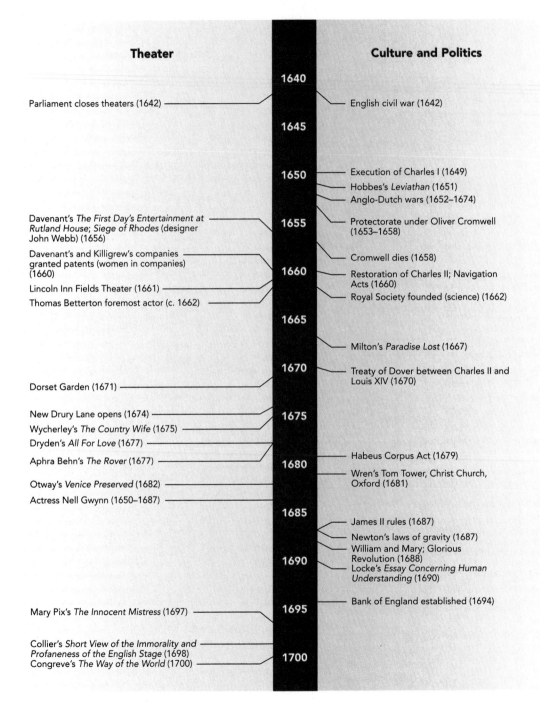

Theater	Year	Culture and Politics
	1640	
Parliament closes theaters (1642)		English civil war (1642)
	1645	
	1650	Execution of Charles I (1649)
		Hobbes's *Leviathan* (1651)
		Anglo-Dutch wars (1652–1674)
Davenant's *The First Day's Entertainment at Rutland House; Siege of Rhodes* (designer John Webb) (1656)	1655	Protectorate under Oliver Cromwell (1653–1658)
Davenant's and Killigrew's companies granted patents (women in companies) (1660)	1660	Cromwell dies (1658)
Lincoln Inn Fields Theater (1661)		Restoration of Charles II; Navigation Acts (1660)
Thomas Betterton foremost actor (c. 1662)		Royal Society founded (science) (1662)
	1665	
		Milton's *Paradise Lost* (1667)
	1670	Treaty of Dover between Charles II and Louis XIV (1670)
Dorset Garden (1671)		
New Drury Lane opens (1674)	1675	
Wycherley's *The Country Wife* (1675)		
Dryden's *All For Love* (1677)		
Aphra Behn's *The Rover* (1677)	1680	Habeus Corpus Act (1679)
		Wren's Tom Tower, Christ Church, Oxford (1681)
Otway's *Venice Preserved* (1682)		
Actress Nell Gwynn (1650–1687)		
	1685	James II rules (1687)
		Newton's laws of gravity (1687)
	1690	William and Mary; Glorious Revolution (1688)
		Locke's *Essay Concerning Human Understanding* (1690)
		Bank of England established (1694)
Mary Pix's *The Innocent Mistress* (1697)	1695	
Collier's *Short View of the Immorality and Profaneness of the English Stage* (1698)	1700	
Congreve's *The Way of the World* (1700)		

Eighteenth Century
Year, C.E.

Theater		Culture and Politics
	1700	War of Spanish Succession in France (1701–1714)
Ferdinando Bibiena introduces angle perspective (c. 1703)		Peter the Great begins westernization of Russia (c. 1701)
Susanna Centlivre's The Busy Body (1709)	**1710**	
		The Spectator begun by Addison and Steele (1711)
		Louis XIV dies (1715)
Gottsched and Neuber meet (1727)	**1720**	Defoe's *Robinson Crusoe* (1719)
Gay's *The Beggar's Opera* (1728)		
Lillo's *The London Merchant* (1731)		Baroque music flourishes (Bach and Handel) (c. 1724)
Voltaire's *Zaire*; London's Covent Garden Theater built (1732)		Swift's *Gulliver's Travels* (1726)
	1730	
English Licensing Act (1737)		John Key's "flying shuttle" loom patented (1733)
Voltaire's *Mahomet*; Macklin's Shylock—an attempt at costume reform (1741)		Rococo style flourishes (1737)
Garrick becomes actor-manager at Drury Lane (1747)	**1740**	Frederick the Great of Prussia, "enlightened despot" (1740)
Goldoni's *The Comic Theater* (1750)		
Hallams in Virginia (1752)		
Voltaire's *Orphan of China* (1755)	**1750**	*Encyclopédie* begun (c. 1750)
Spectators banished from French stage (c. 1759)		French and Indian War (1754)
Boulevard theaters begin to develop in France (c. 1760)		Seven Years' War begins (1756)
Piranesi continues to paint his "prison drawings" using chiaroscuro (1761)	**1760**	Voltaire's *Candide* (1759)
Gozzi's *Turandot* (1762)		Rousseau's *Social Contract*; Catherine the Great of Russia begins reign (1762)
Drottningholm completed; Southwark Theater in Philadelphia (1766)		James Watt patents a steam engine (1769)
John Street Theater in New York (1767)	**1770**	
Lessing's *Hamburg Dramaturgy* (1767–1769) Hamburg National Theater (1767–1769) "Storm and stress" movement (1767–1787)		Declaration of Independence (American Revolution 1775–1783); Adam Smith's *Wealth of Nations* (1776)
	1780	
Goethe's *Goetz von Berlichingen*; Goldsmith's *She Stoops to Conquer* (1773)		Goya's *Don Manuel de Zuniga*; James Watt patents a locomotive (1784)
Sheridan's *The School for Scandal* (1777)		Mozart's *Don Giovanni* (1787)
	1790	French Revolution (1789)
		David's *Murder of Marat* (1793)
Goethe "directs" Weimar court theater; Schiller assists (1798)	**1800**	Consulate of Napoleon (1799)
Schiller's *Mary Stuart* (1800)		

Nineteenth Century, 1800 to 1875
Year, C.E.

Theater		Culture and Politics

Theater

Talma foremost actor in France (c. 1800) — 1800

Goethe's *Faust*, Part I (1810) —
Kleist's *The Prince of Homburg* (1810) —
Pixérécourt and French melodrama flourish (1810)
Edmund Kean's London debut (1814) —
Chestnut Street Theater in Philadelphia becomes first totally gaslit theater (1816)

Daguerre exhibits diorama (1822) —
Charles Kemble's historically accurate *King John*; Shchepkin member of Moscow troupe (1823)

Forrest's New York debut (1826) —
Hugo's *Hernani* (1830) —
Madame Vestris's management of Olympic Theater begins (1831)

Gogol's *Inspector General*; Büchner's *Woyzeck* (1836)

Macready manages Covent Garden (1837) —
Scribe's *A Glass of Water* (1840) —
England's Theater Regulation Act (1843) —

Astor Place Riot (1849) —
Dumas fils's *Camille*; first production of *Uncle Tom's Cabin*; Charles Kean's *King John* (1852)

Adolphe Montigny innovates in directing at Gymnase (c. 1853)

Sardou's *A Scrap of Paper* (1860) —
Edwin Booth's *Hamlet* runs 100 nights in New York (1864)

Duke of Saxe-Meiningen begins reforms (1866)

Booth Theater (1869) —
Henry Irving at Lyceum (1871) —

Zola's *Thérèse Raquin*; preface discussed naturalism (1873)

Paris Opéra building completed (1874) —

Year markers: 1800 · 1810 · 1820 · 1830 · 1840 · 1850 · 1860 · 1870 · 1880

Culture and Politics

Louisiana Purchase (1803)
Napoleon I, emperor of France (1804)

Fulton's paddle steamer *Clermont* navigates on Hudson (1807)
Latin American independence (1808–1826)
Mme. de Stael's *Of Germany*, published in France (1810)
Beethoven's Fifth Symphony (1810)

Battle of Waterloo; Metternich system (1815)
First Factory Act, England (1819)
Greek war of independence (1821)
Monroe Doctrine (1823)
Decembrist uprising in Russia (1825)

Comte's positivism (1830)

Upper middle class enfranchised in England (1832)
Davy Crockett killed at the Alamo (1836)
Victoria of England (rules 1837–1901)
Dickens's *Oliver Twist* (1838)

Second French Empire; Napoleon III (1852)
Crimean War (1853–1865)
Perry in Japan (1854)
Flaubert's *Madam Bovary* (c. 1857)
Darwin's *On the Origin of Species* (1859)
American Civil War (1861–1865); proclamation of the Kingdom of Italy
Bismarck becomes Prussian prime minister (1862)
Dostoyevsky's *Crime and Punishment* (1866)
Marx's *Das Kapital*; extension of suffrage in Great Britain (1867)
Tolstoy's *War and Peace* (c. 1869); American transcontinental railway (1869)
German empire founded; Paris commune (1871)

1875 to 1915
Year

Theater		Culture and Politics

1875

Wagner's Bayreuth Festspielhaus opened (1876)

Telephone patented (1876)

Ibsen's *A Doll's House* (1879)

Edison's incandescent lamp (1879)
Height of Imperialism (1880–1914)
Alexander II assassinated in Russia (1881)

Savoy Theater in London uses electricity (1881)

1880

Antoine's Théâtre Libre (1887)
Strindberg's *Miss Julie* (1888)
Brahm's Freie Bühne (1889)

Trade unions in France legalized (1884)

1890

Grein's Independent Theater (1891)
Lugné–Poë's Théâtre de l'Oeuvre (1893)
Shaw's *Arms and the Man* (1894)
Oscar Wilde's *The Importance of Being Earnest* (1895)

Dreyfus affair in France (1894)

Chekhov's *Sea Gull;* Jarry's *Ubu Roi;* revolving stage in Munich (1896)

1895

Moscow Art Theater (1898)
Appia's *Music and Stage Setting* (1899)

Boer War in South Africa (1899)
Freud's *Interpretation of Dreams* (1900)
Marconi's first transatlantic radiotelegraph message (1901)

1900

Williams and Walker's *In Dahomy* (1902)

Boer War ends (1902)

Chekhov's *Cherry Orchard* (1904)
Synge's *Riders to the Sea* (1904)

Wright brothers make successful airplane flight (1903)

Craig's *The Art of Theater;* Reinhardt succeeds Otto Brahm as director of Deutsches Theater (1905)

1905

Einstein's theory of relativity (1905)

Picasso's *Les Demoiselles d'Avignon* (1907)

First modern Japanese drama presented by Osanai Kaoru (1909)

1910

Indian playwright, Rabindranath Tagore, receives Nobel Prize (1913)

Théâtre du Vieux Colombier (1913)

Stravinsky's *Le Sacré du Printemps* (1913)

Anita Bush founds Lafayette Players (1914)

Provincetown Playhouse (1915)

1915

World War I (1914)

Theater

Culture and Politics

Major futurist productions
at Piccolo Teatro in Rome (1918)

1915

Easter Rebellion in Ireland (1916)
Bolshevik revolution (1917)

Soviet renaissance: Meyerhold,
Vakhtangov, Tairov, Erveinov

Prohibition in United States;
Peace of Versailles (1919);
Women's suffrage in
United States (1920)

Toller's *Man and the Masses*
Pirandello's *Six Characters* (1921)

1920

Joyce's *Ulysses*; Mussolini's
march on Rome (1922)

O'Neill's *The Hairy Ape* (1922)
Dullin's *Atelier* (1922)

Hitler's beer hall putsch in
Munich (1923)

Jouvet in *Doctor Knock* (1923)

Ortega y Gassett's
The Dehumanization of Art;
Kafka's *The Trial*; Thomas
Mann's *The Magic Mountain* (1924)

Stanislavski's *My Life in Art*;
Breton's *First Manifesto*;
O'Neill's *Desire Under the Elms* (1924)

1925

Schoenberg's twelve-tone
music (1926)

Meyerhold's *Inspector General* (1926)

Brecht's *Threepenny Opera* (1928)

Depression begins; Wolfe's *Look
Homeward Angel*; Faulkner's
The Sound and the Fury (1929)

O'Neill's *Mourning Becomes Electra* (1931)

1930

Group Theater, United States (1931)

Spains' monarchy collapses (1931)

Socialist realism declared proper
style in Soviet Union; Brecht and
other German artists emigrate (c. 1934);
Gielgud's *Hamlet* (1934)

Hitler takes power in Germany;
New Deal in United States (1933)

1935

Italy attacks Ethiopia; purges in
Soviet Union; Nuremberg laws
against Jews in Nazi Germany
(1935)

Lorca's *House of Bernarda Alba*,
Giraudoux's *The Trojan War
Will Not Take Place*; Federal
Theater Project in United States (1935)

Spanish Civil War; first television
broadcast (1936)

Tyrone Guthrie appointed
administrator at the Old Vic (1937)

World War II (1939–1945)

1940

Hemingway's *For Whom the
Bell Tolls* (1940)

Artaud's *Theater and Its Double* (1938)

Thornton Wilder's *Skin of Our Teeth* (1942)

Othello with Paul Robeson (1943)

Camus's *Myth of Sisyphus* (1943)

Sartre's *No Exit* (1944)

1945

United States drops atomic bomb
on Japan; United Nations formed
(1945)

1945 to Present
Year

Theater		Culture and Politics

1945

Barrault's Compagnie Madeleine Renaud–Jean-Louis Barrault established (1946) — Nuremberg trials (1946)

Genet's *The Maids*; Williams's *A Streetcar Named Desire* (1947) — Orwell's *1984*; Germany divided (1949)

1950

Ionesco's *The Bald Soprano*; Berliner Ensemble; Miller's *Death of a Salesman*; Arena Stage in Washington (1949) — Korean War (1950–1953)

Vilar at TNP (1951) — Stalin dies (1953)

McCarthy-Army hearings; hydrogen bomb tested (1954)

Beckett's *Waiting for Godot* (1953) —

1955

Thornton Wilder's *The Matchmaker* (1954) — Russia crushes Hungarian revolt; Suez crisis (1956)

Osborne's *Look Back in Anger* Dürrenmatt's *The Visit* (1956) — Sputnik I and II (1957)

Pinter's *Birthday Party*; Laterna Magika (1958) — Belgian Congo granted independence (1960)

1960

Hansberry's *A Raisin in the Sun* Grotowski founds Polish Laboratory Theater (1959) — Berlin Wall (1961)

Cuban missile crisis (1962)

Café La Mama founded; Albee's *Who's Afraid of Virginia Woolf?* (1962) — Warfare escalates between North and South Vietnam; Martin Luther King arrested in Birmingham; John F. Kennedy, president of the United States, assassinated (1963)

1965

National Theater under Laurence Olivier (1963) —

Krushchev resigns (1964)

Lonne Elder's *Ceremonies in Dark Old Men* (1969) — American astronauts walk on moon (1969)

1975

Camp David accord reached between Israel and Egypt (1977)

Muslim revolution in Iran (1979)

Sam Shepard's *Buried Child* wins Pulitzer Prize (1979) — Ronald Reagan elected president (1980)

1985

August Wilson's *Fences* wins Pulitzer Prize (1987) — Chinese government crushes pro-democracy demonstration (1989)

1990

Berlin Wall taken down; eastern Europe democratized (1990)

Neil Simon's *Lost in Yonkers* wins Pulitzer Prize (1991) — Soviet Union dissolves (1991)

Tony Kushner's *Angels in America* wins Pulitzer Prize (1993) — Bill Clinton elected president of the United States (1992)

Eugene Ionosco dies (1994) —

Heiner Meuller dies (1996) — Bill Clinton reelected president (1996)

1995

Wit by Margaret Edson wins Pulitzer Prize (1999) — George W. Bush elected president of United States (2000)

Peter Stein directs *Faust*, Berlin, Germany (2000) —

Topdog/Underdog by Suzan-Lori Parks wins Pulitzer Prize (2002) — Terrorist attack on World Trade Center in New York City (09/11/2001)

2000

Anna in the Tropics by Nilo Cruz wins Pulitzer Prize (2003) — War in Iraq (2003)

Notes

Introduction

1 Bernard Beckerman, *Dynamics of Drama: Theory and Method of Analysis,* Knopf, New York, 1970, p. 129.
2 Robert Edmond Jones, *The Dramatic Imagination,* Theatre Arts, New York, 1941, p. 40.

Chapter 1

1 Jean-Claude van Itallie, *The Serpent: A Ceremony,* written in collaboration with the Open Theater, Atheneum, New York, 1969, p. ix.
2 Gustave Le Bon, *The Crowd: A Study of the Popular Mind,* 20th ed., Benn, London, 1952, p. 23.
3 Ibid., p. 27.
4 Bernard Beckerman, *Dynamics of Drama: Theory and Method of Analysis,* Knopf, New York, 1970, p. 9.

Chapter 2

1 Notes on *King Lear* are from G. K. Hunter's edition of Shakespeare's *King Lear,* Penguin, Baltimore, Md., 1972, pp. 243–244.

Chapter 4

1 The Performance Group, *Dionysus in 69,* Noonday, Farrar, Straus & Giroux, New York (n.p.).
2 Ibid.
3 Material on proscenium, arena, and thrust stages was suggested by

a booklet prepared by Dr. Mary Henderson for the educational division of Lincoln Center for the Performing Arts.
4 Antonin Artaud, *The Theater and Its Double,* Grove, New York, 1958, pp. 96–97.

Chapter 5

1 Richard Findlater, *The Player Kings,* Weidenfeld and Nicolson, London, 1971, p. 25.

Chapter 6

1 Constantin Stanislavski, *An Actor Prepares,* Theatre Arts, New York, 1948, p. 73.
2 Jean Benedetti, *Stanislavski,* Routledge, New York, 1988, p. 217.
3 Mira Felner, *Free to Act: An Integrated Approach to Acting,* Harcourt, Brace, Fort Worth, Tex., 1990, p. 14.
4 Walter Kerr, drama review, *New York Herald Tribune,* January 10, 1961.

Chapter 7

1 Harold Clurman, *On Directing,* Macmillan, New York, 1972, p. 27.
2 Ibid., p. 221.
3 Ibid., p. 30.
4 Ibid.

Chapter 9

1 Arthur Miller, *The Theater Essays of Arthur Miller,* Viking, New York, 1978, pp. 3–5.

2 Friedrich Nietzsche, "The Birth of Tragedy," from *Works in Three Volumes,* Carl Hanser, Munich, vol. 1, pp. 19, 92.

Chapter 10

1 Albert Camus, *Le Mythe de Sisyphe,* Gallimard, Paris, 1942, p. 18.
2 From the book *Waiting for Godot* by Samuel Beckett. Copyright 1954 by Grove Press; renewed copyright 1982 by Samuel Beckett. Used with the permission of Grove/Atlantic, Inc.

Chapter 12

1 Jacki Apple, "Art at the Barricades," *Artwork,* vol. 21, May 3, 1990, p. 21.

Chapter 14

1 Kenneth MacGowan, *A Primer of Playwrighting,* Dolphin, Doubleday, Garden City, N.Y., 1962, p. 62.

Chapte sr 15

1 Jean Anouilh, *Antigone,* Lewis Galantière (trans. and adaptor), Random House, New York, 1946, p. 36. Copyright 1946 by Random House.

Chapter 16

1 Robert Edmond Jones, *The Dramatic Imagination,* Theatre Arts, New York, 1941, p. 25.

Select Bibliography

Allen, John: *Theatre in Europe,* Offord, Eastbourne, England, 1981.

Appia, Adolphe, *Essays, Scenarios, and Designs,* Walther R. Volbach (trans.), Richard C. Beacham (ed.), UMI Research Press, Ann Arbor, Mich., 1989.

Aristotle: *Aristotle's Poetics,* S. H. Butcher (trans.), Introduction by Francis Fergusson, Hill and Wang, New York, 1961.

Aronson, Arnold: *American Set Design,* New York, Theatre Communications Group, 1985.

Artaud, Antonin: *The Theater and Its Double,* Mary C. Richards (trans.), Grove, New York, 1958.

Atkinson, Brooks: *Broadway,* rev. ed., Macmillan, New York, 1974.

Austen, Gayle, *Feminist Theories for Creative Criticism,* University of Michigan Press, Ann Arbor, 1990.

Banham, Martin (ed.): *The Cambridge Guide to the Theatre,* updated version, Cambridge University Press, New York, 1992.

Bank, Rosemarie K.: *Theatre Culture in America, 1825–1860,* Cambridge University Press, New York, 1997.

Bartow, Arthur: *The Directors' Voice: 21 Interviews,* Theatre Communications Group, New York, 1988.

Bay, Howard: *Stage Design,* Drama Book Specialists, New York, 1974.

Beckerman, Bernard: *Dynamics of Drama: Theory and Method of Analysis,* Drama Book Specialists, New York, 1979.

Benedetti, Jean: *Stanislavski: An Introduction,* Theatre Arts, New York, 1982.

Benedetti, Robert: *The Actor at Work,* Prentice Hall, Englewood Cliffs, N.J., 1971.

Bentley, Eric: *The Life of the Drama,* Atheneum, New York, 1964.

_____ (ed.): *The Theory of the Modern Stage,* Penguin, Baltimore, 1968.

Betsko, Kathleen, and Rachel Koenig: *Interviews with Contemporary Women Playwrights,* Beech Tree, New York, 1987.

Bigsby, C. W. E., *Contemporary American Playwrights,* Cambridge University Press, New York, 1999.

_____ , *Modern American Drama, 1945–1990,* Cambridge University Press, New York, 1992.

Bradby, David, and David Williams: *Directors Theatre,* St. Martin's, New York, 1988.

Brandon, James R. (ed.): *Cambridge Guide to Asian Theatre,* Cambridge University Press, New York, 1993.

Brecht, Bertolt: *Brecht on Theatre,* John Willett (trans.), Hill and Wang, New York, 1965.

_____ , and Robert R. Findlay: *Century of Innovation: A History of European and American Theatre and Drama since the Late 19th Century,* 2d ed., Allyn & Bacon, Boston, 1991.

Brockett, Oscar, with Franklin J. Hildy: *History of the Theatre,* 9th ed., Allyn and Bacon, Boston, 2003.

Brook, Peter: *The Empty Space,* Atheneum, New York, 1968.

_____: *The Shifting Point,* HarperCollins, New York, 1987.

Brown, John Russell (ed.): *The Oxford Illustrated History of Theatre,* Oxford University Press, New York, 1997.

Burns, Elizabeth: *Theatricality,* Harper and Row, New York, 1973.

Canning, Charlotte: *Feminist Theaters in the U.S.A.: Staging Women's Experience,* Routledge, New York, 1996.

Carlson, Marvin: *Performance,* Routledge, New York, 1996.

_____: *Theories of the Theatre: A Historical and Critical Survey from the Greeks to the Present,* expanded ed., Cornell University Press, Ithaca, N.Y., 1993.

Case, Sue-Ellen: *Feminism and Theatre,* Chapman and Hall, New York, 1988.

Case, Sue-Ellen (ed.): *Split Britches: Lesbian Practice/Feminist Performance,* Routledge, New York, 1996.

Chinoy, Helen K., and Linda W. Jenkins: *Women in American Theatre,* rev. ed., Theatre Communications Group, New York, 1987.

Clark, Barrett H. (ed.): *European Theories of the Drama,* rev. ed., Crown, New York, 1965.

Clurman, Harold: *On Directing,* Macmillan, New York, 1972.

Cohen, Robert: *Acting Power,* Mayfield, Palo Alto, Calif., 1978.

Cole, Toby: *Playwrights on Playwriting,* Hill and Wang, New York, 1961.

————, and Helen Krich Chinoy: *Actors on Acting,* Crown, New York, 1970.

Corrigan, Robert (ed.): *Comedy: Meaning and Form,* Chandler, San Francisco, 1965.

———— (ed.): *Tragedy: Vision and Form,* Chandler, San Francisco, 1965.

Corson, Richard: *Stage Makeup,* 6th ed., Prentice Hall, 1981.

Dolan, Jill: *The Feminist Spectator as Critic,* Ann Arbor, University of Michigan Press, 1988.

Dukore, Bernard: *Dramatic Theory and Criticism: Greeks to Grotowski,* Holt, New York, 1974.

Edmunds, Lowell, and Robert W. Wallace (eds.): *Poet, Public, and Performance in Ancient Greece,* Johns Hopkins University Press, Baltimore, Md., 1997.

Elam, Harry J.: *Taking It to the Streets: The Social Protest Theater of Luis Valdez and Amiri Baraka,* University of Michigan Press, Ann Arbor, 1997.

Emery, Joseph S.: *Stage Costume Technique,* Prentice Hall, Englewood Cliffs, N.J., 1981.

Esslin, Martin: *The Theatre of the Absurd,* rev. ed., Doubleday, Garden City, N.Y., 1969.

Felner, Mira: *Free to Act,* Holt Rinehart and Winston, New York, 1990.

Fergusson, Francis: *The Idea of a Theater,* Princeton University Press, Princeton, N.J., 1949.

Finney, Gail: *Women in Modern Drama,* Cornell University Press, Ithaca, N.Y., 1989.

Gassner, John: *Masters of the Drama,* 3d ed., Dover, New York, 1954.

———— and Ralph Allen (eds.): *Theatre and Drama in the Making,* 2 vols., Houghton Mifflin, Boston, 1964.

———— and Edward Quinn: *The Reader's Encyclopedia of World Drama,* Crowell, New York, 1969.

Gillespie, Patti P., and Kenneth M. Cameron: *Western Theatre: Revolution and Revival,* Macmillan, New York, 1984.

Goffman, Erving: *Presentation of Self in Everyday Life,* Overlook, New York, 1973.

Goldberg, Roselee: *Performance Art: From Futurism to the Present,* rev. ed., Abrams, New York, 1988.

Goldman, Michael: *The Actor's Freedom: Toward a Theory of Drama,* Viking, New York, 1975.

Grotowski, Jerzy: *Towards a Poor Theatre,* Simon & Schuster, New York, 1968.

Gurr, Andrew: *Playgoing in Shakespeare's London,* 2d ed., Cambridge University Press, New York, 1996.

————: *The Shakespearean Playing Companies,* Oxford University Press, New York, 1996.

Hanawalt, Barbara A., and Michal Kobialka (eds.), *Medieval Practices of Space,* University of Minnesota Press, Minneapolis, 2000.

Hartnoll, Phyllis, and Peter Found (eds.): *The Concise Oxford Companion to the Theatre,* new ed., Oxford University Press, New York, 1993.

Heilman, Robert G.: *Tragedy and Melodrama: Versions of Experience,* University of Washington Press, Seattle, 1968.

Howarth, William D., et al. (eds.): *French Theatre in the Neo-Classical Era, 1550–1789,* Cambridge University Press, New York, 1997.

Izenour, George: *Theatre Design,* McGraw-Hill, New York, 1977.

Jones, Robert E.: *The Dramatic Imagination,* Meredith, New York, 1941.

Kerr, Walter: *Tragedy and Comedy,* Simon and Schuster, New York, 1967.

Kirby, E. T.: *Ur-Drama: The Origins of Theatre,* New York University Press, New York, 1975.

Kirby, Michael: *Happenings,* Dutton, New York, 1965.

Kobialka, Michal, *This Is My Body: Representational Practices in the Early Middle Ages,* University of Michigan Press, Ann Arbor, 1999.

Kolin, Philip C. (ed.): *American Playwrights since 1945: A Guide to Scholarship, Criticism, and Performance,* Westport, Conn., 1989.

Lahr, John, and Jonathan Price: *Life-Show,* Viking, New York, 1973.

Langer, Susanne K.: *Feeling and Form,* Scribner, New York, 1953.

Larson, Orville K.: *Scene Design in the American Theatre from 1915 to 1960,* Fayetteville, Ark., 1989.

Londré, Felicia Hardison, and Daniel J. Watermeier: *The History of North American Theater: From Pre-Columbian Times to the Present,* Continuum, New York, 1998.

Martin, Carol (ed.): *A Sourcebook of Feminist Theatre and Performance,* Routledge, New York, 1996.

Miller, Arthur: *The Theatre Essays of Arthur Miller,* Robert Martin (ed.), Viking, New York, 1978.

Mills, David: *Recycling the Cycle,* University of Toronto Press, Canada, 1998.

Mitchell, Loften: *Black Drama,* Hawthorn, New York, 1967.

Nagler, Alois M.: *Sourcebook in Theatrical History,* Dover, New York, 1952.

Novick, Julius: *Beyond Broadway,* Hill and Wang, New York, 1968.

Oenslager, Donald: *Scenery Then and Now,* Norton, New York, 1936.

Ortolani, Benito, *The Japanese Theatre: From Shamanistic Ritual to Contemporary Pluralism,* rev. ed., Princeton University Press, Princeton, N.J., 1995.

Parker, W. Oren, and Harvey K. Smith: *Scene Design and Stage Lighting,* 4th ed., Holt, New York, 1979.

Partnow, Elaine T.: *The Female Dramatist: Profiles of Women Playwrights from the Middle Ages to Contemporary Times,* Facts on File, New York, 1998.

Perkins, Kathy, and Roberta Uno, *Contemporary Plays by Women of Color: An Anthology,* Routledge, New York, 1996.

Pilbrow, Richard: *Stage Lighting,* rev. ed., Van Nostrand and Reinhold, New York, 1979.

Postlewait, Thomas, and Bruce McConachie (eds.): *Interpreting the Theatrical Past: Essays in the Historiography of Performance,* University of Iowa Press, Iowa City, 1989.

Pottlitzer, Joanne: *Hispanic Theatre in the United States and Puerto Rico,* Ford Foundation, New York, 1988.

Richmond, Farley, et al., *Indian Theatre: Traditions of Performance,* University of Hawaii Press, Honolulu, 1990.

Roberts, Vera M.: *On Stage: A History of the Theatre,* 2d ed., Harper and Row, New York, 1974.

Rodenburg, Patsy, *The Actor Speaks: Voice and the Performer,* St. Martin's Press, New York, 2000

Roemer, Rick: *Charles Ludlam and the Ridiculous Theatrical Company,* McFarland, Jefferson, N.C., 1998.

Roose-Evans, James: *Experimental Theatre: From Stanislavsky to Peter Brook,* 2d ed., Routledge, New York, 1996.

Rovit, Rebecca, and Alvin Goldfarb, (eds.), *Theatrical Performance during the Holocaust: Texts, Memoirs and Documents,* Johns Hopkins University Press, Baltimore, Md., 1999.

Rudlin, John, *Jacques Copeau,* Cambridge University Press, New York, 1986.

Savran, David: *In Their Own Words: Contemporary American Playwrights,* Theatre Communications Group, New York, 1988.

Schechner, Richard: *Environmental Theater,* Hawthorn, N.Y., 1973.

_____: *The End of Humanism: Writings on Performance,* Routledge, New York, 1982.

Schevill, James: *Breakout! In Search of New Theatrical Environments,* University of Chicago Press, Chicago, 1972.

Schuler, Catherine: *Women in Russian Theatre: The Actress in the Silver Age,* Routledge, New York, 1996.

Senda, Akihiko: *The Voyage of Contemporary Japanese Theatre,* J. Thomas Rimer (trans.), University of Hawaii Press, Honolulu, 1997.

Shank, Theodore: *American Alternative Theatres,* St. Martin's, New York, 1982.

Solomon, Alisa: *Re-Dressing the Canon: Essays on Theatre and Gender,* Routledge, New York, 1997.

Southern, Richard: *The Seven Ages of the Theatre,* Hill and Wang, New York, 1961.

Stanislavski, Constantin: *An Actor Prepares,* Elizabeth Reynolds Hapgood (trans.), Theatre Arts, New York, 1936.

Watson, Jack, and Grant F. McKernie: *A Cultural History of Theatre,* Longman, New York, 1993.

Wickham, Glynne: *A History of the Theatre,* Cambridge University Press, England, 1992.

Wiles, David, *Tragedy in Athens: Performance Space and Theatrical Meaning,* Cambridge University Press, New York, 1997.

Wilmeth, Don B., and Christopher Bigsby (eds.): *The Cambridge History of American Theatre,* Cambridge University Press, New York, 1998.

Wilmeth, Don B., and Tice L. Miller (eds.): *Cambridge Guide to American Theatre,* Cambridge University Press, New York, 1993.

Wilson, Edwin, and Alvin Goldfarb: *Living Theater: A History,* 4th ed., McGraw-Hill, New York, ©2004.

Worrall, Nick: *The Moscow Art Theatre,* London, Routledge, 1996.

Young, Stark: *The Theatre,* Hill and Wang, New York, 1963.

Index

Terence, 308

Terrorist attack, September 11, 2001, 20, 26, 415

Terry, Megan, 258

Testa, Mary, 365

Tetralogy, 421

Text (see Script)

Texts for Nothing (Beckett), 63

Texture, 353, 359, 361, 395

Tharp, Twyla, 132

Theater:
    as action, 7, 9, 294
    as art form, 3, 10, 39
    as collaborative art, 166, 184–185, 407
    diversity of, 47, 50–53, 54, 243–263, 264, 412–414
    elements of, 7, 9–10, 407–409
    everyday occurrence of, 1
    focus of, 4–5, 10, 176–177, 187
    future of, 414–415
    "grammar" of, 294
    as group experience, 18–20, 415
    human concerns as subject matter of, 4–5, 10, 176, 294
    immediacy of, 3, 8
    as impulse, universal, 5–7, 10
    and literature, distinguished, 7–8, 9
    meaning in, 409–411
    as metaphor, 27, 35
    observation of, 21–22, 23, 24, 35, 408
    participatory, 21–23, 35
    relationship to film and television, 1, 2, 3, 15, 16–18, 28, 33, 35, 184, 427
    and ritual, 5–7, 10, 78, 79, 257, 258, 264, 305, 317, 318, 319
    selectivity in, 3, 10, 342
    and society, 39–40, 42–44, 54, 182–184, 187, 430
    and technology, 15–16
    spaces (see Stage spaces)
    special nature of, 3, 16–18
    transitory nature of, 7–8, 10
    as unique experience, 407, 414, 415
    and visual arts, distinguished, 7–8

Theater architecture, 70, 71, 74, 78–79, 88

Theater for youth (see Children's Theater)

Theater games, 21, 22

Theater-in-the-round (see Arena stage)

Theater of the absurd, 52, 209, 218, 222, 342, 423
    defined, 219, 428–429
    existential characters, 221
    plots, 219–220
    tragicomedy, 209, 218, 221, 222, 429
    verbal nonsense and non sequitur, 220–221

Theater of cruelty, 52, 429

Theater of diversity, 50–53, 54, 243–263, 264, 414
    African American theater, 51, 53, 177, 243, 244–248, 264, 414
    Asian American theater, 52, 53, 243, 249–254, 264, 414

feminist, 52, 53, 177, 243, 257–258, 259, 264, 414

gay and lesbian theater, 52, 243, 259–260, 261, 264, 414

gender, 15, 243, 260, 264

Hispanic theater, 51, 52, 177, 243, 254–256, 264, 414

multicultural, 15, 50–53, 243, 260, 264

multiethnic, 50–53, 243, 264

Native American theater, 20, 52, 243, 257, 264

websites on, 264

Theater of fact, 33, 429

Theatre Offensive (Boston), 260

Theater Rhinoceros (San Francisco), 52

Theater spaces (see Stage spaces)

Theatre Works (New York), 50

Theatricalism, 429

Theatricality, 1, 2

Theme, defined, 421
    (see also Point of view)

Theme parks, 346

Thespian, 421

Thompson, Douglas, 275

Thoroughly Modern Millie (musical), 46, 239, 377

Three Sisters, The (Chekhov), 123, 170–171, 300, 316

Three Tall Women (Albee), 106

Through line of roles (spine), 124, 134, 136

Thrust stage, 71, 79–83, 84, 88, 89
    advantages of, 79, 83
    defined, 79, 421
    direction on, 156
    history of, 79–83
    structures of, 79, 80, 81, 82, 83

Thumbnail sketch, 354

Thyratron vacuum tube, 387

Tiene la Muerta Atada (Puerto Rican Traveling Theatre), 51

Tilt, 396

Tillinger, John, 210

Time and place, extensive, 309–312

Time and place, restricted, 306–307, 308

Times Square (New York), 46, 48

Tirado, Cándido, 256

Toilet, The (Baraka), 248

Tommy Tune Tonight, 391

Tom Sawyer, 50

"Tonight," 31

Tony Award, 102, 239, 391

Topdog/Underdog (Parks), 31, 39, 179, 244, 248, 392

Top Girls (Churchill), 258

Torch Song Trilogy (Fierstein), 53, 259

Torelli, Giacomo, 74–75

Torres, Bill, 255

Torres, Omar, 255

Touch of the Poet, A (O'Neill), 144

Touring theatre, 46–47

Traditional theater:
    extraordinary characters, 190, 191, 276–279, 289

tragedy, 5, 126, 182–184, 189, 190–192, 194, 198, 202, 203, 225, 276–279, 308, 366

Tragedy:
    comedy, contrast, 198, 207, 215, 218, 222
    defined, 429
    Elizabethan, 182, 183, 190
    Greek, 4–5, 41, 126, 182, 183, 190, 194, 198, 225
    modern, 190, 193–195, 198, 202, 203, 226
    Renaissance, 182, 183, 190
    society's point of view and, 182–184, 194, 203
    theories of, 193–195, 308
    traditional, 5, 126, 182–184, 189, 190–192, 194, 198, 202, 203, 225, 276–279, 308, 366
    websites on, 203

"Tragedy and the Common Man" (Miller), 193–194

Tragic circumstances, 190–191, 203

Tragicomedy, 205, 209, 221, 222
    comedies of menace, 218
    defined, 215–217, 429
    modern, 218
    point of view, 215, 216, 218, 222
    problem play, 216, 217, 427
    theater of the absurd, 209, 218, 219–221, 222, 423, 428–429
    websites on, 222

Tragic effect, 192

Tragic flaw (hamartia), 421

Tragic hero and heroine (tragic figure), 189, 190, 191, 192, 203, 275, 276–277

Tragic irretrievability, 191, 203

Tragic verse, 191–192, 203

Trap, 349, 421

Travolta, John, 101

Treadmill, 349, 421

Treadwell, Sophie, 258

Trestle stage, 80
    (See also Platform stage)

Trilogy, 298, 421

Trip to Coontown, A (musical), 245

Troilus and Cressida (Shakespeare), 147–148

True, Jim, 284

Tryater (Holland), 87

Tryouts (see Preview)

Tucci, Stanly, 29

Tucker, Jennifer Mudge, 24

Turntable (revolving stage), 349, 420

Twentieth-century theater, historical time line, 442–444

Twelfth Night (Shakespeare), 97, 212

Twilight: Los Angeles, 1992 (Smith), 175, 261, 391

Twister (film), 17

Two Trains Running (Wilson), 247, 248

Typecasting, 153

Tyrone Guthrie Theater (Minneapolis), 37, 47, 83, 88, 143, 200, 285, 345, 374